COLLEGE WRITING BASICS

COLLEGE WRITING BASICS

A Progressive Approach   Second Edition

Thomas E. Tyner
Kings River College

Wadsworth Publishing Company
Belmont, California
A Division of Wadsworth, Inc.

English Editor: Angela Gantner
Editorial Assistant: Julie Johnson
Managing Designer: James Chadwick
Print Buyer: Karen Hunt
Designers: Adriane Bosworth and James Chadwick
Compositor: Thompson Type
Cover: James Chadwick

Printed in the United States of America 19

2 3 4 5 6 7 8 9 10—94 93 92 91 90

Library of Congress Cataloging in Publication Data

Tyner, Thomas E., 1944–
College writing basics: a progressive approach/Thomas E. Tyner.
—2nd ed.
p. cm.
ISBN 0-534-12438-0
1. English language—Rhetoric. 2. English language–
–Grammar—1950– I. Title.
PE1408.T95 1990
808'.042—dc20 89–39103
CIP

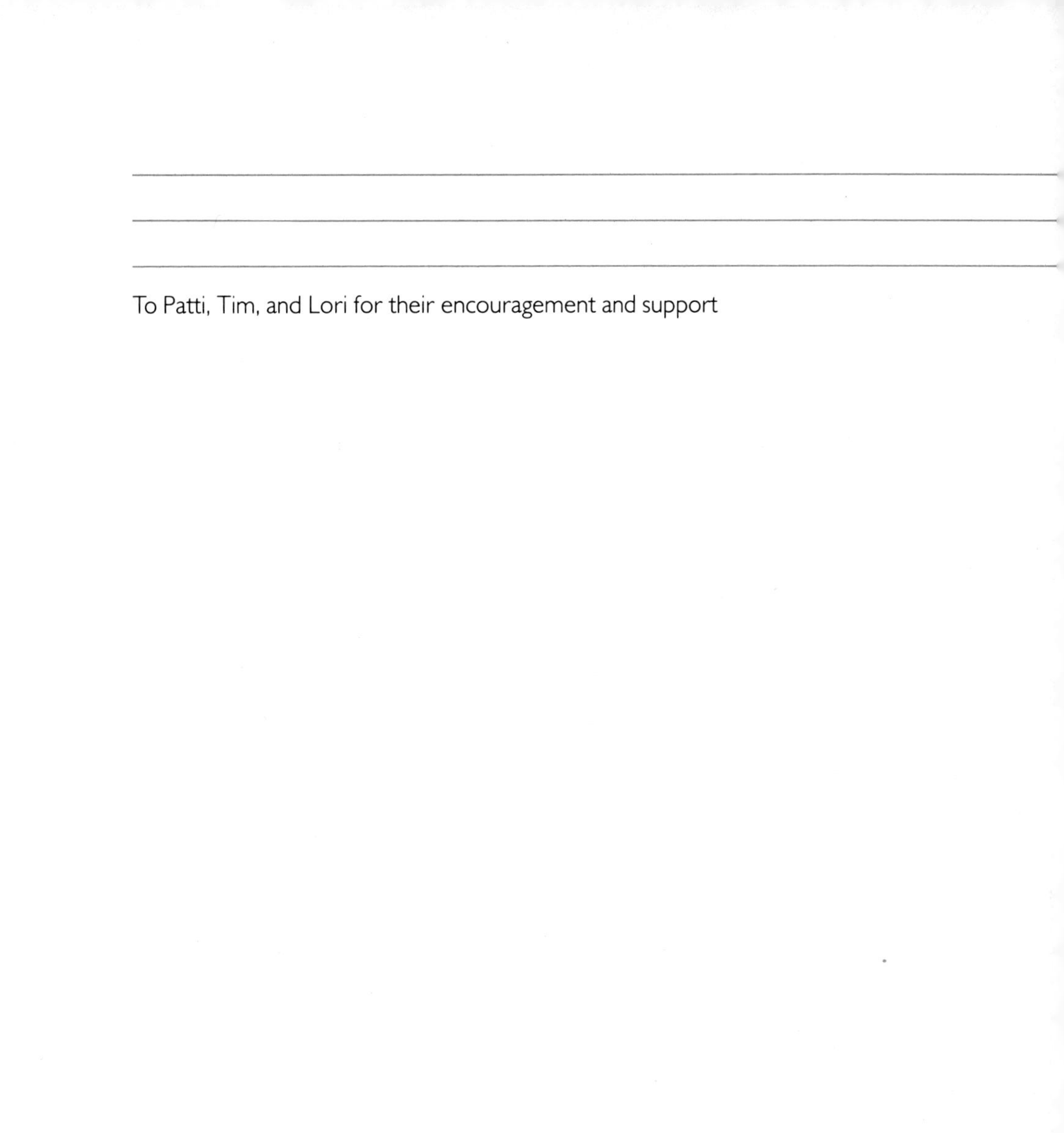

To Patti, Tim, and Lori for their encouragement and support

Preface

In teaching developmental writing courses, I have found that the language and educational backgrounds of students vary greatly, affecting each student's rate of progress in acquiring new writing skills. I have also found that students develop and retain skills best through regular practice and reinforcement, and that as a course progresses, students can handle increasingly sophisticated writing structures and assignments. *College Writing Basics* was designed for developmental writing courses with those three considerations in mind:

- to provide for as much individualization of instruction as is needed,
- to reinforce basic skill learning throughout the text,
- and to gradually increase the difficulty and sophistication of the material as students are ready to handle it.

College Writing Basics has a rather unique format that allows it to meet the needs of developmental writers. It is divided into five "levels" with each level presenting more challenging material as students build their skills and confidence. Each level also covers the same basic skill areas, albeit with increasing sophistication, so that students receive regular skills reinforcement. Finally, each section within a level contains answer-keyed exercises, an end-of-section practice quiz, and an instructor's manual section quiz so that both student and instructor can monitor an individual's progress. Hence, *College Writing Basics* may be used with any degree of individualization that the instructor feels is beneficial for a given class.

College Writing Basics contains a number of features that make it particularly useful for developmental writing courses:

Progressive Skill Development

Each of the five levels is divided into three sections: "The Paragraph," "The Sentence," and "The Word." In Level One, these sections contain very basic material on paragraph unity, simple sentence combining, basic run-on sentence correction, identification of subjects and verbs, using pronouns to replace nouns, and spelling plurals correctly.

By Level Five, the same basic sections on "The Paragraph," "The Sentence," and "The Word" require students to write compositions for specific audiences, to generate compound and complex sentence combinations, to identify and correct dangling modifiers and nonparallel constructions, to identify and correct inappropriate shifts in verb tenses, and to spell difficult "double-letter" words like "occasionally" and "embarrass." The increase in writing sophistication from Level One to Level Five is marked but logical, given the progressive skill development approach in each level.

Process Oriented

In the first section of each level, "The Paragraph," students plan, organize, and draft paragraphs with the emphasis on content. In the following "The Sentence" section, students revise paragraphs for sentence variety, smooth, clear wording, and correct sentence construction. Finally, in "The Word" section, students learn to use correct grammatical constructions and to spell a range of problematic words correctly. Therefore, each level follows the basic writing process, moving from the broader concerns of content and organization to the more specific concerns of expressing ideas in clear, correct prose. Each writing assignment also includes prewriting considerations, audience awareness, revision guidelines, and opportunities for peer editing sessions and the analysis of sample drafts. Since each level follows the same format, the concept of writing as a process is reinforced throughout the text.

Individualized Learning

The text is designed to allow for as much individualization of learning as the instructor desires. The text "talks" to students in clear, direct language and provides simple, straightforward instructions and a multitude of examples that help guide a student independently through a level. The students can check on their progress through the answer keys, the practice quizzes, and the instructor-monitored section quizzes. Through the section quizzes and the end-of-level writing reviews (discussed below under "Writing Component"), an instructor can make sure that students aren't allowed to move from one level to the next without showing real progress. Through instructions in many exercises that require students to share their work with their instructor, the students never feel like they are "going it alone," and the instructor never feels like an intruder in offering his or her help.

Testing Component

Although *College Writing Basics* is a writing-oriented text, it also contains a testing component for both students and instructor to monitor individual progress on a regular basis. The diagnostic quizzes in the instructor's manual can give students an indication of their familiarity with a given topic. The end-of-section practice quiz helps a student prepare for the section quiz. The instructor may use the section quizzes as progress checks, as graded work, or both. All quizzes are multiple choice, require a positive response selection, and can be taken on Scantron cards and electronically graded for instructor convenience. The instructor's manual also contains comprehensive review quizzes at the end of the second, fourth, and fifth levels which may be used as the objective parts of mid-term and final exams.

Writing Component

Throughout each level, students are given numerous writing opportunities. They write individual paragraphs, combine sentences, generate a variety of sentence constructions, and revise textbook sample paragraphs as well as their own writing. In the last two levels, they begin writing compositions and by Level Five, they are writing papers with openings, middles, and conclusions. At the end of each level is a "Writing Review" assignment which requires students to apply what they have learned to a writing assignment following a step-by-step process of draft and revision. These "Writing Review" assignments serve as excellent "exit tests" for determining a student's readiness to move to the next level.

Skill Reinforcement

The text is designed so that students re-encounter the same basic skill areas in each level. For example, the paragraph is introduced in Level One and picked up again at the beginning of Levels Two and Three, with new elements introduced and old elements reinforced in each level. Similarly, students deal with run-on sentence correction, subject-verb agreement, and pronoun usage in every level in the text. By the end of the text, students have had a full semester's exposure to most of the key elements of effective writing. This kind of reinforcement produces optimum student learning and retention.

In addition, *College Writing Basics* seeks to integrate grammar usage into the writing process in a way that helps students understand its relevance. Too many texts isolate grammar sections from real writing so that there is little carryover from doing exercises on dangling modifier correction to eliminating dangling modifiers in a student's writing. *College Writing Basics* deals with grammar in each level as the final phase of the writing process, and the grammar usage topics covered in a particular level are applied immediately to writing assignments through the process of revision. Students begin to understand that grammar has a logical place in the writing process and also an important function—to allow readers to concentrate fully on the writer's ideas.

Special Note on Proficiency Testing

College Writing Basics, Second Edition, addresses in three ways the types of writing sub-skills that are found in a variety of state-instituted standardized diagnostic tests designed to assess students' writing proficiency. To the great extent that *CWB* does prepare students for such writing proficiency tests, it can certainly be recommended for use in colleges for which such tests are administered.

1. The first way in which *CWB* addresses writing proficiency sub-skills is through the writing assignments found throughout the text. Students using *CWB* write on a regular basis on a range of topics. For each topic, students are concentrating on a particular sub-skill or group of sub-skills that are covered in the section in which the assignment occurs.

For example, in the first section on "The Paragraph," students are working on paragraph unity, and the evaluation emphasis for the writing assignments in that section is on writing a unified paragraph. In one section on "The Sentence," students are working on eliminating wordiness and inappropriate language, and the evaluation emphasis for the writing assignment in that section is on revising for wording economy and appropriateness.

As students progress through the text, new sub-skills are introduced and earlier skills are reinforced, so that by Level Three, for example, the draft of a writing assignment might be evaluated on paragraph unity, development, and coherence; sentence structure variety, including compound and complex structures; and specific editing checks on subject-verb agreement and subject pronoun usage.

By the last level of the text, students are writing compositions and evaluating their sub-skill mastery in the areas of thesis statement and support; paragraph organization, unity, development, and coherence, including transitional wording; smooth, clearly worded sentences that include structural variety and parallel constructions and avoid wordiness, inflated language, and misplaced or dangling modifiers; correct standard usage, including subject-verb agreement, correct pronoun usage, correct comparative and superlative adjectives, correct "ly" adverb forms, and avoidance of shifts in tense or pronouns; punctuation, including avoidance of fragments and run-ons and correct comma, apostrophe, semi-colon, colon, quotation marks, and end mark usage; and standard spelling.

2. Second, sub-skills are addressed in specific exercises within each section of the text. Students are first introduced to the new sub-skill, then do text exercises involving the skill, and then apply what they are learning to their writing assignments. Exercises are almost always followed by some type of writing application, which is important for skill transfer to take place.

Another important text feature is that a particular sub-skill is not introduced once and then dropped in the text. For example, there are exercises involving subject-verb agreement, run-on sentence and fragment recognition, and correct pronoun usage throughout the text, with each text level presenting a more complex variation on what was presented previously. Therefore, students are able to practice on specific skills throughout the text, which is important for skill development, rather than at one time in one specific section.

3. Finally, specific sub-skills are also addressed in practice and mastery quizzes at the end of each section, some fifty quizzes throughout the text. Through these "correct answer" or "best response" multiple-choice quizzes, students can check on their own progress (through the practice quizzes and answer keys in the text) and instructors can determine student "mastery" (through quizzes in testing booklet that is a part of instructor's manual). There is also a comprehensive end-of-text) and instructors can determine student "mastery" (through quizzes in the testing booklet that is a part of the instructor's manual). There is also a comprehensive end-of-text multiple choice text which covers the range of sub-skills presented in the text.

Therefore, while *CWB* is not a text designed for "test-takers" but rather for developing writers, and while the emphasis in the text is on writers drafting, evaluating, revising, editing, and drafting some more, the text does address thoroughly the range of content, structure, and editing sub-skills found in numerous standardized diagnostic or mastery tests. Because *CWB* helps students become more proficient writers, it not-so-coincidentally also helps them become more successful test-takers.

Acknowledgments

I am very grateful to a number of reviewers for offering suggestions and insights that helped shape this text. For their help with the first edition, I particularly wish to thank Shain Graham, Orange Coast College; Anthony Garcia, Saddleback College South; Kathryn Osterholm, Clarion University of Pennsylvania; William Condon, Arkansas Technical University; Daniel Lynch, La Guardia Community College, C.U.N.Y.; Larry McDoniel, St. Louis Community College; Gail Hemmeter, East Stroudsburg University; Mark Reynolds, Jefferson Davis State Junior College; and Sandy Meyer, the Pennsylvania State University. For many of the improvements in this second edition, I am indebted to Dolores LaGuardia, San Jose State University; Beatrice Mendez-Egle, Pan American University; Paula Beck, Nassau Community College; Lois Avery, Houston Community College; Barbara Baxter, Memphis State Technical Institute; and Pamela McLagan.

Contents

Level One

Level Two

Level Three

Level Four

Level Five

Alternate Table of Contents

The Paragraph

The Composition

Sentence Construction

Spelling

LEVEL 1

This is the first of five levels in this book. In Level 1, you are introduced to a few basic concepts about writing paragraphs and sentences. You may find many of the Level 1 activities rather easy, but as you progress through the levels, the material becomes more challenging. What you learn in one level helps prepare you for the next level. Working through the book, you develop skills that will help you write more effectively. Level 1 provides your first step toward that goal.

The Paragraph

Section Topic

Paragraph Unity

Paragraph Unity

As a general rule, *a paragraph is a group of sentences that develops one main point or idea.* One important feature of an effective paragraph is *unity: all sentences within the paragraph are related to the main point.*

Following our definitions, which of the following three groups of words are paragraphs and which paragraph is the most unified?

We had a terrible storm last night. The winds blew up to fifty miles an hour, and it rained very hard. Eucalyptus trees by the river blew over, and one tree hit a power line and blacked out the area for five hours. Downtown, the main street was flooded, and cars were left stranded in bumper-deep water. Before morning, the river flooded its banks, and people living nearby were forced to flee their homes with whatever belongings they could gather. It was the worst storm in the country since 1958.

Watching basketball on television is a favorite pastime of mine. In the winter I'll watch two or three games a day on cable T.V. I also enjoy watching college football, but I don't care for professional football as much. Sometimes I'd rather read a magazine than watch television, and I also enjoy going bowling. My average score is 136 per game. I like to eat corn chips and drink Coke Classic, but I don't care for the new Coke. Why did they have to change their formula?

I didn't sleep well last night. I tossed and turned in bed for hours. I'd get hot and throw the covers off and then get cold and put them on again. I'd fall asleep for an hour and then wake up, and it would take me hours to fall asleep again. I had some interesting dreams while I was sleeping. I was in bed for eight hours and probably got about three hours of sleep. On top of that, I've had a stiff neck for a week.

Here are two important features of paragraphs to remember:

1. A paragraph is a group of sentences that develops one main point or idea.
2. A paragraph has *unity* when all of its sentences are related to the main point.

Exercise 1 Circle the letter of the one sentence in each group that is *not* clearly related to the topic for that group of sentences. When you finish, compare your answers to the answer key for Level 1 Exercise 1 in the back of the book. If you don't understand why an answer is incorrect, discuss it with your instructor.

Example *Topic:* I am sick of eating hamburgers.

a. I've been eating hamburgers twice a day all semester.
b. They are starting to taste like dog food.
(c.) I love Big Macs from McDonald's.
d. I'm getting fat from eating greasy hamburgers.
e. I get a stomachache just thinking about eating another hamburger.

1. *Topic:* There are many ways to study for a test.
   a. You can review a few hours the night before the test.
   b. You can study an hour a night the week of the test.
   c. You can study with friends and help each other.
   d. You can get up early the morning of the test and study.
   e. You can improve your grades by attending class regularly.
2. *Topic:* Greensville is a pleasant place to live.
   a. There are three movie theaters in town.
   b. The people are friendly.
   c. There is very little crime.

d. There is a strange smell coming from the sewer plant.

e. There are many places to shop for clothes.

3. *Topic:* The moon was beautiful last night.

a. It was very full.

b. It was bright and lit up the sky.

c. There were a lot of stars out last night.

d. There were shadows on its surface.

e. It had a halo around it.

4. *Topic:* Uncle Fred is very cheap.

a. He only buys old used cars.

b. He is an honest man.

c. He still has the first dollar he made.

d. He's never gone on a vacation.

e. He pulls his own teeth instead of paying a dentist.

5. *Topic:* The quarrel between Suzanne and Maria is stupid.

a. They don't remember what started it.

b. They have always been best friends.

c. They live in Macon, Georgia.

d. They see each other every day.

e. They have been next-door neighbors for ten years.

6. *Topic:* Liquid car wax is a good buy.

a. It can be found in any auto parts store.

b. It is easy to spread on.

c. It goes a long ways.

d. It gives a good shine.

e. It is not expensive.

7. *Topic:* The baby isn't hungry this morning.

a. She keeps spitting out her food.

b. She keeps playing with her food.

c. She turns her head when I try to feed her.

d. Her stomach looks stuffed.

e. She keeps grinning and rubbing her forehead.

8. *Topic:* Registration this semester was confusing.

a. Many of the classes I wanted were closed.

b. I had to go to six different buildings to register.

c. I couldn't find the teachers whose signatures I needed.

d. I had to fill out three different applications.

e. The computer system for registration was efficient.

____

Exercise 2 Each of the following paragraphs contains one or more sentences that are *not* clearly related to the topic for that paragraph. Cross out the *unrelated* sentences so that the paragraph is *unified*. (The first sentence in each paragraph expresses the main point.) When you finish, compare your answers to the answer key in the back of the book.

Example We had a short spring this year. The weather was cold through March and into April due to storms moving down from Canada. There was still snow on the mountains in late April while it is usually gone by the end of March. We had only two nice weeks in May with the temperatures in the low 70s. ~~The winter was unusually mild, however~~. But by mid-May temperatures were in the 90s, and it was hot from then on.

1. The dormitory rooms were unusually large. They were sixteen-foot squares with wide bay windows. The view from the windows was great. The ten-foot-high ceilings added to the feeling of spaciousness, as did the light-colored walls and the mirrored closet doors. There was space in the rooms for two double beds, dressers, a console television, and a sofa and chair. The cupboard space was adequate. They looked twice the size of your average dormitory rooms.

2. Alex loves to jog. He also enjoys soccer. He is slender and has strong legs, so jogging is easy for him. He also has good natural endurance, so he doesn't run out of breath easily and his lungs seldom ache. Since he has loose muscles, he seldom cramps up. He started jogging a year ago to get in shape, but now he runs because he loves it. He has even run in a few marathons, and he enjoys the competition. He disliked running in the Torborg Invitational Marathon last summer.

3. Math II is an easy class. I've gotten nothing but A's and B's on the quizzes without studying. Sixty students were enrolled in the class, and not one person has dropped since it is so easy. The instructor gives two practice tests before the actual test, so everyone knows exactly what to expect by test time. She also expects us to know a lot from our high school math classes. If students are having any trouble with the class, she allows plenty of time for individual conferences. It is the easiest class I've taken in college.

4. My brother is driving me crazy. First, he borrows my razor and doesn't put it back. Then he'll sneak into the kitchen and eat the pancakes I've cooked for myself. He helps me with my homework. Then he borrows my car without asking and returns it with the gas tank empty. Finally, he borrows money from me and never pays it back. I'll be glad when he moves out of the house. My sister is also moving out.

5. Spock is an unusual cat. She has large, flat paws that are twice the size of normal paws. They are great for pouncing on grasshoppers and crickets, and for soft

landings when she jumps from our roof onto the back porch. She has one green eye and one blue eye, and the green one is larger and set closer to her nose. Her whiskers grow long on one side of her nose and short on the other. We call her Spock because of her extra-large, pointed ears. She is a gray, long-haired cat with normal eating habits.

6. Attaching the sink to the wall should be easy. First, we'll attach a bracket to the wall with screws for the sink to sit on. Then we'll slip the sink over the bracket and put the sink pipe into the main pipe leading to the sewer line. Then we'll fasten the pipes together with a metal collar, which will make the sink more secure. Finally, we'll add metal legs to the front of the sink so it can't rock back and forth. Then we'll move on to the shower and caulk the cracks between the tiles.

Exercise 3 Each of the following paragraph topics can be supported by sentences that relate to it. *Write four sentences of your own that relate to the topic* and that would give a paragraph *unity.* When you finish, share your sentences with your instructor.

Examples *Topic:* Harold is a good basketball player.

a. He can dribble with either hand.
b. He can shoot well from anywhere on the court.
c. He is an excellent passer
d. He is a good team player.

Topic: Mildred's front yard is full of flowers.

a. There are rose bushes below the kitchen window.
b. Blooming sweet pea vines cover a trellis to the north of the living room window.
c. Petunias cover the bed in front of the lawn.
d. Pansies grow in pots on the front porch.

1. *Topic:* Lucinda enjoys living away from home in an apartment.

a.

b.

c.

d.

2. *Topic:* The library is a good place to study.

a.

b.

c.

d.

3. *Topic:* It's difficult going to school and working at the same time.

a.

b.

c.

d.

4. *Topic:* I hate the desks in room 36.

a.

b.

c.

d.

5. *Topic:* You should have more confidence in yourself.

a.

b.

c.

d.

6. *Topic:* That is the ugliest dog I've ever seen.

a.

b.

c.

d.

7. *Topic:* I don't like early morning classes.

a.

b.

c.

d.

8. *Topic:* Watching television can be very boring.

a.

b.

c.

d.

Exercise 4 Now you are ready to write your own paragraph. Select one of the following opening sentences to begin a paragraph. Complete the opening sentence in your own words. Then write the "first draft" of your paragraph on the topic presented in your opening sentence.

To help you get started, make a list of five or six ideas that relate to your topic. You may use those ideas to help you develop the paragraph. Here is an example:

Opening Sentence: *The worst day of the week is* Monday.

Ideas: first day of week
hate getting up early
only good Mondays: holidays
can't comb hair
lots of classes
no ride

Opening Sentences:

My favorite class this semester is ______________________.

One of my worst habits is ______________________.

There are many good ways to ______________________.

The worst day of the week is ______________________.

One thing I enjoy doing on weekends is ______________________.

My favorite professional football team is ______________________.

One thing I like about college is ______________________.

When you have finished the first draft of your paragraph, consider the following basic evaluation questions:

1. Is my paragraph unified? Is there anything I need to eliminate or change that does not relate well to my topic?
2. Is there anything I can add—another supporting idea, an example or detail—that would make my paragraph clearer or more interesting to readers?
3. Are my ideas presented in the best order? Are there any sentences that would be more effective in a different location in the paragraph?
4. Do my sentences all make sense? Do I need to add, change, or eliminate any words to make any sentence clearer or smoother?
5. Are my sentences punctuated correctly? Do I have a period at the end of each sentence?
6. Are there any spelling problems? Do I need to look up any questionably spelled words? Have I put the correct endings (*-s, -es, -ed, -ing*) on words that need them?

With a partner or in a small group, analyze the following first draft of a paragraph by applying the six evaluation questions and discussing the kinds of revisions (changes) you might suggest to the author.

My worst day of the week is Monday. Why, I'll tell you why because Monday is the first day of the week. Also because over the weekend we get to sleep in. On a Monday morning we don't like getting up early. The only Mondays I like is when we have a holiday. I also hate Mondays because I hardly have time to comb my hair right like the way I comb it over the weekend. Plus there's the problem of my extra long class schedule on Mondays and trying to find a ride to school at 7:45 in the morning. If I live through Mondays, the rest of the weeks go by real fast.

When you finish analyzing the sample paragraph, reread your own first draft, keeping the evaluation questions in mind. Make notes on the draft of any revisions you'd like to make. You might also have a classmate read your draft for a second opinion. Finally, write your second draft, including all revisions you have noted for improving the paragraph.

Practice Quiz

At the end of each section is a practice quiz to help you prepare for the section quiz. Take the quiz and then compare your answers with the key for the Level 1 Practice Quiz in the back of the book. If you make mistakes on the quiz, review the exercises in this section and also ask your instructor for help. When you are ready for the section quiz on paragraph unity, let your instructor know.

Circle the letter of the one sentence in each group that does *not* relate clearly to the topic given for that group.

Example *Topic:* Your Uncle Bernard is very strong.

a. He has bulging arm and leg muscles.

b. He can lift eight-pound sacks of cement easily.

c. He can beat anyone in arm wrestling.

d. He can lift me over his head with no trouble.

(e.) He is an excellent piano player.

1. *Topic:* It's hard to find a good baby-sitter.

a. Many high school girls go out on weekends.

b. A lot of girls won't work for baby-sitting wages.

c. Our favorite baby-sitter is Clarissa.

d. Baby-sitting is not as popular with girls as it once was.

e. Some girls who baby-sit aren't very responsible.

2. *Topic:* The price of a new car is too high.
   a. A car costs as much as a house used to cost.
   b. Most people can never afford to buy a new car.
   c. Monthly payments on a new car often are over $300.
   d. Some cars are still reasonably priced.
   e. Most people would have to save for years just to buy a new car.
3. *Topic:* Your new hairdo is very attractive.
   a. Your hair color has always been pretty.
   b. Your hair is always in place.
   c. Your hairdo sets off your big eyes.
   d. It gives your face a soft look.
   e. It is the perfect length for your face.
4. Topic: Those weeds in the backyard are hard to pull.
   a. The weeds are waist-high.
   b. Their roots are deep.
   c. They have tiny thorns on them.
   d. They break off at ground level.
   e. There are plenty of flowers in the backyard.
5. Topic: That tree limb should be easy to cut off.
   a. It is not very high.
   b. It is not big around.
   c. The limb next to it is long.
   d. The wood is soft and easy to cut through.
   e. Your chain saw is sharp.
6. Topic: Minkler is a small town.
   a. The population is eighteen.
   b. There are only three buildings in town.
   c. It is located on Highway 101.
   d. The town covers only one quarter of an acre.
   e. It isn't found on any map.
7. Topic: Adding oil to your car is a simple process.
   a. Check the dipstick to see if the oil level is low.
   b. Unscrew the oil cap on top of the engine.
   c. Check the air filter for dirt.

   d. Using a can opener, make two holes in the top of an oil can.
   e. Pour in the oil, replace the cap, and recheck the dipstick.

8. Topic: The swimming pool is in bad condition.
   a. The tiles are covered with a white film.
   b. Algae grows on the steps.
   c. Bugs and leaves float on top of the water.
   d. The plaster is cracking on the bottom.
   e. Pool maintenance is expensive.

The Sentence

In the first section, you learned to write a *unified* paragraph containing sentences that developed one main point. The next step is to look more closely at the individual sentences within the paragraph.

The first time you put your ideas on paper, they don't always come out in clear, smoothly worded sentences. Most writers *revise* their sentences to improve on the original wording. They may change a single word in one sentence, change the word order in another, and completely reword a third sentence.

The section in each level on "The Sentence" provides information and activities that help you to write clearer, stronger sentences. You learn to spot weaknesses in your own writing and to make changes, or *revisions*, that eliminate those weaknesses. Sentence revision is an important task for all writers.

Sentence Variety

Experienced writers have the ability to use a variety of sentence structures to express their thoughts. Less experienced writers may use a few basic structures over and over, which can lead to a monotonous writing style. The sections on "Sentence Variety" will give you the confidence and skill to use a variety of sentence structures to convey your ideas to readers.

Section Topic

Combining Short Sentences

Combining Short Sentences—Method #1

The first time you write a paragraph, you may find some short, choppy sentences in it. Here is an example of a paragraph full of such sentences.

I enjoy Christmas very much. I like shopping. I like decorating the tree. I like giving presents. I enjoy eating on Christmas Day. I enjoy eating turkey. I like a lot of dressing. I like pumpkin pie. I also like being with the family. I like seeing my grandmother. I like seeing my nieces.

The short, similar sentences are choppy and not easy or pleasant to read. Here is a *revised* version of the same paragraph with some of the short sentences combined.

I enjoy Christmas very much. I like shopping and decorating the tree, and I also enjoy giving presents. On Christmas Day, I love eating all the turkey, dressing, and pumpkin pie. Finally, I look forward to being with the family and seeing my grandmother and nieces in particular.

As you can see, the revised paragraph is smoother and more pleasant to read than the first version. The thoughts expressed are the same, but the sentences are smoother and stronger.

Here is a basic method for combining short sentences that will be used in this section:

COMBINING METHOD #1

1. Eliminate words that are repeated in sentences.
2. Group similar words or groups of words together.
3. Use the joining word *and* to combine words or groups of words.
4. Use commas (,) to separate words or groups of words that are joined.

Here are four examples of short sentences combined to form better single sentences. In each new sentence formed, some words have been eliminated and some have been grouped together. Notice the use of commas (,) and *and* in the new sentences.

Short Sentences: Jules is sweet. He is considerate. He is loving.
Combined: Jules is sweet, considerate, and loving.

Short Sentences: Mary went to the store. Julie went to the store. Maria went to the store.
Combined: Mary, Julie, and Maria went to the store.

Short Sentences:	I like your Chevrolet. It is a 1956. It is green. It is a two-door.
Combined:	I like your green, two-door 1956 Chevrolet.
Short Sentences:	Jack applied for a job. He went for an interview. He was hired.
Combined:	Jack applied for a job, went for an interview, and was hired.

Exercise 5 Combine the following groups of short sentences to form single sentences. Use the combining method introduced: Eliminate repeated words, group similar words together, use *and* to join words, and use commas (,), to separate words that have been joined. When you finish, show your sentences to your instructor.

Example Your uncle married my aunt. He is rich. She is poor.

Revised:

1. The large dog jumped over the fence. He landed in a bush.
2. Myra watered the roses. She mowed the lawn. She trimmed the hedge.
3. Henry was invited to the reception. Myrtle was also invited to the reception.
4. You look tired. You look sore. You look angry.
5. The house is small. It is white. It is on the corner.
6. May I borrow your watch? May I borrow your pen? May I borrow your tie?
7. Louise bought a sweater. Freda bought a sweater. Helen bought a sweater. The sweaters were red. The sweaters were wool.
8. That cat is skinny. It has short hair. It is a Siamese. It is spoiled.
9. I like Fred's motorcycle. It is new. It is black. It has chrome fenders. It has a sheepskin seat.
10. I have posters on the wall. I have many of them. They have rock stars on them. The wall is above my bed. I live in the college dormitory.

Exercise 6 Rewrite the following paragraph, and combine pairs or groups of short sentences into single sentences using the Combining Method #1.

Example Swen came home from work early. He was tired. He was depressed. He had worked twelve hours. He had worked them straight through.

Revised: Swen came home from work early. He was tired and depressed. He had worked twelve straight hours.

The horror movie at the drive-in was terrible. The acting was bad. The plot was bad. The sound track was even worse. Every scene was filled with blood. There was blood on the bodies. There was blood on the walls. There was blood in the bathtub. The ending of the movie was the worst part. It was stupid. It was unbelievable. It made no sense. A six-year-old girl poisoned her mother, father, brother, and dog with rat poison. She did it for fun. She did it to amuse her friends. They were wild. They were psychotic. It was the worst movie I've seen in a long time. I went home. I was disgusted. I didn't go to another movie for a month. I didn't watch one on T.V.

____

Exercise 7 Write a paragraph about something you hate to do or hate to have: take out the garbage, shave your legs, take lecture notes, work on weekends, wake up early, get a shot, have a headache, have an unreliable car, and so on. Fill in the following sentence to use as your opening sentence:

I hate to ______________.

Before you write your first draft, list some ideas supporting your topic to include in your paragraph as you did in Exercise 4. Here is an example:

Sample Paragraph

I hate to have a toothache.

Ideas: the pain
not enough pain killer
wait for appointment
trouble with wisdom teeth
teeth pulling
shots

When you have finished the first draft of your paragraph, consider the following evaluation questions:

1. Is my paragraph unified? Is there anything I need to eliminate or change that does not relate well to my topic?
2. Is there anything I can add—another supporting idea, an example or detail—that would make my paragraph clearer or more interesting to readers?
3. Are my ideas presented in the best order? Are there any sentences that would be more effective in a different location in the paragraph?
4. Do my sentences all make sense? Have I used the best words to express my thoughts? Do I need to add, change, or eliminate any words to make any sentence clearer or smoother?

5. Are there any pairs or groups of short sentences that could be improved by being combined into single sentences?
6. Are my sentences punctuated correctly? Do I have a period at the end of each sentence?
7. Are there any spelling problems? Do I need to look up any questionably spelled words? Have I put the correct endings (*-s, -es, -ed, -ing*) on words that need them?

With a partner or in a small group, analyze the following first draft of a paragraph by applying the evaluation questions and discussing the kinds of revisions you might suggest to the author.

I hate to have a toothache in the first place. I hate pain. It seems my whole mouth is sore from cheek to cheek. My dentist never give me enough novocaine, then to make it worst I have to wait for over a week for an appointment. I don't know why we have wisdom teeth in the first place, it's silly to have them and then in our later years get them pulled and tugged and then the pain again inflicts. I hate the thought of the sharp instruments the man uses and those shots that sting for days to come after you feel that terrible pain of a tooth.

When you finish analyzing the sample paragraph, reread your own first draft, keeping the evaluation questions in mind. Make notes on the draft of any revisions you'd like to make. You might also have a classmate read your draft for a second opinion. Finally, write your second draft, including all revisions you have noted for improving the paragraph.

Practice Quiz

Here is a practice quiz to help prepare you for the section quiz. Take the quiz and check your answers with the key in the back of the book. If you have problems, review the exercises in the section and ask your instructor for some help. When you are ready for the section quiz, let your instructor know.

Circle the letter of the best sentence formed from combining the groups of short sentences provided.

Example Mabel bought a dress. She tried it on. She found a hole in one sleeve.

a. Mabel bought a dress, and she tried it on and found a hole in one sleeve.
(b.) Mabel bought a dress, tried it on, and found a hole in one sleeve.
c. Mabel bought a dress which she tried on with a hole in one sleeve.
d. Mabel bought a dress, tried it on, and a hole in one sleeve.

1. Ted's ankles are thin. They are weak. They are wobbly.

a. Ted's ankles are thin and are weak and also wobbly.

b. Ted's ankles are thin, weak, and wobbly.

c. Wobbly are Ted's weak and thin ankles.

d. Weak, thin, and wobbly are Ted's ankles.

2. The cat jumped onto the sofa. It curled up in a ball.

a. The cat jumped onto the sofa and curled up in a ball.

b. The cat jumped onto the sofa, and it curled up in a ball.

c. The cat jumped onto the sofa curled up in a ball.

d. The cat jumped and curled up in a ball onto the sofa.

3. No one went to school today. No one stayed home. No one went to town.

a. No one went to school today, home, or town.

b. No one went to school today or stayed home today or went to town today.

c. No one went to school, stayed home, or went to town today.

d. No one went to school today or stayed home and went to town.

4. There is a statue in the park. It is very large. It is of a grizzly bear.

a. There is a large statue of a grizzly bear in the park.

b. There is a large statue in the park, and it is a grizzly bear.

c. There is a statue in the park of a grizzly bear that is large.

d. There is a statue in the park that is large of a grizzly bear.

5. The Mets ended their season on Tuesday. The Yankees ended their season on the same Tuesday.

a. The Mets and Yanks ended their season on Tuesday.

b. The Mets ended their season on Tuesday with the Yankees.

c. The Mets ended their season on Tuesday as did the Yankees.

d. The Mets ended the Yankee's season on Tuesday.

6. The weather is cold. It is wet. It is chilling. It is ruining the vacation.

a. The cold weather is wet, and it is chilling, and ruining the vacation.

b. The weather is cold and it is wet and chilling, and ruining the vacation.

c. The weather is cold, wet, and chilling and ruining the vacation.

d. The cold, wet, chilling weather is ruining the vacation.

7. The ship anchored in the bay. It took on gasoline. It sailed out to sea.

a. The ship anchored and then took on gasoline and then sailed out to sea.

b. The ship anchored in the bay, took on gasoline, and sailed out to sea.

c. The ship anchored in the bay and sailed out with some gasoline to sea.

d. The ship anchored, took on gasoline, and sailed out to sea in the bay.

8. The train station is filled with people. They are happy. They are noisy. It is New Year's Eve.

   a. The station is filled with people happy and people noisy on New Year's Eve.

   b. The station is filled and with happy and noisy people and on New Year's Eve.

   c. The New Year's Eve station is happy and noisy with people.

   d. The station is filled with happy, noisy people on New Year's Eve.

Clear Sentences

Section Topic

Word Choice

A second important concern in revising sentences is *effective wording*. When you reread a paragraph you have written, you may find ways to make your sentences clearer, more direct, and more accurate. The sections on "Clear Sentences" give you practice revising sentences for wording improvement.

Word Choice

One of the biggest challenges for writers is to find the best combination of words to express themselves in any given sentence. Often a writer will revise a sentence three or four times before finding the best wording. As a writer, you need to reread your sentences carefully, looking for words or groups of words that don't express your thoughts as clearly or accurately as you would like.

Here are some common wording problems that writers face.

COMMON WORDING PROBLEMS

1. Using the wrong word to express a thought.

   Example: I feel very subconscious around strangers.
   Revised: I feel very self-conscious around strangers.

   Example: We will precipitate in the contest.
   Revised: We will participate in the contest.

   Example: We took the wrong fairway outside of Chicago.
   Revised: We took the freeway outside of Chicago.

2. Not choosing the *best* word to express a thought.

   Example: I did a mistake on my income tax form.
   Revised: I made a mistake on my income tax form.

   Example: I got a lot of work to do tonight.
   Revised: I have a lot of work to do tonight.

   Example: It was a humongous diamond.
   Revised: It was a huge diamond.

3. Using the wrong form of a word for a particular sentence.

   Example: I dreamed to be a jet pilot.
   Revised: I dreamed of being a jet pilot.

   Example: George wanted getting to know Teresa better.
   Revised: George wanted to get to know Teresa better.

   Example: He was burying up to his neck in sand.
   Revised: He was buried up to his neck in sand.

4. Using words or groups of words that *don't go together* in the same sentence.

   Example: Although you are late for work, but I don't mind. (*Although* and *but* don't go together in this sentence.)
   Revised: Although you are late for work, I don't mind.

   Example: Since I got the job, so I have money to spend. (*Since* and *so* don't go together in this sentence.)
   Revised: Since I got the job, I have money to spend.

   Example: Ms. Jones helps me how to program a computer. (*Helps* and *how to* don't go together.)
   Revised: Ms. Jones helps me program a computer.

As you can see, there are a number of possible wording problems a writer might face from time to time. Here are some suggestions for working out such problems.

1. When you find a word or *phrase* (group of words) that on rereading doesn't sound right to you, it probably needs revising. You may need to change a single word, change your word order, or totally revise your sentence.

2. If you are not sure of the exact meaning of a word that you have used, look it up in the dictionary. Don't settle for using a word that seems *close* to what you want to express.

3. Try out different ways to express the same thought until you arrive at the most effective wording.

Example: That foreign student doesn't seem to be having much of a time here.

The foreign student doesn't seem to be enjoying herself much here.

The Italian student doesn't seem to be enjoying herself in or out of school here.

The Italian exchange student doesn't seem to be enjoying her stay in the United States.

Exercise 8 Each of the following sentences needs revising for better wording. Rewrite each sentence and *revise the underlined words* by changing, adding, or removing words to improve the sentence. Then show your sentences to your instructor.

Example Matilda learned me how to polish my fingernails.

Revised: Matilda taught me how to polish my fingernails.

1. Hilda thought to be a nurse when she graduated from community college.
2. The grass looks of a dark green.
3. The stripes on the building happen every two feet.
4. The building is built up by glass and marble.
5. Each house is differential in its own way.
6. Many of the yards have a light organization of leaves on the ground.
7. The size of the backyard echoes the size of the front yard.
8. Not nice-looking patios are behind every home on the block.
9. Although John was well fed, but he still looked scrawny.
10. You've never exercised regularly is because you had no place to do it.
11. Dogs barked ravagely at the moon.
12. The differences in the two houses are reflexed by their sizes.
13. One side of the house is all over with ivy.
14. The wall is high enough to accept the huge door.
15. The current of warm air from the fireplace scatters throughout the house.
16. After two months of duty, John could release from the army.
17. Because of the cafeteria's location, it is with convenience for the students.

18. In community colleges also have vocational nursing programs.

19. The cassette recorder "on" button is upper on the right side.

20. Most people want secure for their families.

Exercise 9 Write a paragraph about the best (or worst) job you ever had. Begin the paragraph with a sentence that expresses your main idea. You may want to make a list of supporting points to include in your paragraph before writing it. Here is an example:

Topic: hoeing weeds at the high school
Supporting Points: very hot
hard ground
tough Bermuda grass
blisters
sore back
neverending
get nauseated

When you have finished the first draft of your paragraph, consider the following evaluation questions:

1. Is my paragraph unified? Is there anything I need to eliminate or change that does not relate well to my topic?
2. Is there anything I can add—another supporting idea, an example or detail—that would make my paragraph clearer or more interesting to readers?
3. Are my ideas presented in the best order? Are there any sentences that would be more effective in a different location in the paragraph?
4. Do my sentences all make sense? Do I need to add, change, or eliminate any words to make any sentence clearer or smoother?
5. Are there any pairs or groups of short sentences that could be improved by being combined into single sentences?
6. Are my sentences punctuated correctly? Do I have a period at the end of each sentence?
7. Are there any spelling problems? Do I need to look up any questionably spelled words? Have I put the correct endings (*-s, -es, -ed, -ing*) on words that need them?

With a partner or in a small group, analyze the following first draft of a paragraph by applying the evaluation questions and discussing the kinds of revisions you might suggest to the author.

Hoeing weeds one summer at the high school was the hardest job I ever had. After my sophomore year, I was hired as a part-time groundsman to hoe up the weeds around the trees lining the outside of the football stadium. There were a hundred and fifty trees around the stadium, I counted them, every tree had Bermuda growing around its base with a bunch of Bermuda between trees where the watering ditch was dug. The month I worked, it averaged over 100 degrees in heat, and I'd get so hot, sweaty, and dirty that I'd get sick to my stomach. The weeding wasn't easy, the ground was like hard pan and the Bermuda was as tough as barbed wire. I'd really have to strain to dig the hoe in and depress the Bermuda roots. The end of a day, my hands were blistered and my back was sore and I was stooped over from bending over. And the work seemed endless, looking down that long line of trees and knowing there were just as many on the other side of the stadium was depressing. I finally learned to pace myself and work in the shade as much as possible, but there was no freeing from the heat, the hard work, or the monotonous work. It was the last summer I worked at the high school.

When you finish analyzing the sample paragraph, reread your own first draft, keeping the evaluation questions in mind. Make notes on the draft of any revisions you'd like to make. You might also have a classmate read your draft for a second opinion. Finally, write your second draft, including all revisions you have noted for improving the paragraph.

Practice Quiz

Here is a practice quiz to help prepare you for the section quiz. Take the quiz and compare your answers to the answer key. When you are ready for the section quiz, let your instructor know.

Circle the letter of the best-worded sentence in each group.

Example

a. Sexual freedom has increased a big rate on teenage pregnancies.
(b.) Sexual freedom has caused a big increase in teenage pregnancies.
c. Sexual freedom increased a lot of teenage pregnancies.

1. (a.) My Easter vacation was boring because I worked in the lumberyard.
   b. My Easter vacation was boring which I worked in the lumberyard.
   c. My Easter vacation was boring for working in the lumberyard.
2. a. The weekend went by slowly and hot.
   b. The slowly weekend went by very hot.
   (c.) The hot weekend went by slowly.
3. (a.) The children waded into the water and plunged in.
   b. The children moved out into the water and lunged in.
   c. The children walked out into the water and thrashed in.

4. a. My skin was troubled by a rash.
   b. My skin was irritated by a rash.
   c. My skin was hampered by a rash.
5. a. The siphon narrowed at the bottom and largened at the top.
   b. The siphon got smaller at the bottom and got larger at the top.
   c. The siphon narrowed at the bottom and widened at the top.
6. a. Although the game was almost over, so no one in the stands left.
   b. Although the game was almost over, no one in the stands left.
   c. Although the game was almost over, so no one in the stands emptied.
7. a. Jonathan did a number of errors on his job application.
   b. Jonathan made a number of errors on his job application.
   c. Jonathan put a number of errors on his job application.
8. a. Maria learned us to have a positive attitude.
   b. Maria taught us to have a positive attitude.
   c. Maria taught us to have a possessive attitude.
9. a. They must try to overdo their fear of the water.
   b. They must try to overwhelm their fear of the water.
   c. They must try to overcome their fear of the water.
10. a. When we landed on the beach, but there was no one there to acknowledge us.
    b. When we landed on the beach, there was no one there to welcome us.
    c. We landed on the beach, but there was no one there to accentuate us.

Correct Sentences

Section Topic

Run-on Sentence
Pattern #1

A final concern for all writers is to make sure their sentences are *structurally* correct: each sentence is complete and correctly punctuated. The most common structural problem—the *run-on sentence*—is introduced in this section, and the *sentence fragment* is introduced in a later level. The sections throughout the text on "Correct

Sentences" will help you write complete, correctly punctuated sentences that will communicate your thoughts most effectively.

Run-on Sentence Pattern #1

A complete sentence is set off from other sentences because it begins with a *capital letter* and ends with a *period* or other end mark. However, sometimes a writer will run two or three complete sentences together without separating them with periods, causing a *run-on-sentence*. Here is one of the most typical run-on sentence patterns:

RUN-ON SENTENCE PATTERN #1

1. Two sentences are run together without a period separating them.
2. The second sentence within the run-on sentence often begins with a *pronoun*:

   I he she it you they we

3. Sometimes a *comma* is placed between the two sentences, and sometimes there is no punctuation. A comma by itself does *not* correctly separate two sentences.

Here are examples of pattern #1 run-ons. The *pronoun* beginning the second sentence within the run-on sentence is underlined.

Mary bought four tickets to the rock concert, she planned on inviting her three roommates.

Those trees growing along the freeway are dying they are being killed by pollution.

Your brother should join the circus he is a great animal trainer.

Wendy decided to change her style of dress, she threw away her jeans and bought four dresses.

The news about Sarah's triplets spread rapidly it reached our house last night.

Martha and I have been planning on working all weekend, we need the extra money.

As you can see, each sample run-on sentence contains *two complete sentences* with a *pronoun* beginning the second sentence. The sentences all need correcting to eliminate the run-ons.

There are different ways to correct a run-on sentence. Here is the most common method, which will be used in this section. Other options will be introduced in later levels.

> RUN-ON SENTENCE CORRECTION: METHOD #1
>
> Place a period (.) at the end of the first sentence and *capitalize* the first letter of the second sentence.

Here are the corrected versions of the sample run-on sentences. A period separates the sentences, and a capital letter indicates the beginning of the second sentence.

Mary bought four tickets to the rock concert. She planned on inviting her three roommates.

Those trees growing along the freeway are dying. They are being killed by pollution.

Your brother should join the circus. He is a great animal trainer.

Wendy decided to change her style of dress. She threw away her jeans and bought four dresses.

The news about Sarah's triplets spread rapidly. It reached our house last night.

Martha and I have been planning on working all weekend. We need the extra money.

Exercise 10 Rewrite and correct the following run-on sentences by putting a *period* at the end of the first sentence and *capitalizing* the first letter of the second sentence. Look for *pronouns* that commonly begin the second sentence within a run-on: *I, he, she, it, you, they, we*. Remember, a *comma* does not correctly separate two sentences. When you finish, check your answers with the key in the back of the book.

Example You are invited to attend the church social Friday, you don't need to bring anything.

Revised: You are invited to attend the church social Friday. You don't need to bring anything.

1. The ants invaded the kitchen last night, they crept through cracks in the wall and into the sugar container.
2. Your new sweater is soft and warm, it should be great to wear during football season.
3. The Joneses are renting half of the N Street duplex, they are paying $300 a month.
4. Marcy is trying out a new diet, she is eating only fruit and nuts for seven weeks.
5. Frank has become very attached to his German shepherd Oscar, they go everywhere together.
6. The mercury vapor light on top of the garage roof is bright, it might keep the neighbors awake at night.

7. Let's try to get to the hardware store before five o'clock tomorrow we need to buy a trap for the sink.

8. It is hard to believe you are in need of money, Scott I lent you $15.00 yesterday.

9. The roll of colored film was developed at one of the corner drugstores on the mall it had all of our Niagara Falls pictures on it.

10. The nurses went on strike for better benefits and improved working conditions they returned to work with an improved contract.

Exercise II

The following paragraph contains some run-on sentences. Rewrite the paragraph and correct all run-on sentences by putting a period after the first sentence and capitalizing the first letter of the second sentence. When you finish, compare your answers to the key in the back of the book.

Example Fernando returned to school after the service, he was able to use the G.I. funding bill. He enrolled at Coast College in the electronics program.

Revised: Fernando returned to school after the service. He was able to use the G.I. funding bill. He enrolled at Coast College in the electronics program.

Alicia worked as a secretary for an accounting firm, she started as a typist but later helped with the bookkeeping. After six years as a secretary, she realized that she was doing as much bookkeeping as typing, but she was only making $6.00 an hour. She decided to enroll at the San Joaquin Night School in their accounting program, the classes met four evenings a week for two sixteen-week semesters. Alicia continued working as a secretary during the day and went to school four nights a week for four years. That was the roughest time in her life. Today, Alicia is a certified public accountant she is working for the same firm that hired her as secretary ten years ago. Someday she hopes to be a partner in the firm.

Practice Quiz

Here is a practice quiz to help prepare you for the section quiz. Take the quiz and compare your answers to the key in the back of the book. When you are ready for the section quiz on run-on sentences, let your instructor know.

Circle the letter of the correctly punctuated sentence in each group.

Example

a. You are an exciting young gymnast, Donna, you should set your sights on the Olympics.

b. You are an exciting young gymnast, Donna. You should set your sights on the Olympics.

c. You are an exciting young gymnast, Donna you should set your sights on the Olympics.

1. a. The art students are having a great semester, they have moved into a new art building.

   b. The art students are having a great semester. They have moved into a new art building.

   c. The art students are having a great semester they have moved into a new art building.

2. a. Swimming is a good form of exercise. It requires the use of most body muscles.

   b. Swimming is a good form of exercise, it requires the use of most body muscles.

   c. Swimming is a good form of exercise it requires the use of most body muscles.

3. a. Myra's closet is filled with old, holey sweat shirts, she doesn't like to wear anything else.

   b. Myra's closet is filled with old, holey sweat shirts. She doesn't like to wear anything else.

   c. Myra's closet is filled with old, holey sweat shirts she doesn't like to wear anything else.

4. a. The jury slept at a hotel on Main Street for six weeks, they were allowed to see no one.

   b. The jury slept at a hotel on Main Street for six weeks. They were allowed to see no one.

   c. The jury slept at a hotel on Main Street for six weeks they were allowed to see no one.

5. a. Divorce laws in the U.S. are getting very lenient. They make it easy for a couple to divorce.

   b. Divorce laws in the U.S. are getting very lenient they make it easy for a couple to divorce.

   c. Divorce laws in the U.S. are getting very lenient, they make it easy for a couple to divorce.

6. a. You and I should get together during Easter we could look for summer work together.

   b. You and I should get together during Easter. We could look for summer work together.

c. You and I should get together during Easter, we could look for summer work together.

7. a. The renters objected to the latest rent increase, they hired a lawyer to represent them.

   b. The renters objected to the latest rent increase they hired a lawyer to represent them.

   c. The renters objected to the latest rent increase. They hired a lawyer to represent them.

8. a. The nuclear energy project was costly, the expense was passed on to the taxpayers.

   b. The nuclear energy project was costly. The expense was passed on to the taxpayers.

   c. The nuclear energy project was costly the expense was passed on to the taxpayers.

The Word

In the first section you learned to write *unified paragraphs*. In the second section you worked on *revising* sentences for variety, clearness, and correct structure. In this final section on "The Word," you look at *individual words and their relationship* within a sentence to make sure you aren't making any errors that could bother your readers. You have moved from considering the paragraph as a whole to considering individual sentences within the paragraph to considering individual words within the sentence. The process of writing usually moves roughly in that direction: from the broadest concerns to the most specific.

Verb Forms

Section Topics

Subject-Verb Identification
Basic Subject-Verb Agreement

Writers have more problems with *verbs* than with any other grammatical area. Verbs take many different forms depending on their *tense*, which indicates a particular time period: future, present, or past. Present tense verbs also change form depending on whether the *subject* is singular or plural. Finally, some verbs change their forms in *irregular* ways rather than conforming to the rules. The sections on "Verb Forms" throughout the book introduce the most common and useful verb tenses for writers, beginning with this section on *present tense verbs*.

Subject-Verb Identification

To use *present tense* verb forms correctly, it is important to be able to identify *subjects* and *verbs*, the two main parts of any sentence. Here are some suggestions for identifying subjects and verbs in your sentences.

TO FIND THE *SUBJECT*:

1. Ask yourself, "Who or what is doing the action in the sentence?"
2. Ask yourself, "Who or what is the sentence about?"
3. The subject usually comes *before* the verb.

Examples:

Mary baked a cake Saturday. (Who baked? the subject *Mary*)

The cat leaped onto the mantel. (What leaped onto the mantel? the subject *cat*)

Sarah is very tired today. (Who is the sentence about? the subject *Sarah*)

The garbage can is full. (What is the sentence about? the subject *can*)

Jacqueline ran a mile yesterday. (Who ran a mile? the subject *Jacqueline*)

TO FIND THE *ACTION VERB*:

1. Ask yourself, "What is the action or thought in the sentence?"
2. Ask yourself, "What word tells what the subject is doing?"
3. Ask yourself, "What word changes form with time?" (Today I *eat*. Yesterday I *ate*).
4. The verb usually comes *after* the subject.

Examples:

Wally catches catfish with his hands. (What is the action? the verb *catches*)

The trout swim lazily in the pond. (What do the trout do? the action *swim*)

Allison believes in justice for all. (What is the thought? the verb *believes*)

Truck drivers often stop at our restaurant. (What word changes form with time? the verb *stop*—Yesterday I *stopped*)

Exercise 12 Underline the subject and circle the verb in each sentence. Use the suggestions just provided to help you find the subject and verb. When you finish, check your answers with the answer key in the back of the book.

Example Freddie (buys) his clothes at Penney's.

Who buys? Freddie (subject)
What is the action? buys (verb)
What word changes with time? buys (verb) Yesterday Freddy *bought* clothes.

1. Aunt Clarice makes all of her own dresses.
2. The screen door needs patching.
3. Your trees fell down in the storm.
4. Marvin accepted an invitation to the debate.
5. That hurricane tore the roof off a house.
6. That hamster bit me on the arm.
7. The tallest building collapsed during the earthquake.
8. Your ideas startle everyone.
9. That stop sign shakes all the time.
10. The news bothered Theodore.
11. New shoes make my feet sweat.
12. Your actions speak louder than your words.
13. Terry behaved badly during the ceremony.
14. Your good looks attract lots of attention.
15. One of Jim's slippers fell from the window ledge.
16. That man reads many strange books.
17. To Mike's surprise, a sudden telephone call prevented him from finishing his work.
18. Your nose dripped all morning because of the cold air.
19. Out of all your purchases, the new can opener works the best.
20. At the top of Judy's swing, the head of her golf club flew off.

Exercise 13 Write ten of your own sentences using verbs that show an *action* or *thought* (see "Action Verb" section before Exercise 14 and the type of verbs found in Exercise 14). Use ten different subjects and ten different verbs. Underline the subject and circle the verb in each sentence. When you finish, share your sentences with your instructor.

Examples My cat loves to sleep on my bed at night.

The broken window needs to be replaced in the kitchen.

1.

2.

3.

4.

5.

6.

7.

8.

9.

10.

Subject-Verb Agreement

The *present tense* verb form changes in relation to the subject of the sentence. Here are the main things you need to know to use the correct present tense forms.

1. The *present tense* is used to write about anything that is *currently happening* or *existing*.
2. The *subject* of a sentence may have two different forms: *singular* or *plural*.

   Singular means *one* of anything: a person, a state, one onion, a team, an idea.

   Plural means *more than one* of anything: people, six swans, rooms, bananas, ideas.

   Most plural words end in *s* or *es*: dogs, cats, apples, houses, churches, boxes.

3. Here are the basic rules for subject-verb agreement:
   a. If the subject is singular, the verb ends in *s*.

      Examples:

      Jack enjoys long walks.

      That cat sleeps practically anywhere.

      One player needs to stay back on defense all the time.

   b. If the subject is plural, the verb does not end in *s*.

      Examples:

      The boys enjoy long walks.

      Those cats sleep practically anywhere.

      Two players need to stay back on defense all the time.

4. An exception to rule 3-*b* is verbs that are *s*-ending words: *press, dress, mess, impress, assess, caress, depress*.
5. When *pronouns* are subjects, here are the subject-verb agreement rules:
   a. With *he, she,* and *it* (third persons singular): *verb ends in* s.

      Examples:

      He likes to fish below the dam.

      She prefers fishing in the lake above the dam.

      It takes a lot of courage to admit mistakes.

   b. All other pronouns (*I, you, they, we*): *verb does not end in* s.

      Examples:

      I like to fish below the dam.

      You prefer fishing in the lake above the dam.

      They enjoy eating fish more than catching them.

      We clean the fish for everyone.

Here are examples of sentences with *present tense verbs* and *singular subjects*. Notice that all verbs end in *s*. (Subjects are underlined and verbs are circled.)

Harry enjoys a good spy movie.

Your watch keeps very good time.

The right roller skate needs fixing immediately.

That apple tastes delicious.

Your mother walks across the town every morning.

The pheasant sleeps in the bushes in our backyard.

Here are examples of sentences with *present tense verbs* and *plural subjects. Notice that the verbs do not end in* s.

The boys enjoy a good spy movie.

Your watches keep very good time.

The roller skates need fixing immediately.

Those apples taste delicious.

The two mothers walk across the town every morning.

The pheasants sleep in the bushes in our backyard.

Here is a final tip for solving *most* subject-verb agreement situations.

> When the subject *doesn't* end in *s*, the verb *does* end in *s*.
>
> When the subject ends in *s*, the verb *doesn't* end in *s*.

Exercise 14 Circle the correct present tense verb form that *agrees* with the subject of the sentence. First, locate and underline the subject and determine whether it is singular or plural. Then select the appropriate verb. Remember, if the subject is singular, the verb ends in *s*, and if the subject is plural, the verb does *not* end in *s*. (Remember, only the pronouns *he, she,* and *it* follow the singular subject rule.) When you finish, compare your answers to the answer key in the back of the book.

Example Ted (likes, like) to play Monopoly on Saturdays.

1. My niece (belongs, belong) in a more difficult English class.
2. Those waves (breaks, break) hard against the shoreline.
3. That street (needs, need) repairing before anyone can drive on it.
4. Some foxes (sneaks, sneak) into our hen house around midnight.
5. The stock market (goes, go) up after every presidential election.
6. This college (has, have) a large, well-stocked bookstore.
7. Your high heel shoes (needs, need) polishing.

8. That large man (slips, slip) every time he crosses the newly waxed floor.
9. The new grocery stores (carries, carry) the latest line of men's cosmetics.
10. Miami (hosts, host) the Orange Bowl every New Year's night.
11. The construction company (plans, plan) to remodel the cafeteria this spring.
12. I (enjoys, enjoy) eating Martha's spaghetti.
13. You (belongs, belong) to the Peace and Freedom Party, don't you?
14. She (answers, answer) everyone's questions in a straightforward manner.
15. It (look, looks) like it's going to rain this afternoon.
16. Grandma (sells, sell) homemade medicines in a vacant lot.
17. They (fits, fit) the description of the lost twins.
18. The neighbors (complains, complain) about the smell from the sewer.
19. He (gives, give) his time freely to charitable causes.
20. The blackbirds (eats, eat) our cherries before we can pick them off the tree.

Exercise 15 Fill in a *present tense verb* that agrees with the subject in each of the following sentences. First, locate the subject and decide whether it is singular or plural. Then choose the appropriate form of a verb that makes sense in the sentence. Then when you finish the exercise, show your verbs to your instructor. (Make sure not to add an *-ed* ending to any of your verbs. The *-ed* ending indicates the *past tense*.)

Examples Freda *calls* me every day at this time.
other possibilities: visits, meets, greets, writes, bothers

The companies *send* representatives to the college campuses.
other possibilities: fly, appoint

1. Mary ______ all of her groceries at Hanoian's Market.
2. Henry ______ harder than anyone else on the debate team.
3. That store ______ the best sales in town.
4. The ladies ______ every week in the deserted barn.
5. Those trees ______ taller every week.
6. That boy ______ climbing mountains.
7. The swallows ______ to the mission every spring.
8. Clarence's wig ______ very oddly on his head.

9. My mother _loves_ shopping in malls.
10. Your uncles _play_ the piano very well.
11. That lake _has_ some big trout in it.
12. A cold wind _blows_ through the valley every afternoon.
13. Those bushes _need_ trimming this summer.
14. Your socks always _fall_ down your ankles.
15. That lobster _looks_ at people who try to touch it.

Exercise 16 Rewrite each of the following sentences. Change each singular subject to a plural subject by adding *-s*, and change each plural subject to a singular subject by dropping the *-s*. Then change the present tense verb to agree with the new subject form. When you finish, compare your answers to the key in the back of the book.

Example

The girls knock on my door every morning.
Revised: The girl knocks on my door every morning.

The fire goes out in the evening.
Revised: The fires go out in the evening.

1. Your sisters enjoy a good joke with her friends.
2. The duck waddles across the lawn to the pond.
3. Your long nails scratch me during our fights.
4. The fences along the north side of the pasture need fixing.
5. The dog sleeps in the shade of the oak tree.
6. Your eyebrows arch in a pleasing way.
7. The teachers bring apples to the dental hygiene students.
8. My hamsters bite anyone in the neighborhood.
9. The storm blows through Maine in early February.
10. Your motorcycle leans into every turn on the course.
11. The boxers want to end the year in good health.
12. Chemistry labs last four hours on Wednesday afternoons.

Practice Quiz

Here is a practice quiz to help prepare you for the section quiz. Take the quiz and compare your answers with the answer key in the back of the book. If you have problems, review the exercises in this section. When you are ready to take the section quiz, let your instructor know.

I. Circle the letter of the two words that are the *subject* and *verb* for each of the following sentences. (The subject is always the first word.)

Example Ralph has problems with his geometry proofs.

a. problems with b. geometry proofs c. Ralph has d. Ralph problems

1. The doctor examined six patients in an hour.

   a. the examined b. patients examined c. doctor patients d. doctor examined

2. Harold's jeans shrink in hot water.

   a. Harold's shrink b. jeans hot c. jeans shrink d. water shrink

3. Jogging makes my muscles very tight.

   a. Jogging makes b. muscles makes c. muscles tight d. Jogging muscles

4. The judge hears six cases a day.

   a. the hears b. judge hears c. judge cases d. cases hears

5. The divorce rate climbs every six months.

   a. climbs divorce b. divorce climbs c. rate climbs d. months climbs

6. Easter Sunday falls on different dates each year.

   a. Easter Sunday b. Easter Sunday falls c. dates falls d. year falls

7. Gretchen returned the damaged cans to the store.

   a. Gretchen cans b. cans returned c. store returned d. Gretchen returned

8. Protesters tied themselves to the chain-link fence.

   a. Protesters tied b. fence tied c. Protesters fence d. tied themselves

9. Your uncle plans very mysterious trips.

   a. Your plans b. trips plans c. uncle plans d. plans uncle

10. The Spanish moss hangs from the trees in the Everglades.

    a. trees hangs b. moss hangs c. Spanish hangs d. Spanish moss

II. Circle the letter of the sentence whose subject and verb *agree*.

Examples

a. Your nephew enjoy television reruns.
b. Your nephew enjoys television reruns.

a. The zebras run in large herds.
b. The zebras runs in large herds.

1. a. The sky clears up every morning at about eleven o'clock.
   b. The sky clear up every morning at about eleven o'clock.
2. a. Your cat like to play with my toy poodle.
   b. Your cat likes to play with my toy poodle.
3. a. Those horses needs a good brushing after a long ride.
   b. Those horses need a good brushing after a long ride.
4. a. The eels slither through the water.
   b. The eels slithers through the water.
5. a. The Barnum and Bailey circus come to town this month.
   b. The Barnum and Bailey circus comes to town this month.
6. a. Your wallet fall out of your pocket when you sit down.
   b. Your wallet falls out of your pocket when you sit down.
7. a. The fog usually lift in the late afternoon.
   b. The fog usually lifts in the late afternoon.
8. a. Those spiders spin interesting webs in the bathroom.
   b. Those spiders spins interesting webs in the bathroom.
9. a. That book belong to the school library, doesn't it?
   b. That book belongs to the school library, doesn't it?
10. a. The alligator hide in the shallows of the marsh.
    b. The alligator hides in the shallows of the marsh.
11. a. Your good nature please everyone in the class.
    b. Your good nature pleases everyone in the class.
12. a. The college dormitories provides cheap room and board for foreign students.
    b. The college dormitories provide cheap room and board for foreign students.

13. a. My mother bake delicious cakes and cobblers.
    b. My mother bakes delicious cakes and cobblers.
14. a. The basketball team plays thirty games this season.
    b. The basketball team play thirty games this season.
15. a. Teddy enjoys a good game of dominoes.
    b. Teddy enjoy a good game of dominoes.

Pronouns, Adjectives, and Adverbs

Section Topic

Using Pronouns

Pronouns, adjectives, and *adverbs* are among the most helpful parts of speech available to writers. However, many writers have problems using these kinds of words correctly. In this first section you are introduced to *pronouns*, and in later levels adjectives and adverbs are covered. The sections on "Pronouns, Adjectives, and Adverbs" will help you use these parts of speech effectively and correctly in your writing.

Using Pronouns

A *pronoun* is used to replace another word in a sentence so that word isn't repeated unnecessarily. Here is the way a paragraph might read if there weren't any pronouns:

Jim invited Jim's friends to Jim's house. Jim had food and drink for Jim's friends, and Jim also provided music and games for Jim's friends. Jim's friend had a good time at Jim's party, and some of Jim's friends stayed late into the night.

Now here is the same paragraph with *pronouns* used to replace the frequently repeated words.

Jim invited his friends to his house. He had food and drink for them, and he also provided music and games for them. They had a good time at Jim's party, and some of them stayed late into the night.

Here are two suggestions for using pronouns in your writing:

1. Use a pronoun to replace a word in a sentence rather than repeat the same word unnecessarily.

   Example:

   Instead of June helped June's mother clean the oven.
   Write June helped her mother clean the oven.

   Instead of Matt lives close to Fenway Park, so Matt goes to a lot of baseball games.
   Write Matt lives close to Fenway Park, so he goes to a lot of baseball games.

2. Make sure that when you use a pronoun, there is a *definite word* in the sentence or paragraph that it replaces.

   Instead of We went to the concert last night, and we had a great time.
   Write My roommates and I went to the concert last night, and we had a great time.

   Instead of They took everything with them except their roller skates.
   Write The young boys took everything with them except their roller skates.

   Instead of It looked very stormy outside, and it would soon grow worse.
   Write The weather looked very stormy outside, and it would soon grow worse.

Here is a list of commonly used pronouns and the kinds of words they replace:

USEFUL PRONOUNS

it, its, itself:

used to replace singular things and places

The dinosaur bone was twenty feet long, and it weighed 2,000 pounds.
(*it* replaces *dinosaur bone*)
The plant is very big, and it is still growing.
(*it* replaces *plant*)
The tall bank building lost its roof in a tornado.
(*its* replaces *bank building*)
The turtle flipped over on its stomach by itself.
(*its* and *itself* replace *turtle*)

he, him, his, himself:

used to replace singular male persons

John wanted a better seat at the game, so he sat on a rooftop.
(*he* replaces *John*)
Ralph took six pairs of skates with him to the skating rink.
(*him* replaces *Ralph*)
Manny said that anyone could borrow his grey sweater next weekend.
(*his* replaces *Manny*)
Fred bought himself a new watch.
(*himself* replaces *Fred*)

she, her, herself:

used to replace singular female persons

Gladys was happy when she passed her Spanish final.
(*she* and *her* replace *Gladys*)
Louise didn't do well on the test because she didn't study.
(*she* replaces *Louise*)
Mary didn't find her wallet when she lost it.
(*her* and *she* replace *Mary*)
Valerie gave herself two weeks to complete her term paper.
(*herself* and *her* replace *Mary*)

they, them, their, themselves:

used to replace plural persons, places, and things

The boys bought a horse, and they took it to the racetrack.
(*they* replaces *boys*)
Those benches have just been painted, so don't sit on them.
(*them* replaces *benches*)
Those flashlights are worthless when they lose their power.
(*they* and *their* replace *flashlight*)
Gretchen and Joe found themselves good jobs on campus.
(*themselves* replaces *Gretchen* and *Joe*)

we, us, our, ourselves:

used to replace plural persons when the *writer* is one of the persons

Johnny and I didn't catch a fish all morning, so we went home at noon.
(*we* replaces *Johnny and I*)
Fred and I were stuck at the dance, so our friends brought us home.
(*our* and *us* replace *Fred and I*)
Ricardo and I wanted to play a good game of tennis, so we used our new tennis balls.
(*we* and *our* replace *Ricardo and I*)
Michelle and I have done all of the wallpapering by ourselves.
(*ourselves* replaces *Michelle and I*)

you, your, yourself, yourselves:

used to replace the person or persons that are being directly spoken to

John, you have been doing very well in biology lately.
(*you* replaces *John*)

Students, please meet at 10:00 a.m. in the gym. You will get further instructions there.
(*You* replaces *students*)
Mother, you left your slippers on the porch last night.
(*you* and *your* replace *mother*)
Anthony, you have bought yourself a great used motorcycle.
(*you* and *yourself* replace *Anthony*)

Note: The pronouns, *I, me, my,* and *mine* are commonly used by writers when speaking of themselves, but they do not *replace* other words in the same way that the other pronouns do.

Example: I left my watch on the mantle, and that was a stupid thing for me to do.

Exercise 17 Rewrite each of the following sentences and replace the underlined words with the appropriate pronouns. When you finish, compare your answers with the answer key in the back of the book.

Example Celia got married last summer, and Celia has never been happier.

Revised: Celia got married last summer, and she has never been happier.

Example Those elm trees really need to be pruned before those elm trees block the road.

Revised: Those elm trees really need to be pruned before they block the road.

1. Marge was invited to the business club meeting, so Marge decided to go.
2. Harold wanted more rice for dinner, so Harold opened a new box of Minute Rice just for Harold.
3. The flags were getting damp in the rain, so Randy brought the flags inside.
4. The sun seems to lose some of the sun's power when the sun goes behind clouds.
5. Fred wanted a companion in Fred's dorm, so Fred bought a canary for Fred.
6. Angie and I are very close friends, and Angie and I have known each other for years.
7. The plants are doing well in the house, but the plants would do even better if we put the plants on the patio.
8. The cats were shedding the cats' fur, so I didn't let the cats in the house.
9. The storm is very fierce, and the storm shows no sign of letting up.

10. The girls took the same P.E. class, and the girls took the girls' sweats with the girls.

11. Students, I would like students to work on students' term papers today by students.

12. Ann and I are having problems in math, but Ann and I are trying Ann's and my best to resolve the problems by Ann and me.

Exercise 18 Rewrite the following paragraph and replace with appropriate pronouns any nouns that are unnecessarily repeated. When you finish, compare your answers to the key at the back of the book.

Example The clouds started gathering in the north, and the clouds would soon drop the clouds' moisture on the nearby field. The nearby field would get a good soaking, which the nearby field badly needed.

Revised: The clouds started gathering in the north, and they would soon drop their moisture on the nearby field. It would get a good soaking, which it badly needed.

Rita enjoys living in Rita's new apartment. Rita moved in two months ago with her friend Gwendolyn. Rita and Gwendolyn share the one-bedroom apartment, and Rita and Gwendolyn take turns cleaning the one-bedroom apartment. All of the apartments in the complex have one bedroom, and all of the apartments rent for $250 a month. Rita and Gwendolyn's apartment has a microwave oven, and Rita and Gwendolyn enjoy cooking in the microwave oven. Rita and Gwendolyn do all of Rita and Gwendolyn's own cooking because Rita and Gwendolyn enjoy cooking for Rita and Gwendolyn. Rita would like an apartment of Rita's own some day, but until Rita can afford an apartment, Rita is happy to share an apartment with Gwendolyn.

Exercise 19 Write a paragraph about a situation where you had to share something with at least one other person: an apartment, a bathroom, a car, a locker, a bedroom, a closet, or a pet. Begin your paragraph with this opening sentence:

Sharing a(n) ______________ with ______________ was ______________.

Before you write your first draft, you may want to make a list of supporting ideas that relate to your opening sentence. Here is an example:

Sample Paragraph

Opening Sentence: Sharing a bedroom with my two sisters was very difficult.

Ideas: small room
only one bed
messy room
no privacy
fighting and yelling

When you finish writing your first draft, analyze the following draft with a classmate, using the questions on page 21 to help you.

Sharing a bedroom with my two sisters was very difficult. The room was very small, none of us had enough room for our belongings. There was one double bed for the three of us, and if one of us had a bad night, no one got much sleep. Sheila, my youngest sister, was very sloppy, the room was always a mess. Myra, my oldest sister, was the neat one. She was always yelling at Sheila. I didn't really care how the room looked, but I was the private one, when I wanted to be alone, I treated my sisters as intruders. We did our share of yelling and fighting, but we also grew up very close. I miss my sisters, but I don't miss sharing that small bedroom.

When you finish analyzing the paragraph, read your own first draft, keeping the evaluation questions on page 21 in mind. Note any revisions or corrections you need to make. (You might also share your draft with a classmate.) Finally, write the second draft of your paragraph.

Practice Quiz

Here is a practice quiz to help prepare you for the section quiz. Take the quiz and compare your answers with the key in the back of the book. If you have problems, review the exercises in this section. When you are ready for the section quiz, let your instructor know.

Circle the letter of the best-written sentence in each group.

Example

a. Your shoes look very worn, and your shoes need to be resoled.
(b.) Your shoes look very worn, and they need to be resoled.
c. Your shoes look very worn, and it needs to be resoled.

1. a. Clyde found college difficult, but he wouldn't give up easily.
   b. Clyde found college difficult, but Clyde wouldn't give up easily.
   c. Clyde found college difficult, but they wouldn't give in easily.

2. a. The enchiladas in the cafeteria were cold when the enchiladas were served.
   b. The enchiladas in the cafeteria were cold when they were served.
   c. The enchiladas in the cafeteria were cold when it was served.
3. a. The Amazon is the longest river in the world, and the Amazon flows across South America.
   b. The Amazon is the longest river in the world, and they flow across South America.
   c. The Amazon is the longest river in the world, and it flows across South America.
4. a. The senators could not agree on a pay raise, so the senators got no raise.
   b. The senators could not agree on a pay raise, so they got no raise.
   c. The senators could not agree on a pay raise, so he got no raise.
5. a. Ted's parents went on a trip, so Ted decided to go with Ted's parents.
   b. Ted's parents went on a trip, so he decided to go with them.
   c. Ted's parents went on a trip, so they decided to go with him.
6. a. Harold helped Sue with Sue's math homework, and Sue helped Harold with Harold's typing.
   b. Harold helped Sue with her math homework, and she helped him with his typing.
   c. Harold helped Sue with his math homework, and she helped him with her typing.
7. a. The cheetah is a very swift animal because of the cheetah's great strides.
   b. The cheetah is a very swift animal because of its great strides.
   c. The cheetah is a very swift animal because of great strides.
8. a. The storms dropped their snow across Minnesota.
   b. The storms dropped the storm's snow across Minnesota.
   c. The storms dropped its snow across Minnesota.
9. a. John and I have had our differences, but we have always remained friends.
   b. John and I have had John's and my differences, but John and I have always remained friends.
   c. John and I have had your differences, but they have always remained friends.
10. a. Students, I would like students to take out students' notebooks.
    b. Students, I would like them to take out their notebooks.
    c. Students, I would like you to take out your notebooks.

Spelling

Section Topic

Plural Words

The final section in each level covers a group of spelling words that have common features. The words found in the spelling sections are among the most commonly misspelled words in English.

Spelling is covered at the end of each level because it is often the last consideration that writers give their paragraphs in the revision process. However, checking for spelling errors should also be an ongoing writing practice, and it is wise to circle or correct any questionably spelled word that you notice in your writings. You might also keep a list of spelling words handy that give you particular problems, and you can add to the list as you work through the book.

Plurals

A common error for many writers is to leave off the *-s* or *-es* ending that indicates the *plural* form of a word. Here is a list of plural words to learn for this section, but you will be able to apply the rules for forming plurals to most words you use.

WORD LIST #1

alleys	classes	parties
armies	lessons	places
bodies	men	people
boxes	mice	watches
children	monkeys	women

Here are the basic rules for making singular words plural. These rules will help you with the words in List #1 and with most plural words that you use in your writing.

RULES FOR FORMING PLURALS

1. To form most plurals, add *-s* to the singular word: *boy/boys, dog/dogs, cow/cows, sock/socks, tree/trees, umbrellas/umbrellas.*

2. Add *-es* to singular words when the plural ending adds a *new syllable* (additional sound) to the word: *bench/benches, watch/watches, class/classes, box/boxes, crash/crashes.*

3. If a singular word ends in *-e*, just add *-s* as in rule 1: *place/places, race/races, date/dates, size/sizes.*

4. If a singular word ends in *-y* preceded by a *consonant* (all letters but *a, e, i, o, u*), drop the *-y* and add *-ies*: *army/armies, duty/duties, party/parties*.
5. If a singular word ends in *-y* preceded by a *vowel* (*a, e, i, o, u*), just add *-s*: *donkey/donkeys, monkey/monkeys, toy/toys*.
6. Some singular words form their plurals *without adding -s*. Instead, the words change their spelling to indicate the plural. These plural forms follow no rule, so they need to be memorized: *man/men, woman/women, child/children, mouse/mice, ox/oxen, alumnus/alumni*.

Exercise 20 Write the plural forms for the following singular words. Follow the rules for forming plurals from singular words. Then check your spelling with the key in the back of the book. (Some of these words are from List #1 and some are not.)

Example cat *cats*

1. donkey ____
2. child ____
3. woman ____
4. hutch ____
5. mouse ____
6. fox ____
7. body ____
8. man ____
9. monkey ____
10. salary ____
11. person ____
12. place ____
13. reason ____
14. army ____
15. alley ____
16. class ____
17. party ____
18. grass ____
19. duty ____
20. latch ____

Exercise 21 Here are ten new singular words. Write the plural form for each word following the rules for forming plurals. Then compare your spellings to the answer key in the back of the book.

Example pillow *pillows*

1. jersey ____
2. batch ____

3. lobby ______________ 7. journey ______________

4. glass ______________ 8. fly ______________

5. face ______________ 9. couch ______________

6. lawn ______________ 10. turkey ______________

Practice Quiz

Take this practice quiz to prepare you for the section quiz. Then compare your answers with the correct spellings from List #1. When you are ready for the section quiz, let your instructor know.

Circle the letter of the correctly spelled plural word from each group.

Example (a.) kites b. kitts c. kities d. kitse

	a.	b.	c.	d.
1.	a. partys	b. parties	c. partyies	d. partes
2.	a. clases	b. classe	c. classes	d. class
3.	a. alleies	b. alleys	c. alleyies	d. allys
4.	a. armies	b. armys	c. armes	d. armyies
5.	a. lessones	b. lessonns	c. lessonse	d. lessons
6.	a. places	b. placees	c. placeses	d. placese
7.	a. peoples	b. peopls	c. people	d. peoplies
8.	a. mans	b. mens	c. man	d. men
9.	a. bodys	b. bodeys	c. bodies	d. bodyies
10.	a. boxxes	b. boxes	c. boxs	d. boxses
11.	a. mouses	b. mices	c. mice	d. mousse
12.	a. watchs	b. watches	c. watchez	d. watchses
13.	a. childs	b. childes	c. childrens	d. children
14.	a. womans	b. woman	c. womens	d. women
15.	a. monkeys	b. monkies	c. monkeyies	d. monkees

Writing Review

At the end of each level is a "Writing Review" section that allows you to apply what you have learned to one final paragraph writing assignment. The purpose of all the work you have done in Level 1 is to make you a more effective writer. The following assignment covers those writing skills that you have worked on in Level 1.

Level 1 Paragraph Assignment

Step One Write a paragraph choosing one of the following opening sentences to begin with. Your main concern as you write the paragraph is *unity*: Each sentence in the paragraph should relate to the main idea expressed in the opening sentence. Your paragraph should contain from six to ten sentences.

Opening Sentences: (fill in the blank)

1. The hardest decision I ever made was ______________.
2. The best summer I ever had was ______________.
3. ______________ is a great way to exercise.
4. Living at home is ______________.
5. The biggest problem I face this semester is ______________.
6. One thing I'm looking forward to this semester is ______________.

Note Before you write your paragraph, you may want to make a list of ideas to include that relate to your opening sentence. Here is an example:

Opening Sentence: Living at home is very easy.
Ideas: free food
free laundry
no rent

peace and quiet
lots of room
parents are okay

Step Two When you have written your paragraph, read over your sentences, considering these suggestions:

1. Look for any sentence that does *not* relate well to the opening sentence. If you find one, cross it out or change it.
2. If you come up with other ideas to include in your paragraph as you read it over, add them to your draft.
3. Look for any pairs or groups of short sentences that can be combined to form better sentences. If you find any, underline them.
4. Check your paragraph for any *run-on* sentences: two or more sentences run together without periods (.) to separate them. If you find any, make the necessary corrections.

Step Three Now give your newly written paragraph a final check for wording problems:

1. Check your sentences for words that don't sound or look quite right. Are there better word choices? Have you left any words out? If you find wording problems, eliminate them.
2. Check each sentence for subject-verb agreement with present tense verbs. Remember the basic rule: If a subject is singular, the verb ends in *-s*, and if the subject is plural, the verb does *not* end in *-s*. Correct any errors you find.
3. Check each sentence to make sure you are using *pronouns* to replace words that don't need repeating. Are you using the correct pronouns? Make any necessary corrections.
4. Check your spelling. Are you adding the correct *-s* or *-es* ending to plural words? If you have used any words whose spelling you are uncertain of, look them up in a dictionary. If you can't find a word, ask your instructor. Then correct any spelling errors.

Now write the *final draft* of your paragraph including all the corrections you made in Step Two and Three. Your final draft should be unified, well written, and nearly error free. When you finish, share the paragraph with your instructor.

Sample Paragraph (First Draft)

run-on Combine

Living at home is very easy. I get three meal s a day. I don't have to pay for them. My mom also do all of my laundry, she washes, dries, and irons all of my cloths. It's also nice not having to pay any rent. I can get my studying done easily because there is very little noize. There is also lots of room in the house since I am the only one left besides my parents. Fortunately, I get along pretty well with my mom and dad, my mom and dad are very nice. They are easygoing. My mom and dad are very nice and easygoing.

Final Draft

Living at home is very easy. I get three meals a day and don't have to pay for them. My mom also does all of my laundry. She washes, dries, and irons all of my clothes. It's also nice not having to pay any rent. I can get my studies done easily because there is very little noise. There is also lots of room in the house since I am the only one left besides my parents. Fortunately, I get along pretty well with my mom and dad. They are very nice and easygoing. I'm in no hurry to move out at all.

LEVEL 2

In Level 2, you cover the same basic sections as in Level 1: "The Paragraph," "The Sentence," and "The Word." The topics introduced in each section are either new or add more development to topics presented in Level 1. What you learned in the first level will prepare you for Level 2, but you may find many of the exercises more challenging. Each new level builds on the previous level's work so that you add to your foundation of basic writing skills.

The Paragraph

Each level begins with a section on "The Paragraph," because paragraph writing is central to most writing you may do. In Level 1, you learned that a paragraph develops *one main idea* and that an effective paragraph is *unified*: All sentences relate to the main idea. In this section you learn about the *topic sentence* and about *paragraph development*.

Section Topics

Topic Sentence
Paragraph Development

Topic Sentence

Although you were concentrating on paragraph unity in Level 1, you were also working with *topic sentences* in your paragraphs without realizing it. In this section, you find out exactly what a topic sentence is, why it is useful in most paragraphs that you write, and how it can be worded most effectively.

Here are some important things to know about topic sentences:

1. A topic sentence expresses the main idea of a paragraph.
2. A topic sentence usually states a definite opinion or attitude.
3. A topic sentence provides the reader with a clear understanding of what a paragraph is about.

4. A topic sentence gives *direction* to a paragraph that both the writer and reader can follow.
5. A topic sentence often begins a paragraph or is found near the beginning of a paragraph.
6. Other sentences within a paragraph relate to the topic sentence.
7. The final "wrap-up" sentence in a paragraph often reinforces the topic sentence.

Here are three sample paragraphs with their topic sentences underlined. Notice how each topic sentence expresses a definite opinion or attitude and how the rest of the sentences relate to the topic sentence.

The weather in March was unpredictable. One day there was heavy ground fog, and the next day was clear. It rained for a few days and cleared up, and then it rained again. One day the temperature ranged from 45 degrees to 75 degrees, and the next day the temperature stayed around 55 degrees all day long. It was difficult to plan activities or know what to wear with such unpredictable weather.

Mary Ann is determined to do well in her class this semester. She is not going to miss any classes, and she's going to tape all of her lecture classes as well as take notes. She has blocked out three hours a day on weekdays to study, as well as Sunday afternoons. She has also formed a study group with friends who share her classes and has a tutor for her calculus class. Finally, Mary Ann is declaring her own "dead weeks" two weeks prior to finals for intensive studying since her poor finals preparation last semester hurt her grades badly.

Easter week is going to be terrific. First, I have the whole week off from the stationery store because it's going to be closed. My friends are all staying in town, so there will be plenty to do. We'll go to the arcades during the day and rent movies or go downtown in the evenings. I've also saved enough money to visit my cousin in Buffalo for a couple days, and we always have a good time together. This could be the best Easter week I've had in a long time.

Notice that the topic sentence for each paragraph states a definite opinion. When a topic sentence is definite and clear—"Easter week is going to be terrific"—a writer can easily develop the rest of the paragraph in support of that sentence, and a reader can clearly understand the writer's intention.

Exercise I

Underline the *topic sentence* in each paragraph: the sentence that expresses the paragraph's main idea. The topic sentence will *not* always be the first sentence in the paragraph. When you finish, compare your answers to the answer key.

Example Your sweaters are quite colorful. I like the bright red one you wear to football games. I also like the purple turtleneck sweater you wear every Friday. My favorite is the red, white, and blue striped one you wear on holidays. But the wildest one has to be the fluorescent orange pullover with the pink and black polka dots. I couldn't believe that you wore it to church last Sunday.

1. Freddie is very shy. At parties he sits in a corner by himself all night. When he is in a crowd, you would never notice him. When you talk to him, he looks at the ground and stammers out one-word replies. He never speaks in class, and I've never seen him talk to a girl. He is a nice person, but few people ever get to know him.

2. I'll never work in a commercial laundry again. I spent twelve hours a day one summer loading huge spin dryers with sheets and towels. The wet laundry was very heavy, and each time one load was finished, another one appeared. Sometimes I wouldn't have the dryer balanced right, and it would start kicking and making a racket. I'd have to stop it, rebalance the load, and start it again while a new load backed up behind me. On top of that, the supervisor was a grouch who only paid attention to me when I messed up, and the place paid below minimum wage. I quit after one summer.

3. The sky is a clear blue. Sparrows chirp in the early mornings. The fruit trees in the backyard are beginning to bloom. The hills are turning green, and purple and yellow wildflowers are appearing in the fields. The snow on top of Camel Mountain has all melted. It must finally be spring.

4. I don't like algebra this semester, and I'm not too fond of history. But I'm enjoying my racquetball class a lot. I'm getting a lot of exercise, and I'm also enjoying the game. We usually play partners and compete in small tournaments within the class. The competition is fun, and playing partners keeps it relaxed. I may sign up for intermediate racquetball next semester.

5. Some people like ketchup on their eggs, and other people like hot sauce. Suzette's the only person I know who likes marmalade jelly on her eggs. She scrambles three or four eggs and puts them on a large platter. Then she gets out a big jar of marmalade jelly. She digs in a big spoon and spreads a large gob of jelly all over her eggs. Then she gobbles them down in a matter of seconds. She discovered the combination of eggs and marmalade one morning when she accidentally dropped her toast smeared with marmalade on her eggs.

6. Our old neighborhood is looking better, but there is still a big problem. The sidewalks in the neighborhood are filthy. The melting snow has left a muddy film on the concrete. Garbage is piled up because of the collectors' strike. Packs of dogs have left their waste everywhere. Old newspapers carpet the sidewalks, and neighborhood drunks have left their bottles piled against the buildings. You can't walk anywhere without stepping on something.

What are the ingredients of an effective topic sentence? What makes one topic sentence more effective than another? Here are some suggestions for writing strong topic sentences.

1. A good topic sentence usually states an opinion or attitude that can be *supported* by details and examples:

   Examples: *Topic Sentence:* The weather is miserable today.
   Support: 105-degree temperature
   high humidity
   no breeze
   bad pollution

   Topic Sentence: Ms. Johnson is a good teacher.
   Support: knowledgeable in her field
   excellent lecturer
   fair
   works hard
   helpful

2. A good topic sentence is *specific enough* to be clear and interesting.

   Examples: *Weak Topic Sentence:* The trees in your yard look bad.
   Better Topic Sentence: The elm trees in your backyard look diseased.

   Weak Topic Sentence: Harriet works in politics.
   Better Topic Sentence: Harriet enjoys being in politics.

   Weak Topic Sentence: A school in town is having some problems.
   Better Topic Sentence: Tabor College is having financial problems.

   Weak Topic Sentence: The United States has a different image below the border.
   Better Topic Sentence: The United States' image in Central America is deteriorating.

3. A good topic sentence gives a *definite direction* to a paragraph.

   Weak Topic Sentence: I went on vacation to Pensacola last week. (no direction given for paragraph)
   Better Topic Sentence: I spent a perfect week's vacation in Pensacola. (direction given: describing the "perfect" vacation)

   Weak Topic Sentence: The student council met for the first time Monday. (no direction given)
   Better Topic Sentence: The first student council meeting on Monday was interesting. (direction given: describing the "interesting" meeting)

   Weak Topic Sentence: I can see the mountains this time of year. (no direction given)
   Better Topic Sentence: My view of the mountains in the spring is gorgeous. (direction given: describing the "gorgeous" view)

Weak Topic Sentence:	I own a dog name Biscuit. (no direction given)
Better Topic Sentence:	My cocker spaniel Biscuit is a lazy dog. (direction given: examples of how "lazy" Biscuit is)

Exercise 2 Circle the letter of the *best* topic sentence from each group. Select the sentences that can be supported with details or examples, that are specific enough to be interesting, and that would give definite direction to a paragraph. When you finish, compare your answers to the answer key.

Example

a. Riding horses is something that I do.

(b.) Riding horses is my favorite hobby.

c. Riding horses is a hobby.

1. a. I've seen a lot of alligators in the zoo.
   b. Alligators are not as dangerous as they look.
   c. Alligators are not what they seem like.
2. a. I didn't sign up for the draft last month.
   b. I thought about signing up for the draft last month.
   c. Signing up for the draft is a horrifying thought.
3. a. Barbecuing is one way to cook hamburgers.
   b. Barbecuing hamburgers is one way that I cook them.
   c. Barbecuing hamburgers is the best way to cook them.
4. a. Some day I will graduate from college.
   b. College graduation will be in two years.
   c. I can't wait for the day I graduate from college.
5. a. Driving an ambulance is one kind of job.
   b. Driving an ambulance can be a hazardous job.
   c. Driving an ambulance might be different from what you imagine.
6. a. I eat a lot of homemade ice cream.
   b. Homemade ice cream is my favorite.
   c. I have a homemade ice cream maker.

7. a. Getting up in the morning is something everyone does.
   b. I have to get up early five days a week.
   c. Getting up in the morning is the hardest thing I do.
8. a. Temperatures in the western hemisphere are gradually changing.
   b. Temperatures in the western hemisphere are being studied by scientists.
   c. Temperatures in the western hemisphere are gradually warming.
9. a. I've never been to a punk rock concert.
   b. I'll never go to a punk rock concert.
   c. Punk rock concerts are held every weekend in Los Angeles.
10. a. Gilda is a friend of mine at college.
    b. Gilda and I go to the same college.
    c. Gilda is the best friend I've made this semester.

Exercise 3 Write your own topic sentence that could begin each of the following paragraphs. Choose a sentence that the rest of the sentences in the paragraph support. When you finish, show your sentences to your instructor.

Example First, I lost my notebook. Then I broke the mirror in my compact when I dropped it. I got sick during lunch and flunked my geometry midterm first period after lunch. I cried all the way to the dorms.

Topic Sentence: Yesterday was my worst day of the semester.

1. Open the microwave oven door and put in your leftovers. Then shut the door and set the timer to about two minutes. Then press the "on" button and wait. When the bell goes off, check the leftovers. If they're hot enough, take them out to eat. If they're not hot enough, just close the door and reset the timer for another minute. It's as simple as that.

   Topic Sentence:

2. We tried to get an eighteen-wheel truck bed, but we had to settle for the back of a pickup. We wanted to use real flowers to decorate the float, but we settled for colored toilet paper. We couldn't find a beautiful girl who would ride on it, so my kid sister volunteered. I wanted to drive the vehicle in the parade, but I ended up walking behind it.

   Topic Sentence:

3. First, it sounded like someone was on the roof. Then we heard the back door rattling. Then there were strange noises coming from the north side of the house.

They sounded like dying animals. We rushed down to the basement and then heard footsteps above our heads. We locked the basement door and hid in the closet all night.

Topic Sentence:

4. I passed the history test I'd been dreading. Then I found out I got a B+ on my English term paper. My afternoon classes had been canceled, so I went to the river to relax. That evening I saw one of the best movies I'd ever seen, and I didn't pay a penny to see it. And for the first night in weeks, I slept great.

Topic Sentence:

5. First, you make close to five dollars an hour, which is good summer wages. Then all you do is sit in a chair all afternoon and watch the swimming pool. You have to stay alert, but I only had to go in after a kid once all last summer. Every hour, you get a fifteen-minute break when you can go into the office and relax. When you come back on deck, you rotate to a new station, which breaks the monotony. On top of that, there are a lot of good-looking guys around the pool, so as the only female guard, you can have a lot of fun.

Topic Sentence:

Exercise 4 Write your own topic sentence for each of the following paragraph topics. Write a sentence that expresses a definite opinion or attitude, that can be supported by details and examples, that is specific enough to be interesting, and that would give a paragraph definite direction. When you finish, share your sentences with a classmate who is also finished and with your instructor.

Examples

Paragraph Topic: taking notes
Topic Sentence: I have a hard time taking notes in my history class.

Paragraph Topic: choosing a major
Topic Sentence: Choosing a major is one of the most important things you'll ever do.

Paragraph Topic: having a pet
Topic Sentence: an anteater makes a surprisingly good pet.

1. *Paragraph Topic:* buying a used car

   Topic Sentence:

2. *Paragraph Topic:* a particular rock singer or group

   Topic Sentence:

3. *Paragraph Topic:* parents

   Topic Sentence:

4. *Paragraph Topic:* getting married

   Topic Sentence:

5. *Paragraph Topic:* a season of the year

   Topic Sentence:

6. *Paragraph Topic:* a particular holiday

   Topic Sentence:

7. *Paragraph Topic:* smoking marijuana

   Topic Sentence:

8. *Paragraph Topic:* a particular animal

   Topic Sentence:

Exercise 5 Write a paragraph beginning with one of your topic sentences from Exercise 4, or a topic sentence on another subject you'd like to write about. Select a topic sentence that you can support well in a paragraph. Remember, an effective paragraph has *unity*: All of the sentences should be related to your topic sentence.

Before you begin, you may want to make a list of points that support your topic sentence to include in your paragraph. Some writers find that listing supporting ideas helps them develop a paragraph more easily and effectively. Here is an example:

Sample Paragraph

Topic Sentence: I have a hard time taking notes in my history class.
Supporting Ideas: instructor talks too fast
she talks too softly
nothing written on the board
rambles too much
important things aren't emphasized

After you finish your first draft, meet with a classmate or small group to analyze the sample draft in the text, using the evaluation questions following the paragraph as a guideline.

Sample First Draft

I have a hard time taking notes in my history class. The instructor talks so fast that I can't keep up with her, she also has a soft voice, and I miss a lot of things she says. When I study my notes, I have trouble separating the important material from the rest. She never writes anything on the board like my other instructors do to outline their lectures. She also rambles and get off the subject a lot. I end up writing down unimportant things. Finally, she talks about everything in the same tones and never determines the important points. I've decided to try tapeing the lectures, taking notes isn't working. I'm really frustrated.

Evaluation Questions to Consider:

1. Does the topic sentence express a definite opinion or attitude?
2. Is the paragraph unified? Are there any stray sentences that should be omitted or changed to improve the paragraph?
3. Are there things that could be added—a supporting point, example, or detail—that would make the paragraph more interesting, clearer, or more informative for readers?
4. Are the sentences in the clearest order for the readers to follow? Would any sentence(s) make more sense in a different location?
5. Are the sentences clearly, smoothly worded? Are there any short sentences that could be effectively combined?
6. Are the sentences punctuated effectively? Does a period end each complete sentence?
7. Are there any words whose spelling needs to be checked? Are there any words that have been unintentionally omitted?

When you finish your analysis, reread your own first draft, using the same evaluation questions as a guideline. If you want a second or third opinion, exchange drafts with classmates. Finally, write your final paragraph draft, including all revisions and corrections you have noted.

Paragraph Development

In Level 1, you learned that an effective paragraph has *unity:* All of its sentences relate to the main point. A second important feature of an effective paragraph is *development.* Here are the main qualities of a *well-developed* paragraph:

1. It provides enough *supporting points* for the main idea expressed in the topic sentence to be clearly understood.
2. It provides enough *specific details and examples* to be interesting and informative.
3. It does not leave the readers with *unanswered questions* that could be cleared up with a little more detail or an additional example or two.
4. It concludes with a sentence that clearly "wraps up" the paragraph and relates to the topic sentence in some manner.

Here are examples of four paragraphs that are effectively developed. The main point of each paragraph is in the underlined *topic sentence*.

1. Your sister is an attractive woman. Her large, dark eyes are beautiful. Her complexion is flawless, and she has a lovely big smile. Her long, black hair is full and shiny. She is tall and slender, and her every movement is graceful. She also dresses stylishly, and her assortment of straight skirts and colorful blouses look great on her.

The main point of the paragraph—how *attractive* the woman is—is supported by a number of *specific details:* beautiful eyes, flawless skin, a lovely smile, beautiful hair, graceful movements, and stylish dress. Notice that there is even more specific detail to describe some of these features: large, dark eyes; long, full, shiny black hair; and straight skirts and colorful blouses.

2. There is plenty to do tonight besides watching television. We can invite the neighbors over and play gin rummy. We can catch up on some reading we've been putting off. We can build a fire in the fireplace, roast marshmallows, and pop popcorn. We can get out the old Monopoly board and play a few hours. We can even get out the paintbrushes and repaint the hallway as we've been threatening to do for months.

The main point of the paragraph—that there is *plenty to do*—is supported by a number of *specific examples:* play gin rummy, read, roast marshmallows, play Monopoly, or paint. Five alternatives to watching television are presented in support of the topic sentence.

3. The housing industry in Omaha is not doing well. House sales are down 65 percent from two years ago. The average length a house is on the market before being sold is two years. The average house price has actually dropped $5,000 this year. There has also been no new housing construction within the city limits in the last six months. Two building contractors have gone out of business, and the carpenter's union has sixty-five unemployed members. Lumber sales have dropped over 35 percent, and the local mill has sold three logging trucks and laid off twenty-five workers. It has been the worst period for the housing industry in over thirty years.

The main point of the paragraph—that the housing industry is doing badly—is supported by a number of specific *facts:* Sales are down, house prices are down, construction has stopped, carpenters are unemployed, and lumber sales are down. The last sentence concludes the paragraph by reinforcing just how bad the housing situation is.

4. I just turned fifty, and I'm feeling it. I have a constant ringing in my ears that bothers me when I try to sleep at night. I get winded after thirty minutes of tennis. My back is sore when I get out of bed, and I keep pulling muscles when I try to lift weights. My blood pressure is above normal, and my temples throb when I am under stress. I had my first root canal done last Thursday,

and my gums are showing signs of deterioration. I used to go to one doctor and one dentist, but now I have an internist, a podiatrist, an ear specialist, an ophthamologist, and a dental surgeon that I keep busy. I guess all of this comes with middle age.

The main point of the paragraph—that the writer is feeling his fifty years—is supported by a number of examples: ringing ears, no endurance, sore back, high blood pressure, a root canal, deteriorating gums, and a flock of specialists. The final sentence ties in with the topic sentence: the writer is feeling his age.

Exercise 6 Specific detail is important for the development of most paragraphs. Change the following vague, general sentences into strong, supportive sentences for the topic sentences that are given. When you finish, share your sentences with a classmate who is finished and with your instructor.

Examples *Topic Sentence:* Tenson has a lot to offer for a small town.

a. There is a theater.

a. There is a movie theater downtown with three separate screens.

b. There are things for older folks to do.

b. For the older folks, there is Friday night bingo, checker tournaments at the recreational hall, and bus trips to the city.

Topic Sentence: The conditions are great for surfing.

a. The waves are just right.

a. The waves are about six feet high, and they break every thirty seconds.

b. The weather is good.

b. The temperature is in the 80s, and there is no wind.

1. *Topic Sentence:* Myra hasn't been feeling well lately.

   a. Something's wrong with her throat.

   a. ~~It has been~~ Her throat has been sore & scratchy for two days

   b. Her stomach aches.

   b. When she woke in the morning her stomach ached.

2. *Topic Sentence:* Uncle Fred is getting fat.

   a. You should see his face.

a. His face is as round as a beach ball.

b. His stomach has really changed.

b. His stomach looks like he's 9 months pregnant.

3. *Topic Sentence:* Freda has a lot of hobbies that keep her busy.

a. She knits.

a. She knits vests, & sweaters.

b. She works on dolls.

b. She fixes dolls up for little kids.

4. *Topic Sentence:* Torrance Lake is a beautiful spot.

a. There are trees all over.

a. The trees surround the lake completely

b. The lake is beautiful.

b. The lake is so clear you can see the bottom

5. *Topic Sentence:* Ellen's baby is very advanced for her age.

a. She moves very well.

a. She moves from one room to another without anything holding her up.

b. She has good eyesight.

b. She can see a bird or squirrel in the tree from inside the house

6. *Topic Sentence:* The pirate movie at the Midway Drive-in is exciting.

a. There is a lot of action.

a. There is something happening every eye opening minute

b. The hero of the movie is very brave.

b. The hero not only wrestled a bear & a lion he ran through a pit full of rattle snakes

7. *Topic Sentence:* Although Grandma is eighty-seven years old, she still has a lot of energy.

a. She still works a lot.

a. She makes dinner, cleans house, watches us kids, & still has time for crafts

b. She still dances.

b. Her grandpa really cut a rug at the wedding

8. *Topic Sentence:* The old neighborhood is looking better.

a. The houses look better on the outside.

a. The houses have not only have new siding, they are very nicely landscaped.

b. The street lighting has been improved.

b. They add two more street lights & fixed & replaced the broken ones.

Exercise 7 A well-developed paragraph usually contains both supportive points for the main idea of the paragraph and more specific details to clarify the supportive points. In this exercise, a topic sentence is followed by two main supporting points and two more specific sentences providing detail for each of the supporting points. First, identify the two supporting points for the topic sentence, and second, place the more detailed sentences under the point that they refer to. Put the two main supporting points in A. and B. and the detailed sentences in 1. and 2. beneath A. and B., as shown in the example following. Then compare your answers to the answer key.

Example *Topic Sentence:* The backyard needs a lot of work.
The branches are growing over the back fence.
The trees need trimming.
The pool needs cleaning.
Algae is growing on the bottom.
Some branches are covering the telephone lines.
The tiles are discolored.

A. The trees need trimming.
1. The branches are growing over the back fence.
2. Some branches are covering the telephone lines.

B. The pool needs cleaning.
1. Algae is growing on the bottom.
2. The tiles are discolored.

1. *Topic Sentence:* Alicia is a very funny person.

A She loves to play jokes on friends.

B She's good at imitating people.

1 She painted her roommate's feet green while her roommate was sleeping.

1 She does a great Fat Albert imitation.

2 She can laugh just like Eddie Murphy.

2 She tied a cow to her brother's bed one night.

2. *Topic Sentence:* I have great respect for the ocean.

1 Riptides can take you miles down the coastline.

A Ocean tides and undertow can be very dangerous.

An undertow can carry you far out into the ocean.

The surf can be very powerful.

The surf can hold you underwater for a long time.

The surf can flip you around like a rag doll.

3. *Topic Sentence:* The new restaurant has something for all ages.

Anyone over sixty gets a 50 percent discount.

Each child gets a coloring book.

The restaurant does special things for children.

Anyone over sixty gets seated immediately on arrival.

Each child gets a free dessert with dinner.

Senior citizens get special treatment.

4. *Topic Sentence:* There's a good sale on at Shopmart.

You can buy slips at a 30 percent discount.

There's a two-for-one sale on underwear.

Fishing poles are marked way down.

A $100 weight set costs only $42.99.

The lingerie buys are excellent.

There's also a special sale in the sports department.

5. *Topic Sentence:* Henry is enjoying being in the Marines.

He can do fifty pushups.

Henry is in the best shape of his life.

He likes the fellows in his platoon.

He grew up with many of them.

He can run over three miles without getting exhausted.

They all stick together and help each other.

6. *Topic Sentence:* The nuclear arms negotiations went badly.

The two main negotiators didn't get along.

The United States waited for Russia to make a land missile concession.

One was very emotional and the other very calm.

Neither side wanted to make the first move.

They never trusted each other.

Russia waited for the United States to make a nuclear submarine concession.

Exercise 8 Each of the following paragraphs contains *general statements* in support of the topic sentence but no *details or examples* to clarify the general statements and make the paragraph interesting. In the space provided after each general statement, *add your own details or examples* to make the paragraph more interesting and informative.

Sample Paragraphs (added details and examples underlined)

Aunt Lily was one of the strangest relatives in the family. By our family's standards, she was a wealthy lady. She owned hundreds of acres of land that had been in her family for sixty years. Her husband had also left her hundreds of thousands of dollars in a half-dozen bank accounts around the state. She owned her own home and bought a new Cadillac every year. However, when it came to sharing with her family, Aunt Lily was a tightwad. When her nieces and nephews had birthdays, she'd always give them one brand new dollar bill each. Whenever she went out to dinner with the family, she never once offered to pick up the bill or even leave a tip. As she grew older, my mother waited on her hand and foot for months at a time. The most she ever did in return was to give my mother an old coat that she hadn't worn since before World War II. Finally, when she died at eighty-eight, she gave us one last surprise. Instead of leaving her money and land to the family, she left it all to an old boyfriend of hers whom she hadn't seen in years. Each niece and nephew was left a five-dollar bill, and my mother got all of Aunt Lily's old clothes.

Shopping in the Chicago garment district was an unusual experience. My mother and I went into this old stucco building in a run-down-looking section of town. Inside we found a shopper's dream. The five-story building was full of brand-name outlet shops offering warehouse prices on all their clothing. Going from floor to floor, we found outlets for "Polo," "Guess," "Gucci," "Gunne Sax," "Zag," "Esprit," and "Forenzi" brands. The great shopping opportunities brought a variety of shoppers together. There were wealthy ladies escorted by chauffeurs, gangs of teenagers in punk attire, prostitutes stocking up for spring, wide-eyed tourists, and an ethnic mix of blacks, whites, Puerto Ricans, Chinese, Samoans, Mexicans, Arabs, and East Indians. The only problem shopping in the outlet building was that I feared for my safety. First, the building was a terrible firetrap. There were no windows, the electrical system was ancient, the elevators seldom worked, the stairways were clogged with people, and there were no fire escapes. If a fire broke out, I figured it was all over. Second, there were some sleazy-looking men hanging around. Poorly dressed, bad-smelling men stood along the hallways, and gangs of tough-looking boys roamed around. The whole time I was there, I was worried about getting mugged or getting my purse snatched, but nothing ever happened. I came out safely with five bags of new clothes.

1. I really enjoyed eating at ______________ last night. First, the atmosphere inside the restaurant was ______________. ______________________________

____

Second, the restaurant offered a great variety of ________________. ________________

Third, you get so much food that you ________________. ________________

Finally, the service is ________________. ________________

2. ________________ is the most likable person in my ________________ class.

He/She has a very friendly personality. ________________

________________ also has a great sense of humor. ________________

Finally, ______________ knows how to make a person feel ______________.

3. ______________ has many talents. First, he/she is a great ______________.

______________ is also a good ______________.

Probably ______________'s greatest talent is his/her ______________.

4. Fishing at ______________ last summer was a big disappointment. The lake area was not as pretty as I had expected.

The weather was also a disappointment.

We had nothing but problems with the ______________.

Worst of all, the fishing turned out ______________.

5. Finals week went a lot better than I had expected. First, I had a lot of free time to study during the week.

My ______________ test turned out much easier than I expected.

I really surprised myself on my ________ final. ________

Overall, my grades on final exams were ________. ________

Exercise 9 Choose one topic from the following list for writing a paragraph. Please follow these steps.

1. Write a *topic sentence* expressing the main point to be developed in the paragraph.
2. Write a *well-developed paragraph* beginning with the topic sentence and including supporting points and details or examples to clarify those points.
3. End your paragraph with a *concluding sentence* that wraps up the paragraph and refers back to your topic sentence in some manner.

Paragraph Topics: going to college
eating in the cafeteria
your home town
small foreign cars (or another type)
a particular class
a particular person

dating
raising children

Before you write your first draft, you may want to make a list of supporting points for your topic sentence as you've done in other exercises. However, some writers prefer a more *detailed outline* that contains both supporting points and details in a formal outline structure. The advantage of the outline is that you have both supporting points and details on paper before you write your paragraph. Study both prewriting methods—listing and outlining—in the following sample, and then use the one that you prefer.

Sample Paragraph

Topic: swimming
Topic Sentence: I don't enjoy swimming anymore.

List of Points:
can't swim for fun
hard work
no one to swim with
cold weather

Formal Outline:

I. Can't swim for fun
   A. On swim team for too long
   B. Shoulder problems
II. Hard work
   A. Don't float well
   B. Small hands and feet
III. Cold weather
   A. Freezing winters
   B. No desire to go outside
IV. No one to swim with
   A. None of my friends swim
   B. Don't enjoy swimming alone

When you finish your first draft, analyze the following sample paragraph with a classmate, referring to the questions that follow the paragraph.

I don't enjoy swimming anymore, first, all the fun is gone. I feel I have to swim laps and push myself. I also developed shoulder problems from swimming in high school, and my joints hurt when I do any stroke but breaststroke. Besides, swimming has always been hard work for me. First, I'm what you call a "sinker" because I can't float. Second, I have small hands and feet. Now that I'm living in Minnesota, the wheather is also a trouble. Finaly, where I'm currently living, I don't know of anyone who swims regularly, I won't swim alone.

Questions for Evaluation:

1. Does the topic sentence express a definite opinion or attitude about the topic?
2. Are the supporting sentences strong? Are there enough supporting points to satisfy the reader?
3. Is there enough detail and examples to make the paragraph interesting and informative? Is each main point supported with detail or examples?

4. Does the last sentence refer back to the topic sentence in some manner?
5. Are there any problems with wording, sentence punctuation, or spelling?

Now apply the questions to your own draft and consider any revisions or corrections that will improve your paragraph. (Get a second opinion from a classmate if you wish.) Then write your final draft, with all revisions included.

Practice Quiz

Take this practice quiz to help prepare you for the section quiz. Then compare your answers with the answer key. When you are ready for the section quiz, let your instructor know.

I. Circle the letter of the *best* topic sentence in each group for beginning a paragraph. Remember, an effective topic sentence states a definite opinion or attitude, can be supported in a paragraph, is specific enough to interest readers, and gives definite direction to a paragraph.

Example

a. Disney World is an amusement park in Florida.
b. Disney World is a place where a lot of tourists go.
(c.) Disney World is the most popular attraction in Florida.

1. a. I've lived in Hawaii.
   b. It costs money to live in Hawaii.
   c. Hawaii is a very expensive place to live.
2. a. Commuter train travel is dying out in many states.
   b. Commuter train travel is found in some states.
   c. Commuter train travel is one form of transportation.
3. a. Lucinda was surprised by her SAT scores.
   b. Lucinda took her SAT exam on Saturday.
   c. Lucinda did surprisingly well on her SAT exam.
4. a. Larry could never understand his problem with girls.
   b. Larry could never understand why girls felt as they did about him.
   c. Larry could never understand why girls didn't like him.
5. a. I recently dealt with a high-pressure salesman.
   b. There is one type of salesman I can't stand.
   c. I can't stand high-pressure salesmen.
6. a. Joan is looking forward to the spring semester.
   b. Joan is beginning the spring semester next week.

c. Joan has a definite opinion about the spring semester.

7. a. Fall will soon be coming to Maine.
   b. Fall in Maine is an okay time of year.
   c. Fall in Maine is the loveliest time of the year.

8. a. Scientists experiment on rats and apply what they learn to humans.
   b. Scientists' experimentation on rats has been very useful for humans.
   c. Scientists' experimentation on rats has had an effect on humans.

9. a. Indoor pollution is as dangerous as outdoor pollution.
   b. There is both indoor pollution and outdoor pollution.
   c. Indoor pollution affects people just like outdoor pollution.

10. a. The lottery is a form of gambling.
    b. The lottery has the same effect on people as other forms of gambling.
    c. The lottery is just as bad as any other form of gambling.

II. Circle the letter of the *best-developed* paragraph in each pair.

Example

(a.) Rudy has always worked hard. When he was young, he ran a lemonade stand in the summer. Later, he delivered papers every morning at 4:30. When he was in high school, he worked in a drugstore after school and as a gardener on weekends. At the same time he carried a B average at school and studied at least two hours a day. Now he manages his own store, and he works seventy to eighty hours a week. He's also going to night school to complete a business degree.

b. Sally has a lot of things done for her. Her mother helps her around the house. Her older sister helps her out with school things. Her younger sister shares the outdoor chores. Her boyfriend helps her with finances, and her girlfriend solves her social problems. Even at her job people make some things easier for her. She gets help at home, at school, and at work.

(*Note:* Paragraph *a.* is better developed because it provides a number of *detailed* examples supporting the main point that Rudy works hard. Paragraph *b.* is not well developed because although it provides a number of supporting points, it contains *no details* for the reader to understand the specific things that different people do for Sally.)

1. a. Mel is a great husband. He brings his wife roses at least once a week. Once he brought her some red roses with long stems, and another time he bought her some pink baby roses for the kitchen. He really likes roses, and so does his wife. He loves to give them to her, and she always loves to get them. Mel is a great husband in a lot of ways, but he really brings a lot of roses.

   b. Agnes is a terrible worrier. She worries when things are going badly, and when things go well, she worries that they'll get worse. She worries about her health, her grades, her looks, and getting married. She worries that her cat will run away, that her boyfriend will leave her, that her parents might get divorced, and that her car will be stolen. She worries about nuclear war, world poverty, the President's health, pollution, overcrowded cities, crop failure in Iowa, and thirty-two species of endangered animals. When she vacationed in California, she worried about it falling into the ocean.

2. a. The horse races were boring. All of the favorites finished first, so there wasn't an upset all day. The track was slowed by morning rain, so the times were slow, and no records were set. Fog came in late in the morning, and you couldn't see the far side of the track by noon. Also, the loudspeaker system was broken, so there was no one calling the races. To top it off, the best-known jockeys scheduled to ride didn't show up, and most of the winning riders were unknowns.

   b. The ice hockey game was exciting. There was a lot of action out on the ice. The two teams really went at it. The game was close most of the way, and either team could have won. For a time, there was as much action in the stands as there was on the ice. Some of the fans apparently had too much to drink. The referees even got involved in the action on the ice. I had never seen that kind of thing happen at a hockey match. It seemed like something exciting was happening every minute.

3. a. The laywer made a strong case for his client. He proved that the young woman couldn't have drunk enough beer in an hour to be legally drunk. He proved this in a brilliant way. He also showed that she was not big or strong enough to have punched out the arresting officer. He used some physics experts to prove this. He also proved that the arresting officer had not read his client her legal rights. He did this with some tricky questioning of the officer. With some more tricky questions, he showed that the officer was a sexist who didn't believe that women should be allowed to take a drink in public. He did a lot of smart things for his client.

   b. The prosecuting attorney was very weak. He was so disorganized that he kept losing his place while examining witnesses and had to go back and look at his notes. He had a thin, weak voice that the jury had trouble hearing, and he didn't sound like he had any confidence in the case. In fact, he started every argument with the words, "I hope that the jury will . . ." His cross-examination of the defendant was very weak. He couldn't get her upset or confused with his questions about her drinking habits, and he appeared to be sympathetic to her problems with the arresting officer. Most visitors in the court agreed that his cross-examination of the defendant had helped her case more than hurt it. He did so poorly that at the end of his final arguments, he asked the jury not to be prejudiced by the poor job he had done presenting the case. He finished with tears in his eyes.

4. a. Manny's Market sells practically everything that a family needs. It sells all kinds of food and drinks. It sells lots of clothing. In the rear of the store you can buy automotive products, and on the north side is the gardening section. The kids can also buy school supplies at Manny's, they can play games, and they can rent things to watch on television. Manny's also has a sporting goods section where you can buy all kinds of things. Manny's slogan is "If you can't buy it at Manny's, you don't need it!"

b. Older American-made cars are still a good buy for many people. First, you can buy them very reasonably since the trend is toward smaller, more economical models. You can get a clean 1978 or 1979 Oldsmobile or Chevrolet for two thousand dollars, and you can get slightly older Buicks or Cadillacs for a thousand dollars or under. The cars are roomy and comfortable inside, and most of them drive well because of their weight and big engines. Parts are easy to replace because they are American-made, and there are always plenty of mechanics who prefer working on good old General Motors engines. The big engines give you plenty of power, and although they burn more fuel, you can use regular gas in many of the models. They also burn less oil than cars with smaller higher-compression engines. So if you shop around carefully and look for a car that has been taken care of, you might find an older-model American car to your liking.

5. a. Hal is the biggest eater I know. He'll start the day with four or five eggs and a half dozen pieces of toast for breakfast, and he'll wash it all down with a quart of orange juice. For lunch, he'll have three Big Macs at McDonald's, large fries, a large Coke, a milk shake, a fruit pie, and a box of animal cookies. For dinner he'll eat a whole chicken by himself along with a huge mound of mashed potatoes, eight or nine rolls, and a half gallon of milk. Then from about 8:00 until bedtime, Hal will snack on nuts, potato chips, candy bars, ice cream, soda pop, chocolate chip cookies, and any fruit that is in season. Then by breakfast the next morning he's ready to start over again.

b. Sandy eats barely enough to survive. For breakfast, she eats nothing or very, very little. For lunch she'll have a little something, but nothing more than two or three hundred calories worth, all in fruits or vegetables. For dinner she eats a lot, for her. She'll have up to five hundred calories worth of meats, vegetables, and starches. She may even treat herself to a low-calorie dessert. She almost never snacks in the evening, and when she does, you'd be shocked at how little she eats.

The Sentence

The section in each level on "The Sentence" introduces the next step in effective paragraph writing: revising your sentences to produce the best wording for expressing your ideas. While the section on "The Paragraph" concentrated primarily on *content*—the development of *ideas*—the sections on "The Sentence" concentrate on *form*—the structural shape those ideas take in your sentences. Effective writing is a combination of having something to say (content) and expressing it in the clearest written manner (form).

Sentence Variety

Section Topics

Compound Sentence

Combining Method #2

Each section on "Sentence Variety" introduces different ways to structure and combine sentences to produce the most effective sentences and sentence patterns. This section introduces a new structure—the *compound sentence*—and also shows you how to combine short sentences to form compound sentences.

Compound Sentence

The *compound sentence* is one of the most common and useful sentence structures, and you have no doubt used some compound sentences in your writing. Here are the main features of the compound sentence.

1. A compound sentence contains two *independent clauses* joined by a *coordinating conjunction: and, but, so, yet, for,* and *or.* An *independent clause* contains a subject and a verb and *can stand alone as a sentence.*
2. A *comma* (,) comes *before* the conjunction in a compound sentence.
3. The coordinating conjunction shows the *relationship* between the two halves (independent clauses) of the sentence.

Here are examples of compound sentences with different coordinating conjunctions. Notice that there is a complete sentence (independent clause) on each side of the coordinating conjunction, that there is a comma *before* the conjunction, and that each conjunction shows a different relationship between the two halves of the sentence. (The conjunctions are underlined.)

I'm heading for Chicago tonight, and I won't be back for a month.
I'm heading for Chicago tonight, so I won't be seeing you for a month.
I'm heading for Chicago tonight, but I'll come right back if it's snowing.

Jerry is a good student, yet he could be doing even better.
Jerry is a good student, so he should be able to handle eighteen units this semester.
Jerry is a good student, for he studies hard and grasps concepts well.

The watermelon crop is large this spring, or at least it seems larger than last year's crop.
The watermelon crop is large this spring, so we should have a good harvest.
The watermelon crop is large this spring, yet the melons look pretty small.

Notice that each coordinating conjunction shows a different relationship between the two halves of the sentence. Here is how each is used.

COORDINATING CONJUNCTIONS

and:

joins information together; adds one action or thought to another *without* showing a relationship between them

Examples:

The Joneses moved to Shreveport in 1984, and they have lived there ever since.

Harold is a quiet, private man, and he works for the post office on Q Street.

but:

shows a *contrast* between the two halves of the sentence; the second half is often opposite in meaning to what is expected

Examples:

Harriet looks very weak and tired, but she is actually in perfect health.

Ralph had an F in sociology halfway through the semester, but he worked hard and finished the course with a B.

yet:

similar to *but*; shows a contrast between two thoughts or actions

Examples:

I'm going to the store for you, yet I'd rather stay home and watch cartoons.

Felicia isn't feeling well, yet she is going to work this morning anyway.

so:

shows a *cause-effect* relationship: what happens in the first half of the sentence influences what happens in the second half

Examples:

I am running short of money, so I'm going to have to find a part-time job.

A computer manufacturing plant is opening in Hallsport, so there will be one hundred new jobs available in October.

for:

means "because"; what happens in the second half of the sentence influences what happens in the first half

Examples:

The negotiations were finally called off, for neither side in the wage dispute would budge from their position.

You should wash your hair every day, for it really shines when it is clean.

or:

shows *options*; a choice is available

Examples:

We could call a taxi to get us, or we could walk sixteen blocks to the restaurant.

We'll call you before we come over, or we might just drop by unexpectedly sometime.

Exercise 10 Fill in the best coordinating conjunction to complete each of the following compound sentences. Notice that there is a complete sentence on each side of the conjunction and that there is a comma before the conjunction. When you finish, compare your answers with the answer key.

Example You were late for work this morning, ***and*** you were also late yesterday.

1. Harvey's cat sleeps in the house at night, ______ he usually sleeps on the foot of his bed.
2. It's warm out today, ______ let's wear shorts to the park this afternoon.
3. Geography II is offered at 9:00 on Monday and Wednesday, ______ it is offered at 8:00 on Tuesday and Thursday.
4. Jogging is a popular form of exercise, ______ many doctors don't recommend it.
5. There was smoke coming from apartment 2, ______ the manager didn't seem concerned.
6. A burglar snuck into the Davis home last night, ______ the front door was unlocked.
7. Marian has been married for thirty years, ______ she still feels like a newlywed.
8. Classical music concerts are drawing larger crowds in Lexington, ______ art exhibits are also attracting more people.
9. Black-and-white television sets are inexpensive, ______ they are cheap to manufacture.
10. Cuba's emigration laws are lenient, ______ many Cubans have gone to Florida.
11. Homer is playing out his option with the Redbirds, ______ he still hopes to rejoin them next year.
12. The coast had been badly damaged by the hurricane, ______ thousands of homeowners were evacuated.
13. Perfume filled the air, ______ was it the smell of lilacs blooming?
14. A strong wind changed the course of our sailboat, ______ we lost an hour's time.
15. Your minister must be a Bible scholar, ______ he can quote the most obscure passages.

Exercise 11 Complete the following compound sentences by adding a complete sentence (independent clause) after the coordinate conjunction that ties in with the first half and the conjunction. When you finish, show your sentences to your instructor.

Example I know we've driven through this part of town before, yet I don't recognize it.

1. The Rangers beat the Bruins badly in hockey, yet the Bruins remained optimistik.
2. The geometry class may be held in room 32 tomorrow, or the auditorium depending on the latin Club
3. Please put the plates back in the dishwasher, for they are not done
4. The waves were high and rough, yet they were nice to watch
5. This is the last day of the semester, so I will not have any homework.
6. The hamburgers at the Delport Drive-in are great, and the best tasting in town.
7. I really enjoy reading a good novel in the evening, and a good football game on Sunday afternoon
8. James enjoys his pottery class, but hates his english class.
9. You have gotten good grades on all your tests, so you shouldn't worried about this test.
10. Aunt Matilda is spending the week with us, for ~~has~~ she can not afford a hotel.

Exercise 12 Write your own compound sentences using the coordinating conjunctions provided. Remember, a compound sentence contains two independent clauses, a coordinating conjunction, and a *comma* before the conjunction. When you finish, share your sentences with a classmate who is finished and with your instructor.

Example I used to enjoy staying out late at night, but now I'm contented to come home before midnight.

1. and
2. but
3. yet
4. for
5. or
6. so
7. and
8. but
9. yet
10. so

Donna & I went to the story, and
We bought a pie for dessert
We took a walk for icecream, but
the store was closed.
We made just enough cakes for
the day, yet we still did not
have enough for everyone.
We had brought an umbrella for the
day, for there was a change ~~for~~ rain.
Would you like to go to the movies,
or do you want to go bowling.
We went to the park when it began to
rain, so we turned around & came home.

Combining Method #2

In the "Sentence Variety" section in Level 1, you learned to combine short, similar sentences by eliminating repeated words and joining similar ones. A second method for combining sentences is to join them with a *coordinating conjunction* to form a *compound sentence*. This is perhaps the best way to join pairs of short sentences that would be stronger as a single, revised sentence. Here are some suggestions for combining sentences with coordinating conjunctions.

COMBINING SENTENCES WITH COORDINATING CONJUNCTIONS

1. Combine pairs of shorter sentences that are closely related in meaning.
2. Place the coordinating conjunction that best joins the sentences between them.
3. Place a comma before the coordinating conjunction.
4. Combine sentences *only* when the new compound sentence would be *more effective* than the two shorter sentences.

Here are three examples of pairs of short sentences that could be improved by being combined to form compound sentences. Notice the coordinating conjunction that is used to combine each pair.

Lupe isn't doing well in French. She is thinking about dropping the class.
Lupe isn't doing well in French, so she is thinking about dropping the class.

Henry hadn't driven in fog before. He had no trouble finding his house.
Henry hadn't driven in fog before, but he had no trouble finding his house.

Malcolm is enjoying his teller's job at the bank. He is getting a raise on Monday.
Malcolm is enjoying his teller's job at the bank, and he is getting a raise on Monday.

Maria didn't go on the field trip to the desert. She had a 103-degree temperature.
Maria didn't go on the field trip to the desert, for she had a 103-degree temperature.

Exercise 13 Rewrite and combine the following pairs of sentences with coordinating conjunctions to form compound sentences. Use the conjunction that best joins each pair, and put a comma before the coordinating conjunction.

Example I am tired of staying home every night. I'm going out tonight for a change.
Revised: I am tired of staying home every night, so I'm going out tonight for a change.

1. Let's spend the Fourth of July at Traver Park. Let's spend it at Avocado Lake.
2. It's going to be chilly at the hockey game. We should wear sweaters and jackets.
3. We won't have a chemistry class for a month. Julian blew up the science lab.
4. Doctors are studying the diets of cancer victims. They hope to find a link between diet and cancer.
5. Henrietta is a sweet lady. She has a terrible temper.
6. The Methodist church hired a woman pastor. She won't be in town for nearly three months.
7. Calvin wants the best for his children. He refuses to spend any money on himself.
8. Marian walked to the G Street bus stop. Then she caught a bus to the new museum.
9. Your eyes look terrible. Your tears have smeared the mascara.
10. The fireplace threw out a lot of heat. I still got cold lying on the tile floor.
11. You must be an expert bowler. You must be having beginner's luck tonight.
12. The nursery temperature stays at 76 degrees. The ferns grow best at that temperature.

Exercise 14 The following paragraph contains some pairs of short sentences that could be effectively combined. Rewrite the paragraph and combine pairs of sentences with a coordinating conjunction to form compound sentences. Use the best conjunction to join each pair, and put a comma before the conjunction. When you finish, compare your sentences to the answer key.

Example The freight train passed through town. It didn't stop. Usually it stops at the cattle yard for a half hour.

Revised: The freight train passed through town, but it didn't stop. Usually it stops at the cattle yard for a half hour.

Frank bought ten acres of wheat. He paid $800 an acre. He farmed the land for two years and had fair success. Then there were two years of drought. His crops were very small. He lost money both years and had to borrow from the bank. The next year was a little better. It wasn't good enough for Frank to clear his debt. He put the farm up for sale before he got into a worse financial bind. He sold the farm the next month. He moved to the city and bought a grocery store. He is happy to be free of the farm. He misses living in the country.

Practice Quiz Take this practice quiz to help prepare for the section quiz. Check your answers with the answer key. When you are ready for the section quiz, let your instructor know.

I. Circle the letter of the *best-worded* sentence from each group.

Example

(a.) The river is low in the winter, but it will be full again by spring.
b. The river is low in the winter, so it will be full again by spring.
c. The river is low in the winter, for it will be full again by spring.

1. a. Break dancing is sweeping the nation, or I think it is only a fad.
   (b.) Break dancing is sweeping the nation, but I think it is only a fad.
   c. Break dancing is sweeping the nation, for I think it is only a fad.
2. (a.) The crowd at the Motley Crue concert in Akron was large, yet it wasn't very lively.
   b. The crowd at Motley Crue concert in Akron was large, so it wasn't very lively.
   c. The crowd at the Motley Crue concert in Akron was large, or it wasn't very lively.
3. a. We are going to have to cut down on our phone calls, and our phone bill was $100 last month.
   b. We are going to have to cut down on our phone calls, so our phone bill was $100 last month.

c. We are going to have to cut down on our phone calls, for our phone bill was $100 last month.

4. a. Hal was depressed about his broken arm, so at least it would heal before track season.
   b. Hal was depressed about his broken arm, and at least it would heal before track season.
   c. Hal was depressed about his broken arm, but at least it would heal before track season.

5. a. Miriam had a week's vacation from work, yet she took her family to the mountains.
   b. Miriam had a week's vacation from work, so she took her family to the mountains.
   c. Miriam had a week's vacation from work, or she took her family to the mountains.

6. a. The cows are grazing down in the valley, or there is little grass left in the hills.
   b. The cows are grazing down in the valley, yet there is little grass left in the hills.
   c. The cows are grazing down in the valley, for there is little grass left in the hills.

7. a. Handyman's has a good sale on plywood, for Grossman's has an even better sale.
   b. Handyman's has a good sale on plywood, or Grossman's has an even better sale.
   c. Handyman's has a good sale on plywood, yet Grossman's has an even better sale.

8. a. The kitchen linoleum is getting duller looking, or maybe the light is just growing dimmer.
   b. The kitchen linoleum is getting duller looking, so maybe the light is just growing dimmer.
   c. The kitchen linoleum is growing duller looking, for maybe the light is just growing dimmer.

9. a. Grady failed his entrance exams twice, so he also failed on his third attempt.
   b. Grady failed his entrance exams twice, or he also failed on his third attempt.
   c. Grady failed his entrance exams twice, and he also failed on his third attempt.

10. a. Monroe has dessert with every meal, so he goes through a gallon of ice cream a week.
    b. Monroe has dessert with every meal, yet he goes through a gallon of ice cream a week.

c. Monroe has dessert with every meal, but he goes through a gallon of ice cream a week.

II. Circle the letter of the *coordinating conjunction* that would best join each pair of sentences if they formed a compound sentence.

Example The new school year begins in August. It ends in late May.

a. so b. yet c. and

1. The burritos at Alfred's Restaurant were small. I ate six of them.

   a. but b. or c. so

2. The Senate passed a nuclear freeze resolution. It died in the House of Representatives.

   a. but b. so c. for

3. The Sumerian civilization is one of the oldest known to man. It is also one of the most interesting.

   a. but b. and c. or

4. My carpet needs shampooing. My windows also need cleaning on the inside.

   a. so b. and c. for

5. Todd's family is quite large. They need a van to haul themselves around.

   a. so b. or c. yet

6. Beatrice enjoys her job at the video rental store. She intends to quit next month.

   a. so b. yet c. for

7. That spider has been sitting in the bathtub for a week. I saw it there last Sunday.

   a. so b. for c. or

8. The storm may have reached the mountains last night. It may have reached early this morning.

   a. so b. or c. and

9. Fred and Andy shot a game of pool at the student union. They had nothing better to do.

   a. and b. for c. or

10. We've been acting like strangers for weeks. Let's mend our differences and be friends again.

    a. for b. yet c. so

Clear Sentences

Section Topic

Revising Wordy Sentences

A second important sentence consideration is effective wording. Most writers find that their "first draft" sentences can often be worded more smoothly and economically. In this section you learn to revise sentences that contain unneeded words and phrases.

Revising Wordy Sentences

A common wording problem for writers is using more words than necessary to express a thought. This is particularly true with "first draft" sentences, when you are putting ideas on paper for the first time. Unneeded words in your sentences take away from your ideas and make the reader's job more difficult.

Here are two of the most common reasons for wordy sentences.

1. Repeating the same or similar words in a sentence.

   Examples: (repeated or similar words underlined)

   At the beach we can do a lot of things at the ocean. (get rid of "at the ocean")

   My backyard is the place behind my house where I store my garden tools. (get rid of "the place behind my house")

   I'll be ready at 10:00 a.m., so please pick me up at 10:00 a.m. (get rid of second "at 10:00 a.m.")

   He went for a walk in the park just to relax walking in the park. (get rid of "walking in the park")

   My sister she always seems to be in a bad mood in the morning. (get rid of "she")

2. Using more words than necessary to say something effectively.

   Examples: (wordy phrases underlined)

   We got a flat tire due to the fact that we ran over some glass. (replace phrase with "because")

   Swimming is a sporting type of activity that is good for you. (replace phrase with "sport")

John is the kind of a person you know who never gets in trouble (replace phrase with "someone")

The wind that came down to us from up in the mountains was cold. (replace phrase with "from the mountains")

The house that you are at present residing within used to belong to the Smiths. (replace phrase with "that you live in")

We ordered an ethnic food of Italian derivation at the bazaar. (replace phrase with "Italian food")

Here are some basic suggestions for revising wordy sentences. You may come up with alternatives that are as effective.

1. Eliminate words that are unnecessarily repeated in a sentence.

   Example: Sally was thinking about *quitting school*, and she did *quit school*.

   Revised: Sally was thinking about quitting school, and she did.

2. Find simpler ways to express a thought that is needlessly wordy.

   Example: Henry's stool that he sat on when he milked was thirty years old.

   Revised: Henry's milking stool was thirty years old.

Exercise 15 Revise the following sentences by eliminating unnecessary words and finding simpler language to replace wordy expressions. When you have revised a sentence, there should be no word in it that is not needed to express the thought. Show your revised sentences to your instructor.

Example Mother used to spank us when we did things that mother didn't approve of herself.
Revised: Mother used to spank us for doing things she didn't like.

The sand on the beach is a dark brown color.

1. The sand on the shore is a dark brown color on the beach.
2. The blue water seems to never end with miles of blue water to be seen.
3. On the shore there are different sizes of people of different heights and weights on the shore.
4. I have an average-size room that is twelve-by-twelve feet, and it is painted a white color.

5. The birds were flying very high up in the sky way up there in the blue.
6. I am going to explain to anyone who reads this how to play the game of pool.
7. Before you get started in playing the game of pool, chalk up your cue stick.
8. Now you are ready to take the test, which is on algebra, and which is in room 32.
9. This game of Parcheesi I used to play a lot, and I enjoyed it a lot when I used to play.
10. The main reason why I like her is because of the fact that she doesn't let people down.
11. The two of us we are both the same age and born the same year.
12. We weren't too happy and not too pleased with the jobs we were working in.
13. We got to know a lot of things about each other, and we got to know our likes and dislikes.
14. The cattle huddled together all of them underneath the tree that was of an elm species.
15. The plaster didn't dry itself very fast or quickly in the cold, wet, damp air.

Exercise 16 Write a paragraph on one of the following topics, beginning with a topic sentence that expresses a definite opinion or attitude. Before writing your first draft, you might make a list of ideas relating to your topic sentence or an outline of main points and supporting details to follow in your draft.

Topics: a particular sport
a particular kind of weather
a problem you face
a change needed at your school
a course you'd recommend
living on a tight budget

After you finish your first draft, meet with a classmate or small group to analyze the sample draft in the text, using the evaluation questions following the paragraph as a guideline.

Sample Draft Water polo is a very exciting and fun game to play. Although concidered rougher and more enduring than most sports. Water polo provides lots of fun with many hours of hard work. For instance, in one days practice you might swim two to three thousand yards and then practice running drills. Keep in mind that you don't get out of the water and stand around, as you do in most other sports, so your constantly moving around for about two or three hours.

The game of water polo is very difficult to play. In order to play the game well you must be quick and very low key about what you do. You must also have a very cool temper because people can make you very mad and cause you to be suseptible to commiting a foul witch might have you ejected from the game for thirty seconds. Thee of these ejections and your out of the game for good. On the whole, water polo is a very phisical and rough game. It is also fun if you don't get to up tight about it.

Evaluation Questions to Consider:

1. Does the topic sentence express a definite opinion or attitude? Does the paragraph support the topic sentence well?
2. Is the paragraph unified? Are there any stray sentences that should be omitted or changed to improve the paragraph?
3. Are there things that could be added—a supporting point, example, or detail—that would make the paragraph more interesting, clearer, or more informative for readers?
4. Are the sentences in the clearest order for the readers to follow? Would any sentence(s) make more sense in a different location?
5. Are the sentences clearly, smoothly worded? Are there any short sentences that could be effectively combined? Are there any "wordy" sentences that could be revised effectively?
6. Are the sentences punctuated effectively? Does a period end each complete sentence?
7. Are there any words whose spelling needs checking? Are there any words that have been unintentionally omitted?

When you finish your analysis, reread your own first draft, using the same evaluation questions as a guideline. If you want a second or third opinion, exchange drafts with classmates. Finally, write your final paragraph draft, including all revisions and corrections you have noted.

Practice Quiz

Take this practice quiz to help prepare you for the section quiz. When you finish, compare your answers with the answer key. Then when you are ready for the section quiz, let your instructor know.

I. Circle the letter of the best-worded sentence in each group.

Example

a. My sister married a guy that she was very much in love with this guy.

b. My sister married a guy that was the one whom she really loved.

c. My sister married a guy she was very much in love with.

1. a. The ice on the wings of the airplane caused the airplane to fly lower in the sky than normal.
   b. The ice on the wings of the airplane caused it to fly lower.
   c. The ice-winged airplane flew lower.
2. a. Your Aunt Mattie from Texas just borrowed my socks that I newly bought in a store.
   b. Your Aunt Mattie from Texas just borrowed my new socks I just bought.
   c. Your Aunt Mattie from Texas just borrowed my new socks.
3. a. No one can match Freda's record of shooting twenty free throws in a row and making twenty free throws.
   b. No one can match Freda's record of shooting and making twenty free throws in a row.
   c. No one can match Freda's record of shooting twenty free throws in a row and making them also.
4. a. The downtown drugstore that was downtown had its exterior redone, fixing up the outside.
   b. The downtown drugstore had its outside exterior redone.
   c. The downtown drugstore had its exterior redone.
5. a. The minister at the new Lutheran church used to be the minister from the small church that is up the road.
   b. The minister at the new Lutheran church used to work at the other small church up the road from here.
   c. The minister at the new Lutheran church used to work at the small church up the road.
6. a. Your income taxes should go up with your income this year.
   b. Your income taxes should go up this year as your income did the same.
   c. Your income taxes should go up because your income went up and they go together.
7. a. I only put in thirty-six hours of work this week, so my pay will be less than usual.
   b. I only put in thirty-six hours of work this week, so my paycheck will be lower than if I had worked longer.
   c. I only put in thirty-six hours of work this week, so my pay will show it in less than usual money.
8. a. The tile on the bathroom floor hasn't dried to the floor, so don't walk on the bathroom floor.
   b. The tile on the bathroom floor hasn't dried, so don't walk on it.

c. The tile on the bathroom floor hasn't dried, so don't walk.

9. a. News of Jones's release from prison threw fear into his enemies when they heard of his release from prison.

   b. News of Jones's release from prison frightened his enemies when they heard about it.

   c. News of Jones's release from prison frightened his enemies.

10. a. The Super Bowl was played in the area of Northern California that year of 1985.

    b. The Super Bowl was played in the Northern California area this year.

    c. The Super Bowl was played in Northern California in 1985.

Correct Sentences

Section Topic

Run-on Sentence Pattern #2

The sections on "Correct Sentences" introduce you to the two most common structural problems writers have: *run-on sentences* and *sentence fragments*. In this section you are shown a second common run-on sentence pattern and two methods for correcting it.

Run-on Sentence Pattern #2

In the first "Correct Sentences" section, you learned that pronouns—*I, he, she, it, you, we, they*—often begin the second sentence within a run-on sentence. The second most common run-on pattern involves a group of common introductory words. Here is the pattern:

RUN-ON SENTENCE PATTERN #2

1. Most run-ons have *two sentences* run together without a period separating them.
2. The second sentence *within* the run-on begins with one of the following introductory words: *there, then, the, that, these, those.*

3. Sometimes there is *no punctuation* between the two sentences within the run-on, and sometimes there is a comma. *A comma does not separate sentences.*

Here are examples of run-on sentences involving this pattern. The words that begin the second sentence are underlined. Some run-ons have a *comma* between the two sentences and some have no punctuation.

The library is all the way across campus, <u>the</u> bookstore is next to the library.

Please eat all of the peas in the bowl on the kitchen table <u>those</u> are the last peas from the garden.

Mayor Garcia is running for governor, <u>then</u> he plans on running for Congress in four years.

The history of Latin America is full of revolutions <u>the</u> opposition is always trying to remove the party in power.

Strip mining in Colorado has been destructive, <u>there</u> are entire mountains that have been leveled.

Bring your parents to school on Friday at 7:00 p.m. <u>that</u> is open house day for the district.

Each of the sample sentences is a run-on sentence containing two complete sentences. The sentences need to be revised and correctly punctuated. Here are two ways to correct run-on sentences:

CORRECTING RUN-ON SENTENCES

1. As you learned in Level 1, place a period (.) after the first sentence and capitalize the first letter of the second sentence. (This is done most frequently when the sentences within the run-on are fairly *long* and can be effectively separated.)
2. *Join* the two sentences with a *coordinating conjunction—and, but, so, or, for,* or *yet*—to form a *compound sentence* from the run-on sentence. (This is done most frequently when the sentences within the run-on are *shorter* and can be effectively combined.)

Here are the revised versions of the sample run-on sentences. Notice that some of the run-ons have been separated to form two complete sentences, and others have been joined with a coordinating conjunction to form a compound sentence.

The library is all the way across campus, and the bookstore is next to the library.

Please eat all of the peas in the bowl on the kitchen table. Those are the last peas from the garden.

Mayor Garcia is running for governor, and then he plans on running for Congress in four years.

The history of Latin America is full of revolutions, for the opposition is always trying to remove the party in power.

Strip mining in Colorado has been destructive. There are entire mountains that have been leveled.

Bring your parents to school on Friday at 7:00 p.m., for that is open house day for the district.

Exercise 17 Correct the following run-on sentences by putting a period after the first sentence and capitalizing the first letter of the second sentence. Then compare your answers with the answer key.

Example I've heard of the restaurant we are going to tonight, there must be some reason its name is familiar to me.

Revised: I've heard of the restaurant we are going to tonight. There must be some reason its name is familiar to me.

1. Thelma is helping Clyde study for his geometry test, the test will be given on Tuesday.
2. This dense fog is slowing down the traffic on the freeway, the trucks are even slowing down.
3. Your cousin won the long jump at the district meet, this is a very good event for her.
4. Hal's collie is a beautiful, intelligent dog of breeding, there must be some way he would sell her to me.
5. The curfew in the dorms this semester is 1:00 a.m. on weekends, the curfew last semester was only 11:30 p.m.
6. The Stop 'n Go market by my house was robbed Thursday evening, there was over $500 taken from the vault.
7. Three couples that I know well are getting married in the spring, that must be a good season for matrimony.
8. We listened to tapes by the Grateful Dead for three hours, then we went to the Tina Turner concert in Central Park.

Exercise 18 Correct the following run-on sentences by joining them with coordinating conjunctions—*and, but, so, or, for,* or *yet*—to form compound sentences. Then compare your answers with the answer key.

Example We left for Texas on Friday, the weather was bad all the way.

Revised: We left for Texas on Friday, and the weather was bad all the way.

1. Maria was getting married on Wednesday, but then something happened to change her mind.
2. Harry likes loud music, and the louder the music is, the better Harry likes it.
3. The television will be off for the evening, so there is really no reason to turn it on.
4. Your uncle is going bowling tonight, and your aunt is free to play bridge.
5. Detroit is a large, sprawling city, for the population is over eight million.
6. Kingsburg is a very small town, yet there are over fifty churches.
7. Julie had her wisdom teeth pulled yesterday, so her mouth was swollen for a week.
8. Henry's model plane was airborne for an hour, and that's the longest he's ever flown it.

Exercise 19 The following paragraph has a few run-on sentences in it. Rewrite the entire paragraph and correct the run-on sentences. Correct longer run-ons by separating the sentences with a period and beginning the new sentence with a capital letter. Correct shorter run-ons by joining the sentences with *and, but, so, or, for,* or *yet* to form compound sentences. Then show your paragraph to your instructor.

Example Joseph had trouble with his ears every summer, there was something wrong that he couldn't understand. His ears rang all the time for no reason, he went to the doctor. The doctor told him there was nothing that could be done.

Revised: Joseph had trouble with his ears every summer. There was something wrong that he couldn't understand. His ears rang all the time for no reason, so he went to the doctor. The doctor told him there was nothing that could be done.

Maria had faced the same problem for years, there was always one girl on the track team who was better than she. No matter how hard she worked, she always came in second to a teammate. One year she was the second best sprinter in the entire valley, the best runner happened to be her teammate Valerie. Her senior year she finally felt she had a chance to be the best. She could beat everyone on the team in the 100-yard dash then in the middle of the

season, a freshman transferred from Michigan. She had been the Michigan state sprint champion in her age group. Once again, Maria was the second fastest on the team.

Practice Quiz

Take this practice quiz to help prepare you for the section quiz. Then compare your answers with the answer key. When you are ready to take the section quiz, let your instructor know.

Circle the letter of the correctly punctuated sentence in each group. (Circle *one* letter for each group.)

Example

a. You should go to the gift shop this morning, there is a sale on walnut jars.
(b.) You should go to the gift shop this morning. There is a sale on walnut jars.
c. You should go to the gift shop this morning There is a sale on walnut jars.

1. a. The mountains are hard to see this morning, there is a layer of fog covering them.
   b. The mountains are hard to see this morning there is a layer of fog covering them.
   (c.) The mountains are hard to see this morning. There is a layer of fog covering them.
2. (a.) We voted for the gun control initiative, and then we waited for the election results.
   b. We voted for the gun control initiative, then we waited for the election results.
   c. We voted for the gun control initiative then we waited for the election results.
3. (a.) Take a trip down to Joon's Department Store on Broadway. The coat sale they're having is great.
   b. Take a trip down to Joon's Department Store on Broadway, the coat sale they're having is great.
   c. Take a trip down to Joon's Department Store on Broadway the coat sale they're having is great.
4. a. Harriet hung from her teeth and twirled on a suspended ring, that's not easy to do.
   (b.) Harriet hung from her teeth and twirled on a suspended ring, and that's not easy to do.
   c. Harriet hung from her teeth and twirled on a suspended ring that's not easy to do.
5. a. Hal plans on going to Mexico for Christmas this year, this is his first trip outside the United States.

b. Hal plans on going to Mexico for Christmas this year. This is his first trip outside the United States.

c. Hal plans on going to Mexico for Christmas this year this is his first trip outside the United States.

6. a. Hal will probably take a jet plane to Mexico. There is not enough vacation time to drive.

b. Hal will probably take a jet plane to Mexico, there is not enough vacation time to drive.

c. Hal will probably take a jet plane to Mexico there is not enough vacation time to drive.

7. a. The men with foot problems are in that line, those with back problems are in the next line.

b. The men with foot problems are in that line those with back problems are in the next line.

c. The men with foot problems are in that line, and those with back problems are in the next line.

8. a. Mark Spitz won five gold medals in the 1976 Olympics, then he retired from swimming.

b. Mark Spitz won five gold medals in the 1976 Olympics then he retired from swimming.

c. Mark Spitz won five gold medals in the 1976 Olympics, and then he retired from swimming.

9. a. That shoe salesman is having a great day, that is the fiftieth pair of shoes he has sold.

b. That shoe salesman is having a great day. That is the fiftieth pair of shoes he has sold.

c. That shoe salesman is having a great day that is the fiftieth pair of shoes he has sold.

10. a. It snowed all night at Sumner Ridge, the slopes were covered with fresh powder.

b. It snowed all night at Sumner Ridge, so the slopes were covered with fresh powder.

c. It snowed all night at Sumner Ridge the slopes were covered with fresh powder.

The Word

As a rule, the process of writing moves from large, general concerns in the early stages to smaller, more specific concerns in the final stages. In this level, your first concern was writing unified, well-developed paragraphs. Your next concern was writing clear, smooth, correctly structured sentences. In this final section in Level 2, your main concern is to make sure the individual words within your sentences are grammatically sound and correctly spelled.

Although this final stage is not the most exciting part of writing, it is important to eliminate the kinds of errors that can weaken your effect on your readers. The fewer errors readers find in a paragraph, the more they can concentrate on what you have to say.

Verb Forms

Section Topics

Sentences Beginning with *There*

Regular Past Tense Verbs

Sentences Beginning with *There*

In the "Verb Forms" section of Level 1, you learned that *present tense verbs* must *agree* with their *singular* or *plural* subjects. It is sometimes difficult to determine subject-verb agreement in sentences beginning with *there* followed by a form of the verb *to be: is, are, was,* or *were*. Here are some suggestions for using the correct form of *to be* in sentences beginning with *there*.

1. The introductory *there* is *not* the subject of the sentence. The subject comes *after* the verb *is, are, was,* or *were*.

   Examples: (subject underlined)

   There is a bird on your head.
   There are seven days in a week.
   There were cobwebs hanging from Dan's boots.

2. If the subject is *singular*, use *is* in the present tense and *was* in the past tense. (*Was* and *were* are the only *past tense* verbs that change with the subject.)

   Examples: (subject underlined, verb circled)

   There is one habit I would like to break.
   There is a lesson to learn from our experience.
   There was a strong wind last night.
   There was no one in the hallway when I awakened.

3. If the subject is *plural*, use *are* in the present tense and *were* in the past tense.

   Examples: (subject underlined, verb circled)

   There are two women standing outside in the rain.
   There are many bad habits I would like to break.
   There are lessons to learn from our experience.
   There were strong winds blowing last night.
   There were no people in the hallway when I awakened.

Exercise 20 Fill in the correct form of *to be*—*is, are, was, were*—in each sentence. First, underline the subject and decide whether it is singular or plural. You will find the subject *after* the space for the verb. Use *was* or *were* if the sentence is written in the *past tense*—about something that has already happened. When you finish, compare your answers with the answer key.

Example There *were* six geese bathing on the lawn last night.

There *are* many ways to cook chicken.

1. There ______________ no school today because of the terrible fog.
2. There ______________ no school yesterday because of the bomb threat.

3. There ________________ four kinds of pizzas offered on the menu today.
4. There ________________ only three kinds of pizzas offered on yesterday's menu.
5. There ________________ a fly in my soup, waiter!
6. There ________________ a gnat in my soup last night.
7. There ________________ a large crowd at the President's inauguration right now.
8. There ________________ a large crowd at the President's inauguration a year ago.
9. There ________________ forty guests invited to the Newcomb's wedding in Chapel Hill.
10. There ________________ twenty guests who called and said they couldn't come.
11. There ________________ one river that flows into the Dead Sea.
12. There ________________ one river that used to flow into the Herring Sea.
13. There ________________ two men standing outside my window.
14. There ________________ some neighborhood children playing in the yard a few minutes ago.
15. There ________________ a fine mist falling outside.
16. There ________________ a heavy mist falling outside an hour ago.
17. There ________________ many questions students have on birth control.
18. There ________________ many questions about birth control that came up at last night's seminar.
19. There ________________ spiders crawling up and down the bathroom curtains.
20. There ________________ a few hundred ships anchored in the bay yesterday.

Exercise 21 Complete the following sentences, making sure your subject *agrees* with the verb given. Share your sentences with a classmate who is finished and with your instructor.

Example There is a new job opening up at the warehouse in June.
There were six apples left in the sink this morning.

1. There are ____
2. There is ____
3. There was ____
4. There were ____

5. There is ______________________________

6. There are ______________________________

7. There were ______________________________

8. There was ______________________________

____

Regular Past Tense Verbs

The *past tense* is the most common verb tense used by writers. Here are some basic things to know about past tense verbs.

1. The *past tense* is used to write about anything that already happened. It may have happened a minute ago, an hour ago, a day ago, or years ago.
2. The regular past tense ending is *-ed*. The *-ed* ending is the same whether the subject is singular or plural.

   Yesterday I walked six miles to school.
   We crossed the river at its narrowest point.
   The park filled with spectators awaiting the parade.
   First I thanked the host, and then I departed.

Here are the rules for adding the past tense *-ed* ending to verbs.

RULES FOR ADDING *-ED* TO VERBS

1. For most verbs, just add *-ed* to the main verb: *play/played, fish/fished, walk/walked, wish/wished, dream/dreamed, call/called.*
2. For verbs ending in *-y* preceded by a *consonant*, change the *y* to *i* and add *-ed: fry/fried, cry/cried, dry/dried, rely/relied, carry/carried.*
3. For verbs ending in *-y* preceded by a *vowel* (*a, e, i, o, u*), keep the *y* and add *-ed*: *annoy/annoyed, enjoy/enjoyed, display/displayed, destroy/destroyed.*
4. Most short verbs ending in a consonant *double the last letter* and add *-ed*: *ram/rammed, stop/stopped, skip/skipped, cram/crammed, tan/tanned, beg/begged, plan/planned, flop/flopped, mar/marred, ship/shipped, top/topped.*

Exercise 22 Write the correct past tense form for the following regular verbs. Follow the rules for adding *-ed* to verbs. Then compare your spellings to the answer key.

Examples kill *killed*

annoy *annoyed*

1. talk ______________
2. free ______________
3. deny ______________
4. fry ______________
5. hate ______________
6. delay ______________
7. display ______________
8. skate ______________
9. pray ______________
10. love ______________
11. use ______________
12. slip ______________
13. dry ______________
14. anger ______________
15. rob ______________
16. sob ______________

Exercise 23 The following sentences are written in the *present tense*. Rewrite the sentences in the *past tense* by changing all present tense verbs to their past tense forms. Then compare your answers to the answer key.

Example I enjoy working in the office at night.

I enjoyed working in the office at night.

1. We work well together on science projects.
2. The tree looks huge in the small yard.
3. The weather changes constantly in February and March.
4. The ships destroy nuclear targets far out in the Pacific.
5. The boy scouts learn survival skills in the wilderness.

6. The news from Des Moines about the kidnappings disturbs everyone.

7. The paramedics remove victims from the crumbling confines of the building.

8. The crowd plans to hold a rally for peace in the square.

9. Layers of dirt cover the ruins of the ancient city.

10. The large ship rams into the flimsy dock at Manila Bay.

11. You bake the most wonderful spice cookies.

12. Joan and Bill deny ever knowing the man who collects uncut diamonds.

Exercise 24 The following paragraph is written in the *present tense*. Rewrite the paragraph in the *past tense* by adding the appropriate *-ed* ending to regular past tense verbs. Then compare your paragraph with the answer key.

Example The news about his brother's illness bothers Theodore.
The news about his brother's illness bothered Theodore.

Mabel believes in the basic goodness of people. She accepts them with their faults, and she never tries to change anyone. She enjoys talking to people, and she never tires of listening to their problems. Because of her kindness, people love Mabel. They show her only their best side. They act kinder and behave more gently around her than normally. Men purchase gifts for her, and women sew her clothing. She lives in Plaines, Illinois, and everyone who visits her remembers her well. Mabel offers everyone her best, and she receives the same in return.

Exercise 25 Write a paragraph about at least five different things you remember doing as a child with your friends, brothers, sisters, or family. Begin your paragraph by completing a topic sentence similar to this one: When I was about ______________, I remember doing a lot of ______________ things.

You might want to make a list of some things you remember doing to include in your paragraph. Here is an example:

Sample Paragraph

Topic Sentence: When I was about five years old, I remember doing a lot of exciting things.

Things to Remember:
playing in the trees
baseball in the backyard
riding bikes
going to the high school
playing in the vacant lot

When you finish your first draft, analyze the following sample draft with a classmate or small group, using the evaluation questions on page 91 as a general guideline.

Sample Draft

When I was about five years old, I remember doing a lot of exciting things. We had large walnut trees growing behind our house, my sister and I climbed them in the summer. One time I fell out of one of the trees and landed on my head. We also play baseball in the backyard with the neighbor kids, and I remember we used my mother's dishes for home plate and the bases. We rode our bikes all over the north end of town, and we race through the alleys after a rain, splattering water and mud on each other. The high school was only a block away, so we walked there in the summer, we jumped the fence, and we skated around the cement corridors at the school until a custodian chased us out. Finally, there was a big vacant lot beside our house where we played cowboys and Indians almost every Saturday, it seems like I did nothing but play when I was young.

Now reread your own draft, considering the evaluation questions on page 91. (Also check your past tense verb endings.) Exchange drafts with a classmate and get a second opinion. Then write the final draft of your paragraph, including all revisions and corrections you noted.

Practice Quiz

Here is a practice quiz to help prepare you for the section quiz. Take the quiz and compare your answers with the answer key. When you are ready for the section quiz, let your instructor know.

I. Circle the letter of the sentence from each pair whose subject and verb agree.

Example

a. There is six geese swimming in your pond.

(b.) There are six geese swimming in your pond.

1. a. There was thousands of mosquitoes down by the river last evening.
   b. There were thousands of mosquitoes down by the river last evening.
2. a. There are many reasons for John's success in politics.
   b. There is many reasons for John's success in politics.
3. a. There were a hummingbird hovering above your rose bush this morning.
   b. There was a hummingbird hovering over your rose bush this morning.
4. a. There is many women waiting in line for their priority registration cards.
   b. There are many women waiting in line for their priority registration cards.
5. a. There is only one way you are going to get that car washed and waxed tonight.
   b. There are only one way you are going to get that car washed and waxed tonight.
6. a. There were deep ravines on both sides of the narrow mountain road.
   b. There was deep ravines on both sides of the narrow mountain road.
7. a. There is at least six bus stops on Cady Street in a one-mile stretch.
   b. There are at least six bus stops on Cady Street in a one-mile stretch.
8. a. There are only one seat left in the back of the classroom.
   b. There is only one seat left in the back of the classroom.

II. Circle the letter of the correct *past tense* verb form to complete each sentence.

Example The mosquitoes ______________ the hikers.

a. bothers (b.) bothered c. bother

1. Our track team ______________ five women in the long jump finals.
   a. place b. placed c. placeed
2. The buzzing sound from the heater ______________ the students.
   a. annoys b. annoyed c. annoied
3. The first graders ______________ rope during morning recess.
   a. skipped b. skips c. skiped
4. Dark thunderclouds ______________ in the eastern sky.
   a. formed b. forms c. formmed
5. The large policeman ______________ traffic at the congested intersection.
   a. stoped b. stops c. stopped
6. Ted ______________ the incident about the stolen van without any anger.
   a. related b. relates c. relateed

7. No one ______________ Fran's new beehive hairdo.

   a. envyed b. envies c. envied

8. The long-legged frogs ______________ from one lily pad to another.

   a. hoped b. hopped c. hops

9. Our water polo team ______________ on superior conditioning to win games.

   a. relied b. relies c. relyed

10. Students ______________ the main building because a bomb threat had been made.

   a. evacuated b. evacuateed c. evacuate

Pronouns, Adjectives, Adverbs

Section Topic

Subject Pronouns

Subject Pronouns

There are certain pronouns that are *always* used as *subjects* in sentences. These *subject pronouns* are *I, he, she, it, you, they,* and *we*.

There is another group of pronouns called *object pronouns* that are *never* used correctly as subjects. These *object pronouns* are *him, her, me, them,* and *us*.

If a pronoun is a *single* subject, there is seldom any problem using the correct form. Here are some examples of sentences with pronouns as single subjects:

I am not going to the store with you today.

We are not going to leave Samantha alone another night.

They have decided to buy a new car this month.

I talked to Reuben about his grades, and he was not really concerned.

You bought a new binder at the bookstore, but I couldn't find one.

The problem in using the correct subject pronoun form comes in sentences with *two or more subjects*, called *compound subjects*. Compound subjects are usually joined by the conjunction *and*. Writers often incorrectly use *object pronouns* in compound subjects. Here are some examples of common pronoun errors and the correct revised forms:

Wrong: Teddy and me don't belong in this tough algebra class.
Right: Teddy and I don't belong in this tough algebra class.

Wrong: Her mother and her are always together in the afternoons.
Right: Her mother and she are always together in the afternoons.

Wrong: The Willises and us are the best of friends.
Right: The Willises and we are the best of friends.

Wrong: Ralph and him belong to the same fraternity.
Right: Ralph and he belong to the same fraternity.

Here is a good way to decide on the correct subject pronoun form in a compound sentence when you aren't certain: If a pronoun is part of a *compound subject*, treat it as the *only* subject when you decide what pronoun to use. Cross out the other subjects in your mind and decide which pronoun form sounds best.

Examples Fred and (I, me) go to the same barber. (Would you write "I go to the barber" or "Me go to the barber"? I is obviously correct.)

Her mother and (her, she) left for the coast. (Would you write "Her left" or "She left"? She is obviously the correct pronoun.)

Terence, Maria, Freddie, and (we, us) are invited to the snow party. (Would you say "We are invited" or "Us are invited"? We is obviously correct.)

That German shepherd and (he, him) are inseparable. (Would you say "He is" or "Him is"? He is obviously correct.)

Exercise 26 Circle the correct subject pronoun for each of the following sentences. Refer to your list of subject pronouns. Also, follow the suggestion of ignoring any subject *except* the pronoun in a compound subject and deciding which pronoun form sounds best. Check your answers with the answer key.

Example Marvis and (I, me) take a long time showering. (Would you say "I take" or "Me take"?)

1. The opposing team and (us, we) played the longest game of the season yesterday.
2. Mother and (me, I) invited all the relatives to the park for a picnic.
3. Phyllis, Freda, and (she, her) like to cruise Main Street in a 1956 Ford.

4. The Little family and (us, we) go to the opera together in the summer.
5. No one knows if Julie and (he, him) are engaged or just going steady.
6. Everyone met at the library, but then Sam, Frank, and (she, her) left together.
7. Do you have any idea when Harry and (I, me) are supposed to take our SAT exams?
8. The bear and (he, him) wrestled for an hour at the school fair.
9. Jerome, Freda, and (them, they) have always lived north of the railroad tracks.
10. Our guests and (we, us) had to abandon the house when the flood came.
11. Susie, Sara, (he, him), and (we, us) all enjoy long, free summer afternoons.
12. Margaret and (me, I) looked all afternoon for a candidate for debate club president.

Exercise 27 Fill in your own subject pronouns in the following sentences: *I, he, she, you, they,* or *we*. Try to use all of the different subject pronouns at least once. Then show your answers to your instructor.

Example Gladys and ___*I*___ want the best out of life for Clarence.

1. All of the students from Cambria and ________ met at the statue for a tug-of-war.
2. Ruth, Ted, and ________ belong to the same gymnastics group.
3. I don't believe that Sarah and ________ are in this class anymore.
4. The Brookses told us that Mr. Gomez and ________ left for Texas yesterday.
5. Your lovely mother and ________ were just talking about you.
6. That horse and ________ make a great pair.
7. I'd like to find a reason to cut class, but since Ted and ________ are going, I'd better go.
8. Malcolm, Patti, Sheila, and ________ have been waiting for Henrietta all morning.
9. The Weavers, the Browns, the Fernandezes, and ________ play bridge on Wednesdays.
10. The boy in the green shirt and ________ look very nice together.

Exercise 28 Some of the following sentences contain subject pronoun errors that need correcting. Rewrite any sentence with a pronoun problem and replace the incorrect pronoun with the correct subject pronoun form. If the sentence is correct, mark *C*. Check your answers with the answer key.

Example Howard and me don't care about going to the play tonight.
Revised: Howard and I don't care about going to the play tonight.

1. I believe that Phyllis and him don't care much for each other's company.
2. Gertie and me don't care about going to visit the museum today.
3. Do you think that Sarah, Henry, and me have a chance in the math contest?
4. Mr. Sanchez and him don't seem to get along at all.
5. Your mother and I have had a long talk about your wonderful grades.
6. Do you know whether Karen and he are coming to the house for dinner?
7. My dog Clyde and me go for long walks on Saturdays.
8. Henry and her go bicycling at the stadium on weekends.
9. Tad, Sam, Sue, Marv, Mick, and me all have short names.
10. Freddie and I are leaving when Melissa and her arrive.

Practice Quiz Take this practice quiz to prepare for the section quiz. Then compare your answers to the answer key. When you are ready for the section quiz, let your instructor know.

Circle the letter of the sentence with the correct subject pronoun(s).

Example
a. That new girl in class and I have never met.
b. That new girl in class and me have never met.

1. a. The woman from the dress shop and me go to lunch together on Mondays.
   b. The woman from the dress shop and I go to lunch together on Mondays.
2. a. Your aunt and me don't see eye to eye on a lot of things.
   b. Your aunt and I don't see eye to eye on a lot of things.
3. a. I believe that Freddie and him are half brothers.
   b. I believe that Freddie and he are half brothers.
4. a. Do you know where Andrew, Sarah, and she do their Christmas shopping?
   b. Do you know where Andrew, Sarah, and her do their Christmas shopping?

5. a. I'll try the new math class next semester if her and him try it.
   b. I'll try the new math class next semester if she and he try it.
6. a. Those new neighbors and us don't know each other very well.
   b. Those new neighbors and we don't know each other very well.
7. a. Them and us had a good game of darts yesterday at the student union.
   b. They and we had a good game of darts yesterday at the student union.
8. a. Don't invite Fred to your house because his brother and him clean out the refrigerator.
   b. Don't invite Fred to your house because his brother and he clean out the refrigerator.

Spelling

Section Topics

-ing Ending

There, Their, and *They're*

-ing Ending

Words ending in *-ing* are commonly misspelled by many writers. The problem that writers have is deciding what to do with the last letter of the word before the *-ing* ending. Do they keep it, drop it, or double it? These simple rules will help you add the *-ing* ending correctly.

1. If the word ends in *-e*, drop the *e* before adding *-ing* (*bore/boring, care/caring, face/facing, have/having, dare/daring*)
2. If the words end in *-y*, keep the *y* and add *-ing*. (*study/studying, play/playing, carry/carrying, fly/flying*)
3. If a verb ends in a consonant (any letter but *a, e, i, o, u*) preceded by a *short vowel* (*cŭt, hĭt, păt, pĕt, hŏp*), double the last letter and add *-ing*. (*cut/cutting, hit/hitting, pat/patting, pet/petting, hop/hopping*)
4. *In all other cases,* keep the last letter and add *-ing* (*dream/dreaming, fight/fighting, faint/fainting, eat/eating, sleep/sleeping*)

Exercise 29 Add *-ing* to each of the following words. Follow the rules for adding *-ing* when deciding what to do with the last letter of the word. Then compare your answers to the answer key.

Example eat *eating*

1. care ______
2. jump ______
3. plan ______
4. begin ______
5. date ______
6. delay ______
7. study ______
8. cut ______
9. come ______
10. run ______
11. wait ______
12. enjoy ______
13. carry ______
14. hit ______
15. have ______
16. fly ______
17. wear ______
18. drive ______
19. write ______
20. put ______

Exercise 30 Fill in *-ing* ending words in each of the following blanks in the paragraph. Spell the words correctly, and use words that make sense to complete each sentence. Then show your answers to your instructor.

Example I was *running* down the street last night.

Last night I was ______ in an old chair ______ a movie on television. The movie was very scary, and I began ______ strange noises outside. I turned the channel on the television, but I couldn't help ______ about the movie. Then I heard someone ______ on the front door. I was afraid to answer it, so I peeked out the front window to see who it was. There was no one there. The wind was ______ fiercely, and everything outside seemed to be ______. Then I thought I heard someone ______ through the back door of the house. I quickly hid behind the sofa in the ______ room and began

____________ my escape. I would make a run for the car and drive immediately to the police station. But before I could move, there was a shadowy figure ____________ in the room. The figure called my name, and it was my brother's voice. He had knocked on the front door to get in, but then he went around to the back because I hadn't opened the door. I was very relieved, but my heart was still ____________, and I was ____________ rapidly. I remember ____________ nightmares on and off all night long.

There, Their, They're

Three of the most commonly confused words in English are *there, their,* and *they're*. Most writers use one or another of these words incorrectly on occasion. Here are the basic uses for each of the three words. Once you understand their different meanings, you should have little trouble distinguishing among them.

there:

location—The books are over <u>there</u>. <u>There</u> on the table is my cap.
introductory word—<u>There</u> is a fly in my soup. <u>There</u> are cats everywhere.

their:

possessive of *they*—<u>Their</u> car was stolen. <u>Their</u> luggage is new.

they're:

contraction form for *they are*—<u>They're</u> always late for supper.
<u>They're</u> looking for their brothers.

Exercise 31 Fill in the blanks in the following sentences with *there, their,* and *they're*. Then compare your answers with the answer key.

Example <u>Their</u> books are over <u>there</u> in the corner.

1. ____________ are a lot of geese flying over the marsh this afternoon.

2. ______________ tennis shoe size was not in stock in a regular shoe store.
3. ______________ going to lose a lot of money on the horse races tonight.
4. ______________ answers to the math questions were very complicated.
5. ______________ is my watch underneath the bunk bed.
6. I think ______________ worried about the recent stock market drop.
7. ______________ are lots of ways to beat ______________ soccer team.
8. ______________ having a party at ______________ new apartment.
9. Put the new books ______________, ______________, and ______________.
10. Couples keep carving ______________ initials on the elm tree over ______________.

Exercise 32 Write your own sentences using *there, their,* and *they're* as indicated. Then show your sentences to your instructor. (Use the words anywhere in your sentences.)

Examples their *I want their address and telephone number.*

they're there *They're having trouble with the window over there.*

1. there
2. their
3. they're
4. there their
5. there they're
6. there there
7. they're their
8. there their they're

Practice Quiz Take this practice quiz to prepare for the section quiz. Then compare your answers with the answer key. When you are ready for the section quiz, let your instructor know.

I. Circle the correctly spelled word in each group.

Example a. dareing b. darring (c.) daring

	a.	b.	c.
1.	a. haveing	b. having	c. havving
2.	a. dating	b. dateing	c. datting
3.	a. studying	b. studing	c. studeing
4.	a. runing	b. running	c. runeing
5.	a. writeing	b. writting	c. writing
6.	a. begining	b. begineing	c. beginning
7.	a. waiting	b. waitting	c. waiteing
8.	a. comeing	b. coming	c. comming
9.	a. siting	b. sitting	c. siteing
10.	a. planning	b. planeing	c. planing
11.	a. carrying	b. carring	c. carreing
12.	a. flying	b. flyying	c. fliing
13.	a. practiceing	b. practicing	c. practiccing
14.	a. craming	b. cramming	c. crameing
15.	a. delaying	b. delayying	c. delaing
16.	a. watering	b. waterring	c. watereing
17.	a. shiping	b. shipeing	c. shipping
18.	a. mixing	b. mixxing	c. mixeing
19.	a. useing	b. ussing	c. using
20.	a. bottleing	b. bottling	c. bottlling

II. Circle the letter of the sentence that correctly uses *there, their,* or *they're*.

Example (a.) There are many ways to cook a chicken.
b. Their are many ways to cook a chicken.

1. a. There is a fire that is spreading rapidly in the foothills.
   b. Their is a fire that is spreading rapidly in the foothills.
2. a. Their belongings were destroyed after sparks ignited the roof of their home.
   b. There belongings were destroyed after sparks ignited the roof of their home.
3. a. They're currently living with their grandparents in Texas.
   b. There currently living with their grandparents in Texas.

4. a. Their neighbors were also burned out in the fire.
   b. There neighbors were also burned out in the fire.
5. a. There were two hundred acres of foothill pasture burned.
   b. They're were two hundred acres of foothill pasture burned.
6. a. Winds from the ocean did their share in spreading the fire.
   b. Winds from the ocean did there share in spreading the fire.
7. a. Their were over five hundred firemen fighting the blaze at its peak period.
   b. There were over five hundred firemen fighting the blaze at its peak period.
8. a. They're still trying to find out who or what started the fire.
   b. There still trying to find out who or what started the fire.

Writing Review

At the end of each level is a "Writing Review" section where you apply what you have learned to paragraph writing assignments. The following paragraph assignment takes into account everything that has been covered in the first two levels.

Level 2 Paragraph Assignment

Choose one of the following topics for writing a paragraph:

1. a special relative
2. a particular classmate
3. a bad habit
4. something that annoys you
5. a particular kind of music
6. a season of the year
7. a particular place

Step One

1. Decide on a *specific subject* for the topic that you selected.
2. Write a tentative *topic sentence* expressing a definite opinion or attitude about the subject.
3. Make a list of at least six points that support your topic sentence or make a formal outline.

Example

Topic Area: a particular job
Specific Subject: working at McDonald's restaurant
Topic Sentence: Working at McDonald's is very tiring.

List of Supporting Points:
1. always customers to be served

Formal Outline:
I. Always customers to be served
   A. Never a break
   B. Always under pressure

2. have to put together order yourself	II. Have to put together orders yourself A. Run all over the place B. Easy to get sloppy
3. always moving at a fast pace	III. Always moving at a fast pace A. Must uphold image B. Angry customers
4. only one break every four hours	IV. Only one break every four hours A. Not enough time to rest B. Gets you more tired
5. manager keeps the pressure on	V. Manager keeps the pressure on A. Watches you like a hawk B. Fires people

4. Write your first draft beginning with your topic sentence and including your supporting points within the paragraph. Your final sentence should bring your paragraph to a definite conclusion for your readers.

Step Two Read your first draft and consider these questions:

1. Is my topic sentence strong? (Does it express a definite opinion or attitude? Can it be supported easily? Does it give *definite direction* to the paragraph? Make any change in the topic sentence that will strengthen it.)
2. Is my paragraph unified? (Do all of the sentences relate to the topic sentence? Does any sentence need crossing out or changing?
3. Is my paragraph well developed? (Are there plenty of good supporting points? Are there enough details and examples to develop the supporting points? Add any new ideas or specific details or examples that will make your paragraph clearer, more interesting, or more informative.)
4. Are my sentences in the best possible order for expressing my thoughts? Would any sentence(s) be more effective in a different location?

Step Three Now go over your individual sentences and follow these suggestions:

1. Look for any pairs or groups of *short sentences* that could be combined to form stronger, more informative sentences. If you find any, underline them to be revised.
2. Check your wording within each sentence. Are there words or phrases that need replacing with better word choices? Underline anything that sounds awkward or unclear to you and needs to be revised. Also, check for overly wordy sentences that can be improved by omitting words or rewriting the sentence in a simpler form.
3. Check your paragraph for run-on sentences: two or more sentences run together without a period separating them. Look for the types of words that frequently begin the second sentence within a run-on (*I, she, he, we, they, it, then, the, there, this, that, these, those*) and for *commas* that have been placed between complete sentences instead of periods. To correct run-ons, put a period between complete

sentences and capitalize the new sentence, or *join* the shorter run-ons with a coordinating conjunction (*and, but, so*) to form compound sentences.

Step Four Now give your paragraph a final check for wording errors:

1. Check each sentence for *subject-verb agreement*, particularly with sentences beginning with *There is* and *There are*. If the paragraph is written in the *past tense*, make sure you've added the *-ed* ending on all regular past tense verbs.
2. Check your *pronouns* in the paragraph. Are you using them to replace words that don't need repeating? Are you using the correct subject pronoun forms?
3. Check your spelling. Are you adding a correct *-s* or *-es* ending to all plural words? Are you spelling *-ing* ending words correctly? If you aren't sure how a word is spelled, look it up in the dictionary. If you can't find a word, ask your instructor for help. Correct all spelling errors.

Step Five Write the *final draft* of your paragraph, including all sentence improvements and error corrections that you noted. Then share your paragraph with your instructor.

First Draft

Working at McDonald's is very tiring. First, there are always customers to be served. I work in a downtown McDonald's that gets lots of traffic, as soon as I serve one customer, there is always another one ready to order. There is constant pressure because of the fact that I can never step back for a few minutes and relax. Second, I have to put together all of the orders myself. Also, I must always move at a fast pace. McDonald's has an image to uphold, its workers must scurry about like ants. If I don't move fast enough, some customers will say, "Hey, speed it up," or "I thought McDonald's had *fast* service." And with all of this nonstop work. I only get one ten-minute break every two hours. First, ten minutes isn't enough time to rest and feel like getting back to work. It only gives me enough time to realize how tired I am, so I go back to work depressed. Finally, my manager really keeps the pressure on. By the end of the day, I'm emotionaly and phisically drained, like everyone else, and we all head out the door grumbling.

Final Draft

Working at McDonald's is very tiring. First, there are always customers to be served. I work in a downtown McDonald's that gets lots of traffic, and as soon as I serve one customer, there is always another one ready to order. There is constant pressure because I can never step back for a few minutes and relax. Second, I have to put together all of the orders myself. To do that, I have to move all over the serving area: french fries on one side, drinks on the other, and burgers in the middle. It's easy to get sloppy and spill a Coke or throw french fries on the floor. Also, I must always move at a fast pace. McDonald's has an image to uphold, and its workers must scurry about like ants. If I don't move fast enough, some customer will say, "Hey, speed it up," or "I thought McDonald's had *fast* service." And with all of this nonstop work, I only get one ten-minute break every two hours. First, ten minutes isn't enough time to rest and feel like getting back to work. It only gives me enough time to realize how tired I am, so I go back to work depressed. Finally, my manager really keeps the pressure on. He watches us like a hawk, and every time I do something wrong, he seems to catch it. He also has a reputation for firing people, and he never lets any of the workers feel that their jobs are safe. By the end of the day, I'm emotionally and physically drained, like everyone else, and we all head out the door grumbling.

LEVEL 3

Writing is a process that requires making choices. You have to decide what you want to communicate, how you want to express your thoughts, and what combination of words and sentence structures will best convey those thoughts. One of the purposes of Level 3, as well as the entire book, is to make you aware of different options available to the writer. The more sentence structures you feel comfortable using, the more wording choices you have to consider, the more organizational patterns you are aware of, and the more potential problems you learn to avoid, the more effectively and confidently you will write.

The Paragraph

In the sections on "The Paragraph" in the first two levels you learned that effective paragraphs are *unified, well-developed,* and have strong *topic sentences*. In this section you learn that effective paragraphs are *clearly organized* and contain *transitional wording*.

Section Topics

Paragraph Organization
Using Transitions

Paragraph Organization

As you learned in the first two levels, a paragraph is a group of related sentences that develop one main idea. A final important feature of an effective paragraph is *coherence*: The sentences within a paragraph are *logically organized* and *tied together* with words that show the sentences' relationship to one another. There are two important parts of coherence—*paragraph organization* and *transitional wording*.

There are a number of ways that a paragraph may be organized, but the most important concern is this: The sentences should follow each other in the most *sensible order* for developing the main idea of the paragraph.

Here are the five most common ways that writers organize their paragraphs:

Time

Sample Paragraph: (topic sentence underlined)

Sunday was a long day. I had to get up at 5:00 a.m. to attend an Easter sunrise service. Then I had duties at the church the rest of the morning. In the afternoon I visited the Manor Rest Home and talked to shut-ins who seldom have visitors. Then I went to my aunt's for dinner and played cards with Uncle Herman until about 9:00 p.m. Then I drove up into the hills with my family for a special Easter midnight chapel service in the pines. We stayed in a mountain cabin with ten other people that night and didn't get to sleep until after 2:00 a.m. I was exhausted after twenty-one hours of activity.

The paragraph follows the *time* (chronological) order in which the events took place. Here are examples of topics that could be ordered *chronologically*:

how to change a tire on a tractor
how to get from the bookstore to the cafeteria
what you did on Saturday
how Harvey made his first $1,000

Space

Sample Paragraph: (topic sentence underlined)

My bedroom is very cozy. It is a small room with thick carpeting and light blue walls. Below the north window is my double bed covered with an imitation leopard skin bedspread. To the left of the bed against the wall is a walnut nightstand with a reading lamp, a clock, and a radio. At the foot of the bed is a wooden stand holding my portable black-and-white TV and stereo. In all four corners of the room my speakers are mounted just below the ceiling. Behind the wooden stand and in front of the closet are three red bean bag chairs that are sagging from years of use. On the east and west walls are posters of rock groups, and a family of stuffed monkeys sits on the north and south window ledges. My room is small and cluttered and has that "lived-in" feeling I like.

The details within the paragraph are ordered according to their *location* within the description. Details may be ordered right to left, near to far, up to down, north to south, side to side, and so on. Here are examples of topics that could be ordered *spatially*:

describe your English classroom
describe Maria's looks
describe the new housing development
describe one area in Central Park

Size

Sample Paragraph: (topic sentence underlined)

<u>Professional football players come in all sizes</u>. Your smallest players, who range in height from 5′6″ to 5′11″, are your wide receivers. Next come your defensive backs, who are 5′10″ to 6′2″ and very slender and agile. Your running backs are about the same height as defensive backs, but they are heavier, averaging about 215 pounds. Quarterbacks are a bit taller, averaging about 6′3″, but they are often lighter than running backs. Next come your linebackers, who are from 6′1″ to 6′4″ and weigh an average of 230 pounds. Then come the big guys. Your offensive linemen range from 6′1″ to 6′6″ and average over 260 pounds. Your defensive linemen have similar size, but some are as tall as 6′8″ and as heavy as 300 pounds. Obviously, football has a place for all sizes of athletes.

The items within the paragraph are ordered according to their size: smallest to largest in this case. Here are examples of other topics that could be ordered by *size*:

animals in a zoo
members of a basketball team
items in a living room
countries in a hemisphere

Importance

Sample Paragraph: (topic sentence underlined)

<u>Our apartment needs lots of fixing up</u>. First, we've got to fix the leaky roof before the September rains come. Next, we need to patch the big holes in the bedroom walls and then strip the peeling paint off the walls. Then we can repaint the apartment. After the walls are painted, we can work on replacing the linoleum squares in the kitchen that are loose or cracked. Later, the living room carpet needs shampooing, and we should replace that old swaybacked sofa. Then we won't be embarrassed to have company over once in a while.

The items in the paragraph are ordered according to how *important* they are to the topic, in this case from the most important item to the least important. Here are other examples of topics that could be ordered by *importance*:

reasons for dropping the school paper
why dieting can be dangerous
reasons for living away from home
why students work and go to school at the same time

Category

Sample Paragraph: (topic sentence underlined)

Claudia is destined to be an excellent long-distance runner. First, there are her physical attributes. She is long-legged and has a tremendous stride. She also has great natural endurance and an at-rest heart rate of sixty beats per minute. Next comes her mental toughness. She is a tremendous competitor who will extend herself to exhaustion to win a race. She has the strength to block out pain and concentrate on her race during those last few hundred yards where most runners tend to wilt. Finally, Claudia surpasses most athletes in dedication. She runs five to ten miles a day in morning and evening sessions at least five days a week. She maintains this schedule ten months out of the year, and while most high school athletes sit out the summer, Claudia trains and competes in AAU competition. If she can maintain this dedication for another two years, she has an outside chance of being invited to the Olympic trials.

The items in the paragraph are ordered according to *common groupings*: Claudia's physical abilities, her mental toughness, and her dedication. In ordering a paragraph by *category*, you group similar details in a particular category. (For example, in describing a person, details could be grouped under "looks," "personality," and "interests." In explaining the qualities of a good volleyball player, details could be grouped under "physical skills," "mental skills," and "emotional makeup.") Here are examples of topics that could be ordered by *category*:

why the baseball team is successful
why the lifeguarding job is bad
why geometry class is interesting
qualities of a successful salesman

Exercise 1 Put each of the following lists of details in the order suggested. Then check your order with the answer key.

Example *Topic Sentence:* My morning schedule on Monday is rough.

Order:	*Unordered*	*Ordered List*
Time	up at 5:00	1. up at 5:00
	drive to work at 11	2. work from 6:00 to 7:00
	classes from 8 to 11	3. classes from 8 to 11
	work from 6 to 7	4. drive to work at 11
	work from 11:30 to 12:30	5. work from 11:30 to 12:30

1. *Topic Sentence:* The meadow is full of life in the spring.

Order:	*Unordered List*	*Ordered List*
Size	blue jays everywhere	1. 3
	deer in herds	2. 6
	rabbits and squirrels	3. 4
	lizards darting around	4. 2
	an occasional fox	5. 5
	crickets chirping	6. 1

2. *Topic Sentence:* John's shoe store isn't doing very well.

Order:	*Unordered List*	*Ordered List*
Importance	electric bill going up slightly	1. 5
	store needs some fixing up	2. 2
	monthly income way down	3. 1
	good help hard to find	4. 3
	special sales aren't working	5. 4

3. *Topic Sentence:* Swimming is excellent exercise.

Order:	*Unordered List*	*Ordered List*
Category	good for the heart	1. 5
	good for the muscles	2. 4
	lose weight	3. 8
	builds endurance	4. 1
	loosens tendons	5. 2
	doesn't hurt body joints	6. 3
	shrinks waistline	7. 7
	good for the lungs	8. 6

4. *Topic Sentence:* It's a lovely day at the park.

Order:	*Unordered List*	*Ordered List*
Space	sun peeking through clouds	1. 2
	lush green grass	2. 7
	large, sunken lake in middle	3. 6
	white, puffy clouds	4. 1

	ducks on the lake	5. 5
	tall elm trees everywhere	6. 4
	birds flying above the trees	7. 3

5. *Topic Sentence:* Sheila has a lot to do before the wedding tonight.

Order:	*Unordered List*	*Ordered List*
Time	drive an hour to the party	1. 8
	buy a dress	2. 1
	shower	3. 3
	put on makeup	4. 5
	wash her hair	5. 4
	get dressed	6. 6
	buy wedding gift	7. 2
	pick up her sister	8. 7

Exercise 2 Pick two topics from the following list and do these things:

1. Select your general topic.
2. Select a specific subject within your general topic.
3. Write a topic sentence expressing a definite opinion or attitude regarding your subject.
4. Write an unordered list of items to support your topic sentence.
5. Write an *ordered* list of items following one of the ordering methods.

Topics:
1. a childhood friend
2. a place to relax
3. a disgusting kind of food
4. getting to a particular place from the college
5. how to play ________
6. what it takes to be successful at ________
7. an enjoyable experience you *recently* had
8. a favorite television show

Example *Topic:* a childhood friend
Specific Subject: Uncle Robert
Topic Sentence: Uncle Robert was my favorite uncle.

Unordered List	*Ordered List*
always brought ice cream	1. acted young for his age
paid me lots of attention	2. had a good sense of humor
had a good sense of humor	3. visited often
acted young for his age	4. played games with us
visited often	5. always brought ice cream
played games with us	6. paid me lots of attention

(This ordered list was done according to *category*: how the uncle acted, what he did, how he treated writer.)

Example *Topic:* kind of food
Specific Subject: burritos at Sal's restaurant
Topic Sentence: The best burritos in the valley are at Sal's.

Unordered List	*Ordered List*
contain large hunks of pork	1. very big
very big	2. contain large hunks of pork
soft, light tortilla	3. good chile verde sauce
good chili verde sauce	4. soft, light tortilla
good price	5. good price

(This ordered list was done according to *importance*: from the most important detail to the least.)

Exercise 3 Now write one paragraph on an Exercise 2 topic beginning with the topic sentence and following the ordered list. End your paragraph with a concluding sentence that ties back to the topic sentence in some manner. When you finish your first draft, analyze the following sample first draft with a classmate or small group and come up with revision suggestions. Consider its unity (all sentences relating to the topic), development (examples and details to support main points), organization (some sense of an organizational pattern), wording (smooth, clearly worded sentences), sentence structure (correctly punctuated and well developed), and correctness (spelling, verb endings, pronoun usage).

Uncle Rob was my favorite uncle. Although he was past fifty, he acted much younger. He still had a lot of energy for jogging or bicycling, he could go strong on four or five hours of sleep a night. He also had a good sense of humor. Uncle Rob visited us at least once a month, and he always took the time to play with his nephews and nieces. Aunt Harriet would also join us. She loved cards more than anyone. He'd spend hours playing poker, canasta, or Parcheesi with us. On top of that, he'd bring us a few quarts of our favorite flavors of ice cream from the creamery where he worked. Finally, Uncle Rob was my favorite because he paid a lot of attention to me and made me feel special. No one took more interest in my life than Uncle Rob, I really miss him. One of the funniest things he ever did was fill my dad's closet with old tennis balls. When dad opened the doors, he was bombarded by a few hundred green balls.

Now reread your own draft, considering the same areas of evaluation you used for the sample draft. Also exchange drafts with classmates and get their opinions.

Before writing your final draft, consider one other suggestion. As you have done your writing assignments in the course, you may have noticed your paragraphs growing longer and longer, to the point where a single paragraph you write might be a page or longer. If you get to that point, you should consider dividing your writing into two or maybe three separate paragraphs so that readers can follow your thoughts most effectively.

While essay writing will be covered in detail in Levels 4 and 5, here are some suggestions you can use now for dividing paragraphs that run on a page or longer:

1. If you are relating an experience, you can change paragraphs when you move to a new part of the experience: a different time, place, or incident.
2. If you are developing a number of supporting points, you can change paragraphs when you move to a new point.
3. If you are describing a process, you can change paragraphs when you move to a new step in the process.
4. In general, you can change paragraphs when you have brought something to an end and are beginning something new.
5. While there is no set rule for how often to start a new paragraph, you could effectively divide one hand-written page into two or three paragraphs, depending on how large you write.

For practice, meet with a classmate and go over the following "longish" paragraphs: each would run beyond a hand-written page. Make marks (¶) where you might divide each writing into two or three paragraphs.

[1]Wednesday was a perfect day at the beach. [2]First, the weather was ideal. [3]The temperature was in the high 70s, so it was cool enough to lie out comfortably yet warm enough to enjoy the water. [4]There was a gentle breeze that kept the air from getting muggy. [5]There were just enough clouds floating by to cover the sun every fifteen minutes or so and give sunbathers a break. [6]The crowd was also perfect. [7]There were a lot of people on the beach, but it wasn't badly crowded. [8]You had plenty of room to lay out your mats and umbrellas, and the body surfing area wasn't too congested. [9]Yet, there were enough people around of all ages to make things interesting. [10]There were tanners, surfers, frisbee tossers, joggers, volleyballers, boogie boarders, and body builders. [11]The best thing about the day was the water. [12]The water temperature was around 70 degrees, just right for staying in without getting cold. [13]The waves were breaking regularly, and they were about three to four feet high, just right for body surfing. [14]They were also breaking close enough to the shore that you didn't have to swim half a mile to catch them. [15]There

was no riptide or undertow to worry about, so the conditions were about as safe as possible.

[1]Using the dish washer in the apartment is pretty easy. [2]First, I rinse all of the dishes, silverware, and glasses before putting them in the dishwasher. [3]I do this because a dishwasher won't take off anything that is dried on to a surface. [4]I usually sponge off the plates with a scouring rag and fill the glasses with water and then empty them. [5]Next, I load the washer. [6]I pull out the glass rack on top first and fill it with glasses. [7]I fill it from back to front for the easiest loading. [8]I also make sure to turn the glasses bottoms down so they won't fill with water when they are washed. [9]Then I push the glass rack back in and pull out the dish rack. [10]I load the plates and smaller dishes in the side racks and the bowls in the special bowl rack in the back middle. [11]Then I put the silverware, bigger ends down, into the silverware container in the front middle section and push the rack in. [12]Now I'm ready to start the wash cycle. [13]First, I put a cup of soap in the soap container on the inside lid of the door. [14]Then I close the dishwasher and push in place the closing bar that secures the door. [15]Then I turn the wash cycle knob to the "on" position and it begins its cycle. [16]A half hour later, the cycle is completed, and the dishes are clean, dry, and ready to unload.

[1]Our house was robbed the other night, and it still scares me to think about it. [2]Sometime in the middle of the night the thief came through our back gate into the yard and then jimmied the lock on the sliding glass door of the living room. [3]While we were sleeping, he went inside, probably using a small flashlight, and stole a video recorder, two purses, a wallet, a few small wooden boxes, and five sets of keys hanging from a key rack. [4]He must have been in the house at least five minutes, but we never heard a thing. [5]Then he moved to the garage. [6]He went in through the open side door and took some Pepsis from the refrigerator. [7]He also went through the washing machine, probably looking for money or a wallet, and tossed all the clothes on the floor. [8]Before leaving, he spotted my chain saw partially hidden in a corner and took it, along with three extra chains in a bag. [9]For some reason, he also took a half-full bag of dry cat food by the garage door. [10]Finally, he went to the front of the house where the cars were parked and stashed all of his loot in the white Oldsmobile. [11]Then he used a set of keys he'd stolen from the house, started the Olds, and drove off. [12]A week later the car was found, unharmed, at the end of an alley, but all of the stolen items were gone, including a brief case that had been in the trunk of the car. [13]None of the stolen property was ever found, but we were relieved to get our car back. However, I haven't slept well since the night of the break-in.

Finally, consider the length of your own first draft and decide whether it is long enough to be divided into two or more paragraphs. (If you're uncertain, your instructor could advise you.) Then mark your draft for paragraph changes and write your final draft, indenting each new paragraph and including any revisions and corrections that will make your writing clearer and more interesting for readers.

Using Transitions

Transitions are useful words for helping a reader understand how thoughts are connected in a paragraph. Specifically, transitions can (1) show the *order* in which actions, steps, or thoughts take place, (2) show the *relationship* that one thought or action has to another, or (3) help introduce a number of details or thoughts on the same subject. Transitions *help move the reader smoothly* through a paragraph, and they serve as *signposts to guide the reader from one thought to the next.*

Although any word or phrase that helps tie a writer's thoughts together may be considered transitional, here is a list of words and phrases that are most commonly identified as *transitions*.

TRANSITIONS

1. The following transitions are used to show movement through a *time* or *step* sequence: *after, afterwards, always, before, finally, first, last, next, now, second, still, then, when.*

   Sample Paragraph: (transitions underlined)

   To sell your used car, first get it in the best shape possible. Wash and wax it, clean the interior and shampoo the carpet, and have the engine tuned up. Then place an ad in the "for sale" section of the paper and also put "for sale" signs with your phone number on the inside of a window. Next, find a place to park your car during the day where it can be seen by the most motorists. Lock your car and leave it there during the day, and pick it up before dark. When someone calls to come and see your car, take time to dust it off and run the engine a few minutes so it will start smoothly. Finally, set your price a few hundred dollars higher than you are willing to settle on so the buyer can bargain with you and feel he or she has gotten a good deal.

2. The following transitions are used to *add a number of ideas together: additionally, also, another, first, finally, in addition, on top of, one, other, second, third.*

   Sample Paragraph: (transitions underlined)

   There are a lot of different living situations available around Landsford College. There are dormitories on campus, and there is also off-campus housing run by the college. There are a number of apartment complexes located behind the campus in addition to the new duplexes that are being built across the street from the college library. Another living option is the boarding houses on Pleny Avenue, where you can get both room and board. There are also the fraternity and sorority houses located beside the new football stadium. Finally, there are a number of families living in the Wildwood Heights suburb who rent out a single bedroom along with bathroom and kitchen privileges to college students. If you take the time to look, you can find a living situation that suits your needs.

3. The following transitions are used to show *relationships* between thoughts in a paragraph: *as a matter of fact, as you can see, by the way, consequently, despite, for example, furthermore, however, incidentally, in fact, in spite of, nevertheless, on the contrary, on the other hand, therefore.*

Since many of these transitions are not commonly used by all writers, here is a brief introduction to some of the most useful ones:

as you can see: means "the facts show"; used at the conclusion of the supporting ideas.

I have presented ten reasons for your not dropping out of school. As you can see, staying in school opens many opportunities for you.

by the way: used to shift to a new but related thought.

I'm really enjoying my visit to Horseshoe Bay. By the way, how is the weather here in the winter?

consequently: similar to "therefore" or "so."

It is cold and windy. Consequently, I'm going to postpone the picnic for a week.

however: means "but," "yet," or "in spite of."

It is cold and windy; however, I'm still going to wear my bathing suit to the game.

in fact: used to emphasize a point by restating it in even stronger or more specific terms.

I am really tired this morning; in fact, I've never been this tired in my life.

nevertheless: similar to "however," "in spite of," "but," or "yet."

It is cold and windy. Nevertheless, I'm still going to run ten miles this afternoon.

on the other hand: shows a *contrast*; similar to "however."

I'm really enjoying my first classical music concert. On the other hand, I'd still rather be at the Grand Ole Opry.

therefore: means "so" or "for that reason," or "because of this."

It is cold and windy today; therefore, I'm going to wear a jacket to the game.

Notice that a *semicolon* (;) is often used before a transition. A semicolon is used to join two complete sentences that are related in thought. Since a transition usually ties the second sentence to the first one, a semicolon is the ideal punctuation mark because it does not physically separate the sentences like a period and a capital letter do. Although semicolons are only touched upon in this section, they will be covered at length in Level 5.

Here is an example of a paragraph that uses a number of transitions from the lists in this section. The paragraph follows a step-by-step process, so transitions used to show a "step sequence" are used most frequently. (Transitions are underlined.)

Eating in the college cafeteria can be great if you know what you are doing. First, go early in the week, on Monday or Tuesday, when the best food is served. Next, order everything a la carte since complete meals are too expensive. Start off with a big sandwich, like turkey or barbecued beef. In addition, order a basket of french fries. A large basket costs only fifty cents, and the fries are the best in town. However, some people don't like them because they are greasy, so try a couple before you order a basket. Next, take a look at the desserts, which are baked fresh at the college. The cafeteria has the best fruit and cream pies I've eaten. In fact, they are better than my mom bakes. Always save enough money for at least two desserts to top off a meal. Finally, order a glass of milk since you get two free refills and pay only forty cents for the first glass. As you can see, you can eat well in the cafeteria; furthermore, you don't have to leave campus.

To see how useful the underlined transitions are in smoothly tying thoughts together in the paragraph, try reading it without the transitions. It reads more choppily, and the thoughts seem disconnected. Transitions are valuable in any writing you may do.

Exercise 4 Fill in the blanks in the following paragraph with *transitions* from the list on pages 131–132. Choose words and phrases that tie the ideas together sensibly. Then compare your answers to the answer key.

Example You need to work on your serve, Dave. You *also* need to work on your backhand. *However*, your forehand is almost perfect.

Teaching young children to swim requires patience. ________, help them get used to the water. ________ have them put their faces in the water. ________, a lot of youngsters hate getting their faces wet, so you have to motivate them. ________ way is to put coins on the bottom step of the shallow end. ________ let them "dive" for the coins, keeping whatever they can get. ________ they put their heads under, they ________ need to learn to kick properly. With their legs straight and toes pointed, help them kick across the shallow end. Once they can kick across with only the aid of a kickboard, you can work on their arm stroke.

First, move their arms for them. Then have them move their arms by themselves as you hold them in the water. Next have them swim to you, and then stay in front of them so they feel secure. Second, always encourage their efforts and praise them for whatever progress they make each day. ~~Examine~~ After your best efforts, don't be surprised if some youngsters come along slowly. Finally, once a child makes it across the pool alone, you'll feel richly rewarded.

Exercise 5 You have probably had the least experience using transitions from the "relationship" list on page 132. Using nothing but words from this list, fill in the blanks in the following paragraph, and don't use the same transition twice. Notice the use of the semicolon in the middle of some sentences. When you finish, compare your answers with the answer key.

Example The weather this morning was terrible, however, it got much better by noon.

Shopping at Monroe's Clothing Mart can be rewarding; nevertheless, you have to know what you're doing or you'll miss the bargains. In fact, take some time to study their sales in the newspaper each week. They always have certain brands on sale; however, many items have been marked down up to 75 percent, so you can get great bargains. By the way, I bought a blouse one day for $7.95 that retailed for $50. Therefore, I bought a pair of designer jeans for $10 that retailed for $65. as you can see, shopping at Monroe's can be rewarding; Consequently, I'd suggest you give it a try.

Exercise 6 The following paragraph contains no transitions to tie sentences together. Rewrite the paragraph inserting transitions where they would be most useful. In the middle of at least one sentence, try using a semicolon (;) before a transition from the "relationship" list. When you finish, show your paragraph to your instructor.

Making tacos is very easy. Get out all of your ingredients, including tortillas, hamburger meat, onions, cheese, tomatoes, and lettuce. Put your hamburger meat in a pan on the stove and break it into small pieces. Cook the meat until it is brown. Fry the tortillas in a flat pan with a thin layer of grease covering the bottom. Don't fry them too long or they become brittle. Cut up your tomatoes, lettuce, cheese, and onions, and put them in separate bowls. Take a cooked tortilla and fill it with hamburger meat. The tortilla is probably soft, and the bottom can break out of it easily. Don't pile the meat on too high. Add your sliced tomatoes, lettuce, cheese, and onions. You may add hot sauce or avocados if you wish. Fold the sides of the tortilla around the filling. You're ready to eat. Take a small bite first to make sure you haven't put on too much hot sauce.

Exercise 7 Write a paragraph explaining how to do something that you do well: build a cabinet, bake something special, play a particular game, bathe an animal, do something to a car, work a word processor, and so on. Use *transitions* from the list in this section to tie your sentences together and show how the process unfolds. Keep in mind the main points of effective paragraphing: a definite topic sentence, a unified paragraph (all sentences relate to the topic), a well-developed paragraph (ample details and examples to support the topic sentence and a good concluding sentence), and a well-organized paragraph (in this case, one that follows the *time* order of the process being explained).

Write this paragraph for readers who have never done the process you are explaining.

Sample Final Draft (transitions underlined)

How to Start a Fire in a Wood Stove

Starting a fire in a wood-burning stove isn't that difficult. First, get about eight pieces of kindling—any wood scraps will do—and some newspaper. Then open the stove, wad up a few pieces of newspaper, and lay them inside. Next, put a few of the thinnest pieces of kindling on top of the paper. Then add a second layer of paper on top of the kindling. Finally, put the bigger kindling on the second layer of paper. Now take a long match, strike it, and light both layers of paper in a number of places. Once the paper is going, close the door of the stove to intensify the heat. Then open it in a few minutes to make sure the kindling has caught fire. If it has, you can now add pieces of firewood on top of the burning kindling and close the door. Your fire is on its way, as simple as that. Just check your fire every half hour or so, and add more firewood as it is needed.

When you complete your first draft, exchange paragraphs with a classmate, checking each other's use of transitional wording. Also evaluate how clearly and well detailed the process is described, how effectively the steps in the process are ordered, and how well the draft is written and punctuated. Then share comments with your partner and consider possible revisions.

Finally, decide whether your writing is long enough to be divided effectively into two or more paragraphs. If it is, decide at what step(s) in the process you want to begin a new paragraph. Then write your final draft.

Practice Quiz

Take this practice quiz to prepare you for the section quiz. Then compare your answers with the answer key. When you are ready for the section quiz, let your instructor know.

I. Circle the letter of the *best-organized* list of details to support each topic sentence provided.

Example *Topic Sentence:* Putting things off is a bad habit you can overcome.

a. take hardest task first
set a daily work schedule
work about an hour per task
no days off
reward yourself later

b. set a daily work schedule
work about an hour per task
reward yourself later
no days off
take hardest task first

c. no days off
take hardest task first
reward yourself later
work about an hour per task
set a daily work schedule

1. *Topic Sentence:* Changing a flat tire is not difficult.

a. get jack out
jack up car
remove tire
put on new tire
let car down
tighten nuts

b. get jack out
remove tire
put on new tire
jack up car
tighten nuts
let car down

c. get jack out
jack up car
put on new tire
remove tire
tighten nuts
let car down

2. *Topic Sentence:* My room is a terrible mess.

a. dust on blinds
junk all over floor
cobwebs cover ceiling
closet a mess
bed needs making

b. junk all over floor
cobwebs cover ceiling
closet a mess
bed needs making
dust on blinds

c. junk all over floor
dust on blinds
bed needs making
cobwebs cover ceiling
closet a mess

3. *Topic Sentence:* The ancient city was difficult to attack.

a.
- large canal outside city
- high wall around city
- guards on wall
- stone buildings
- large food supply inside

b.
- large canal outside city
- guards on wall
- stone buildings
- high wall around city
- large food supply inside

c.
- high wall around city
- stone buildings
- large food supply inside
- large canal outside city
- guards on wall

4. *Topic Sentence:* Allison is an excellent basketball player.

a.
- very intelligent
- understands the game
- loves to compete
- very quick
- very strong
- very skilled
- tall
- slender
- well muscled

b.
- understands the game
- loves to compete
- well muscled
- tall
- very quick
- very strong
- slender
- very skilled
- very intelligent

c.
- very intelligent
- well muscled
- loves to compete
- tall
- very quick
- very skilled
- slender
- understands the game
- very strong

5. *Topic Sentence:* The beach has changed since 1978.

a.
- not as much fun
- fewer people around
- narrower beach strip
- not much wildlife
- sand is packed harder
- kind of depressing
- thinner layer of sand

b.
- thinner layer of sand
- narrower beach strip
- sand is packed harder
- not much wildlife
- fewer people around
- not as much fun
- kind of depressing

c.
- thinner layer of sand
- narrower beach strip
- not much wildlife
- fewer people around
- sand is packed harder
- not as much fun
- kind of depressing

6. *Topic Sentence:* I almost killed myself trying to cross Seventy-sixth Street.

a.
- walked with "on" sign
- got halfway across
- car made right turn
- car didn't see me
- I dived out of way
- almost hit by another car
- crawled to safety

b.
- walked with "on" sign
- got halfway across
- car didn't see me
- car made right turn
- almost hit by another car
- I dived out of way
- crawled to safety

c.
- walked with "on" sign
- got halfway across
- I dived out of way
- car made right turn
- car didn't see me
- crawled to safety
- almost hit by another car

7. *Topic Sentence:* States in the United States come in all sizes.

a. Rhode Island
Maine
New York
Michigan
California
Texas
Alaska

b. California
Rhode Island
Maine
Michigan
Alaska
Texas
New York

c. Rhode Island
Maine
California
Michigan
New York
Alaska
Texas

8. *Topic Sentence:* Going to college can be beneficial.

a. get a good-paying job
meet interesting people
meet future husband or wife
better understanding of world
social life
greater security for future

b. get a good-paying job
greater security for future
better understanding of world
meet interesting people
meet future husband or wife
social life

c. meet interesting people
better understanding of world
greater security for future
meet future husband or wife
get a good-paying job
social life

II. Circle the letter of the sentence(s) that are most smoothly tied together with transitions.

Example

a. I used to live in the country; now I live in the middle of Chicago.

b. I used to live in the country; I live in the middle of Chicago.

c. I used to live in the country; in addition, I live in the middle of Chicago.

1. a. First, get out some old rags and paint thinner. Next, put your brushes in the thinner.

   b. First, get out some old rags and paint thinner. However, put your brushes in the thinner.

   c. First, get out some old rags and paint thinner. Put your brushes in the thinner.

2. a. Leave your brushes in the thinner for a while. Then take them out.

   b. Leave your brushes in the thinner for a while. However, take them out.

   c. Leave your brushes in the thinner for a while. Another is to take them out.

3. a. Wipe your brushes off with a rag. Always make sure to get all the paint out.

   b. Wipe your brushes off with a rag. By the way, make sure to get all the paint out.

   c. Wipe your brushes off with a rag. As a matter of fact, make sure to get all the paint out.

4. a. Wipe your brushes off thoroughly. Afterwards, throw away the rag because it is flammable.

b. Wipe your brushes off thoroughly. Therefore, throw away the rag because it is flammable.

c. Wipe your brushes off thoroughly. Throw away the rag because it is flammable.

5. a. I've described one way to clean a paintbrush. Another way is to use water.
   b. I've described one way to clean a paintbrush. A way is to use water.
   c. I've described one way to clean a paintbrush. Finally, another way is to use water.

6. a. Water cleans off a water-based paint. In addition, it softens the bristles.
   b. Water cleans off a water-based paint. However, it softens the bristles.
   c. Water cleans off a water-based paint. Next, it softens the bristles.

7. a. Cleaning paintbrushes is very easy; therefore, it does take some time.
   b. Cleaning paintbrushes is very easy; first, it does take some time.
   c. Cleaning paintbrushes is very easy; however, it does take some time.

8. a. Taking good care of brushes saves you money; therefore, it is a good habit to practice.
   b. Taking good care of brushes saves you money; nevertheless, it is a good habit to practice.
   c. Taking good care of brushes saves you money; however, it is a good habit to practice.

9. a. Many people don't take good care of paintbrushes. As a matter of fact, they abuse them.
   b. Many people don't take good care of paintbrushes. However, they abuse them.
   c. Many people don't take good care of paintbrushes. By the way, they abuse them.

10. a. You may paint only once or twice a year; nevertheless, it's still smart to clean your brushes.
    b. You may paint only once or twice a year; in fact, it's still smart to clean your brushes.
    c. You may paint only once or twice a year; therefore, it's still smart to clean your brushes.

The Sentence

The process of writing usually develops in stages. In the early stages, most writers are concerned with putting their ideas on paper with some sense of organization and development. How these ideas are worded and put into sentences is not a main concern. Later, as writers see their thoughts taking shape on paper, the wording and structuring of ideas becomes most important.

It is not enough to have a composition full of good ideas. It is equally important that those ideas reach the readers in the clearest, smoothest, most effective way. The purpose of each section on "The Sentence" is to help you develop language and structural choices that best communicate your thoughts to your readers.

Sentence Variety

Section Topic

Complex Sentence

Complex Sentence

In Level 2, you wrote *compound sentences* using coordinating conjunctions (*and, but, so, or, yet, for*) to join their halves together. A second useful sentence structure is the *complex sentence*, which can be used to show a number of relationships between thoughts or actions. Here are the main features of the complex sentence.

1. A complex sentence has two main parts: a *dependent clause* and an *independent clause*. While each clause contains a subject and verb, the *dependent clause* begins with a *subordinating conjunction* that shows the relationship between the clauses.

2. The *dependent clause* (beginning with the *subordinating conjunction*) may either begin the sentence or end it, depending on what clause the writer wants to emphasize. When the dependent clause *begins* a sentence, a *comma* is placed after it.

   Example: (subordinating conjunction underlined)

   While you were out running around town, I was home taking care of your chores. (comma after dependent clause)
   I was home taking care of your chores while you were out running around town. (no comma—dependent clause *ends* sentence)

3. The clause beginning with the subordinating conjunction is *dependent* because it depends on the *independent clause* to complete its meaning; by itself, it is an incomplete thought, a *fragment*. The *independent clause* can stand alone as a complete thought, or sentence.

   Example: (complex sentence—subordinating clause underlined)

   While you were out running around town, (dependent clause—makes little sense alone) I was home taking care of your chores. (independent clause—makes sense alone)

The subordinating conjunctions in this section show "time" or "place" relationships: *when, before, after, as, until, while, whenever, where,* and *wherever.* Here is how each *subordinating conjunction* is used in a complex sentence.

"TIME AND PLACE" SUBORDINATING CONJUNCTIONS

before: one thought or action *precedes* (comes before) another
Before you go to town, please wash the motorcycles.
Sam was at the party before anyone else arrived.

after: one thought or action *follows* another
After the semester is over, let's relax for a few days.
Tom reviewed his notes after he attended ten biology lectures.

when: two thoughts or actions occur *at the same time* in a sentence
When you called the other night, I was sound asleep.
When you go to the polls today, take along your own pencil.
I decided to support Carlos' candidacy when I saw you supporting him.

whenever: means *at any time* or *every time*
Whenever you want to study for the test, I'll be ready. (at any time)
We'll all go to the races whenever you are free. (at any time)
Whenever you call me, I'm busy with company. (every time)
Whenever Millie is late, she blames her hair. (every time)

as, while: both words mean *during that time*; indicate two thoughts or actions occurring within the same period of time
As we were waiting for a ride, three taxi cabs pulled up to the curb.
While you entertain our guests, I'll slip into the bedroom for a nap.
Please take roll for the class as the students begin to arrive.
I've been reading a new novel while you have been washing dishes.

until: means *up to that time*; one thought or action depends on another thought or action occurring
Until I hear from you, I'll sit here by the telephone.
We'll keep on painting in the garage until you bring us dinner.
Until this class is over for the semester, I'll keep sitting in the back row by the door.

where: one specific location
Where the road makes a hairpin turn, two cars plunged off the cliff.
I'd like to eat again where we ate last Tuesday.
I don't have any idea where you and I first met.

wherever: means *at any location*
I'll meet you wherever you want me to.
Wherever Myrtle travels, Theodore is not far behind.
Wherever the Giants are playing, Lois and Ted are likely to be found.

Exercise 8 Complete the following sentences with one of the following subordinating conjunctions: *when, whenever, before, after, as, while, until, where, wherever.* Also, notice the *punctuation* of a complex sentence: When the *subordinating conjunction begins the sentence, a comma is placed in the middle*, and when the subordinating conjunction comes in the middle, there is *no comma*. Check your answers with the answer key.

Example When you put on your tie, button the top button of your shirt.

1. As the sun began to set, I took out my camera.
2. ~~After~~ When your alarm goes off, please get up and feed the dog.
3. After a hard day at the sawmill, Sam's arms are very tired.

4. I won't answer any of your questions until you've given them more thought.

5. Before I was about to leave the dance, I got cramps in both of my thighs.

6. While everyone sat around and talked for hours, Ted sat on top of the roof and meditated.

7. We all stood at attention whenever the flag was raised up the pole.

8. Whenever you want to go to the mountains, let me know.

9. After you have raised chickens for a while, you'll be ready to raise turkeys.

10. Check the answers for this practice before you go on to the next one.

11. I'll be glad to plant your roses wherever you want me to.

12. Please sit wherever you have been sitting all week.

Here are five subordinating conjunctions associated with "cause and effect" relationships in complex sentences: *because, since, if, although,* and *unless*. Here is how each of these subordinating conjunctions is used in a complex sentence:

"CAUSE AND EFFECT" SUBORDINATING CONJUNCTIONS

because:

one action or condition *causes* another

I want to buy a new car because my old one doesn't run. (The action—buying a new car—is *caused* by the condition—the old car doesn't run.)

Because you have been so helpful, I want to buy you lunch. (The first action—being helpful—causes the second action—getting lunch.)

since:

similar to *because*: one action or condition *causes* another

I'll pick you up for school today since I have my brother's car. (First action—taking someone to school—is caused by the condition—having the brother's car.)

Since it is snowing outside, let's stay indoors and keep warm. (First action—snowing outside—causes second action—staying indoors.)

also means "during the time" or "from the time"

Since we have known each other, you have never lost your temper with me. ("during the time")

I have known Thelma since we were in the first grade together. ("from the time") *if:*

one action or condition *depends* on another occurring or existing

If you want to improve your typing speed, you'll have to practice more. ("Improving" *depends* on "more practice.")

The tires on the truck will last a long time if you drive sensibly. ("Tires lasting" depends on "sensible driving.")

although:

shows a *contrast*; one action or condition occurs *despite* another

Although it is snowing hard outside, we'll still go for a walk in the park. ("We'll go for a walk" *in spite of* the snow.)

My uncle still works ten hours a day although he is eighty years old. ("Uncle works hard" *despite* his age.)

unless:

one action or condition depends on another one *not* occurring

Unless you study for the test, you won't pass it. (If you *don't* study, you won't pass.)

I'll go to the theater today unless Aunt Allie comes over. (I'll go to the theater if she *doesn't* come over.)

Exercise 9 Fill in each complex sentence with a *subordinating conjunction* that best shows the relationship between the two parts of the sentence: *because, since, if, although,* or *unless*. Also, if the subordinating conjunction *begins* the sentence, put a *comma* after the first clause. When you finish, compare your answers with the answer key.

Examples You may leave class early ___if___ you have completed the density experiment.

___Although___ you have completed the project, you still need to stay and help clean up.

1. ___Since___ you don't know where the counseling office is I'll be glad to show you.
2. The wheat harvest was delayed two weeks ___because___ the cool weather had slowed growth.
3. ___If___ the city rezones R Street no restaurants can be built along it.
4. You can stay in London cheaply this summer ___although___ the accommodations won't be fancy.

5. Since Charles has lived in the mountains he hasn't come down to the city once.
6. The art show closed at the Tucor Museum because two paintings were vandalized.
7. If Willie Nelson shaves off his beard his fans won't recognize him.
8. Your rent will not be raised next month seance you are paying all you can afford.
9. I'll be glad to drive you to the dentist tomorrow unless you would rather walk.
10. If the price of milk goes any higher we'll have to switch to powdered milk.
11. Since I have known Samantha she has always been generous with her time and money.
12. I'd suggest that you buy the purple sweater although the green one also looks good on you.

Exercise 10 Complete the following complex sentences by filling in the missing clause so that it makes sense with the rest of the sentence. Put a *comma* after the first clause if the sentence begins with a subordinating conjunction. Share your sentences with your instructor.

Example Because the garage sale begins at 8:00 a.m., we'd better get there by 7:30.

1. Because you have written more compositions than any other student, you have not homework tonight
2. Nancy moved back with her mother since her marriage was going so badly.
3. Do not ride your bikes unless the road to the dam is closed.
4. If the penicillin doesn't clear up your cold, you won't be in the game next week
5. Unless we earn more money selling Christmas trees than we did last year, we won't be able to get the computer

6. Her house always looks dirty
although she cleans it every week.

7. The neighborhood has changed
since you went into the army four years ago.

8. Although the sink is draining all right today please do not use it.

9. As the moon began to rise the sun went down.

10. Before you meet David and his wife you did not have any married friends.

11. The parrots were sitting in their cage while I changed their water.

12. After I heard about your illness I just had to see you.

13. While John was baking cookies, he burnt the pan.

14. I won't do any more work on my car until the weather gets nice.

15. You may put the fertilizer wherever, there are alot of weeds.

16. Whenever Melissa is really feeling depressed, she takes a walk down to the lake.

Exercise 11 Write your own complex sentences using the subordinating conjunctions provided. Remember, if a subordinating conjunction *begins* a complex sentence, put a *comma* after the first clause. When you finish your sentences, show them to a classmate who is finished and to your instructor.

Examples although (in beginning) a soft drink

Although I liked the old Coke taste, I don't like the new taste at all.

because (in middle) passing English

Shirley is certain to pass English this semester because she has the highest grades in the class.

1. although (beginning) Although they love each other alot they still fight.
2. because (middle) Only half the team showed, because the other half had the flu.
3. unless (beginning) Unless ten people sign up, the class will be canceled.
4. if (middle) We can go out to the park, if you finish all your veggies.
5. since (beginning)

6. while (beginning) While riding to school, we saw a car accident.
7. as (beginning) As we walked hand in hand, we talked about our future together
8. before (middle) We went to the movies before we met her parents for dinner.
9. after (beginning) After the prom was over, we went to a party.
10. until (middle) We walked in the mall, until the rain stopped.

Practice Quiz Take this practice quiz to prepare for the section quiz. Then compare your answers with the answer key. When you are ready for the section quiz, let your instructor know.

Circle the letter of the complex sentence with the most appropriate *subordinating conjunction*.

Example

a. If you want to study with me tonight, meet me in the library at 7:00.

b. Unless you want to study with me tonight, meet me in the library at 7:00.

c. Although you want to study with me tonight, meet me in the library at 7:00.

1. a. I'm not going to Fred's birthday party because I've heard it is going to be terrific.

   b. I'm not going to Fred's birthday party if I've heard it is going to be terrific.

   c. I'm not going to Fred's birthday party although I've heard it is going to be terrific.

2. a. The city council voted against enclosing the downtown mall because the project was too expensive.

   b. The city council voted against enclosing the downtown mall although the project was too expensive.

   c. The city council voted against enclosing the downtown mall unless the project was too expensive.

3. a. Margie's stamp collection was stolen because she had it stored in a safe.

   b. Margie's stamp collection was stolen if she had it stored in a safe.

   c. Margie's stamp collection was stolen although she had it stored in a safe.

4. a. Because the water supply is checked for contamination, I wouldn't drink it.

   b. Unless the water supply is checked for contamination, I wouldn't drink it.

   c. Since the water supply is checked for contamination, I wouldn't drink it.

5. a. Since we've owned those white rats, they've doubled in size.

   b. Because we've owned those white rats, they've doubled in size.

   c. Unless we've owned those white rats, they've doubled in size.

6. a. Because pesticide poisoning is a big problem, acid rain is an ever greater one.
   b. Although pesticide poisoning is a big problem, acid rain is an even greater one.
   c. Unless pesticide poisoning is a big problem, acid rain is an even greater one.
7. a. Before you sit down to play the saxophone, please buy a new reed.
   b. After you sit down to play the saxophone, please buy a new reed.
   c. While you sit down to play the saxophone, please buy a new reed.
8. a. After all of the plans for the boat trip were made, they were changed.
   b. When all the plans for the boat trip were made, they were changed.
   c. Before all of the plans for the boat trip were made, they were changed.
9. a. While you are taking a nap on the sofa, I'll take one on the floor.
   b. Before you are taking a nap on the sofa, I'll take one on the floor.
   c. After you are taking a nap on the sofa, I'll take one on the floor.
10. a. The jewel thief was caught until he returned to the scene of the crime.
    b. The jewel thief was caught when he returned to the scene of the crime.
    c. The jewel thief was caught unless he returned to the scene of the crime.
11. a. Julie broke out in a terrible rash wherever she was vacationing in the mountains.
    b. Julie broke out in a terrible rash where she was vacationing in the mountains.
    c. Julie broke out in a terrible rash when she was vacationing in the mountains.
12. a. Until I find a better way to watch crawfish, I'll keep using my net.
    b. As I find a better way to catch crawfish, I'll keep using my net.
    c. Before I find a better way to catch crawfish, I'll keep using my net.
13. a. Whenever the plane circled over Harriet's house, she shook her fist at it.
    b. Until the plane circled over Harriet's house, she shook her fist at it.
    c. Before the plane circled over Harriet's house, she shook her fist at it.
14. a. Where you want me to plant the elm tree saplings, I'll be glad to plant them.
    b. Wherever you want me to plant the elm tree saplings, I'll be glad to plant them.
    c. As you want me to plant the elm tree saplings, I'll be glad to plant them.

Clear Sentences

Section Topic

Concrete Language

Not only should your sentences be varied enough to best express your thoughts and maintain reader interest, they should also be worded as clearly and directly as possible. In the "Clear Sentences" sections, you learn to analyze your writing for wording weaknesses and to *revise* your sentences to make them stronger.

Concrete Language

The writer recreates his or her experiences for readers. The more clearly the readers can see, hear, and feel what the writer experienced, the more accurately they can understand the experience. One way to recreate an experience is to use *concrete language*: words that clearly and accurately describe what is seen, heard, and felt. The use of concrete language allows readers to *visualize* the writer's experiences in the most vivid way.

The opposite of concrete language is *vague, general* language that leaves readers both bored and poorly informed. Here are examples comparing *concretely* worded sentences to *vaguely* worded sentences describing the same basic situations:

Vague: That dog looks bad.
Concrete: That old cocker spaniel looks tired and frail.

Vague: The girl moved down the sidewalk.
Concrete: The young girl skipped down the old, cracked sidewalk.

Vague: When I was younger, we moved from one area to another.
Concrete: When I was eight years old, we moved from Detroit to a farm in Ohio.

Vague: Allen decided to work for a new relative.
Concrete: Allen was nervous about working for his father-in-law.

Vague: The paint you used on the chairs looks terrible.
Concrete: The white paint you used on the lounge chairs is full of runs and bubbles.

Vague: The boy put his books on the floor and left the room.
Concrete: Jason threw his books on the floor and stormed out of the classroom.

Vague: Mary felt strange after the test because she felt she could have done differently.

Concrete: Mary was angry with herself after the math test because she knew she could have done better.

Vague: Monroe's jokes upset a lot of people.
Concrete: Monroe's jokes are filthy, racist, and sexist.

Here are suggestions that will help you write more concrete, descriptive sentences:

1. As a rule, use the most *specific* word you can to describe something: Use *German shepherd* instead of *dog*; use *petunias* instead of *flowers*; use *Boeing 747* instead of *airplane*; use *Uncle Harvey* instead of *relative*; use *Porsche* instead of *sports car*; use *a headache and stomach cramps* instead of *sick*; use *pineapple upside-down cake* instead of *dessert*; use *F* instead of *a bad grade*; and use *17 degrees below zero* instead of *very cold*.

2. *Verbs* are among the most expressive words in any language. Using a verb that most vividly describes an action brings a sentence to life.

   Weak Verbs: The boys walked into the room and sat down on the sofa.
   Revised: The boys trudged into the room and plopped down on the sofa.

   Weak Verbs: The drunk walked down the street and fell to the ground.
   Revised: The drunk staggered down the street and collapsed to the ground.

   Weak Verbs: The men did badly under the pressure and went out the door.
   Revised: The men panicked under the pressure and bolted out the door.

   Weak Verbs: I don't care for lima beans and choose not to eat them.
   Revised: I hate lima beans and refuse to eat them.

   Weak Verbs: The Jaguar went around the corner and went faster down the straightaway.
   Revised: The Jaguar tore around the corner and jetted down the straightaway.

3. Use words that are clear and appropriate for the topic. Don't use words that aren't common in conversation, and, in particular, avoid *inflated language*: big words that are used to impress the reader rather than to communicate ideas clearly.

   Inflated Language: John displayed an element of delight over the acquisition of a stereo system of unquestionable quality.
   Revised: John was thrilled to buy a high-quality stereo system.

   Inflated Language: The couples moved in varying and unpredictable patterns the length and breadth of the floor designated for dancers.
   Revised: The couples boogied crazily all over the dance floor.

   Inflated Language: The quality of your ocular sensibilities is diminishing.

Revised: Your eyesight is getting worse.

4. Whenever possible, *show* the reader something instead of *telling* him or her about it.

Telling: John is a good student.
Showing: In college, John has a 3.8 GPA over five semesters.

Telling: Myrtle has a good sense of humor.
Showing: Myrtle loves to tell funny stories about her navy years and to play practical jokes on her friends.

Telling: Sally is a good seamstress.
Showing: Last month, Sally made two miniskirts and a blouse that looked professionally sewn.

Telling: The math test was easy.
Showing: The math test had only fifteen true-false questions, and all of the answers came from the first five pages of the book.

Telling: Matthew put up a good fight against the bully.
Showing: Matthew bloodied the bully's face and knocked him down once before getting knocked out.

Exercise 12 Rewrite the following sentences by replacing the vague underlined words with more specific, concrete words. Then show your sentences to your instructor.

Examples The sunset was very nice.
Revised: The sunset streaked the western sky with purple and pink.

Your relative is nice to me.
Revised: Your aunt Bessie always stops and talks to me at the college.

1. A man entered the room.
2. That car you were driving is a mess.
3. I had a very big breakfast.
4. Gertrude has a lot of interesting hobbies.
5. The look on your face frightens these people.
6. The movie playing at the theater was bloody.
7. My relative visits our home infrequently.
8. That habit of yours is a problem for you.

Exercise 13 Replace the weak, underlined verbs with stronger, more vivid ones. When you finish, show your sentences to your instructor.

Examples The arrow left the bow and landed in the target.
Revised: The arrow flew from the bow and pierced the target.

I look forward to the day I can depart from this job.
Revised: I long for the day I can quit this job.

1. Mitchell walked up quietly behind his sisters and made a sound like a wolf.
2. The swimmers moved across the water to the finish line and lay down from exhaustion.
3. The long jumper moved high into the air and came down in the sand pit.
4. The rocket left from the launching pad and went up into the sky.
5. The ducks walked into the pond and moved off in a line.
6. The racing car went into the wall, turned around in the air, landed on the ground, and went bang.
7. You concern me with your dangerous schemes but affect me with your accomplishments.
8. The boxer moved forward wildly and put a glove into his opponent's face.

Exercise 14 Reword the following sentences that are full of *inflated language* with clear, conversational language. Then compare your answers with the answer key.

Example Those unkept dogs meander around in large groups in the vicinity of our dwellings.
Revised: Packs of wild dogs roam our neighborhood.

1. Those lately purchased chairs that rock to and fro were of a very steep price.
2. The cars on the large, multilaned expanse moved without great velocity through the dense ground cloud that greatly limited visibility.
3. The man who is your wife's father enjoys inhaling smoke from long, brown tobacco-filled tubes.
4. It greatly taxes one's paycheck to acquire an automobile of latest vintage.
5. The peach trees of smaller proportions were in the best state of health.
6. The skaters moved with great rapidity across the smallish body of water covered by a thin layer of frozen water.

Exercise 15 Write a paragraph describing a place you find attractive: a yard, room, a place on campus, an area in a park, a spot in the mountains or the city. Describe the area using *concrete language* so that a reader could *recognize* the place by your description.

Another technique for generating ideas for a paragraph is called *brainstorming:* writing down everything you can think of associated with your topic, without distinguishing main points from details or examples. Here is a sample brainstorming list of a student describing the yard of her apartment complex.

Brainstormed List:
shade
walkway
cobblestone
well-kept lawn
picnic table
enclosed half of yard
wading pool
other half
flowers around border
fence
large trees (location)
roof
Spanish style
color of building
rose garden

From her list, the student grouped her main points and details and presented them in the order she wanted to write about them:

Large poplar trees by road (provide shade)
Enclosed half of yard
- wrought-iron fence
- wading pool
- picnic table

Open half of yard
- manicured lawn
- bordered by pansies

Building area
- rose garden beside building
- cobblestone walkway separates yard and garden
- light tan building (dark trim)
- Spanish-style roof

Before writing your first draft, brainstorm a list of items associated with your topic and then put your list in an order that shows the relationship among your items, adding or deleting things as you choose. Then write the first draft of your paragraph.

Before revising your paragraph, meet with a classmate and evaluate the following sample first draft. Consider the following evaluation questions:

1. Is the subject vividly described? Is there plenty of "concrete language" to help readers picture what the subject looks like?

2. Is the description organized so that readers can picture the location of everything?
3. Is the paragraph unified (all sentences related), well developed (all main points supported by detail or example), and well written (clear, smooth, correctly punctuated sentences, with correct grammar usage and spelling)?
4. Is the paragraph long enough to consider dividing into two paragraphs or more? If so, where might a new paragraph(s) begin?

Sample First Draft

The front of my apartment building is quite attractive. Three tall, full popular trees grows beside the sidewalk and shade the small yard, the east half of the yard is enclosed in by a white wrought-iron fence, and inside the fenced area within is a round, built-in cement wading pool, a redwood picnic table with attached benches, and a built-in used brick barbecue pit. The west half of the yard is a manicured bluegrass lawn bordered around with blue and yellow pansies. There is also a rose garden. The front of the two-story building has a fresh coat of light tan paint. A cobblestone walkway separate the rose garden from the yard area. The slopeing red-tile roof overhangs the building a couple of feet and adds to the Spanish style. The entire area is a clean and colorful one, and nicely laid out. The dark brown doors and matching trim sets off the light colored building, as well.

Now reread and evaluate your first draft, applying the questions for evaluation. Mark your draft for revisions, corrections, and, if needed, paragraph divisions, and then write your final draft with all improvements included.

Practice Quiz

Take this practice quiz to prepare for the section quiz. Then compare your answers with the answer key. When you are ready for the section quiz, let your instructor know.

Circle the letter of the clearest, most descriptive sentence in each group.

Example

(a.) The Smiths quarreled over the weather and what brand of shampoo to buy.
b. This family quarreled over the smallest things.
c. The Smiths were two people who argued a lot over nothing.

1. a. Johnson wore double-breasted suits, wide lapels, and wide ties.
   b. Johnson dressed rather conservatively.
   c. Johnson dressed as if he lived in the 1940s.
2. a. One of your tables needs some fixing up.
   b. The redwood table in your patio is warped and cracking.
   c. The big table in back of your house doesn't look like it's new.

3. a. Dark clouds gathered in the east and slowly moved across the plain.
   b. Clouds of a deeper color accumulated themselves in the eastern skies and made their way together across the flat land.
   c. Clouds gathered in the sky and made their way across the area.
4. a. Your relative from another state loves Italian food.
   b. Aunt Lucy from Iowa loves pizza and lasagna.
   c. Your female relative from Iowa likes foreign food.
5. a. The bird perched on some wood and made a sound.
   b. The blue-breasted bird sat on a fence and called.
   c. The robin perched atop a fence post and chirped to her mate.
6. a. The woman working in the cafeteria also works downtown on other days.
   b. One of the cooks in the cafeteria works downtown at the bank on her days off.
   c. Mildred Jones, a cafeteria cook, works at the Wells Fargo Bank on Saturdays.
7. a. The horses moved from the starting gate and went around the first curve.
   b. The many horses took off from the starting gate and moved around the first curve.
   c. Twenty horses exploded from the starting gate and raced around the first curve.
8. a. What your mother cooked this morning tasted just right to me.
   b. Your mother's cooking this morning was sweet and delicious.
   c. The apple pie your mother baked this morning was delicious.
9. a. The clock on the wall made quite a sound every hour.
   b. The large wooden clock on the living room wall made a "gonging" sound every hour.
   c. The clock of wooden construction and large proportion made a sound not unlike that of a gong every hour on the hour.
10. a. Please feed the scraps to the animals.
    b. Please feed the potato peels to the goats.
    c. Please feed the peelings from the eaten potatoes to the animals of a goat species.

Correct Sentences

Section Topic

Sentence Fragment

The sections throughout the book on "Correct Sentences" cover the two most common sentence structure problems writers have: run-on sentences and sentence fragments. Two common run-on sentence patterns were covered in Levels 1 and 2. In this section, you are introduced to the sentence fragment and taught how to distinguish it from a sentence.

Sentence Fragments

There are different kinds of sentence fragments, but they all have one thing in common: A fragment is *not* a *complete sentence*. In this section, you learn to recognize the difference between a fragment and a sentence. In other levels, you are introduced to common types of sentence fragments and shown how to correct them.

Here are some ways to tell the difference between a fragment and a sentence:

1. *A sentence expresses a complete thought.* A fragment does *not* express a complete thought. Something is missing.
2. *A sentence can stand alone and make sense.* By itself, a fragment does *not* make sense. It needs sentences around it to give it meaning. Example: I am not interested in going to the theater. Unless you are going. (Fragment "unless you are going" makes no sense without the accompanying sentence.)
3. *A sentence has a subject and a verb.* A fragment is often *missing* a subject, a verb, or a helping verb. (A *helping verb* is needed with some verb forms, like *-ing* ending verbs. Example: "The man walking to town" is a fragment. "The man was walking to town" is a sentence.)
4. *A sentence does not leave the reader with an unanswered question.* A fragment *often* leaves the reader with an *unanswered question.*
5. *A sentence is the proper writing structure for expressing thoughts.* A fragment is *not* a correct writing structure. It should be *revised* to form a complete sentence.

Here are a number of different sentence fragments that leave the reader with unanswered questions. Each fragment is followed by a complete sentence formed by adding words to the fragment.

The man in the grey flannel jacket. (Who is he?)
The man in the grey flannel jacket is my uncle. (complete sentence)

The dog that you left on the porch. (What happened to it?)
The dog that you left on the porch disappeared last night.

Walking to school on a cold, wintry day in November (Who was walking?)
Four boys from the neighborhood were walking to school on a cold, wintry day.

Because you are such a kind, generous person. (What will happen?)
Because you are such a kind, generous person, you will always have friends.

Although John didn't enjoy going to school at night. (What happened?)
Although John didn't enjoy going to school at night, he never missed a class.

The grapes that were left on the kitchen table last night. (What happened to them?)
The grapes that were left on the kitchen table last night were eaten by my cat.

A neighbor of mine from the south side of Chicago. (What happened to her?)
A neighbor of mine from the south side of Chicago married her French teacher.

If you want to do well on the quiz tomorrow. (What should you do?)
If you want to do well on the quiz tomorrow, get a good night's sleep.

In the back of the pickup on the driver's side. (What is there?)
In the back of the pickup on the driver's side is a stack of firewood.

Exercise 16 Write *F* for fragment or *S* for sentence in front of each of the following groups of words. Remember, a sentence expresses a *complete thought*—no question is left unanswered. A fragment does *not* express a complete thought—the reader is left with a question. Check your answers with the answer key.

Examples __S__ I am going to visit my brother in Akron next summer.

__F__ Visiting my brother in Akron next summer.

1. ________ If you want a very good deal on a pair of used roller skates.
2. ________ The pond located in the middle of Central Park in New York.
3. ________ A young woman with three small children and a dog has her hands full.
4. ________ Covering all the things that we have to do for dinner this afternoon.
5. ________ I am quite satisfied with the way that you cut Gertrude's bangs.
6. ________ All of the raindrops collecting in that jar on your patio.

7. ________ I am not very hungry because I just ate half a watermelon.
8. ________ Whenever you call on Maria to babysit on weekends.
9. ________ To do the best that you can in all of your classes this semester.
10. ________ A tired, old dog dragging himself home from a fight in the alley.
11. ________ The last man who tried to have a debate with Deborah Carter.
12. ________ The bone that you just cleaned is perfect for my dog.
13. ________ In back of the old Smith house are wild raspberry vines.
14. ________ A bottle of whiskey in back of the old Shell service station.
15. ________ You look charming in your new sun dress.

Exercise 17 Complete the following sentence fragments by adding words to make them complete sentences. Add words that make sense with the groups of words provided. Then show your sentences to your instructor.

Example If you want to find out how strong you are, *you can try lifting that boulder.*
The boy who works for me *is an excellent mechanic.*

1. The woman who spent her life raising chickens ________________
____
2. A good way to cook chicken ________________
3. While the moon was out last night ________________
____
4. The people who left their luggage at the train station ________________
____
5. In the next half hour ________________
6. The best time to run the sprinkler in the front yard ________________
____
7. To get to the restaurant by 6:00 p.m. ________________
____
8. The ticket with the lucky number on it ________________
____

9. One reason that people don't like to read in the library ______

______

10. When you get to the next bend in the road ______

______

11. A woman in pink leotards and purple tennis shoes ______

______

12. My nephew from the southern tip of Florida ______

______

______

Exercise 18 The following paragraph contains some *sentence fragments.* First, go through the paragraph and underline the fragments. Then rewrite the paragraph and *add words* to each underlined fragment to form a *complete sentence*, or attach the fragment to a sentence it belongs with. Remember, a fragment does *not* express a complete thought. Something is missing, and the reader is left with an unanswered question. When you finish, share your paragraph with your instructor.

Example You are invited to the grand opening of the pub. At five o'clock this afternoon.

You are invited to the grand opening of the pub. It begins at five o'clock this afternoon.

Mary is a very determined woman. A woman who gets what she wants. When she was forty-eight years old, she went to college for the first time. Received a bachelor's degree in science in four years. At age fifty-two, she entered medical school. The oldest student in her class. She spent six years in medical school and finished in the top twenty-five percent of her class. At fifty-eight, she began interning in an Oakland hospital. Working ten-hour shifts in the emergency ward. When she completed her internship, she stayed on in the emergency ward as a fully licensed physician. The most thrilling achievement of her life. She worked at Oakland General Hospital for three years and then opened a small practice in her hometown of Clintsdale. She practiced medicine until she was seventy-five years old. A truly remarkable person.

______

Practice Quiz Take this practice quiz to prepare for the section quiz. Then compare your answers with the answer key. When you are ready for the section quiz, let your instructor know.

Circle the letter of the *complete sentence* among the fragments in each group.

Example

a. Before taking a trip to the Grand Canyon next month.
(b.) Before taking a trip to the Grand Canyon, you must get your car fixed.
c. Before taking a trip to the Grand Canyon and getting your car fixed.

1. a. The man who delivers our milk every day at 5:00 a.m.
   b. The man delivering our milk every day at 5:00 a.m.
   c. I don't know the man who delivers our milk every day at 5:00 a.m.
2. a. If there is a way to get tickets to the Prince concert.
   b. I don't know if there is a way to get tickets to the Prince concert.
   c. Getting tickets to the Prince concert before tomorrow night.
3. a. A man with a strong will to succeed in life.
   b. John is a man with a strong will to succeed in life.
   c. A strong will to succeed in life and the support of his family.
4. a. Because the hills are covered by the morning fog.
   b. We can't see the wildflowers because the hills are covered with fog.
   c. The hills covered with fog every morning in June.
5. a. The politicians meeting in the back room of the hotel.
   b. The politicians in the back room of the hotel beside the airport.
   c. The politicians are meeting in the back room of the hotel.
6. a. With your right hand raised high above your head.
   b. Raising your right hand high above your head and standing on your toes.
   c. You might raise your hand above your head to stretch your arm muscles.
7. a. The Milky Way can be clearly seen tonight with a telescope.
   b. Seeing the Milky Way tonight with a powerful telescope.
   c. The woman who is looking through the telescope at the Milky Way.
8. a. While I was trying to get the attention of the judge.
   b. While I was getting the judge's attention, the jury left.
   c. Trying hard to get the judge's attention before the jury left.
9. a. A day for everyone to relax and enjoy the bright sunshine.

b. Today is a great day to relax and enjoy the sunshine.

c. If you want to relax today and enjoy the nice breeze.

10. a. Your aunt who invited us to her eightieth birthday party.

b. Your aunt who invited us to her birthday party is very kind.

c. Your aunt who invited us to her eightieth birthday party in the park.

The Word

The material presented in "The Word" section of each level is associated with the *proofreading* phase of the writing process. When you proofread a paper, you give it a final check to catch any spelling or grammar errors you may have missed earlier in the process. Proofreading for errors is normally the last step in the writing process, and it is an important step for eliminating those nuisance errors that can bother readers.

Verb Forms

Section Topics

Compound Verbs
Irregular Verb List #1

Compound Verb

Some writers have subject-verb agreement problems in sentences with a *compound verb*. A sentence with a *compound verb* has two or more main verbs, usually joined by *and*. Here are the basic subject-verb agreement rules for a sentence with a compound verb:

1. *Each present tense verb* within a *compound verb* must *agree* with the subject.

   Example: George goes to college during the week and works on weekends. (The verbs *goes* and *works* agree with the singular subject *George*.)

2. Subject-verb agreement rules for verbs within a compound verb are the same as for single verbs:

   1. If the subject is *singular*, the present tense verb ends in *-s*.
   2. If the subject is *plural*, the present tense verb does *not* end in *-s*.
   3. Here are three exceptions to the rules:

      a. The singular first person pronoun *I* and the second person pronoun *you* fall under the *plural subject* rule: Their verbs do *not* end in *-s*.

      b. The *past tense* verbs *was* and *were* must agree with their subjects like present tense verbs: *was* with a singular subject and *were* with a plural subject.

      c. The only verbs ending in *-s* with a plural subject are words like *press, dress, kiss, miss, caress,* and *dismiss*.

Here are examples of sentences with singular subjects and compound present tense verbs. Notice that since the subjects are *singular*, each underlined verb within the compound verb ends in *-s*.

Maria walks to school every day and rides home on the bus.

Fog covers the valley in the morning and burns off in the afternoon.

Marianne directs, produces, and performs in her own plays.

The sandwich tastes stale and looks a bit moldy.

Your retainer arrives at the orthodontist office some time today and needs to be picked up.

Here are examples of sentences with *plural subjects* and compound present tense verbs. Notice that since the subjects are *plural*, each underlined verb within the compound verb does *not* end in *-s*.

Maria and her sister walk to school every day and ride home on the bus.

Fog and haze cover the valley in the morning and burn off in the afternoon.

The Gomez sisters direct, produce, and perform in their own plays.

The sandwiches taste stale and look a bit moldy.

Your retainers arrive at the orthodontist office some time today and need to be picked up.

Exercise 19 Underline the subject and circle the verbs within the *compound verb* in each sentence. Then compare your answers with the answer key.

Example That mother cat eats all of her daughter's food and then sleeps the rest of the day.

1. The new boarder comes and goes quietly.
2. The racing car spins out of the turn and crashes into the hay bales.
3. Your mother wants your help with the vacuuming and also needs you to dust the furniture.
4. Ivan believes in the goodness of people and preaches his belief to others.
5. The rocket lifts off the ground, veers toward the west, and crashes to the ground.
6. We are very tired from the long trip and want to be left alone.
7. No one knows the location of the treasure map or cares.
8. The sun drops toward the ocean and turns a deep orange.
9. I observe students in the library and record their study habits.
10. Teachers expect a lot from Minerva, encourage her efforts, and are seldom disappointed.

Exercise 20 Fill in your own *present tense verbs* in the blanks. Remember, if the subject is singular, the verb ends in *-s*, and if the subject is plural, the verb doesn't end in *-s*. Then show all of your answers to your instructor.

Example The quarterback *drops* back to pass and *throws* the ball.

1. The instructor _____________ out the tests and _____________ instructions.
2. Willie _____________ at the market and _____________ home fresh vegetables.
3. Those trains _____________ on time in the winter but _____________ late in the fall.

4. Ted and Frank _participate_ in rodeos and _~~won~~ wins_ trophies.
5. Your salamander _~~took~~ looks_ ill and _~~died~~ acts_ strangely.
6. Your families _lived_ on the same block and _~~were~~ are_ good friends.
7. That wall _~~was~~ looks_ eight feet high and _~~was~~ is_ made of used brick.
8. Mattie always _goes_ to class and _like_ her friends.
9. Two planes _fly_ at the same time and _land_ at the same time.
10. Tuna fish _sells_ well at the market but _spoils_ too fast.
11. Your grandma _loves_ fried chicken and _hates_ fried fish.
12. Those wallets _are_ brand new and _hold_ a lot of money.
13. Melissa _loves_ her old high school and _visits_ often.
14. My tennis shoes _are_ very ugly but _fit_ just fine.
15. The plaster _is_ falling off the wall and _keeps_ making a mess.

Exercise 21 On the topics given, write your own sentences using compound *present tense* verbs. After you write each sentence, underline your verbs. When you finish, share your sentences with your instructor.

Example two things you do at school every day

Every day we meet in the cafeteria at noon and eat lunch.

1. two things you do every evening
Every evening I cook dinner and then do the dishes.
2. three things the airplane does during every flight
During every flight you get a snack, watch a movie and get a meal.
3. two things the monkeys do at the zoo every day
At the zoo you can see the monkeys play & climb trees.
4. three ways that Albert studies for his tests
Albert reads his text, studies his notes, & has someone ask him questions when studying for a test.
5. five things that football players do every game
Football players every game run, block, guard, fall, and most of all show off.
6. two things movie actors do for their fans
Movie actors are great ~~for~~ their fans by making guest appearance & signing autographs

Irregular Verb List #1

As you learned in Level 2, most verbs form their *past tense* by adding the *-ed* ending. However, there are a number of verbs that form their past tense differently. Instead of adding *-ed*, these verbs form their past tense by *changing their spelling*. Since different verbs undergo different changes, these verbs are called *irregular verbs*.

The following list of irregular verbs is the first of four lists in the book. Each list is grouped according to a similar spelling change for the past tense forms of the verbs.

Simple Form	*Past Tense*	*Past Participle*
feed	fed	fed
find	found	found
have	had	had
hear	heard	heard
hold	held	held
lay	laid	laid
lead	led	led
make	made	made
pay	paid	paid
read	read	read
say	said	said
sell	sold	sold
stand	stood	stood
tell	told	told
win	won	won

These words are grouped together because their past tense and past participle forms are *the same* and because they end in *-d* (exceptions: *made* and *won*). Aside from these similarities, the verbs change their spellings from their "simple form" in different ways, and you need to memorize the past tense and past participle forms.

Here are the distinctions between the "past tense" and "past participle" forms:

1. The simple *past tense* verb indicates an action or condition that is past and completed. The past tense form does *not* require a *helping verb* before it.

   Examples: Jan read six books last summer.

   Frank won first prize in the Pillsbury sweepstakes.

I stood outside all day yesterday waiting for you.

2. The *past participle* form is used most commonly with the helping verbs *has, have,* and *had* to form the *present perfect* and *past perfect* tenses. Here are examples of each tense and how it is used.

   a. Present perfect tense: *has* + past participle (with singular subject)

      have + past participle (with plural subject)

      The *present perfect* is used to indicate an action or condition that *began* in the past but *continues* into the present. The action or condition is *not* completed as with the *past tense*.

      Examples: I have sold a lot of furniture lately.

      Maria has done her best on every math quiz.

      Sam has been very tired since he returned from vacation.

   b. Past perfect tense: *had* + past participle

      The *past perfect* is used to indicate an action or condition that was completed in the past, often due to a *change of circumstances*.

      Examples: I had enjoyed going to college until last semester.

      I had wanted to meet Jan until I heard her lecture on television.

      Sara had paid for her magazine subscription regularly, but she quit paying when the rate went up.

      I had made special plans for Mollie's birthday party to be held in the amusement park, but they didn't work out because of the rain.

Exercise 22 Fill in the blanks with the *past tense, present perfect,* or *past perfect* tense of each verb in parentheses. Use the tense that best fits the situation in the sentence. Remember, the present perfect form is *has* or *have* + past participle, and the past perfect form is *had* + past participle. The past tense requires no helping verb. When you finish, compare your answers with the answer key.

Examples

Mildred (feed) ___fed___ the pigs last night.

Mildred (feed) ___has fed___ the pigs every year since she was twelve.

Mildred (feed) ___had fed___ the pigs every year until she went to college.

John (sell) ___sold___ his Toyota pickup for $2,000.

John (sell) ___has sold___ a lot of cars in the last two months.

John (sell) had sold a lot of cars before going into the insurance business.

1. Yesterday we (find) ________ the spare keys to the station wagon.
2. We (find) ________ every set of keys we have lost this month.
3. We (find) ________ all the keys up until the time we lost the house key.
4. Everyone (hear) ________ of the new rock group "Twisted Sister."
5. Last night I (hear) ________ on the radio that it was going to snow today.
6. Sam (hear) ________ that it was going to snow, but the report was wrong.
7. Marty (lay) ________ her books on the cafeteria table every day until she had them stolen.
8. Marty (lay) ________ her books on the same table every day this week.
9. Marty (lay) ________ her books on the table yesterday.
10. We (stand) ________ here all day waiting for Grace and Barney.
11. Yesterday we (stand) ________ in line for an hour waiting for our tickets.
12. Yesterday we (stand) ________ in line for six hours, but we finally gave up.
13. Jack (win) ________ his only race yesterday.
14. Jack (win) ________ most of his races this year.
15. Jack (win) ________ sixty races in a row before losing.

Irregular Verb List #2

Here is the second list of irregular verbs, all of which share a common ending.

Simple Form	*Past Tense*	*Past Participle*
bring	brought	brought
buy	bought	bought
build	built	built
catch	caught	caught
fight	fought	fought
keep	kept	kept
leave	left	left
lose	lost	lost

meet	met	met
send	sent	sent
sit	sat	sat
sleep	slept	slept
spend	spent	spent
teach	taught	taught
think	thought	thought

Notice that each of these irregular verbs has the same past tense and past participle form. Also notice that all the past tense forms end in the letter *t*.

Exercise 23 Fill in the *best tense* of the verb in parentheses—*past, present perfect,* or *past perfect*—to complete each of the following sentences. Remember, the past tense takes no helping verb, the present perfect takes *has* or *have*, and the past perfect takes *had*. Spell the irregular verb forms correctly. When you finish, check your answers with the answer key.

Examples (bring) I *brought* my sister to the game last night.

(bring) I *have brought* my sister to every game this entire year.

(bring) I *had brought* my sister to every game until the last one.

1. (buy) I ________ soap in liquid form for the last two years.
2. (buy) I ________ soap in liquid form last night for the first time.
3. (buy) I ________ soap in liquid form until I realized how expensive it was to use.
4. (catch) Maria ________ a cold at the ice rink this morning.
5. (catch) Maria ________ a cold every time she went down to the ice rink.
6. (catch) Maria ________ a cold at the ice rink before I could warn her to dress warmly.
7. (keep) Sammy ________ much busier before he was given help at the dry cleaners.
8. (keep) Sammy ________ busy all of last week at the dry cleaners.
9. (keep) Sammy ________ busy every week he's worked at the dry cleaners.
10. (teach) Sarah ________ her dog six tricks last week.
11. (teach) Sarah ________ her dog a number of new tricks lately.
12. (teach) Sarah ________ her dog over twenty tricks before she sold him.

Exercise 24 Fill in the correct past tense or past participle verb form of each irregular verb in parentheses. Then compare your answers to the answer key.

Example (bring) Jonathan has _brought_ in five bundles of firewood.

1. (think) Recently Dr. Hall has _thought_ a lot about retiring at the end of the year.
2. (teach) The lifeguarding instructor _taught_ the class how to rescue a struggling victim.
3. (spend) Myrtle and Clyde have _spent_ long afternoons in the park.
4. (sleep) No one has _slept_ in that motel since last summer's fire.
5. (sit) Have you _sat_ in that left-handed desk all semester?
6. (send) I have _sent_ back the roach spray because it didn't work at all.
7. (meet) Gertrude _met_ all of the requirements for her pilot's license.
8. (lose) Max Farley hasn't _lost_ a law case in the last four years.
9. (leave) We should have _left_ the rock concert ahead of the main crowd.
10. (keep) You have _kept_ very quiet about your recent bowling tournament successes.
11. (fight) Monroe County _fought_ hard to maintain its own separate fire department.
12. Jerry has (win) _won_ every prize given for debate.
13. I (tell) _told_ you that you'd do well in badminton.
14. Joe (stand) _stood_ in line for two hours before the World Series game.
15. Have you (sell) _sold_ your motor scooter yet?
16. Mr. Cepeda has (say) _said_ nothing about a test on Friday.
17. Everyone (read) _read_ about Javier's wedding in last night's paper.
18. We (pay) _paid_ $150 to have our kitchen floor stripped and waxed.
19. Have you (make) _made_ plans for Sunday afternoon yet?
20. The basketball team (lead) _led_ all the way until the final minute.
21. We (lay) _laid_ out everything on the table that we had in the icebox.
22. Have you (hold) _held_ the Smiths' chubby new baby yet?

23. Has anyone (hear) heard whether Hortensia is in town tonight?

24. I (have) had a bad headache after work yesterday.

25. Have the neighbors (find) found their garden hose yet?

Practice Quiz

Take this practice quiz to prepare for the section quiz. Then compare your answers with the answer key. When you are ready for the section quiz, let your instructor know.

I. Circle the letter of the sentence with correct subject-verb agreement from each pair.

Example

(a.) We buy our groceries at Joe's Market and sell them to strangers.

b. We buy our groceries at Joe's Market and sells them to strangers.

1. (a.) The movie begins in about a half hour and ends at 5:00 p.m.
   b. The movie begin in about a half hour and end at 5:00 p.m.

2. a. Your lawn need to be edged this morning and need to be watered this afternoon.
   (b.) Your lawn needs to be edged this morning and needs to be watered this afternoon.

3. a. The trolley car leaves the depot in the morning and arrive back at noon.
   (b.) The trolley car leaves the depot in the morning and arrives back at noon.

4. a. My sisters work at the diner across from the college and makes pretty good wages.
   (b.) My sisters work at the diner across from the college and make pretty good wages.

5. (a.) Your landscaping class meets by the ocean this morning and lasts until evening.
   b. Your landscaping class meet by the ocean this morning and last until evening.

6. a. Those winds comes in every morning at this time and stays all day.
   (b.) Those winds come in every morning at this time and stay all day.

7. a. Your detergent works better than mine and are milder on the hands.
   (b.) Your detergent works better than mine and is milder on the hands.

8. (a.) The motorcycle jumps over the hill and lands on its front wheels.
   b. The motorcycle jump over the hill and land on its front wheels.

9. a. The smells from the dump is sickening and lingers on your clothes.
   b. The smells from the dump are sickening and linger on your clothes.

10. a. Those new uniforms look silly and need to be returned for alterations.
    b. Those new uniforms looks silly and needs to be returned for alterations.

II. Circle the letter of the sentence with the correctly spelled irregular verb.

Example

a. We winned the Monopoly tournament last week.

(b.) We won the Monopoly tournament last week.

1. a. Have you feeded your baby sister yet today?
   b. Have you fed your baby sister yet today?

2. a. George has found a better way to catch mice.
   b. George has finded a better way to catch mice.

3. a. I haved a strange dream last night about invaders from Pluto.
   b. I had a strange dream last night about invaders from Pluto.

4. a. Have you heared about the new rock group called Night Crawler?
   b. Have you heard about the new rock group called Night Crawler?

5. a. Those sails holded up better in the storm that I would have expected.
   b. Those sails held up better in the storm than I would have expected.

6. a. Jenny just layed her books on the desk and watched television all day.
   b. Jenny just laid her books on the desk and watched television all day.

7. a. The priest leaded John through the chapel garden into the confessional area.
   b. The priest led John through the chapel garden into the confessional area.

8. a. Millie has maked plans for Easter vacation already.
   b. Millie has made plans for Easter vacation already.

9. a. Gertrude has stood by her husband much longer than most wives would have.
   b. Gertrude has standed by her husband much longer than most wives would have.

10. a. The art instructor sayed that everyone would be making pots this semester.
    b. The art instructor said that everyone would be making pots this semester.

11. a. Have you readed about the new theater they're building on campus?
    b. Have you read about the new theater they're building on campus?

12. a. John payed a lot of money for that lot on Q Street by the beach.
    b. John paid a lot of money for that lot on Q Street by the beach.

13. a. Jones has leaved nothing to chance in preparing for the debate.
    b. Jones has left nothing to chance in preparing for the debate.
14. a. Have you thinked much about transferring to Amherst next semester?
    b. Have you thought much about transferring to Amherst next semester?
15. a. Malcolm sleeped through the movie in biology and was awakened by the bell.
    b. Malcolm slept through the movie in biology and was awakened by the bell.
16. a. The new glass factory has brought many new jobs to our valley.
    b. The new glass factory has brung many new jobs to our valley.
17. a. No one has builded a better teaching reputation at Monmount College than Dr. Toews.
    b. No one has built a better teaching reputation at Monmount College than Dr. Toews.
18. a. Have you sitted in on a lecture by the foreign language teacher from Calcutta?
    b. Have you sat in on a lecture by the foreign language teacher from Calcutta?
19. a. Donella hasn't spended much time by herself this entire year.
    b. Donella hasn't spent much time by herself this entire year.
20. a. You could have catched that flu bug from practically anyone at the office party.
    b. You could have caught that flu bug from practically anyone at the office party.
21. a. We've fought hard to get ramps built at the school for all handicapped students.
    b. We've fighted hard to get ramps built at the school for all handicapped students.
22. a. Have the Newmans buyed tickets for the philharmonic concert in May?
    b. Have the Newmans bought tickets for the philharmonic concert in May?
23. a. I've keeped out of trouble all semester in Dr. Pindkey's health class.
    b. I've kept out of trouble all semester in Dr. Pindkey's health class.
24. a. No one has spent more time getting signatures for the recall election than Susan.
    b. No one has spended more time getting signatures for the recall election than Susan.

Pronouns, Adjectives, and Adverbs

Section Topics

Pronoun-Antecedent Agreement

Good/Well, Bad/Badly

In this section on "Pronouns, Adjectives, and Adverbs," you are introduced to an important aspect of pronoun usage—*pronoun-antecedent agreement*—and you also learn to distinguish the adverbs *well* and *badly* from the adjectives *good* and *bad*.

Pronoun-Antecedent Agreement

As you learned in previous levels, a *pronoun* is used to replace another word in a sentence. The word that the pronoun replaces is called its *antecedent*. Here are the basic rules to follow for *pronoun-antecedent agreement:*

1. A pronoun agrees *in number* with its antecedent. If the antecedent is singular, the pronoun is singular. If the antecedent is plural, the pronoun is plural.

   Examples: (pronouns underlined with arrow drawn to antecedents)

   John left his wallet in the theater. (The singular pronoun *his* replaces the singular antecedent *John*.)

   The boys left their wallets in the theater. (The plural pronoun *their* replaces the plural antecedent *boys*.)

2. If more than one pronoun replaces an antecedent, all pronouns must agree in number with their antecedent.

   Example: (pronouns underlined with arrow drawn to antecedents)

   The women didn't bring their golf clubs with them today. (The plural pronouns *their* and *them* replace the plural antecedent *women*.)

3. The following words are *always singular: each, one, everyone, someone, everybody, somebody, either, neither, none*. A pronoun replacing any one of these words must be *singular*.

   Examples: (antecedent and pronouns underlined)

   Each of the girls took her skates to the rink on Saturday. (The singular pronoun *her* replaces the singular antecedent *each*.)

One of the buildings lost its roof in the hurricane. (The singular pronoun *its* replaces the singular antecedent *one*.)

4. If an antecedent is a *singular person* who may be male *or* female, the pronouns replacing it should be *he or she, him or her,* or *his and hers.*

   Example: (antecedent and pronouns underlined)

   If a student attends classes regularly, he or she will stand a good chance of passing. (The singular pronouns *he or she* replace the singular antecedent *student.*)

5. To avoid awkward repetition of *he and she* or *his or her* in a sentence, make the antecedent *plural* so that *they* or *their* may be used. (Instead of "A student should use *his or her* time wisely," write, "Students should use *their* time wisely.")

Here is a list of pronouns that are used with singular and plural antecedents:

1. singular male antecedent (boy, man, football player): *he, him, his, himself*
2. singular female antecedent (girl, woman, ballerina): *she, her, hers, herself*
3. singular neutral antecedent (spoon, building, hat): *it, its, itself*
4. plural antecedent for male, female, or neutral: (boys, girls, buildings, men, women, hats) *they, them, their, theirs, themselves*
5. plural antecedent that includes writer: (Ralph and I, Sarah and I, my brothers and I) *we, us, our, ours, ourselves*

Here are examples of sentences that include pronoun-antecedent agreement for all antecedent situations: (antecedents and pronouns underlined)

Mary brought her calculator to math class so that she could use it on the test.
(Singular pronouns *her* and *she* replace singular female antecedent *Mary.*)

When Bob takes his baby sister shopping with him, he attracts a lot of attention.
(Singular pronouns *him* and *he* replace singular male antecedent *Bob.*)

The snail left its trail across the sidewalks, and then it started creeping across the lawn.
(Singular pronouns *its* and *it* replace singular neutral antecedent *snail.*)

The men and women at the bus stop have their bus tokens ready, for they want to board the approaching bus quickly.
(Plural pronouns *their* and *they* replace plural antecedent *men* and *women.*)

Malcolm and I took our sleeping bags to the gymnasium, for we were going to sleep there over the weekend.
(Plural pronouns *our* and *we* replace plural antecedent *including writer, Malcolm and I.*)

A person should watch his or her luggage carefully in bus depots, or it may get stolen.
(Singular pronouns *his* or *her* replace singular *person*; singular pronoun *it* replaces singular *luggage*.)

Exercise 25 Fill in each blank with a pronoun that agrees with its antecedent in the sentence. Also, underline the antecedent for the pronoun. Remember, *each, one, everyone, anyone, either,* and *neither* are always *singular* antecedents, and a singular antecedent that may be male *or* female is replaced by *he or she, him or her,* and *his or her.* When you finish, compare your answers with the answer key.

Example The girls took their cars to the dance so they could leave whenever they wanted to.

1. John lost his car keys in the parking lot, but he found them the next day.
2. The weather has been very warm lately, but it should cool off this weekend.
3. The Garcias took all of ~~our~~ their belongings to Texas with them last night.
4. Each of the umbrellas has a large hole in it.
5. Everyone in the building needs to find their coat before leaving.
6. One of the sixteen female puppies in the litter hasn't opened his eyes yet.
7. Ralph, Terry, and I bought all of your fishing bait today so that we could get an early start to the lake tomorrow.
8. A person should do his best to make others feel welcome in a company.
9. People entering this museum should leave their names with the registrar before they leave.
10. That car in the lot needs its interior cleaned before it is sold.
11. The waves crashed into the pier, and it knocked down part of the railing with its immense force.
12. That painting hanging in the hall had its frame stolen during the auction.

Exercise 26 The following sentences are written without pronouns. Rewrite each sentence and use pronouns to replace words that are unnecessarily repeated. Make sure your pronouns agree with their antecedents. When you finish, compare your answers to the answer key.

Example Aunt Mildred took Aunt Mildred's temperature with a baby thermometer.

1. All of the women invited all of the women's friends to the lawn party by the river.
2. Ted enjoyed eating Ted's breakfast on the back porch.
3. The female rats in the far cage won't touch the female rats' food this morning.
4. One of your uncles has put your uncle's pipe on my clean glass table.
5. A person needs to know a person's strengths and weaknesses to be most successful.
6. Students have been cutting students' classes too often this semester.
7. Everyone in the stadium rose to everyone's feet when Willie Mays walked into the stadium.
8. The dust is thick in the air tonight, and the dust is getting thicker every hour.
9. A man at the saloon brought a man's horse inside with the man.
10. Cats shouldn't be kept inside in the summer, for cats' fur gets all over the carpet and furniture.

Exercise 27 Complete the following sentences and include *at least one pronoun* to replace each underlined antecedent. When you finish, show your sentences to a classmate who has finished and to your instructor.

Example Make sure that the pronouns ____________

1. The boys standing in front of the school ____________
2. One of the female giraffes ____________
3. The girl in the pink bikini ____________
4. Those peaches on the kitchen table ____________
5. My watch that I left with you ____________

6. Those two families from Italy ______________________________
7. Everyone in the bank ______________________________
8. A person who is looking for bargains ______________________________
9. The fourteen men in the blue sweat suits ______________________________
10. Mandy and I ______________________________

____

Good/Well and *Bad/Badly*

Many writers have trouble deciding when to use the adverbs *well* and *badly* instead of the adjectives *good* and *bad*. The two adverbs are seldom misused as adjectives, but the two adjectives are frequently misused as adverbs. Here are some suggestions to help you use these four common words correctly.

1. *Well* and *badly* are *adverbs* used to tell *how* something is done.

   Examples: Sammy hits a tennis ball well. (*Well* tells *how* he *hits the ball.*)

   Mary played badly in the tournament. (*Badly* tells *how* she *played.*)

   You have done well with your babysitting. (*Well* tells *how* you *have done.*)

   I chipped my tooth badly on the drinking fountain. (*Badly* tells *how* you *chipped your tooth.*)

2. *Good* and *bad* are *adjectives* that *describe* a person, place, or thing.

   Examples: Martina Navratalova is a very good tennis player. (*Good* describes the person.)

   That was a bad lecture I just sat through. (*Bad* describes the lecture.)

   That is a good picture of Sue on the wall. (*Good* describes the picture.)

   Those are bad angles to serve a tennis ball from. (*Bad* describes the angles.)

3. Certain *linking verbs* are followed by the adjectives *good* and *bad* and *not* the adverbs *well* and *badly: taste, look, feel, sound, seem, smell,* and forms of *to be: am, is, are, was,* and *were.*

   Examples: That watermelon tastes good.

I don't feel as bad as I did yesterday.

You always look good in leotards.

That new Sting album sounds pretty bad.

The weather seems good for jogging this morning.

That new teacher is good with problem children.

Exercise 28 Fill in the correct word—*good* or *well*—to complete each of the following sentences. Then compare your answers to the answer key.

Examples You performed *well* on the trampoline last night.

You are really *good* on the trampoline.

1. That was a ________ deal you made on your bicycle.
2. That ball that just sailed out of the park was hit ________.
3. Those red licorice sticks taste ________ compared to these black ones.
4. I think we all did ________ on the quiz considering how hard it was.
5. Everyone at the office speaks ________ of Harriet and her family.
6. Samantha is a ________ stenographer.
7. None of the dogs at the pet show behaved as ________ as their owners had hoped.
8. You are really ________ at making that frisbee sail.
9. The orchestra played extremely ________ the entire year.
10. That is a ________-looking piano that you have stored in your garage.

Exercise 29 Fill in the correct word—*bad* or *badly*—to complete each of the following sentences. Then compare your answers with the answer key.

Example Sammy hit the golf ball *badly* during the first round of the tournament.

1. Marian has a ________ cold and sore throat.
2. Your mother has never baked ________ in her life.

3. You look ________ this morning after having gone three days without sleep.
4. Ted played ________ in the chess tournament because he couldn't concentrate.
5. The entire class did ________ on the essay question about free will.
6. That was a ________ storm that we júst suffered through.
7. The Museum of Natural Art in Des Moines has a________ reputation among collectors.
8. The blister that Wendy got while hoeing the garden hurts ________.
9. I feel ________ about the way I've been treating my youngest sister.
10. No one did as ________ as I did with Sunday's crossword puzzle.

Exercise 30 The following paragraph contains some errors in both *pronoun-antecedent agreement* and in the use of *good/well* and *bad/badly*. First, read the paragraph and underline the errors. Then rewrite the paragraph so that all pronouns agree with their antecedents and so that the adverbs *well* and *badly* and the adjectives *good* and *bad* are used correctly. When you finish, compare your paragraph with the answer key.

Example One of the girls in the band played their flute very good.
Revised: One of the girls in the band played her flute very well.

Six women were in their lanes for the start of the Olympic backstroke event. When the starter shot his gun, five of the women stretched her bodies far out over the water. One woman, however, lost their footing on the wall and slipped bad. Going into the turn, three of the women were tied for first place, her arms stroking in unison. The woman in lane four hit her turn good, and she came out ahead of the others. The woman in lane five hit her turn bad, and she slipped back to fifth place. On the home stretch, every person in the stands was on their feet cheering. At the finish, the woman from Australia in lane four touched out their nearest competitor from Japan in lane three. Every one of the swimmers did their best time for the race.

Exercise 31 Write a paragraph comparing any two of the following subjects. Include a statement of which one you would recommend to your classmates and also tell why. Before you write your first draft, you may want to make a list of points for comparison to include in your paragraph. Here is an example:

Comparing Honda Accords to Toyota Camrys

	Honda	*Toyota*
looks	smooth lines	boxier
performance	quick, smooth handling	not as quick, smooth
interior	roomy, good-looking	tighter, average looks
ride	smooth to 95 mph	fairly smooth to 85
price	$13,000–$16,000	$11,000–14,500

Topics:
Compare any of the following:

1. Two instructors
2. Apartment vs. dormitory living
3. Two fast-food burger restaurants
4. Four-year vs. community college
5. Two work shifts (day vs. swing, swing vs. graveyard, etc.)
6. Two different diets
7. Two popular forms of exercise
8. Two kinds of music
9. Two clothing stores

After you've written your first draft, meet with a classmate or small group and analyze the sample first draft, referring to the evaluation questions following it.

First Draft

The Toyota Camry and Honda Accord are cars that both sell well. The Accord has a slightly longer front and more sharply angled rear end, giving it a sleeker, sportyer look. The Camry is boxy looking by comparison. The Honda is also quicker than the Camry, with about 20 more horsepower in its fuel-injected model, but in traffic both cars handle about the same. The interior of the Honda are plusher looking, with thicker carpeting, smooth, rich seat apholstery, and a space-age dash, the Toyota's apholstery is not as nice, and its dash is like GM cars. Both cars rides smoothly, but the Honda has a little more weight and rides more smoother on rougher roads and at higher speeds. While the Honda is priced slightly higher, when you consider all the options available with the Honda along with its durability, looks, performance and ride. They are certainly worth the extra money.

Questions for Evaluation:

1. Does the paragraph cover the most important points of comparison for the reader? Are there other important points to be considered?

2. Are the points of comparison presented in the most effective order? Could any point be more effectively located?

3. Is each point of comparison supported with adequate details or examples? Does the reader clearly understand the comparisons?

4. Does the writer show a definite preference in the paragraph? Is the preference well supported?

5. Are the sentences well worded? Are there short sentences that could be combined or wordy sentences that could be effectively shortened? Are there any problems with run-on sentences or fragments?

6. Is the paragraph long enough to consider dividing into two or three paragraphs? If so, where might it be divided? Why?

7. Check for any errors in spelling, subject-verb agreement, punctuation, and grammar.

Practize Quiz

Take this practice quiz to prepare for the session quiz. Then compare your answers with the answer key. When you are ready for the section quiz, let your instructor know.

I. Circle the letter of the sentence in which the pronoun(s) agrees with its antecedent.

Example

a. The new women's PE teacher is trying their best to get the girls in shape.
(b.) The new women's PE teacher is trying her best to get the girls in shape.
c. The new women's PE teacher is trying the teacher's best to get the girls in shape.

1. a. Henry had a difficult time paying its monthly installments on the new pickup.
   b. Henry had a difficult time paying his monthly installments on the new pickup.
   c. Henry had a difficult time paying their monthly installments on the new pickup.

2. a. Tuition is a big expense this semester, for it was raised to $300.
   b. Tuition is a big expense this semester, for they were raised to $300.
   c. Tuition is a big expense this semester, for tuition was raised to $300.

3. a. Fish is one food most recommended by nutritionists, for they are low in fat.
   b. Fish is one food most recommended by nutritionists, for fish is low in fat.
   c. Fish is one food most recommended by nutritionists, for it is low in fat.

4. a. Every person in the aerobics class dropped their active heart rate by ten beats per minute.
   b. Every person in the aerobics class dropped his or her active heart rate by ten beats per minute.
   c. Every person in the aerobics class dropped its active heart rate by ten beats per minute.

5. a. The students who study the hardest will do her best on the essay section of the test.

b. The students who study the hardest will do their best on the essay section of the test.

c. The students who study the hardest will do his best on the essay section of the test.

6. a. A man who lived here last year dropped by to return their key to the landlady.

   b. A man who lived here last year dropped by to return his key to the landlady.

   c. A man who lived here last year dropped by to return the man's key to the landlady.

7. a. Each of the petunias in the garden lost their flowers in the same week.

   b. Each of the petunias in the garden lost its flowers in the same week.

   c. Each of the petunias in the garden lost our flowers in the same week.

8. a. John and I are worried about the cannery shutting down, for we don't want to lose our jobs.

   b. John and I are worried about the cannery shutting down, for John and I don't want to lose our jobs.

   c. John and I are worried about the cannery shutting down, for they don't want to lose their jobs.

9. a. The pronouns in the sentences must agree in number with its antecedents.

   b. The pronouns in the sentences must agree in number with their antecedents.

   c. The pronouns in the sentences must agree in number with our antecedents.

10. a. Students who register early have a good chance of getting all of their classes.

    b. Students who register early have a good chance of getting all of the student's classes.

    c. Students who register early have a good chance of getting all of his or her classes.

II. Circle the letter of the sentence with the correct adjective or adverb.

Example

a. You know how to work that combination lock good.

(b.) You know how to work that combination lock well.

1. a. The negotiations for the latest baseball contract appear to be going bad.

   b. The negotiations for the latest baseball contract appear to be going badly.

2. a. Mark's campaign for city dogcatcher is off to a badly start.

   b. Marks' campaign for city dogcatcher is off to a bad start.

3. a. The child sitting in the back of the room does well with finger paints.

   b. The child sitting in the back of the room does good with finger paints.

4. a. Attempts to reduce the federal deficit are going bad this year.
   b. Attempts to reduce the federal deficit are going badly this year.
5. a. That's a very well-looking shirt you are wearing.
   b. That's a very good-looking shirt you are wearing.
6. a. The corn crop isn't looking too well for this time of the season.
   b. The corn crop isn't looking too good for this time of the season.
7. a. The Midwestern region of the United States needs about three weeks of rain bad.
   b. The Midwestern region of the United States needs about three weeks of rain badly.
8. a. New York City did a good job of settling the garbage collectors' strike last year.
   b. New York City did a well job of settling the garbage collectors' strike last year.
9. a. Muriel performed bad on the treadmill test, but she did good on the other stress tests.
   b. Muriel performed badly on the treadmill test, but she did well on the other stress tests.
10. a. No one has done as good a job of organizing the city art festival as Jane.
    b. No one has done as well a job of organizing the city art festival as Jane.

Spelling

Section Topics

Contractions

Possessives

A final proofreading consideration for writers is correct spelling. Before sharing your writing with others, it is a good idea to go over your sentences one last time checking for any spelling problems. If you find a word that doesn't look quite right to you, there is a good chance that it is misspelled. Look up the word in a dictionary to find the correct spelling, and if you can't find the word, get some help from your instructor.

Contractions

Some of the most commonly misspelled words are *contractions*: words that are formed by combining two words and replacing the left-out letters with an apostrophe ('). Here is a list of commonly misspelled contractions and the two words that each contraction is formed from.

	Contraction		*Contraction*
he is	he's	is not	isn't
she is	she's	are not	aren't
it is	it's	was not	wasn't
I am	I'm	were not	weren't
you are	you're	will not	won't
they are	they're	has not	hasn't
we are	we're	have not	haven't
you have	you've	had not	hadn't
they have	they've	does not	doesn't
we have	we've	do not	don't
there is	there's	can not	can't
that is	that's		

Here are some basic points to help you spell contractions correctly:

1. A contraction is a *single word* formed from combining two words.
2. A contraction *always contains an apostrophe*.
3. *The apostrophe replaces* the letter(s) left out when the words are combined.
4. The apostrophe is placed where the left-out letter(s) would go. (Example: in *don't*, the apostrophe replaces the *o* in *not*; in *he's*, the apostrophe replaces the *i* in *is*.)

Exercise 32 Write the contraction form for each pair of words given. Make sure to spell correctly. Then compare your spellings with the list of contractions.

Example you are *you're*

1. do not *don't*
2. they are *they're*
3. he is *he's*
4. does not *doesn't*
5. will not *won't* ~~*willn't*~~
6. they have *they've*
7. are not *aren't*
8. it is *it's*
9. can not *can't*
10. she is *she's*
11. we have *we've*
12. they are *they're*
13. have not *haven't*
14. is not *isn't*
15. you are *you're*
16. that is *that's*

Exercise 33 Fill in the blanks with appropriate contractions from the list on page 185. Spell the contractions correctly. Then share your fill-ins with your instructor.

Example *We're* tired of having our seats taken at the arena.

1. *That's* one thing about Claudia that everyone admires.
2. Do you know that *you're* running for class secretary my last semester of school?
3. We *don't* have to turn in our bug collections until May 20th.
4. It seems that *you've* had a lot of bad luck with your new car.
5. *They've* been returning all of the old newspapers John has sent to them.
6. *Isn't* that a flamingo standing beside the shallow pond?
7. *Haven't* any of you ever seen a cross-eyed leopard?
8. *We're* going to our grandparents for Thanksgiving this year.
9. *I'm* having a few friends over to my house this evening.
10. It *doesn't* look like *it's* going to rain today.

Possessives

Possessive words are often spelled incorrectly because the apostrophe showing possession is either omitted or put in the wrong place. Here are some basic points to help you spell possessive words correctly:

1. A possessive word *shows ownership*. The word following the possessive word "belongs" to it:

   the boy's coat (the coat belongs to the boy)
   Maria's cat (the cat belongs to Maria)
   today's weather (the weather of today)
   the ambulance's siren (the siren of the ambulance)

2. If the possessive word is *singular*, add -*'s* to show possession:

   the boy's coat
   the girl's sweater
   a cloud's lining
   a dog's collar

3. If the possessive word is *plural*, add the apostrophe *after* the *s* (*s'*):

   many boys' sweaters
   fourteen girls' books
   the clouds' moisture (more than one cloud)
   the dogs' territory (more than one dog)

4. If the possessive word forms its plural *without* adding -*s*, add -*'s* to show possession:

   men's club
   women's stores
   children's manners
   people's dreams
   oxen's yoke

5. *Possessive pronouns* such as *yours, his, hers, theirs,* and *ours* do *not* take apostrophes since their form indicates possession. However, indefinite pronouns such as *one, anyone, everyone, somebody,* and *nobody* require an apostrophe to show possession: one's money, everyone's future, nobody's fault.

6. Don't put apostrophes on plural words that are *not* possessive. If a word is *not followed* by something belonging to it, it is not possessive:

   dogs and cats
   four coats and six umbrellas
   the doctors, the nurses, and the orderlies
   many Sundays ago

Exercise 34 Put an apostrophe in each possessive word that requires one, following the rules for singular and plural possessive. If a word is *not* possessive, *don't* add an apostrophe. Check your answers with the answer key.

Example the ladies room

the ladies' room

1. your sisters ring
2. a trouts coloring
3. my pastors home
4. many pigeons droppings
5. six soldiers bunks
6. dogs and rabbits
7. yours and ours
8. a streets number
9. a newspapers headline
10. both parents blessings
11. the mens pockets
12. Marias slacks
13. Clydes horoscope
14. all of the students desks
15. the boxes lids
16. cups and saucers
17. his wallet
18. the winds whistle
19. the schools policy
20. your grandparents Model T

Exercise 35 Put an apostrophe in each possessive word that requires one in the following sentences. Then compare your answers to the answer key.

Example All of the childs toys were scattered around his room.

All of the child's toys were scattered around his room.

1. Mildred blew a months salary on a new red dress.
2. I think we have lost the custodians key.
3. A girls locket was found in the trash can at the station.
4. Some squirrels nuts were found hidden in Mitchells sofa.
5. Your uncles house is located close to my doctors apartment.
6. The childrens belongings were sent to the womens charity ward for sorting.
7. I don't think that a years supply of soap is going to last the troops.
8. Your hamsters teeth just bit into my brothers pant leg.

9. A nations defense depends on all civilians support of the military.
10. All of the lilies in this field wouldn't cover Sallys front yard.

Exercise 36 Write your own sentences using the *possessive forms* of the following phrases. Spell your possessive words correctly. Then show your sentences to your instructor.

Examples the books belonging to Harry

Harry's book about Africa is very interesting.

the dog belonging to Mary

Mary's dog is a Doberman pinscher.

1. the toys belonging to the children
2. the weapons belonging to the soldiers
3. a blouse belonging to Nadine
4. the supplies belonging to the government
5. the motion of the waves
6. the nurses of the doctors
7. the courage of Clyde
8. the story belonging to the newspaper
9. the horn belonging to the old Chevrolet
10. the blackboards belonging to all of the classes

Practice Quiz Take this practice quiz to help prepare for the section quiz. Then compare your answers to the answer key. When you are ready for the section quiz, let your instructor know.

I. Circle the letter of the correctly spelled conjunction in each group.

Example	a. dont	(b.) don't	c. dont'
1.	a. shes	b. shes'	c. she's

2. a. youve — b. you've — c. youv'e
3. a. theyre — b. theyr'e — c. they're
4. a. weren't — b. were'nt — c. werent'
5. a. havn't — b. haven't — c. have'nt
6. a. thats — b. thats' — c. that's
7. a. isnt — b. is'nt — c. isn't
8. a. Im — b. I'am — c. I'm
9. a. are'nt — b. arent — c. aren't
10. a. dosen't — b. does'nt — c. doesn't
11. a. there's — b. theres — c. ther'es
12. a. havn't — b. have'nt — c. haven't
13. a. hes — b. hes' — c. he's
14. a. its — b. it's — c. its'
15. a. youre — b. your'e — c. you're

II. Circle the letter of the correctly punctuated possessive in each group.

Example a. a boys sweater — b. a boy's sweater — c. a boys' sweater

1. a. a girls' room — b. a girls room — c. a girl's room
2. a. six merchants ware — b. six merchant's ware — c. six merchants' ware
3. a. a ducks' feathers — b. a duck's feathers — c. a ducks feathers
4. a. four sisters husbands — b. four sisters' husbands — c. four sister's husbands
5. a. a men's lounge — b. a mens' lounge — c. a mens lounge
6. a. my mothers perfume — b. my mother's perfume — c. my mothers' perfume
7. a. two coaches wives — b. two coache's wives — c. two coaches' wives
8. a. a trips expenses — b. a trip's expenses — c. a trips' expenses
9. a. many doctors' careers — b. many doctor's careers — c. many doctors careers

Writing Review

At the end of each level is a "Writing Review" section where you have the opportunity to apply what you have learned to a paragraph-length assignment. The following paragraph assignment draws upon everything that has been covered in the first three levels.

Level 3 Paragraph Assignment

Select one of the following topics for writing a paragraph:

1. a style of dress
2. one type of student
3. a person you admire
4. a great movie
5. fixing something up
6. something to look forward to
7. something to dread
8. an unusual relationship

Step One

1. Select one topic from the list you'd like to write on.
2. Write a tentative topic sentence expressing a definite opinion or attitude about your subject.
3. Do some type of prewriting work—brainstorm for ideas, make a list of supporting points, or devise a formal outline including supporting points and details. Choose the prewriting technique that would be most useful for your subject.
4. Organize your brainstormed material in the best manner for your subject: chronologically (time), spatially, categorically, by importance, or by size.

Example

General Topic: a particular kind of weather
Specific Subject: foggy weather
Topic Sentence: I hate to drive in foggy weather.

Brainstorming	*Ouline (from Brainstorming)*
crazy drivers	I. Dangerous
poor visibility	A. Poor visibility
fogs up inside	B. See cars at last second
slow drivers	C. Can't see divider or sides
dangerous	II. Cars drive at different speeds
can't see cars	A. Slow cars
moisture on windows	B. Crazy drivers
can't see lines	III. Windows fog up
	A. Outside moisture
	B. Inside moisture

5. Write your first draft of the paragraph. Your audience—the person you are writing for—is a particular classmate. Keep this person in mind as you write.

Step Two When you finish your first draft, read it over carefully and apply the following questions:

1. Is my topic sentence strong? (Does it express a definite opinion or attitude about your subject that your paragraph supports? Can it be improved?)
2. Is my paragraph unified? (Make sure that each sentence is related to your subject. If any sentence strays off topic, either delete the sentence or change it.)
3. Is my paragraph well developed? (Is your topic sentence well supported? Do you have enough examples and details to develop your subject clearly? Are examples or details provided for all general statements?)
4. Is my paragraph well organized? (Are your sentences in the best order for developing your subject? Do you have a definite organization: time, space, size, category, or importance?)
5. Do I use *transitional words* to tie my sentences together? (Common transitions include *first, second, next, then, another, also, therefore, however,* and so on.)
6. Do I end with a concluding sentence(s) that wraps up the paragraph and ties back to the topic sentence in some manner?
7. Have I kept my audience (classmate) in mind as I wrote the paragraph? (Is the paragraph written like something you would share with a good friend? Is it interesting? Does it share honest feelings?)
8. Is my paragraph long enough to consider dividing into two or more paragraphs? If so, where might I divide it?

Step Three Go over each individual sentence in your paragraph and follow these suggestions:

1. Look for any pairs or groups of *short sentences* that could be combined. Underline them to revise in your final draft.
2. Check your wording within each sentence. Make sure each sentence is clear and direct. Underline any sentence that is awkward, overly wordy, or vague to revise in your final draft.

3. Check your paragraph for run-on sentences and fragments. Separate run-ons with periods and correct fragments by adding words to make them sentences or by joining them to the sentence they belong with.

4. Check your punctuation. Do you have periods after all sentences? Do you have a question mark after any sentence that asks a question? Do you have *commas* before a coordinate conjunction (*and, but, so, for, yet, or*) in a compound sentence, between clauses in a complex sentence beginning with a subordinate conjunction (*because, after, when, while, as, if, since, although, unless, until*), and between words in a series? Add or change punctuation marks as needed.

Step Four Now give your paragraph a final check for wording errors. Follow these suggestions:

1. Check sentence for subject-verb agreement, for the past tense *-ed* verb ending on regular past tense verbs, and for correct irregular verb spelling.

2. Check your use of *pronouns*, making sure that you are using correct subject pronouns and that you are using the correct pronouns to replace words that don't need repeating.

3. Finally, check your spelling. Are you adding *-s* or *-es* endings to plural words? Are you spelling *-ing*-ending words correctly? Are you using *there, their,* and *they're* correctly? Are you spelling *contractions* and *possessives* correctly? Circle any word you are unsure of, and look it up in a dictionary. Correct all spelling errors.

Step Five Write your final draft of the paragraph, including all improvements and corrections. When you finish, share your paragraph with your classmate you wrote it for and with your instructor.

Sample Final Draft

I hate to drive in foggy weather. It is the most dangerous weather for driving because the fog covers everything. I have driven in fog so bad that I couldn't see the next white line in front of me on the road. It's impossible to see cars coming toward you or cars in front of you until the last second, which greatly increases the chances for accidents. Furthermore, cars travel at different speeds in the fog. Some drivers barely creep along, and others drive as if they have X-ray vision, so accidents often occur when faster cars ram into slower ones. To add to the problems, the windows often fog up on the inside and film over with mist on the outside, forcing you to work the windshield wipers and defroster while straining to see the road. Every time I go out on a foggy night, I feel I'm risking my life, and when the visibility gets too bad, I just pull way off the road and wait for the fog to lift.

LEVEL 4

Now that you have worked with individual paragraphs for three levels, you are ready to begin on *compositions*: longer writings consisting of a number of paragraphs. Instead of writing a single paragraph on a topic, you will write three or more paragraphs, each developing a *different aspect* of the topic.

Everything you learned about writing paragraphs in the previous levels will be useful for writing compositions. Paragraphs within a composition often begin with a *topic sentence*, and the principles of unity, development, and coherence are still important. You will also learn that the paragraphs within a composition have a similar relation to the sentences within a paragraph. Paragraphs are organized within a composition and relate to its topic as sentences are organized within a paragraph and relate to the topic sentence.

The Composition

Section Topics

Basic Paragraphing

Controlling Idea

Most writing that people do usually requires more than one paragraph: letters, stories, newspaper or magazine articles, essay exams, or even diaries. From Level 4 on, a *composition*, or *essay*, will mean any written assignment on a single topic developed in a number of paragraphs. While individual paragraph writing limits how much you can do with a topic, composition writing allows you to develop a topic in as much depth and detail as you like.

Basic Paragraphing

A composition is divided into *paragraphs* in order to present the writer's ideas most effectively. Paragraphs within a composition help to *separate* and *organize* a writer's ideas so that they stand out clearly to readers.

Here are some basic suggestions for dividing a composition into paragraphs:

1. Change paragraphs when you move to *something new* in a composition: a new idea, a new step, a new location, or a different time.
2. Each paragraph within a composition often develops a different point, step, idea, or situation.

3. Most paragraphs within a composition begin with a *topic sentence* that expresses the main point of the paragraph.
4. Paragraphs within a composition follow the same basic principles as the individual paragraphs you have worked with: They are unified, well developed, organized, and tied together with transitional wording.
5. Most compositions begin with an *opening paragraph* introducing the topic for the composition and the *controlling idea*: the main idea the writer is developing. The controlling idea directs a composition like a topic sentence directs a paragraph.
6. Compositions often have concluding "wrap-up" paragraphs, which will be covered in detail in Level 5.

Here are three sample compositions divided into *paragraphs*. The prewriting before each composition shows the topic, the controlling idea, and the main point developed in each paragraph in support of that idea.

Sample Composition One

Topic: the downtown mall
Controlling Idea: The downtown mall is in bad condition.
Main Points for Paragraph:
1. vacant buildings
2. dirty and run-down
3. attracting undesirable people

Composition: (The controlling idea is in brackets ([ ]) and topic sentences are underlined. In Level 5, the controlling idea will be contained in a separate opening paragraph.)

I hadn't shopped downtown in Telleport for over a year, going instead to more convenient suburban malls. So when I finally went downtown to do some shopping, I was shocked at what I saw. [The downtown shopping mall in Telleport is really in bad condition.]

<u>The vacant buildings scattered throughout the mall show how bad things are.</u> Large chain stores have moved their businesses to the newer suburban malls that attract more affluent customers. Other businesses are reluctant to move in, so large buildings stay vacant month after month. The vacant buildings are a sign that the downtown mall is dying out.

<u>The mall is also more run-down than ever before.</u> The city has reduced its maintenance budget, and there aren't enough workers to keep the mall up. The sidewalks are littered, and the once lovely fountains don't work. The iron sculptures are rusting, and other artwork has been vandalized. There is graffiti on the sides of buildings and on the sidewalks, and many of the windows in the vacant buildings are broken or boarded up.

<u>There are also some undesirable people that have moved into the mall.</u> Transients in ragged clothes can be found on most of the benches and lawn areas, and their wine bottles are strewn everywhere. Prostitutes who used to stay four blocks west of downtown have slowly made their way to the mall and

hang out at the north end. There are also teenage gangs that roam the mall in the evening, and the crime rate in the area is up. These new elements obviously don't help attract customers to the mall.

Sample Composition Two

Topic: Kaeding Park

Controlling Idea: Kaeding Park is Manley's most popular summer attraction.

Main Points for Paragraph:
1. the zoo
2. picnic areas
3. evening cruises

Composition: (Controlling idea in brackets ([ ]); topic sentences underlined)

There's not much you can do today for entertainment that doesn't cost a lot of money. Movies, amusement parks, bowling, or miniature golf are all expensive. However, in Monroe, there's one place people can still go and have a good time very cheaply: the city park. [Every summer, Kaeding Park attracts thousands of visitors.]

<u>The main attraction is the zoo located in the center of the park</u>. For fifty cents apiece, a family can spend the day enjoying the animals. The zoo covers twenty acres, and the animals live in areas resembling their natural habitats. Zebras and antelope roam the plains, and bears and deer can be spotted on pine-covered hills. Elephants drink at a large man-made watering hole while hippopotamuses float along its surface. The animals stay healthy and alert because they have room to move around. The zoo attracts over 500,000 people a summer, and over half of them are children.

<u>Picnicking is the main family activity in the park</u>. The park has over one hundred picnic areas complete with tables, benches, and barbecue facilities. Some of the areas are covered and lit for nighttime use. Large family reunions are held in the park every weekend, but there are also smaller picnic areas for couples or small families. Between the picnic areas are open fields where picnickers can play volleyball or baseball or toss a Frisbee, and thousands of oak, elm, and maple trees provide plenty of shade from the summer heat.

<u>Finally, the main evening attraction at Kaeding Park is cruising</u>. Every summer evening, hundreds of cars full of teenagers creep slowly through the winding park roads with stereos blasting. The park is the number one summer spot for teenagers to meet, show off their cars, and play their music. Despite all the cars and people, there is seldom any trouble, and the local police prefer that teenagers cruise the park rather than the main boulevards of the city.

Sample Composition Three

Topic: Harriet's second semester of college

Controlling Idea: Harriet changed her habits second semester.

Main Points for Paragraph:
1. attended class regularly
2. studied more
3. took a lighter load

Composition: (Controlling idea in brackets ([ ]); topic sentences underlined)

When Harriet went to college, she couldn't handle all the freedom. She started missing classes, and she didn't know how to manage her free time. Consequently, her first semester grades were a disaster. [After doing badly her first semester in college, Harriet decided to make some changes the next semester.]

First, she began attending class regularly. The first semester, she cut a lot of classes and got far behind in her work. Now she never misses a class, so she knows what's going on. She was also smart enough to avoid the 8:00 daily classes that she had missed so often the first semester. Her first class begins at 10:00 every day.

Next, Harriet started studying regularly for the first time in her life. She read all her assignments and did her homework. She turned in all her projects on time, and she put in long hours the night before a test. She never went out from Monday through Thursday nights so that she could study at least four hours those evenings. She also set aside Sunday afternoon to catch up on her reading assignments.

Harriet also chose her classes more wisely second semester. The first semester she took five tough three-unit classes that all required a lot of preparation. The second semester she took three tough classes—political science, psychology, and English 10—and two easier ones—aerobic dance and pottery. She could spend most of her time studying for the harder classes and just enjoy the other two. With her easier schedule and improved habits, Harriet was passing all of her classes at midterm report.

Notice that the three sample compositions have the following features in common:

1. Each composition opens with a paragraph that introduces and presents the controlling idea for the composition: the condition of the shopping mall, the attractions of the park, or the changes in Harriet's college habits.
2. Each paragraph within the composition develops *one supporting point* on the topic. (Look at the "main points for paragraph" before each composition.)
3. Each paragraph contains a topic sentence (underlined) that expresses the main point of the paragraph.
4. Each paragraph develops in detail the main point expressed in the topic sentence.

Exercise 1 Each of the following compositions contains *four paragraphs*. Put the paragraph symbol (¶) in front of the sentences that begin the second, third, and fourth paragraphs, and underline the *controlling idea* in the opening paragraph and the *topic sentence* for the next three paragraphs. When you finish, compare your paragraphing with the answer key.

Example Americans often have a low opinion of politicians. However, there are some politicians who stand out above the rest. These good politicians possess a few strong qualities. First, they are intelligent. The business of government is complex, and it takes a sharp-minded person to understand what's going on. They must also be bright enough to weigh the pros and cons of an issue and make decisions in the best interests of the people they represent. They must be able to separate the important issues from the trivial ones, and they must be smart enough to know what can be accomplished and what can't.

Good politicians are also hard workers. They put in twelve- to sixteen-hour days handling all the work they must do to serve their district or state. They have to read all the bills that go before the legislature, research the issues, develop and present their own legislation, meet with their constituents and numerous lobbying groups, and meet all the public relations obligations that go with the job. The best politicians all share a common schedule: long, hard working days.

Finally, good politicians are honest. Politicians that gain the reputation of being dishonest are seldom trusted or reelected. The temptation to tell every person exactly what he or she wants to hear is strong, but politicians who talk out of both sides of their mouths aren't listened to for very long. A politician can lie and get away with it for a while, but eventually the lies come back to the source. The only way a politician can hope for a long or effective career is to be honest.

1. I was raised with the help of one Italian grandmother and one Mexican grandmother. Our family lived close to the Japanese section of San Jose and across the street from a Greek delicatessan. Consequently, I grew up eating spaghetti, enchiladas, sushi, and pastrami sandwiches. Today, I love all kinds of different ethnic foods. Italian food is one of my favorites. I like pizzas with thick crusts and lots of tomato sauce and cheese. My favorite pizza has everything on it: sausage, salami, pepperoni, olives, onions, peppers, and anchovies. I also like spaghetti with rich, spicy meat sauce smothered in Parmesan cheese. On special occasions, I enjoy veal parmigiana with tender veal covered with spaghetti sauce and melted cheese. I also like lasagna, but only the way my grandma cooks it with extra ricotta cheese and meat. Japanese food is my second favorite. When I eat at a Japanese restaurant, I always order the same thing: teriyaki chicken and beef with tempura-style vegetables and shrimp. I love the sweet, tangy flavor of meat marinated in teriyaki sauce, and the light, crisp tempura batter makes drab vegetables like carrots and squash taste delicious. I also like to eat sushi and fish soup, but I stay away from raw fish and octopus. Probably my favorite ethnic food is Mexican. I eat Mexican food at least once a week at home or at a restaurant. My favorite dish is chili verde burritos with rice and beans. I love the soft tortillas, the big chunks of pork, and the hot chili verde sauce. At one restaurant I eat nothing but chicken dishes: chicken tacos, chicken tostados, chicken enchiladas, and chicken mole, a chicken casserole with thick, spicy sauce. I also like to eat machaca and chili colorado, and I'm learning to eat menudo, a soup made with tripe. Because of my eating background growing up, I'm willing to try about anything.

2. I dream more than most people, and I often remember my dreams vividly. In many dreams I'm a time traveler, jumping into the future or back in time. For example, in a dream I had the other night, I traveled back in time to the 1950s. When I went to school, the students looked like the cast from the movie "Grease." The boys had flattops with ducktails. They wore Levi's with rolled-up cuffs, madras shirts with the shirttails out, and penny loafers with white socks. The girls had ponytails and pageboy cuts, and they wore poodle skirts, tight sweaters, and

saddle oxfords with bobby socks. The cars parked in the school lot were vintage 1950s. There were two-tone blue and white '55 Chevies, '54 Fords lowered in the front, '58 Impalas with pinstripes and tuck 'n roll interiors, and an occasional '57 T-bird or '58 Corvette. There were also a lot of "papa and momma" cars: Dodge, Buick, and Oldsmobile four-door sedans with black walls. There wasn't a foreign car on the lot—no Hondas, Toyotas, or Volkswagens—except for one '57 MGB sports car. When I went to a department store downtown, I got my biggest shock. Looking through the clothing department, I found Levi's for $7 a pair and polo shirts for $2.95. Dresses went from $8 to $20, and you could buy any pair of shoes for under $18. Sport coats ranged from $25 to $35, and women's coats were just a bit higher. Before I woke up, I had bought ten shirts, five pairs of peg-legged cords, and two pairs of wing tips, all for under $50.

3. Summer jobs are important to most students. However, those jobs vary tremendously in the kind of work available and how much you can make. It's not always wise to jump at the first job opportunity you find. When looking for a summer job, there are a few things you should consider. First, find out about the pay and benefits for a job. While most summer employers pay only minimum wage, others pay from $.50 to $1.50 above minimum. Some also give midsummer raises. Other jobs require piecework wages, where your earnings depend on how much you produce. Calculate how much you can actually make by working at an average speed. It is also good to check on any benefits. Some employers may give health insurance benefits for three months or end-of-summer bonuses based on profits. Look at all these financial angles before deciding on a job. Second, it's important to find out about the hours. You have to be able to get enough hours per week for the job to be worth your time. Find out if the job is a guaranteed forty-hour week, if there is overtime, and if your hours are the same each day. If you have a job working with fruit or produce, find out how steady the hours will be and how long the job will last into the fall. Before you decide on a job, multiply the hourly rate by the number of hours in an average workweek to have a clear picture of your earnings. Finally, it is important to look into the working conditions. Are you going to be working outside or inside? If you're working outside, will you get regular breaks and plenty of water? Will you start in the morning to avoid the hottest part of the day? If you are working inside, check on the cooling system. Also see if the lighting is adequate for the kind of work being done. Make sure the machinery is safe and looks in good operating condition. Also check to see how clean the place is. If the work site is filthy, that tells you something about your employer. Since you will be spending an entire summer at your work location, make sure that the conditions are safe, comfortable, and clean enough for you.

4. Some people should never get out of bed in the morning. My friend Monte is one of those people. Since I've known him in grade school, he's always been accident prone: broken fingers from baseball games, twisted ankles from roller skating, bruises and gashes from falling off his bike or down a stairway. But Monte saved the "worst" for high school. He had a rash of accidents his junior year you wouldn't believe. In PE class the first semester, he was doing the rope climb in the gym when the rope came off the ceiling hook. Monte fell to the hardwood floor and broke his left arm. He went to the doctor in great pain, with his bone below the elbow cracked in two. His arm was in a cast for two months, and he missed the cross-country season. Then during Christmas vacation, Monte went ice skating at Mill Pond. Unfortunately, he skated onto the thin ice near the east edge of the

pond and crashed through it into the icy water. He went all the way underwater and struggled for about fifteen seconds trying to gain his footing. Luckily, the water only turned out to be waist deep, but Monte still caught a bad cold and was in bed the rest of the vacation. Monte's worst mishap came in the spring. On his way down from the mountains, he lost his brakes on his Ford and went off the road into a ravine. The car landed on top of a bushy oak, which helped to pad the landing and probably saved Monte's life. However, he was still in the hospital for a month with a broken collarbone, cracked ribs, a dislocated shoulder, and a cracked jaw. He missed the last part of school and had to do summer make-up work to get credit for his classes.

Exercise 2 Each of the following topics has one supporting point that would develop into a paragraph in a composition. Add a *second, third,* and *fourth* supporting point under each topic in the space provided. Add points that support the controlling idea and that could be developed into a paragraph in a composition. When you finish, show your supporting points to your instructor.

Example *Topic:* car maintenance
Controlling Idea: There are four things you should do to keep your car in good shape.
Supporting Points for Paragraph: 1. changing the oil regularly
2. annual tune-ups
3. tire maintenance
4. cleaning and waxing

1. *Topic:* being successful in college
   Controlling Idea: Being successful in college doesn't come by accident.
   Supporting Points for Paragraph:
   1. studying for tests
   2. making use of spare time
   3. keeping good notes
   4. showing up for class
2. *Topic:* my old high school
   Controlling Idea: There's a lot that can be done to improve my old high school.
   Supporting Points for Paragraph:
   1. get rid of lazy teachers
   2. allow students to be more involved
   3. change the appearance

4. get parents involved

3. *Topic:* budgeting your money
   Controlling Idea: It's possible to survive on a tight budget.
   Supporting Points for Paragraph:

   1. write out a monthly budget
   2. bring your lunch to work
   3. buy only the necessities
   4. allow yourself to go out once a month

4. *Topic:* alligators
   Controlling Idea: An alligator could make a great pet.
   Supporting Points for Paragraph:

   1. better than a watchdog
   2. ______________________
   3. ______________________
   4. ______________________

5. *Topic:* Haskell
   Controlling Idea: Haskell is an unusual person.
   Supporting Points for Paragraph:

   1. strange sense of humor
   2. ______________________
   3. ______________________
   4. ______________________

6. *Topic:* spring semester
   Controlling Idea: Spring semester drags on forever.
   Supporting Points for Paragraph:

   1. not many breaks
   2. to many outdoor things to do
   3. to many distractions
   4. thoughts of summer break

7. *Topic:* Christmas
   Controlling Idea: Christmas can be a bad time of year.
   Supporting Points for Paragraph:

   1. not enough money to buy things
   2. homeless people

3. no work
4. death rate up

8. *Topic:* living at home
Controlling Idea: Living at home while going to college has its advantages.
Supporting Points for Paragraph:

1. no rent
2. no distracting parties
3. no sharing the bathroom
4. family support

Exercise 3 Now write a third and fourth paragraph for one of the following compositions using *two* of the supporting points you listed in Exercise 2 for that particular topic. Begin each paragraph with a *topic sentence* that expresses the main point for that paragraph and then develop the paragraph with strong supporting sentences.

Sample Composition

Topic: car maintenance

There is no mystery to getting a long life from your car. However, some people send their cars to the graveyard prematurely. If you aren't getting at least 100,000 miles from a car, you are one of these people. There are four basic things you can do to keep your car in good shape.

First, you need to change the oil regularly. Most mechanics recommend that you change the oil at least every 3,000 miles. However, you might want to change it even more often than that. Check your oil regularly, and if it is showing very black on the dipstick, that indicates that it is dirty enough to be changed. The oil serves as the lubricant for your engine to keep all parts running smoothly, and when the oil becomes dirty, it does a poorer job; consequently, your engine won't last as long.

Next, you need to have your engine tuned up at least once a year. With a typical tune-up, the spark plugs and distributor points are replaced, the carburetor is adjusted, and all engine fluids—oil, radiator coolant, brake and transmission fluid—are checked. This is also a good time to have all of your hoses replaced and your brakes checked for wear. The annual tune-up is basically a preventive measure to keep your car in good running condition and to keep everything from running down or wearing out at an unexpected time.

Third Paragraph:

Another important part of auto care is tire maintenance. More accidents are caused by bad tires than by any auto malfunction. It's important to start with a good set of tires on your car, preferably steel-belted radials for the greatest safety and best wear, and to check them regularly for leaks or uneven wear. Have your tires rotated every 3,000 to 4,000 miles for the most even wear, and have them balanced if the car starts to vibrate at higher speeds. Taking good care of your tires is the best way to get 30,000 to 40,000 miles out of them and to ensure your safety.

Fourth Paragraph:

Finally, it pays to keep you car cleaned and waxed. Washing a car regularly keeps substances off the car, like grease or bird droppings, that can stain or spot the paint. If you clean the chrome every week or two, there is less chance that it will become water stained. Cleaning and vacuuming the interior will make the car more pleasant to ride in and will help your seats and carpeting last longer. Waxing the car at least twice a year protects the paint against oxidation, helps prevent rusting, and keeps the car looging good. Moreover, all of these things will keep the car looking better longer, which will add to its resale value.

1. *Topic:* my old high school

After being out of high school for four years, I can look back at it pretty objectively. While I enjoyed going there, I realize now that Lincoln High had its problems. There is a lot that can be done to improve my old high school.

First, I'd get rid of the entire English department. There are some very nice people on the English staff, but they do a lousy job of teaching English. In four years of high school English classes, I was asked to write about four papers. The rest of the time was spent doing grammar exercises, vocabulary sheets, and all kinds of workbook fill-ins. When I got to college, I was competing with students from other high schools who had written hundreds of papers during high school. While they were whipping out their writing assignments, I was struggling to put a few poorly chosen words on paper. My college experience has taught me that you can't learn to write very well without doing it, and the students are not doing it at my high school. The school board should bring in some new English teachers who will have the students write.

Next, I'd have some new and interesting classes added to the curriculum. There is not one exciting class offered at the high school. While some high schools offer classes in computer programming, backpacking, marine biology, or environmental protection, my high school plugs along with the basic college prep and vocational courses. Each year I ended up taking the same selection of courses—one from English, one from science, one from math, one from history, and one from foreign language. If a student could take just one interesting or unusual class a semester, it would sure make school less boring and routine.

Third Paragraph:

Fourth Paragraph:

2. *Topic:* Christmas

Christmas is the best time of year for everyone. That's what we want to believe, at least. However, Christmas time doesn't always hold the joy that people would like it to. In fact, more people become depressed around Christmas time than any time of year. Although it may sound strange, Christmas can end up being a bad time of year.

The last couple of Christmases, I haven't had enough money to buy much of anything. It's no fun going shopping for Christmas presents when you can't afford 90 percent of the things in the stores. I hate giving cheap presents to my relatives and friends, so sometimes I don't buy them anything. They understand the problem, but it doesn't make me feel any better, especially when I get nice things from other people.

I also don't like the cold weather around Christmas time. I like to do things outdoors, and when it's cold and wet out, I usually stay cooped up inside. I get bored and grouchy and wind up irritating everyone in the house. When there is a rare sunny day, I'll go for a long walk downtown or play some basketball at one of the school grounds. But most of the days around Christmas are cold, drizzly, and sunless, so I just lie around the house and get depressed.

Third Paragraph:

Fourth Paragraph:

Controlling Idea

Just as a paragraph has a main point to center on, a composition has a main idea that helps shape the paper for the writer and reader. Since it is this main idea that controls what goes into a composition, it is called the *controlling idea* for the composition.

Here are the main features of an effective *controlling idea* for a composition:

1. The controlling idea is the *main idea* that the writer is developing in a composition. The controlling idea usually expresses a definite opinion or attitude about the topic for the composition. (Please read the bracketed ([ ]) controlling idea statements for the compositions on pages 197–199.)

2. The controlling idea can be *supported* within the paragraphs of a composition. (For example, if a writer's controlling idea on the topic of tariffs is "the United States needs strong tariffs on foreign goods to protect American industries," the writer needs to be able to support that controlling idea in a number of well-developed paragraphs.)
3. The controlling idea gives *direction* to the composition. It lets the reader know what to expect, and it gives the writer a *definite focus* for the entire composition.
4. The paragraphs within a composition are related to the controlling idea like the sentences within a paragraph are related to its topic sentence. It is the controlling idea that ties all the paragraphs together and makes them a part of the larger composition concept.
5. Without a controlling idea, a composition lacks focus. The writer has nothing to center the composition on, and the reader may ask, "What is the writer's point?"

Here are examples of a number of *controlling ideas* for specific composition topics.

General Topic: animals
Specific Subject: horses
Controlling Idea: Raising horses is an expensive hobby.

General Topic: college
Specific Subject: aeronautics department
Controlling Idea: The college aeronautics program is one of the most innovative in the country.

General Topic: weather
Specific Subject: summer in the southern states
Controlling Idea: Summer weather in the Deep South can drain a visitor.

General Topic: sex
Specific Subject: premarital sex
Controlling Idea: Sexually transmitted diseases are changing the sexual habits of millions of singles in the United States.

General Topic: exercise
Specific Subject: aerobic dancing
Controlling Idea: Aerobic dancing classes waste a person's time and energy.

General Topic: state
Specific Subject: Alaska
Controlling Idea: Alaska beckons adventurers as the last great American frontier.

General Topic: insects
Specific Subject: ants
Controlling Idea: Nobody works harder than an ant.

Exercise 4 Select the letter of the best controlling idea for a composition from the choices given. Then compare your answers with the answer key.

Example

a. Drinking and driving is a problem some people have.
(b.) Drunk driving is the leading cause of fatal accidents in the United States.
c. People who drive drunk cause problems for other drivers.

1. a. Divorce is something that many people go through.
   b. Divorce in the United States is increasing alarmingly.
   (c.) Divorce is the legal dissolution of a marriage.
2. a. Acid rain is occurring in the United States.
   b. Acid rain is rainfall with chemicals in it.
   (c.) Acid rain is one of the leading environmental problems today.
3. a. There is a difference between U.S. exports and imports.
   b. The United States is in the import and the export business.
   (c.) The large gap between American exports and imports is hurting the economy.
4. (a.) Millions of Americans are still risking their health by smoking.
   b. Smoking is a habit that millions of Americans have.
   c. Smoking is still a topic for discussion in the United States.
5. a. We visit Uncle Charlie once a year at Christmas.
   (b.) Our Christmas visit to Uncle Charlie's is usually a disaster.
   c. We visit Uncle Charlie in Baton Rouge when we vacation.
6. a. I remember going to grandma's in the summer.
   (b.) I have special memories of visiting grandma in the summer.
   c. Visiting grandma in the summer was something I used to do.
7. a. There are overcrowded schools across the country.
   b. Overcrowding in the classrooms means there are too many students per class.
   (c.) Overcrowded classrooms create major educational problems across the country.

8. a. Some children learn to play the piano early.
   b. There are benefits in a child learning to play the piano early.
   c. Children learn to play the piano at different ages.

9. a. Our phone bill for March was over $100.
   b. We got a high phone bill this last month.
   c. March's $100 phone bill is a mystery to all of us.

10. a. We have one car for our family.
    b. Having only one car for a family of six creates problems.
    c. Everyone in our family of six drives one car.

Exercise 5 Write a *controlling idea* for the following specific subjects. Decide on a definite opinion or attitude about the topic that you could support in a composition. When you finish, show your controlling ideas to your instructor.

Examples

General Topic: music
Specific Subject: classical music
Controlling Idea: Teenagers are taking more interest in classical music than ever before.

General Topic: car repairs
Specific Subject: charging a battery
Controlling Idea: Charging a battery is a simple process.

1. *General Topic:* breakfast
   Specific Subject: the importance of breakfast
   Controlling Idea: Breakfast gives you body the energe needed to start the day.

2. *General Topic:* crime
   Specific Subject: drug-related crime
   Controlling Idea: Drug-related crime has become a big problem in our cities.

3. *General Topic:* vacation
   Specific Subject: planning a weekend vacation
   Controlling Idea: When planning a weekend vacation you must be very organized.

4. *General Topic:* cars
   Specific Subject: fast cars
   Controlling Idea: In neighborhoods & cities fast cars are becomeing more & more dangereous.

5. *General Topic:* marriage

   Specific Subject: when to marry

   Controlling Idea: When to marry is question many of us ask.

6. *General Topic:* major in college

   Specific Subject: selecting a major

   Controlling Idea: When selecting a major, you should pick something of interest to you.

Exercise 6 In this exercise, you are given the *general topic* only. First, decide on a *specific subject* within the general topic area, and then write a *controlling idea* for that specific subject. When you finish, show your subjects and controlling ideas to your instructor.

Examples

General Topic: winter sport
Specific Subject: skiing
Controlling Idea: snow skiing is an expensive sport to take up.

General Topic: leisure-time activities
Specific Subject: video games
Controlling Idea: video games are declining in popularity.

1. *General Topic:* food

   Specific Subject: fruit

   Controlling Idea: Fruit is not only a nutrious food but its all natural too.

2. *General Topic:* grades

   Specific Subject: above average

   Controlling Idea: Above average shows interest & more dedication than an average student

3. *General Topic:* occupation

   Specific Subject: Bankers

   Controlling Idea: Banking is an ever changing field.

4. *General Topic:* religion

   Specific Subject: catholic

   Controlling Idea: There are things about the catholic religion I do not like.

5. *General Topic:* family

   Specific Subject: brother or sister

   Controlling Idea: I would not want to grow ~~[illegible]~~ up without a brother or a sister

Opening Paragraph

Most compositions begin with an opening paragraph that introduces the topic and controlling idea to give the readers a sense of what lies ahead. Here are the features that most effective openings have in common.

1. An opening paragraph provides some *lead-in* information to the topic. The lead-in may include any of the following:
   a. a personal experience or observation
   b. factual information related to the topic
   c. an incident or event that is related to the topic
   d. background information important to the topic
   e. an invented situation that dramatizes the importance of the topic
2. An opening paragraph *clearly introduces the topic* of the composition to the readers.
3. An opening paragraph often concludes with the *controlling idea* for the composition so readers understand where the composition is heading. The *controlling idea* often states a definite opinion or attitude about the topic.
4. An opening paragraph creates *interest* in the topic for the readers and emphasizes the *importance* of the topic. Interest is often created in the *lead-in* to the topic, and a topic's importance is often shown by how the topic relates to the readers.
5. An opening paragraph usually does *not* get into the *supporting points* for the controlling idea in any detail. These come in the paragraphs *following* the opening.

Here are examples of a number of opening paragraphs for compositions. The underlined sentence expresses the controlling idea for the composition. Read each opening paragraph carefully before going on to the next exercise.

Topic: one bad rabbit (personal experience lead-in)

A year ago I saw an ad in the paper for a 1980 Volkswagen Rabbit with only 22,000 miles on it. The asking price was $4,000, so I drove to the listed address to take a look at the car. The car looked in good shape and was very clean. When I took it for a test drive, it performed well. So I offered the man $3,500 for the Rabbit and he took it. Little did I know then that within a year I would have put another $2,000 into the car just to keep it running. <u>That Volkswagen Rabbit turned out to be the worst car I ever owned.</u>

Topic: Sarah's sandwich shop (factual information lead-in)

In the last five years, four different people have owned the sandwich shop on the corner of G and Tate. One owner put in new booths, another added an ice cream parlor, and the third added hot sandwiches to the menu. However, none of them made enough money to keep the sandwich shop going, so they all sold out. The current owner, Thelma Sayer, is doing twice the business of the other owners, and she hasn't changed one thing in the shop. She has put all of her money into area-wide advertising, and that is why the sandwich shop is doing a good business.

Topic: the need for CPR training (invented situation lead-in)

If you were at a restaurant with a friend who started choking on a piece of meat, how would you help him? If you pulled an unconscious child out of a swimming pool, how would you try to revive her? You never know when you might be in an emergency situation where someone's life depends on what you do. Without the proper training, you may have little luck helping the choking person or the unconscious child. However, if you had been trained in CPR (Cardio-Pulmonary Resuscitation) procedures, your chances of helping would have been excellent. Since you never know when someone may need your help, you should take a CPR course as soon as possible.

Topic: changing student attitudes (background information lead-in)

Fifteen years ago, *Trend* magazine surveyed a large group of college seniors about their career choices. In order of importance, their main concerns were to find a career that was interesting, that benefited others, and that paid the bills. Fifteen years later, in 1985, *Trend* conducted the same survey on the latest senior class. In order of importance, their main concerns were a career that paid very well, that provided security, and that offered good benefits. The results of the survey showed a definite change of attitude among college seniors about their career concerns. Today's students are more oriented toward money and security than students fifteen years ago.

Topic: the nonbook bookstore (personal experience lead-in)

This summer I was browsing through a bookstore in the mall hoping to find a good novel to read. I found lots of dieting and exercise books, books showing me how to get rich fast, photo books with close-ups of any part of the human anatomy you wanted, popular magazines, cassette tapes, computer software, travelogues, sex guides, and books on tape. Finally, in a back corner of the bookstore, I found a small section of real books: novels and short story collections written by skilled authors. I suddenly realized that in today's bookstore business, the least important piece of merchandise is a good book.

Notice that all the sample opening paragraphs have similar features: lead-in information that relates to the topic, introduction of the topic, and a controlling idea for the composition at the end of the paragraph. The first paragraph begins with a personal experience lead-in, the second with factual information, the third with invented incidents, the fourth with background information, and the fifth with a personal experience.

For a final opening paragraph example, here are three opening paragraphs written for the *same* topic, with each paragraph providing a different kind of lead-in. With classmates, discuss which opening you feel is most effective and why.

Sample Paragraphs

Topic: buying a used car

Controlling Idea: You need to follow a few basic rules to help you find a good used car.

First Opening Paragraph: (factual information lead-in; controlling idea underlined)

Over a million Americans will buy a used car this year. Some of them will get good deals and drive their cars for many years. Others, however, will wind up with real "lemons," cars that create nothing but costly problems. There is always some risk involved in buying a used car off a car lot or from an individual, but people who know something about buying used cars minimize that risk considerably. For anyone who is thinking about buying a used car, there are a few basic rules to follow for getting a good deal.

Second Opening Paragraph: (personal experience lead-in; controlling idea underlined)

Three years ago our family bought a 1978 Oldsmobile station wagon from a dealer in Akron. We wanted a wagon so that our family of six could travel more comfortably, and the Oldsmobile was roomy and priced right. We paid cash for the wagon, got the pink slip, and our problems began. The first trip we took out of town, the transmission went out completely, and we spent our $300 of vacation money on a rebuilt transmission. We also began to notice a vibration throughout the wagon when we drove over sixty miles an hour. We bought new tires to smooth out the ride, but the vibration was still there. We took it to a mechanic, and he noticed that the front end of the wagon had been repainted. He looked underneath the car and said, "This car has been in a bad accident, and the frame is badly bent. There's not much you can do about the vibration." As the year wore on, we also discovered that our Oldsmobile was a gas hog and an oil user. We finally unloaded it on another unsuspecting party, but we lost nearly $2,000 overall. We learned the hard way that buying a used car is a risky business. However, since then we've learned to follow a few basic rules for buying used cars, and we've come out a lot better.

Third Opening Paragraph: (invented situation lead-in; controlling idea underlined)

Here you stand at Honest Harley's Used Car Heaven, the biggest used car dealership in the city. In front of you sit hundreds of gleaming used cars just waiting to be driven home. On all sides of you are honest-looking salesmen swearing that there isn't a bad buy on the lot. How can you go wrong? The truth is, if Honest Harley's is a typical used car lot, there are some good used cars on the lot and some real dogs, and it's hard to tell the difference by their freshly waxed paint jobs. You could drive away the proud owner of a reasonably priced, reliable car or the depressed owner of an overpriced piece of junk. Although there is always risk involved in buying a used car, there are a few basic rules to follow that will help you separate the good buys from the "lemons."

Exercise 7

Write your own opening paragraph for one of the following topics. Decide on a *controlling idea* for a composition. Then decide on the best kind of lead-in for your subject, using one (or a combination) of the lead-ins introduced on pages 211–212. Then write your opening paragraph, concluding with your controlling idea.

Sample Opening Paragraph

Topic: fixing up a neighborhood

Controlling Idea: If neighbors work together, they can turn a run-down neighborhood into the best-looking block in the area.

Opening Paragraph: (personal experience lead-in; controlling idea underlined)

Walking down Peach Street in my old neighborhood the other day, I was pleasantly surprised. For a stretch of two blocks, every house on both sides of the street looked great. The houses were freshly painted, had new composition shingle roofs, were landscaped with lawns and shrubs, and showed little evidence of their fifty years of wear. Beyond those two blocks, the houses looked like what I had expected: chipped and peeling paint, sagging roofs, and weed-filled yards. Talking to a friend who lived in one of the renovated houses, I found out that the neighbors formed a work force and helped each other restore their homes. If neighbors work together like they did in my old neighborhood, they can turn a block of run-down houses into one of the best-looking neighborhoods in town.

1. *Topic:* choosing a college to attend

   Controlling Idea:

   Opening Paragraph: (kind of lead-in: ____________ ____________)

2. *Topic:* premarital sex

   Controlling Idea:

   Opening Paragraph: (kind of lead-in: ____________________)

3. *Topic:* choosing a major

   Controlling Idea:

   Opening Paragraph: (kind of lead-in: ____________________)

4. *Topic:* teenage drinking

   Controlling Idea:

   Opening Paragraph: (kind of lead-in: ____________________)

5. *Topic:* a particular TV show

   Controlling Idea:

   Opening Paragraph: (kind of lead-in: ____________________)

6. *Topic:* a particular concert

   Controlling Idea:

   Opening Paragraph: (kind of lead-in: ____________________)

7. *Topic:* a special person

   Controlling Idea:

   Opening Paragraph: (kind of lead-in: ____________________)

8. *Topic:* a career you're interested in

   Controlling Idea:

   Opening Paragraph: (kind of lead-in: ____________________)

Exercise 8 Select a topic from Exercise 5, 6, or 7 to write a composition on. Consider a *controlling idea* for your composition, and make a list of *three* or *four* supporting points, ideas, or steps for your controlling idea. Then write a first draft following these suggestions:

1. Begin your composition with an opening paragraph that includes your controlling idea.
2. Develop each main point, idea, or step in a *separate paragraph*.
3. Begin each paragraph with a *topic sentence*.

4. Follow the same guidelines for effective paragraphing that you used to write individual paragraphs in Levels 1 to 3: unity, development, organization, and transitional wording.

5. Write the composition for your classmates to read.

Sample Composition

Topic: a special person
Controlling Idea: Uncle Al was the weirdest relative I ever had.
Supporting Points:
1. strange looks
2. always scaring us
3. unpredictable

Sample First Draft

The first time I met Uncle Al was on our family trip back to Missisipi when I was ten. The relatives I was used to being around were pretty normal. Uncle Al was a big surprise. From the first time I saw him I knew he was going to be weird.

Uncle Al was a strange looking man. He had these big, wild eyes that he stared at you with. And a mouth that was always turned up in an evil-looking crooked kind of smile. He was a tall, bony man with huge hands and ears a red face and a bunch of white hair growing in every direction. He also had a big nose with red veins all over it. The first time I saw him I was already a little bit scared.

To make matters worse, Uncle Al loved to scare my younger sister and me. He'd call us over to where he was sitting on the front porch and, tell us not to go behind the house because there was a crazy man with an ax waiting for us. Or he'd ask us if we'd found the snake that was running around the house, Uncle Al would scared us to death, and when he'd see that he'd shock us good, he'd laugh and cackle and giggle til tears came to his eyes. And he'd say, "You kids from Arizona will believe anything!" One time he showed us where his little toe was missing and said that an aligator that lived under the house had bit it off one time.

Uncle Al was also unpredictable. Some days we wouldn't see him at all, he'd never said where he'd been or what he'd been doing. Some afternoons he'd just rock on his porch for hours and never speak to anyone. Other times he'd round everyone up to play cards or, he'd play the guitar for us and sing his hillbilly songs.

But when he got that gleam in his eye, you knew he was up to mischief, and someone in the family was in for trouble. My mom says he was always kind of whacko since he was just a kid but, that his bark was a lot worse than was his bite. He died the summer when I turned eleven a few weeks before we were going back to visit.

After you finish your first draft, meet with a classmate or small group and analyze the sample first draft, using the following questions as a guide.

1. Does the composition have a definite opening paragraph? What is accomplished? Is there a controlling idea for the composition?

2. Check the paragraphing. Is a different idea, point, step, or incident developed in each paragraph? Do any paragraphs need combining or separating?
3. Check each individual paragraph. Is there a topic sentence? Are the sentences in the clearest order for the reader? Could an example or detail be added anywhere to make a point more interesting?
4. Check individual sentences. Are there any awkward or wordy sentences that need revising? Are there any run-ons or fragments that need correcting? Are there any questionable word choices?
5. Correct any errors in spelling, grammar usage, or punctuation.
6. What is your overall impression of the composition? What did you find interesting? What did the author do well?

When you finish, reread your own draft, using the evaluation questions as a guideline for possible revisions and corrections. Then exchange papers with a classmate or two and analyze each other's drafts. When you are ready, write your final draft, including all revisions and corrections you feel will improve the composition.

Practice Quiz

Take this practice quiz to help prepare for the section quiz. Then compare your answers to the answer key. When you are ready for the section quiz, let your instructor know.

I. Circle the letter that indicates the *best paragraphing* for each composition.

Example

[1]I get to the coast about once a year, and when I went in July, the first couple of days were cold and foggy. [2]Then the wind came up in the middle of the week, and you needed a jacket just to walk the beach. [3]However, the trip wasn't a total waste. [4]The last day I was there was a perfect day at the beach. [5]First, the weather was ideal. [6]The temperature was in the high 70s, so it was cool enough to lie out comfortably yet warm enough to enjoy the water. [7]There was a gentle breeze that kept the air from getting muggy. [8]There were just enough clouds floating by to cover the sun every fifteen minutes or so and give sunbathers a break. [9]The crowd was also perfect. [10]There were a lot of people on the beach, but it wasn't badly crowded. [11]You had plenty of room to lay out your mats and umbrellas, and the body surfing area wasn't too congested. [12]Yet, there were enough people around of all ages to make things interesting. [13]There were tanners, surfers, Frisbee tossers, joggers, volleyballers, boogie boarders, and body builders. [14]The best thing about the day was the water. [15]The water temperature was around 70 degrees, just right for staying in without getting cold. [16]The waves were breaking regularly, and they were about three to four feet high, just right for body surfing. [17]They were also breaking close enough to the shore that you didn't have to swim half a mile

to catch them. [18]There was no riptide or undertow to worry about, so the conditions were about as safe as possible.

(a.) Begin paragraphs with sentence numbers 1, 5, 9, and 14.

b. Begin paragraphs with sentence numbers 1, 9, and 13.

c. Begin paragraphs with sentence numbers 1, 7, 12, and 15.

1. [1]I've worked during the summer since I was in high school. [2]I worked at a playground one summer and at a video store another. [3]When I applied for a gas station job the summer of my second year in college, I didn't know what to expect. [4]Working at Premium Gas Station turned out to be a rough job. [5]The weather was terrible. [6]There was a five-week heat wave of 100+ degree temperatures, and the asphalt around the station added another ten degrees. [7]The garage area was enclosed on three sides so that the heat didn't escape well, and by mid-afternoon it felt like an oven. [8]I was drenched in sweat most of the time and longing for even the mildest breeze. [9]Another problem was the gas line. [10]A new resort had opened in the hills above town, and hundreds of cars and vans streamed through town and into the station. [11]It was a never-ending job pumping gas, checking oil, airing tires, and making out tags. [12]Sometimes I'd go five or six hours at the pump without a break. [13]To top things off, I had foot problems most of the summer. [14]I was not used to standing on hard pavement eight to ten hours a day, and my feet got very sore. [15]I have small feet and weigh around 220 pounds, so my feet are really overloaded. [16]I limped around most of the time, but it never was bad enough to quit working. [17]Besides, I needed the money. [18]But that constant pain in my feet kept me on edge a lot of the time.

a. Begin paragraphs with sentence numbers 1, 8, and 15.

(b.) Begin paragraphs with sentence numbers 1, 5, 9, and 13.

c. Begin paragraphs with sentence numbers 1, 4, 8, and 12.

2. [1]Summer school has always been a drag: long, boring classes and lots of work. [2]I'd go to summer school to catch up on some units or get a requirement out of the way. [3]However, last summer was different. [4]I really enjoyed summer school for the first time. [5]I was only taking one class—Film Appreciation—so I wasn't pressed. [6]Normally I take two classes which run from 8:00 to 12:00. [7]With one class, I was finished by 10:00 and had plenty of time to study or relax before going to work at 3:00. [8]Taking one class instead of two made a big difference. [9]I also enjoyed the class a lot. [10]We got to see films every day, and some of them were great. [11]We saw a lot of classics, like *Gone with the Wind, Citizen Kane,* and *High Noon*, and some bizarre foreign films with English subtitles, like Fellini's *8½*. [12]We also got to go to two movie sets in New York and watched a film being shot on location in New Jersey. [13]It was a perfect class for the summer. [14]I also learned to be a better film critic. [15]Before taking the class, I couldn't tell a bad film from a good one. [16]Now I look for all kinds of things in a movie: lighting, camera techniques, acting, and realism. [17]I don't enjoy some

movies the way I would have before, but it's nice to have more insight into film making than most movie-goers.

a. Begin paragraphs with sentence numbers 1, 5, and 11.

b. Begin paragraphs with sentence numbers 1, 5, 9, and 14.

c. Begin paragraphs with sentence numbers 1, 4, 8, and 12.

II. Circle the letter of the sentence with the best *controlling idea* for a composition.

Example

a. The new auditorium was built just last summer.

b. The new auditorium replaced the old one that was torn down.

c. The new auditorium is a big improvement over the old one.

1. a. Summer break is coming up in two weeks.

   b. I am really looking forward to summer break this year.

   c. Summer break comes between the spring and fall semesters and lasts three months.

2. a. The college is increasing the cost of tuition.

   b. The tuition increase at the college is unfair.

   c. The college has a new tuition rate for students.

3. a. Some people wait until they are in their 30s to have children.

   b. Some people have children in their 20s and some have them in their 30s.

   c. There are advantages to a couple waiting until their 30s to have children.

4. a. Baking chocolate chip cookies is something I do.

   b. I eat most of the chocolate chip cookies that I make.

   c. Making chocolate chip cookies is fun and easy.

5. a. Soviet bloc countries are becoming more westernized.

   b. Soviet bloc countries are changing in one way.

   c. Soviet bloc countries are being influenced by some countries.

6. a. Penicillin is a common drug.

   b. Penicillin is a prescription drug that I use.

   c. Penicillin is the most widely used prescription drug in America.

7. a. We took a trip to Nashville last summer.

   b. Our trip to Nashville last summer took a week.

   c. Our trip to Nashville last summer was wonderful.

8. a. The six-week drought caused severe problems for farmers.

   b. The six-week drought had an effect on farmers.

   c. The drought in this area lasted six weeks.

9. a. I took a math final on Friday.
   b. Friday's math final was the worst I've ever taken.
   c. Friday's math final is over.

10. a. Dealing with terrorists is a complex problem.
   b. Terrorists are a group that we deal with.
   c. There are terrorists in the world today.

III. Circle the letter of the best opening paragraph for a composition from each group.

Example

a. When I first enrolled at Harvey College, I thought I had the expenses figured out for the semester. I knew how much tuition would cost, and I knew what my share of the apartment rent was. I had budgeted a certain amount of money to live on each month based on the average expenses I had figured. However, after the first month, I had spent $100 over my budget, and I was in trouble. There are a lot of hidden expenses in going to college that I hadn't counted on.

b. When I first enrolled at Harvey College, I thought I had the expenses for the semester figured out. Boy, was I wrong!

c. When I first enrolled at Harvey College, I thought I had the expenses figured out for the semester. I had figured out all of my college costs and my living costs and written them down. However, after a month of school, I found out I didn't have a few things figured in the budget. This set me back financially, and I still had four months to go.

1. a. When I was in high school, most of the students were about the same. They were in their teens, they dressed alike, they had similar interests, and they were from the valley. However, when I went to college, I had students in my classes who were in their forties and fifties, students from Nigeria and the Philippines, students wearing everything from bathing suits to sarongs, and students with widely different interests and backgrounds. I realized that in college, there is a place for anyone who wants to attend.

   b. When I was in high school, everything was about the same. Nothing stood out as being different from anything else. However, when I went to college, many things were different. I enjoy college more than I did high school because of these differences.

   c. When I was in high school, most of the students were about the same. They were in their teens, they dressed alike, they had similar interests, and they were from the valley. However, when I went to college, the students weren't the same. College students are different from high school students. That is why I enjoy college more than high school.

2. a. Since my mom has gotten on a health kick, she no longer cooks a lot of things we loved to eat. Now we are eating something different, and lots of it. She thinks that this food is better for us than what we used to eat, and she can buy it more cheaply. One thing I've found out since mom started serving one item: there are a lot of different ways to cook it.

b. Since my mom has gotten on a health kick, she no longer cooks a lot of things we loved to eat, like pork chops, roasts, spareribs, and steaks. Now we get one kind of meat almost every day—chicken. Mom thinks that chicken is the best thing for us to eat, and it's also fairly cheap. One thing I've learned since we've started on this new diet: There are a lot of good ways to cook chicken.

c. Since my mom has gotten on a health kick, she no longer cooks a lot of things we loved to eat, like pork chops, roasts, spareribs, and steaks. Now we get one kind of meat every day—chicken. Mom thinks that chicken is good for us, and it's also fairly cheap. It costs about half as much as most of the meats mom used to buy. We used to eat very little chicken, but now we eat it all the time.

3. a. I've tried a lot of different exercises, but walking is the best exercise for me.

b. I've tried a lot of different exercises, but I've never stuck with any of them. I swam for a while, but when the weather got cold, I quit. I tried jogging, but that really wore me out. I played racquetball for a few months, but I couldn't find a person to play with regularly. Then I read about a form of exercise that I didn't even consider exercise. I tried it for a month, and it was so easy that I kept doing it. This exercise is great for me because it keeps me in shape without killing me.

c. I've tried a lot of different exercises, but I've never stuck with any of them. I swam for a while, but when the weather got cold, I quit. I tried jogging, but that really wore me out. I played racquetball for a few months, but I couldn't find anyone to play with regularly. Then I read in a magazine that just plain walking was a great exercise. I started walking a half hour a day, and it didn't hurt at all. I can walk at a good pace, enjoy the scenery, talk to people I meet, and come back home feeling great. For people who want to exercise without killing themselves, walking is the way to go.

4. a. I love watching television on Saturdays, and I'll watch just about any sports program that's on. I love watching football and basketball because of all the action. I also enjoy track, swimming, bowling and golf on TV. I'll even watch big-time wrestling or roller derby on a late Saturday afternoon. However, there is one sport that I can't stand watching on television. The game is just too slow for me to sit through. Of all the sports on TV, that one is the worst.

b. I love watching television on Saturdays, and I'll watch just about any sports show that's on. However, the one sport that I can't stand to watch on TV is baseball. Baseball is a very slow game to watch. If the pitchers are doing well, you may not see anything but a ball being pitched back and forth for a few hours. When there is some action, it only lasts a few seconds and then it's back to watching nine guys stand around with mitts on. I usually fall asleep sometime during the game and miss the grand slam home run or triple play that is fun to watch. However, 99 percent of the time, I can sleep during a baseball game and miss nothing.

c. I love watching television on Saturdays, and I'll watch just about any sports show that's on. I love watching football and basketball because of all the action. I also enjoy track, swimming, bowling, and golf on TV. I'll even watch big-time wrestling or roller derby on a late Saturday afternoon. However, there is one sport that I can't stand watching on TV, and that is baseball. There is nothing more boring than watching Saturday's baseball "game of the week" on the tube.

5. a. In England a year ago, a man poisoned his wife. That may sound like a simple murder case, but it wasn't. The woman had painful terminal cancer and was in agony. She had lived a long life, and all she wanted was to die. She asked her husband of fifty years to end her life for her, and they signed a pact to that effect. The husband administered a shot of lethal chemical into her blood system, and she went to sleep and never woke up. Did the husband commit a murder to be punished for or an act of mercy to be commended? Mercy killing, or euthanasia, is a complex subject for which there are no easy answers.

   b. In England a year ago, a man poisoned his wife. That may sound like a simple murder case, but it wasn't. The woman had an illness, and she was in pain. She wanted her husband to end her life for her, and he agreed to. He gave her something that killed her, but he did it because he loved her. It is difficult to judge his act.

   c. In England a year ago, a man poisoned his wife. That may sound like a simple murder case, but it wasn't. There were circumstances surrounding the murder that put it in a different light. Some people felt the murder was an act of mercy. The man and woman had lived together for fifty years, and she had agreed to the murder. The whole situation raises some complex legal questions.

6. a. In Texas and Arkansas last month, over one hundred children's beauty contests were held. In those contests many children of all ages competed for awards. Some of the contestants competed more than once. Children's beauty pageants are becoming very popular, particularly in one section of the country. Very young girls are getting all fixed up to be judged on certain attributes. Many people think that these pageants are fine, but others don't. Are children's beauty pageants good or bad?

   b. In Texas and Arkansas last month, over one hundred children's beauty contests were held. Many psychologists think that these contests do more harm than good. Do these pageants benefit children or exploit them?

   c. In Texas and Arkansas last month, over one hundred children's beauty contests were held. In those contests, over one thousand children from the age of six months to ten years competed for trophies and ribbons, and half of those contestants competed in at least two of the contests. Children's beauty pageants are becoming very popular, particularly in the southern states. Very young girls are putting on makeup, bathing suits, and big smiles to be judged on their beauty and poise. Most of the mothers and fathers of the contestants think that these pageants are wonderful, but some child psychologists believe they do more harm than good. Are children's beauty pageants harmless diversions for children or a dangerous form of child exploitation?

The Sentence

As a writer, you are judged by your readers in two ways: by your ideas and how you express them. Since many writers, including yourself, have interesting experiences and good ideas to share with readers, it is the ability to *express those ideas effectively* that separates the better writers. Each section on "The Sentence" is concerned with how you put your thoughts in writing: the structures you use and the wording you choose to communicate with your readers.

Sentence Variety

Section Topic

Complex Sentences with Relative Clauses

To write most effectively, you need to be familiar with a variety of sentence structures. Another useful structure is introduced in this section: the complex sentence with the *relative clause*.

Complex Sentences with Relative Clauses

In Levels 3 and 4, you have written complex sentences containing *subordinating conjunctions* such as *when, before, as, because, if,* and *although*. Another type of complex sentence contains a *relative clause*, so named because it begins with a *relative pronoun: who, which,* or *that*.

Here are the key features of complex sentences with relative clauses.

1. These complex sentences contain two parts: a *relative clause* beginning with a relative pronoun and an *independent clause* that can stand alone as a sentence.
2. The relative *clause* begins with a *relative pronoun: who, which,* or *that.*
3. The relative clause *modifies* the word that it follows in the independent clause:

   The man who invited us to dinner is a sharp dresser. (The relative clause *who invited us to dinner* modifies *man.*)

   The chair that you just sat in is fifty years old. (The relative clause *that you just sat in* modifies *chair.*)

   Samsonite luggage, which is reasonably priced, is a popular graduation gift. (The relative clause *which is reasonably priced* modifies *luggage.*)
4. The relative clause may modify a word at the beginning, in the middle, or at the end of the independent clause:

   A duck that just flew by here had orange tail feathers.

   I met a man who lives in Missouri when I flew from Houston to Shreveport.

   You are all invited to the surprise party that begins at 7:00 p.m.
5. If you remove the relative clause from a complex sentence, a *complete sentence* remains:

   Mr. Javier, who is the mayor of Salem, was born in France.
   Mr. Javier was born in France.

   The woman that I just met belongs to six charity organizations.
   The woman belongs to six charity organizations.

The relative pronouns *who, that,* and *which* are used in the following ways in complex sentences:

*who:** used with *people*, whether *named* or *not identified by name*

The Miller twins, who bought the Sutter house, are not from this area.
The women who live together on I Street are cousins.
Gladys Ormsby, who teaches mechanical drawing, also has her law degree.

The fellow who brought you home is still parked outside.

that: used with *things*

The building that caught on fire was condemned a month ago.
The trees that you pulled out were over two hundred years old.
The lake that Freddie lives by is man-made.

used (interchangeably with "who") with *people* who are *not identified by name*

The children that go to the academy school have learning handicaps.
The men that belong to the lodge raise money for many charities.
I'd like to meet the boy that won the district speech contest.

which: used with *things*

The Alexander Bridge, which was built in 1927, spans the Feather River.
The party which you threw for my birthday was really wild.
Our car is parked in the Hagar Lot, which is a mile from the high school.

(*Note: Which* and *that* are interchangeable in modifying "things" except when the modified word is named or specifically identified. In that case, *which* is always used:

Pine Flat Dam, which is above the Kings River, is two hundred feet high.
The Duerkson Science Building, which was built a month ago, has sixteen classrooms.)

**Whom* is the object form of *who*. It is used most frequently *just before the subject of the relative clause:*

The man whom we met yesterday is an electrician. (subject *we*)
The girl whom I introduced you to is stunning. (subject *I*)
Is that the musician whom you wanted me to meet last night? (subject *you*)

Exercise 9 Fill in the best relative pronouns—*who, which,* or *that*—to complete each of the following complex sentences. Also, *underline* the relative clause. When you finish, compare your answers with the answer key.

Examples Sam Ortega, *who* swims for Ladera Oaks, qualified for Senior Nationals.

The groceries *that* you just bought should last for weeks.

The Eiffel Tower, *which* is a tourist attraction, is a Paris landmark.

1. The sweater ______ I bought at Macy's shrank two sizes when I washed it.
2. The men ______ own the C Street realty office buy a lot of land for themselves.
3. Jack's mother, ______ owns a downtown delicatessen, is also a seamstress.
4. The Mecha Christmas party, ______ has become an annual event, is always well attended.
5. Sarah's grandfather enjoys playing shuffleboard, ______ requires a good touch.
6. I'd like to meet the guy ______ put toilet paper in the top of my sycamore tree.
7. A game ______ requires little skill but is fun to play is called Spoons.
8. Murphy Madlock, ______ collects rare stamps, is also a volunteer fireman.
9. The Vietnamese family ______ moved into the neighborhood last week could use some help getting settled.
10. Everyone in town wants to see the traveling Nutter Family Vaudeville Extravaganza, ______ opens next week at the park.
11. Uncle Elmo, ______ posed for *Playgirl* magazine, gets lot of fan mail.
12. The rains of February 1955, ______ were the heaviest ever recorded, are remembered well by long-time residents.

Exercise 10 Fill in your relative clause beginning with *who, which,* or *that* to complete each of the following complex sentences. Then show your sentences to a classmate who is finished and to your instructor.

Examples The crime wave *that has been sweeping the city* is finally on the decline.

Manny Jones, *who is a freshman at Dartmouth*, lives in Santa Rosa Dormitory.

1. The young boy ______ is my nephew.
2. The new house ______ was burglarized last month.
3. The Tule River, ______, is famous for its rapids.
4. I'd like to see those rare white whales ______.
5. The new Secretary of the Interior, ______ is a Democrat.
6. Your sister Sarah, ______, is a very outgoing person.
7. The tall woman ______ is a great runner.

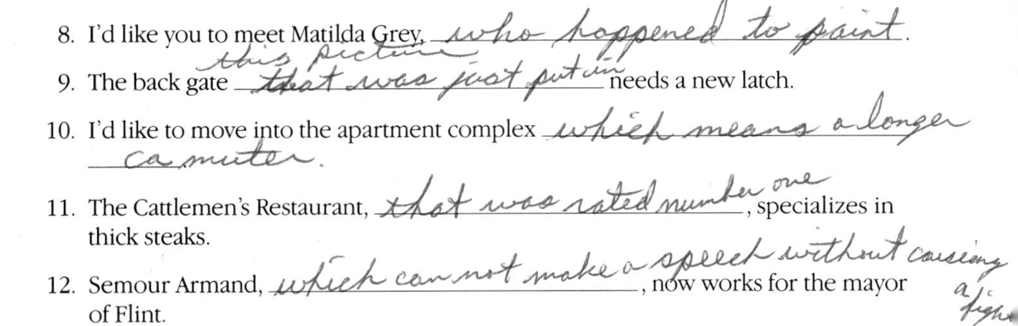

8. I'd like you to meet Matilda Grey, ______________________.
9. The back gate ______________________ needs a new latch.
10. I'd like to move into the apartment complex ______________________.
11. The Cattlemen's Restaurant, ______________________, specializes in thick steaks.
12. Semour Armand, ______________________, now works for the mayor of Flint.

Before you write your own complex sentences with relative clauses, you need to know a few rules of punctuation. Here are the rules for comma usage with relative clauses:

1. If the modified word is *clearly named or identified without* the help of the relative clause, put commas before and after the clause:

   Alex Morgan, who used to live in Albany, has moved to Ontario, Canada. (*Alex Morgan is clearly named, so the relative clause is set off by commas.*)

   Friant Dam, which is located above the Swann River, was built in 1978. (*Friant Dam* is clearly named, so the relative clause is set off by commas.)

   The R Street peach cannery, which opened last week, operates throughout July and August. (*The R Street peach cannery* is clearly identified.)

   The Guillen twins, who attend the same college, do not room together. (*The Guillen twins* are clearly named.)

2. If the modified word is *not* clearly named or identified without the help of the relative clause, the clause is *not* set off by commas. In other words, if the relative clause is *needed* to clearly identify the modified word, don't use commas:

   The man who brought you the roses used to work at Zak's Hardware Store. (*Who brought you the roses* identifies which man.)

   The turnips that you cooked for dinner were delicious. (*That you cooked for dinner* identifies which turnips.)

   The woman who stole my purse should be arrested. (*Who stole my purse* identifies which woman.)

3. *Never use commas* with a relative clause *beginning with that.*

   The man that sent you the dynamite is no friend of mine.
   The dress that you wore to the party looked great on you.
   The horse that is in the big corral is too wild to ride.

Exercise 11 Punctuate the following complex sentences correctly by putting in commas where necessary. If a sentence needs no commas, mark *C* for correct. (*Note:* If a relative clause *ends* the sentence, you only insert *one comma*. Example—I'd really like to meet Nadine, who has a reputation for giving good advice.) When you finish, compare your punctuation with the answer key.

Examples Mary Ann Doeppler, who used to work in the bank, believes in flying saucers.

C The girl that used to work in the bank believes in flying saucers.

C 1. That trip that I just took to Mule Mountain was inexpensive.
C 2. The new cough medicine that I picked up at the drugstore contains no codeine.
3. Yellowstone National Park, which is located in Wyoming, is famous for its geysers.
4. Sally, is going to marry Clyde Walker, who just graduated from, Missouri State Teachers College.
C 5. My friends who took me to the mall last weekend are from Pittsburgh.
6. Emily Lewis, who used to work at a 7-11 store, now manages the new antique store in town.
7. My old 1956 Ford, which was the best car I ever owned, is probably a rusted heap of junk by now.
C 8. The carpet store that opened last week on Broad Street is having a sale on throw rugs.
9. I'd like to meet Phil Collins, who seems like a funny man on his videos.
10. The paintings that were causing the most excitement at the museum were painted, by Ferdie.

Exercise 12 Write your own complex sentences including the relative clauses provided. Make sure the relative clause comes directly after the word it modifies. Remember to put *commas* before and after the relative clause *if the modified word is clearly named or identified*. Otherwise, do not separate the clause with commas. When you finish, share your sentences with a classmate who has finished and with your instructor.

Examples that I brought to school

The bug collection that I brought to school was over four years old.

who lives on Feed Street

Jenny Long, who lives on Feed Street, is in two of my classes.

which runs through the center of town

The Stanley River, which runs through the center of town, is free of pollution.

1. that is good for your teeth
2. who live in the Mojave Desert
3. who ran for president in 1988
4. which dropped eight inches of rain last week
5. who lives on a four-acre dairy farm
6. that crawl around my kitchen
7. who used to work for Sears
8. which is known for its outstanding pizza and spaghetti
9. that any child can learn to play
10. who is an excellent athlete

Exercise 13 Write your own complex sentences with relative clauses, using the relative pronouns and comma instructions provided. When you finish, show your sentences to your instructor.

Examples *who* clause with commas

Sylvia Plath, who was a respected poet, committed suicide at the height of her success.

that clause (*that* clauses are never set off by commas)

The movie that I saw on cable TV last night was about an owl named Hortensia.

which clause with commas

The C Street mission, which is open all day on Saturday, is closed on Sunday.

1. *that* clause
2. *which* clause with commas
3. *who* clause without commas
4. *who* clause with commas
5. *that* clause
6. *which* clause with commas

7. *who* clause with commas

8. *who* clause without commas

Practice Quiz

Take this practice quiz to prepare for the section quiz. Then compare your answers with the answer key. When you are ready for the section quiz, let your instructor know.

I. Circle the letter of the complex sentence containing the appropriate *relative pronoun*.

Example

a. Marty Shaw, who runs the gas station on R Street, is my grandfather.
b. Marty Shaw, that runs the gas station on R Street, is my grandfather.

1. a. The finals that I took on Thursday were more difficult than I expected.
   b. The finals who I took on Thursday were more difficult than I expected.
2. a. Mary Slade, which is the mother of twins, is a twin herself.
   b. Mary Slade, who is the mother of twins, is a twin herself.
3. a. College tuition, that is a student's biggest expense, is increasing every year.
   b. College tuition, which is a student's biggest expense, is increasing every year.
4. a. The roast beef who I got at the cafeteria was tough as leather.
   b. The roast beef that I got at the cafeteria was tough as leather.
5. a. Those new exercises that you do for strengthening your lower back make you more flexible.
   b. Those new exercises who you do for strengthening your lower back make you more flexible.
6. a. I would like you to meet Angie Goodard, that is a sports columnist for the Delta Star.
   b. I would like you to meet Angie Goodard, who is a sports columnist for the Delta Star.
7. a. The Statue of Liberty, which is a symbol of freedom, has recently been restored.
   b. The Statue of Liberty, that is a symbol of freedom, has recently been restored.
8. a. The young women which work at the new drive-up bank are very courteous.
   b. The young women who work at the new drive-up bank are very courteous.
9. a. An issue who is receiving much debate in the legislature is the legalization of marijuana.

b. An issue that is receiving much debate in the legislature is the legalization of marijuana.

10. a. Arthur Grover, which has been farming the delta for twenty years, is selling his farm this year.

    b. Arthur Grover, who has been farming the delta for twenty years, is selling his farm this year.

II. Circle the letter of the correctly punctuated complex sentence in each group.

Example

a. The man who does the weather reporting for channel 47 used to work for channel 9.

b. The man who does the weather reporting for channel 47, used to work for channel 9.

c. The man, who does the weather reporting for channel 47, used to work for channel 9.

1. a. Vancouver which is the capital of British Columbia is divided into a north and south section.

   b. Vancouver, which is the capital of British Columbia, is divided into a north and south section.

   c. Vancouver which is the capital of British Columbia, is divided into a north and south section.

2. a. The water, that you are drinking from the well, flows from a natural spring.

   b. The water that you are drinking from the well flows from a natural spring.

   c. The water that you are drinking from the well, flows from a natural spring.

3. a. Jenny Slade, who models for *Seventeen* magazine is from Peoria, Illinois.

   b. Jenny Slade, who models for *Seventeen* magazine, is from Peoria, Illinois.

   c. Jenny Slade who models for *Seventeen* magazine is from Peoria, Illinois.

4. a. The Oriental silk screen display that is showing at the Crispex Gallery has been widely acclaimed.

   b. The Oriental silk screen display that is showing at the Crispex Gallery, has been widely acclaimed.

   c. The Oriental silk screen display, that is showing at the Crispex Gallery, has been widely acclaimed.

5. a. The Stone Pony, which is a rock group from England, just completed its first U.S. tour.

   b. The Stone Pony which is a rock group from England just completed its first U.S. tour.

   c. The Stone Pony, which is a rock group from England just completed its first U.S. tour.

6. a. The hamburger joint that just opened on Clovis Avenue is offering nineteen-cent burgers.
   b. The hamburger joint that just opened on Clovis Avenue, is offering nineteen-cent burgers.
   c. The hamburger joint, that just opened on Clovis Avenue, is offering nineteen-cent burgers.
7. a. The economists, who predicted an increase in the gross national product, were wrong.
   b. The economists who predicted an increase in the gross national product were wrong.
   c. The economists, who predicted an increase in the gross national product were wrong.
8. a. Millie Abrams who used to race dragsters on the salt flats, now races speedboats.
   b. Millie Abrams who used to race dragsters on the salt flats now races speedboats.
   c. Millie Abrams, who used to race dragsters on the salt flats, now races speedboats.
9. a. Guaranteed student loans, which most state colleges offer, have excellent payback terms.
   b. Guaranteed student loans, which most state colleges offer have excellent payback terms.
   c. Guaranteed student loans which most state colleges offer, have excellent payback terms.
10. a. My good friend Gwendolyn who reads her poetry in the student union, just had her first book of poems published.
    b. My good friend Gwendolyn, who reads her poetry in the student union, just had her first book of poems published.
    c. My good friend Gwendolyn, who reads her poetry in the student union just had her first book of poems published.

Clear Sentences

Section Topic

Misplaced Modifiers
Dangling Modifiers

"Clear Sentences" sections help you word your sentences as smoothly, clearly, and directly as possible. In this particular section, you are introduced to the problems of *misplaced* and *dangling modifiers* and shown how to avoid them in your writing.

Misplaced Modifiers

The first time a writer expresses a thought in a sentence, the words don't always come out in the best possible order. A common wording problem involves *misplaced modifiers*, descriptive groups of words that are placed in an awkward or confusing place in a sentence, often some distance from the modified word. Here is some useful information about misplaced modifiers and how to handle them:

1. A modifier is a group of words that describes something in a sentence. A modifier may *identify* (the woman in the green coat, the hat that you just bought, the boy with the green beanie), *locate* (the book on the table, the theater on Monroe Boulevard), *set in time* (They arrived at 9:00 p.m. The roses bloomed in May.) or *tell how something happened* (John played the piano like a drunken gorilla, Maria combs her hair with great care.)
2. As a general rule, a modifier should come *directly after the word it modifies:*

   The creek running through town is almost dry.
   The catalog that you just ordered won't arrive for weeks.
   The seats in the back of the theater are ours.
3. Occasionally, a modifier is best located *directly before* the word it modifies:

   Happy and excited, the children searched the room for Easter eggs.
   Tired, sore, and hungry, the miners trudged home long after dark.
   Bothered by the hard rain, the gardeners quit working for the day.
4. A misplaced modifier is often found some distance away from the word it describes. To correct the problem, the modifier should usually be moved directly behind the word it modifies:

Misplaced: Your aunt just borrowed my lawn mower from Milwaukee. (What's from Milwaukee? the lawn mower?)

Revised: Your aunt from Milwaukee borrowed my lawn mower.

Misplaced: The man is my English teacher who lives next to you. (*who lives next to you* is in an awkward location)

Revised: The man who lives next to you is my English teacher.

Here are examples of sentences with *misplaced modifiers* followed by corrected versions with the modifiers in the right places. The modifiers are underlined.

Misplaced: That dog just ate all of my roses that lives next door.
Revised: That dog that lives next door just ate all of my roses.

Misplaced: The small cars are selling better than ever with four-wheel drive.
Revised: The small cars with four-wheel drive are selling better than ever.

Misplaced: Mary finally had to cancel her first singing recital bothered by a cold.
Revised: Bothered by a cold, Mary finally had to cancel her first singing recital.

Misplaced: That woman just bought her dog a milk shake in the plaid blouse.
Revised: That woman in the plaid blouse just bought her dog a milk shake.

Misplaced: The poker game was illegal in the back room that you just played in.
Revised: The poker game that you just played in the back room was illegal.

Exercise 14 Rewrite the following sentences and place the *misplaced modifiers* next to the words they describe. Your revised sentences should be easier to understand. When you finish, compare your answers to the answer key.

Example The odor is strong and unpleasant from the old refrigerator.
Revised: The odor from the old refrigerator is strong and unpleasant.

1. The treatment is expensive, lengthy, and painful for implanting hair.
The treatment for implanting hair is Expensive,
2. Please get the firewood and bring it into the house that is on the back porch.
3. John showed up for his job interview at the Ajax Employment Agency nervous and excited.
4. John took to the interview twenty letters of recommendation with him.
5. The president interviewed him personally in his office of the Ajax Employment Agency.
6. When you get to the top of the hill, the cool breeze feels good from the ocean.

7. They wash in the shallow water all of their clothes on the rocks.
8. The new rug is an attractive burnt-orange color in the den.
9. There is a meadow that I love to visit just beyond that hill in the summer.
10. The results weren't made public until ten minutes ago of the election.
11. I'd like to exchange the medium-sized shirt for a larger one that you gave me.
12. The man I was just talking to used to be my butcher on the patio.
13. The woman also invited me and sixteen other people to her party who invited you.
14. The old cat hasn't moved for six hours sleeping in her basket.
15. Those clouds are going to drop a lot of rain on the city blowing in from the north.

Exercise 15 Each of the following sentences is followed by a *modifier* that belongs with the sentence. Rewrite each sentence and insert the modifier next to the word that it describes. Then compare your answers with the answer key.

Example The rock singer is my cousin. in the dark glasses
Revised: The rock singer in the dark glasses is my cousin.

1. The new students are from Vietnam. that you introduced me to
2. All of the plants need pruning and watering. in the back of the classroom
3. That chair is very difficult to move through doorways. that we just bought
4. I want to find the guy. who stole my French notes
5. Please go to the back of the house and turn off the water. running in the garden
6. The hotel manager was very kind to his bellhops before he left. that moved to Naples
7. All of the players raced to the locker room. from the opposing team
8. Marta waited for the results from her X-rays. relaxed and confident
9. I'd like to thank the man at last night's office party. who introduced us
10. Everyone was sent home from the dance last night. in pink pajamas

Dangling Modifiers

The *dangling modifier* is usually an *introductory phrase* that does not go with the subject of the sentence. These phrases are called *dangling* modifiers because they have nothing to modify.

Here is what you need to know about dangling modifiers in order to avoid them:

1. Almost all *dangling modifiers* begin sentences.

   Surprised by the cold weather, our sweaters were left in the car. (*surprised by the cold weather* doesn't modify *sweaters*.)

2. Almost all dangling modifiers are phrases beginning with an *-ing*-ending word (gerund) or with an *-ed*-ending word (past participle):

   Walking to school, my nose got very cold.
   Thrilled by her good grades, a party sounded great to Sarah.

3. If an introductory phrase *does not* modify the subject of the sentence, it is a dangling modifier:

   Rushing to class, the books fell all over the stairs. (*Books* can't rush to class; the phrase *rushing to class* doesn't modify the subject *books*.)

   Troubled by a sore ankle, the track meet was out of the question. (A *track meet* can't have a sore ankle. The subject doesn't go with the phrase *troubled by a sore ankle*.)

   Walking to his room in the dorms, the floor was very slippery. (A *floor* can't walk; the phrase *walking to his room in the dorms* doesn't modify the subject *floor*.)

4. There are two ways to correct a dangling modifier:

   a. Change the subject of the sentence so that it goes with the modifying phrase. (Corrected revisions of sentences in 3.)

      Rushing to class one morning, I dropped my books all over the stairs.
      Troubled by a sore ankle, Joan couldn't compete in the track meet.
      Walking to his room in the dorms, Freddie almost slipped on the wet floor.

   b. Change the dangling phrase into a subordinate clause by adding a *subordinating conjunction* and a *subject*. Leave the rest of the sentence alone. (Corrected revisions of sentences in 3.)

      While I was hurrying to class one morning, my books fell all over the stairs.
      Since Joan was troubled by a sore ankle, the track meet was out of the question.
      When Freddie walked to his room in the dorms, the floor was very slippery.

Here are examples of sentences with dangling modifiers followed by their corrected versions. Notice that each problem can be corrected two ways: by changing the subject or by changing the dangling phrase to a subordinate clause.

Wrong: Taking five hard classes in one semester, Joe's grades dropped a lot. (*Grades* can't take classes.)
Right: When Joe took five hard classes in one semester, his grades dropped a lot.
Right: Taking five hard classes in one semester, Joe knew that his grades would drop a lot.

Wrong: Sitting around the dinner table, the discussion was lively. (*Discussion* can't sit around a dinner table.)
Right: While the family sat around the dinner table, the discussion was lively.
Right: Sitting around the dinner table, the family had a lively discussion.

Wrong: Troubled by a lack of steady income, a job was more important than college. (A *job* can't be troubled by a lack of income.)
Right: Because Mary was troubled by a lack of steady income, a job was more important than college.
Right: Troubled by a lack of steady income, Mary felt a job was more important than college.

Wrong: Picketing outside the school board office, increased tuition was being protested. (*Increased tuition* can't picket.)
Right: As students picketed outside the school board office, increased tuition was being protested.
Right: Picketing outside the school board office, the students protested the increased tuition.

Wrong: Excited by his new diet, ten pounds were lost in the first two weeks. (*Ten pounds* can't be excited by a diet.)
Right: Because John was excited by his new diet, ten pounds were lost in the first two weeks.
Right: Excited by his new diet, John lost ten pounds in the first two weeks.

Wrong: Rushing to the basketball game at the convention center, the police gave John a ticket. (The *police* weren't rushing to the basketball game.)
Right: As John was rushing to the basketball game at the convention center, the police gave him a ticket.
Right: Rushing to the basketball game at the convention center, John got a ticket from the police.

Exercise 16 Each of the following sentences contains a dangling modifier. Rewrite the sentence and correct the dangling modifier by adding a subordinating conjunction and subject to the phrase to make it a subordinate clause. (The subject is provided in parentheses if it is not found anywhere in the sentence.) Leave the rest of the sentence alone. When you finish, compare your sentences with the answer key.

Examples Returning to college after ten years, the students seemed very young. (Ruth)

When Ruth returned to college after ten years, the students seemed very young.

Being the mayor of a large city, the workdays were long and strenuous. (Mac)

When Mac was mayor of a large city, the workdays were long and strenuous.

1. Playing on the monkey bars on the playground, the weather turned sultry. (children)
2. Trying to pass a bill on child abuse through Congress, his wife became his secretary. (Milton)
3. Delighted by his new tractor rig, a second one was purchased. (Simon)
4. Planning for the hot days ahead, the weather suddenly cooled. (Mary)
5. Traveling through six cities in one week, their luggage was lost twice. (Ted and Celia)
6. Inspired by the beautiful countryside, her sketches were better than ever. (Grace)
7. Worried about her failing health, her doctor's glowing report was welcome. (Alice)
8. Finding a place to display his statues on the courthouse lawn, tourists followed him around. (Harvey)

Exercise 17 Correct the dangling modifiers in the following sentences by changing the subject of each sentence to go with the introductory phrase. Then change the rest of the sentence after the new subject so that the sentence makes sense. Then show your sentences to your instructor.

Examples Worrying about his dental appointment, the doctor's appointment was forgotten. (Ted)

Worrying about his dental appointment, Ted forgot his doctor's appointment.

Relieved by her good semester grades, the summer was a time to relax. (Allison)

Relieved by her good semester grades, Allison decided to relax for the summer.

1. Surprised by the size of the concert audience, everyone was thanked for coming. (Mick)
2. Worried over her business losses, four workers were laid off. (Sarah)
3. Excited by a rise in the stock market, ten shares of computer stocks were bought by Fran.
4. Shocked by the cost of new cars, a used car seemed the best buy to Harriet.
5. Rushing to get to work on time this morning, her wallet was left in the house. (Sally)
6. Treating his friends rudely, they weren't invited to Hal's party.
7. Trying to keep her marriage together, a marriage counselor was hired by Marty.
8. Growing along both sides of the river, the fisherman enjoyed the shade of the oak trees.

____

Exercise 18 Complete the following sentences so that the introductory phrases correctly modify your subjects. The word following the introductory phrase should be the subject. When you finish, share your sentences with a classmate who is finished and with your instructor.

Examples Rushing to get on the school bus, Harvey caught his tie in the bus door.

Defeated by the Rice Owls in soccer, the Harvard team went home disappointed.

1. Trying to find a cure for the common cold, ____
2. Vacationing in Mexico for the first time, ____
3. Trying to find an apartment near the college, ____
4. Repairing the garbage disposal in the kitchen, ____
5. Borrowing money from the local savings and loan, ____

6. Troubled by constant backaches, ______________________________

____

7. Excited by her Uncle Ned's visit, ______________________________

____

8. Bothered by a thorn in its paw, ______________________________

____

9. Cleaned by a full week of rain, ______________________________

____

10. Delighted by the low interest rate on her loan, ______________________________

____

____

Exercise 19 Write a short essay on the value that you place on any one of the following aspects of life. Before writing your first draft, do a "free writing" on your subject to get some ideas on paper. Free writing is like brainstorming in sentences: write whatever comes to mind about your topic without regard for organization, structure, or logical connections.

Topics: money, family, career, religion, leisure, public service

Free Writing Sample One

Family has always been important to me. I guess it always will be. Having a husband and kids. Watching the kids grow up and raising them to be good people. Having a mate who will stick with you over the years, someone to love and to count on. Someone to grow old with. Then the kids grow up and there are grandchildren around and family reunions. Family is like security. There are always people who care about you and whom you care about. Being alone in this world sounds pretty bad. What good is money or a great job if you have no one to share your life with and no one to bring into this world to keep life going. That is one of our reasons to exist, to perpetuate life. A big family portrait with all my kids and their husbands and wives and my grandchildren and husband. I'd like that hanging on my wall in thirty years. That would tell the best story of my life and what I value. Family is forever.

Free Writing Sample Two

Family is really overrated. It can really be a mess with so much divorce and kids living with a single parent or a stepparent or being moved from one house to another. Then there's child abuse and wife beating and all the terrible things that people in families sometimes do to one another. Loving, perfect families are on TV, not in real life. Dads who drink too much and don't give a damn about their kids. Single mothers who have to work so hard to raise a family and work two jobs just to make ends meet. Single life doesn't seem bad. No hassles, no commitments, no lives to screw up but your own. People have kids they don't want and get married when they don't want to. Families are expensive, too. Houses cost so much and doctor bills and a college education. Too much pressure on families. Maybe get married in your thirties or forties when you know what you really want. People marry too early. It can be a mess.

When you finish your free writing, read it over and see what you have. Is there a main idea running through your writing? Is there some good support for your main idea? Is there a way to organize your free writing thoughts so that readers can follow them clearly? What needs eliminating? What might need expanding? Once you have a main idea in mind and some sense of structure to follow, write your first draft.

Sample Draft

Family will always be very important in my life. I was raised in a loving family, and I could always count on my mom and dad to be there when I needed them. I still can. I don't think there's anything in life that provides the joy and security that family does.

I want to get married and have children. I'm looking forward to a long, loving relationship with my husband. I'll marry someone who is family oriented like I am and who believes that marriage is forever. We'll grow old together and always have each other to count on through the good times and the bad.

My children will be a big part of my life. I don't care if I have one or five, I'll give them lots of love and try to raise them to be good people. I'll look forward to teaching them things and going to their school activities or Little League games or dance lessons. Part of our reason for living is to perpetuate life, and I look forward to that responsibility. My kids will always be able to count on me, just like I could with my parents.

Later in life I'll look forward to grandchildren and big family reunions and everyone coming to our house at Christmas and Thanksgiving. Maybe I'll live long enough to enjoy a four-generation reunion with my kids, their kids, and their kids' kids. That would be great. We'd have a big family portrait taken, and it would represent to me what life is all about: family being together, counting on one another, and giving love and security. Family is forever.

When you finish your first draft, read it over and consider the following:

1. *Paragraphing:* Do you have a main idea in your opening that you support in the composition? Does each paragraph develop a particular point or thought? Is each paragraph well developed and organized effectively?
2. *Sentences:* Are your sentences clearly worded? Are there any problems with wordiness, dangling or misplaced modifiers, or awkward phrasing? Could any sentences be effectively combined? Are there any run-ons or fragments to eliminate?
3. *Correctness:* Check your verb endings, pronoun usage, comma usage, and spelling.

Share drafts with a classmate and exchange revision suggestions. When you are ready, write the final draft of your composition, including all revisions you have noted for making it clearer or more interesting for readers.

Practice Quiz

Take this quiz to prepare for the section quiz, and then compare your answers with the answer key. When you are ready for the section quiz, let your instructor know.

I. Circle the letter of the most clearly worded sentence in each group.

Example

a. That duck loves to squawk at golfers with the green neck.
(b.) That duck with the green neck loves to squawk at golfers.
c. That duck loves to squawk with the green neck at golfers.

1. a. The boy got into a fight at school with a scar on his temple.
   b. The boy with a scar on his temple got into a fight at school.
   c. The boy at school got into a fight with a scar on his temple.
2. a. Marta was bothered by a sore shoulder that she got in a car accident.
   b. Marta was bothered by a sore shoulder in a car accident that she got.
   c. Marta by a sore shoulder was bothered in a car accident that she got.
3. a. The chairs need to be moved to the front of the hall in the back of the hall.
   b. The chairs in the back of the hall to the front of the hall need to be moved.
   c. The chairs in the back of the hall need to be moved to the front of the hall.
4. a. Your friend from Cleveland looks like she belongs in college.
   b. Your friend looks like she belongs in college from Cleveland.
   c. Your friend in college from Cleveland looks like she belongs.
5. a. He hit the ball with an aluminum bat over the fence from Sears.
   b. He hit the ball from Sears with an aluminum bat over the fence.
   c. He hit the ball over the fence with an aluminum bat from Sears.
6. a. The way to Joey's heart is through his stomach.
   b. The way is through his stomach to Joey's heart.
   c. Through Joey's heart to his stomach is the way.
7. a. The secretary pleases at work her boss with her efficiency.
   b. The secretary pleases with her efficiency at work her boss.
   c. The secretary pleases her boss with her efficiency at work.

8. a. The filing cabinet in the closet is full of old documents.
   b. The filing cabinet is full of old documents in the closet.
   c. The filing cabinet is in the closet full of old documents.

9. a. The news about the bomb threat spread rapidly across campus.
   b. The news spread rapidly about the bomb threat across campus.
   c. The news across campus about the bomb threat spread rapidly.

10. a. Call me and tell me everything in the morning about your new job.
    b. Call me about your new job and tell me everything in the morning.
    c. Call me in the morning and tell me everything about your new job.

11. a. You should leave the park on the same bus that you came on.
    b. You should leave the park that you came on on the same bus.
    c. You should leave on the same bus that you came on to the park.

12. a. That bird is an ostrich at the zoo with its head stuck in the sand.
    b. That bird is an ostrich with its head stuck in the sand at the zoo.
    c. That bird at the zoo with its head stuck in the sand is an ostrich.

II. Circle the letter of the sentence in each group that does *not* contain a dangling modifier.

Example

(a.) Coming to the same amusement park every week, Thadeus spends hundreds of dollars on rides.
b. Coming to the same amusement park every week, hundreds of dollars are spent on rides by Thadeus.
c. Coming to the same amusement park every week, the rides cost Thadeus hundreds of dollars.

1. a. Hoping to spend little money on clothes, the Salvation Army store was Ted's first stop.
   b. Hoping to spend little money on clothes, Ted stopped first at the Salvation Army store.
   c. Hoping to spend little money on clothes, the first step for Ted was the Salvation Army store.

2. a. Frustrated by the high cost of housing, the dorms seemed the best place for Cleo.
   b. Frustrated by the high cost of housing, Cleo felt the dorms would be the place to live.
   c. Frustrated by the high cost of housing, the best place to live for Cleo was the dorms.

3. a. Pleased by her parents' financial help, they were taken out to dinner by Millie.
   b. Pleased by her parents' financial help, a dinner out was their gift from Millie.
   c. Pleased by her parents' financial help, Millie took them out to dinner.
4. a. Since Meg wanted to get to the graduation party on time, the gathering at her parents' house had to be short.
   b. Wanting to get to the graduation party on time, the gathering at her parents' house had to be short.
   c. Wanting to get to the graduation party on time, her parents had to shorten the gathering at their house.
5. a. Since Mal was having trouble selling his pottery, painting became his new hobby.
   b. Having trouble selling his pottery, painting became Mal's new hobby.
   c. Having trouble selling his pottery, Mal's new hobby became painting.
6. a. Fascinated by fantastic stories of America, there are a lot of disappointed immigrants when they arrive.
   b. Fascinated by fantastic stories of America, a lot of immigrants are disappointed when they arrive.
   c. Fascinated by fantastic stories of America, the country disappoints a lot of immigrants when they arrive.
7. a. As the legislature got tougher on crime, a law was passed increasing bail for violent crimes.
   b. Getting tougher on crime, a law was passed increasing bail for violent crimes.
   c. Getting tougher on crime, bail was increased for violent crimes.
8. a. Spilling over the floodgates of the dam, the mist from the water was sprayed a mile downriver.
   b. Spilling over the floodgates of the dam, spraying a mile downriver was a mist from the water.
   c. Spilling over the floodgates of the dam, the water sent a mist spraying a mile downriver.
9. a. Trying to stay cool in the heat, the flower beds provided the best sleeping places for the cats.
   b. Trying to stay cool in the heat, the cats slept in the flower beds.
   c. Trying to stay cool in the heat, the best sleeping places for the cats were in the flower beds.
10. a. Tired of having to drink bottled water, Enrique bought a water-purifying unit for his kitchen sink.
    b. Tired of having to drink bottled water, a water-purifying unit was bought by Enrique for his kitchen sink.

c. Tired of having to drink bottled water, Enrique's kitchen sink now has a water-purifying unit on it.

Correct Sentences

Section Topics

Split Complex Sentences
Run-on Sentence Correction Options

Along with sentence variety and clear wording, a third important sentence consideration is proper structure. The two most common structural problems—run-on sentences and fragments—are covered in the "Correct Sentences" section of each level. In this section, you cover fragments involving split complex sentences, and you learn some new ways to correct run-on sentences. It is important that you eliminate all run-ons or fragments from your writing since they may cause readers confusion.

Split Complex Sentences

One of the most common fragment problems is caused by splitting a complex sentence. When you split the two clauses of a complex sentence into separate sentences, *the dependent clause beginning with the subordinating conjunction is a fragment*.

Here are examples of fragments caused by split complex sentences. *The clause beginning with the underlined subordinating conjunction is the fragment.* Following each split complex sentence is the correct form.

Wrong: We left for the laundromat at 6:00. After we shopped at the supermarket.
Right: We left for the laundromat at 6:00 after we shopped at the supermarket.

Wrong: The crowd gathered in front of the pet shop. Because there was an iguana in the window.
Right: The crowd gathered in front of the pet shop because there was an iguana in the window.

Wrong: Let's walk to the museum today. Unless it starts raining before we get started.
Right: Let's walk to the museum today unless it starts raining before we get started.

Wrong: While you were out hunting for an apartment. I was checking the ads in the paper.

Right: While you were out hunting for an apartment, I was checking the ads in the paper.

Wrong: If John arrives home by nine tonight. Please ask him to call me immediately.

Right: If John arrives home by nine tonight, please ask him to call me immediately.

Wrong: When you check your interest on your savings. See if the rate has increased.

Right: When you check your interest on your savings, see if the rate has increased.

Here are some basic suggestions for identifying, correcting, and avoiding fragments caused by split complex sentences:

1. The dependent clause beginning with a subordinating conjunction *can't stand alone as a sentence*. By itself, it is a fragment that needs to be *added on* to the second clause in the sentence.

   Fragment: Before you have to leave.
   Sentence: Before you have to leave, please read me some of your poetry.

   Fragment: Because it is raining outside.
   Sentence: Because it is raining outside, I won't have to water the lawn.

   Fragment: If you want me to go to the delicatessen with you.
   Sentence: If you want me to go to the delicatessen with you, I'll be glad to.

2. In a split complex sentence, the fragment may be the *first clause* or the *second clause*, depending on where the subordinating conjunction is.

   You finished the test. Before I was halfway through. (second part is fragment)

   Before I was halfway through the test. You were already finished. (first part is fragment)

3. The correction for a split complex sentence is simple: Join the two clauses to form the complex sentence. *No words need to be added.*

   Wrong: I don't want to take the test today. Because I have been absent too much.
   Right: I don't want to take the test today because I have been absent too much.

   Wrong: If you really want to get a job after school. I'll talk to my uncle.
   Right: If you really want to get a job after school, I'll talk to my uncle.

4. To avoid fragments, double check your sentences *containing subordinating conjunctions* to make sure you haven't split a complex sentence.

Exercise 20 The following groups of words contain two complete sentences and one fragment beginning with a *subordinating conjunction* (*because, while, if, although, when, until, unless,* and so on.). Correct the fragment by adding it to the sentence it belongs with to form a complex sentence, and write out the new complex sentence. Put a *comma* between clauses when the sentence begins with a subordinating conjunction. Then compare your answers with the answer key.

Example Jan's mother's illness is a great mystery. Because the doctors can't figure out what's wrong with her. Meanwhile, Jan's mother continues losing weight and having headaches.

Complex Sentence: Jan's mother's illness is a great mystery because the doctors can't figure out what's wrong with her.

1. Aunt Hilda worries about her roses. When the neighbors' boys are playing outside. Last spring they played golf using the rosebuds as balls.
2. When the Olympic games were in Los Angeles. Air pollution was minimal. The improvement was possible because of the cooperation of heavy industry in the area.
3. The beaver ducked under the lily pads below the waterfall. Then it surfaced twenty yards downstream. Where the river splits in half.
4. Thelma's backyard is covered with water. When she was asleep last night. Her dog broke a sprinkler line, and water gushed out all night long.
5. The thief broke into the house through the back door. While the family was sleeping inside. Then he exited through the front door and stole the car in the driveway.
6. While drought and starvation continued in Ethiopia. American and British rock groups raised millions of dollars through concerts televised worldwide. The money was to be spent for food, clothing, and medicine.
7. Haley collects beer bottles. He has accumulated over two hundred bottles from all over the world. Since he began collecting three years ago.
8. The National Organization of Women ran Sarah Howell as their candidate for the legislature. When the election results were in. Sarah had run a close second to the incumbent.
9. If you want to go to Harvey's barn party tonight. I'll be glad to pick you up. Just give me a call an hour in advance.
10. Mark's health science lab was canceled yesterday. Because the instructor was ill. Therefore, Mark had driven thirty miles to the college for nothing.

Exercise 21 Complete the following complex sentences and punctuate them correctly to *avoid fragments*. Remember, a *comma* goes between the clauses of a complex sentence *beginning with a subordinating conjunction*. When you complete the sentences, show them to a classmate who is finished and to your instructor.

Examples Before Clyde could go out for tennis, he had to pass a physical exam at the college.

Sally could not participate in golf until she had also passed the physical.

1. Before you decide on what college to attend ____________________
2. While you were working in the backyard yesterday ____________________
3. If you want to go bowling tonight ____________________
4. John wants to be a dentist someday although ____________________
5. Susan has voted in every election since ____________________
6. You don't have to baby-sit my children tonight unless ____________________
7. When the lottery first began in Michigan ____________________
8. No one knows where the lodge meeting will be held because ____________________

Exercise 22 Rewrite the following paragraph and correct any fragments by joining split complex sentences and putting in needed *commas*.

Example Before the family reunion could begin. The relatives from Texas had to arrive. Their plane had been delayed for two days by dense ground fog.

Revised: Before the family reunion could begin, the relatives from Texas had to arrive. Their plane had been delayed for two days by dense ground fog.

After Sam took a health education class at Monmart College, he changed some of his ways. He realized he had been eating too much fat and sugar, so he cut down on red meat and desserts. He began eating more fish and chicken. Because they are very low in fat. He began using sugar substitutes like saccharin or honey to sweeten his food and drinks. He also started exercising. Before he took the class. Sam had never run a hundred yards without stopping. Now he is running a mile a day and trying to build up to two miles. He is also doing morning and evening calisthenics. Whenever he doesn't have time to run. Sam's health education class made him realize the importance of proper diet and exercise for healthy living. He is happy he took the class. Because it changed his life.

Run-on Sentence Correction Options

As you learned in previous levels, a run-on sentence is two or more sentences run together without proper punctuation. Run-on sentences need to be corrected because they are incorrect sentence structures and because they cause readers problems.

Here are four different ways to correct run-on sentences and some suggestions for when to use each.

1. If the sentences within a run-on are fairly long, put a period after the first sentence and capitalize the first letter of the second sentence. This is the most common run-on correction.

   Example:

   Sociologists did a three-year study on criminals serving time in a maximum security prison in London, they reached the conclusion that a person commits crimes due to a combination of environmental conditions and genetic traits.

   Revised:

   The sociologists did a three-year study on criminals serving time in a maximum security prison in London. They reached the conclusion that a person commits crimes due to a combination of environmental conditions and genetic traits.

2. If the sentences within a run-on are shorter and related in thought, the sentences can be *combined* to form a compound or complex sentence by adding a coordinating conjunction (*and, or, but, so, for, yet*) or a

subordinating conjunction (*because, since, while, when, before, as, if, although, until, unless*).

Run-on: The rain was going to last for a while, clouds covered the entire sky.
Revised: The rain was going to last for a while *because* clouds covered the entire sky.

Run-on: The test is going to be very difficult, just do the best you can on it.
Revised: The test is going to be very difficult, *so* just do the best you can on it.

3. Another correcting option for two short, closely related sentences within a run-on is the *semicolon*. A *semicolon* (;) is used to join two related sentences. It takes the place of a period and capital letter or a joining word.

Run-on: We went to the park this morning, then we went to the museum this afternoon.
Revised: We went to the park this morning; then we went to the museum this afternoon.

Run-on: Harry wouldn't make a good professional negotiator he doesn't have the patience.
Revised: Harry wouldn't make a good professional negotiator; he doesn't have the patience.

Run-on: Your hat is sitting on my kitchen table, you left it there last night.
Revised: Your hat is sitting on my kitchen table; you left it there last night.

4. If a run-on contains *three or more* short, similar sentences, they may be combined to form a single sentence by eliminating unnecessary words and joining similar words.

Run-on: Samantha is smart she is good-looking, she is married.
Revised: Samantha is smart, good-looking, and married.

Run-on: Meet me at the bank, meet me at 8:00 a.m., meet me by the Versatel machine.
Revised: Meet me at the bank at 8:00 a.m. by the Versatel machine.

Run-on: Julia is my sister, she is twenty-six years old, she lives in Manhattan.
Revised: My twenty-six-year-old sister Julia lives in Manhattan.

Exercise 23 Correct each of the following run-on sentences using the method suggested for that set of run-ons. When you finish, compare your answers with the answer key.

Example Combine with coordinating or subordinating conjunctions to form compound or complex sentences:

I'm very tired this evening, it was a long day at the office.

Revised: I'm very tired this evening, for it was a long day at the office.

The movie will last at least three hours, let's bring our own popcorn and candy.

Revised: The movie will last at least three hours, so let's bring our own popcorn and candy.

A. Correct the first three sentences by using periods and capital letters to separate sentences:

1. Many farmers are having trouble making payments on their bank loans this year, they are asking for loan extensions, which the banks are reluctant to give.
2. The tides have been changing along the southern coast of Oregon, the cause for the change is being studied by a team of geologists.
3. We used to go into the city to shop at least once a week, now we are lucky to go there once a month.

B. Correct the next run-ons by adding coordinating or subordinating conjunctions to form compound or complex sentences:

1. It's a good day to dry the clothes outside, there's a nice breeze and no clouds.
2. I'm having difficulty understanding the photosynthesis process, would you please help me?
3. We could study at the library until 9:00 p.m. we could stay here and study in the dormitory lobby.

C. Correct the next run-ons by separating the sentences with a semicolon (;).

1. The Indian statue was removed from the park, it was shipped to the Smithsonian Institute to be preserved.
2. The music business is in great shape today, television videos are a big reason.
3. You might invest $100 in computer stocks they are as secure an investment as anything.

D. Correct the next run-ons by eliminating unnecessary words and joining similar words to form one good sentence:

1. Ted is short, he is handsome, he is lonely.
2. Mary is from Missouri she is fifteen years old, she is a blonde.
   Mary is a fifteen year old blonde from Missouri.
3. The tide came in, it went out it changed with the moon.

Exercise 24 Correct each of the following run-on sentences by using one of the four methods suggested in this section: separating sentences with a period, joining them with a conjunction, separating them with a semicolon (;), or combining three or more sentences to form one good sentence. Use the method that seems most appropriate for correcting each run-on, and use all four methods at least once during the exercise. When you finish, compare your sentences with the answer key.

Examples Lucy decided to go on for her master's degree in English after having completed her bachelor's degree, she felt that a master's degree would provide her with more teaching opportunities after graduation.
Revised: Lucy decided to go on for her master's degree in English after having completed her bachelor's degree. She felt that a master's degree would provide her with more teaching opportunities after graduation.

The ice around the sides of the pond is melting, the ice in the middle is still firm.
Revised: The ice around the sides of the pond is melting, but the ice in the middle is still firm.

You have a very gentle way with children, you should consider being an elementary school teacher.
Revised: You have a very gentle way with children; you should consider being an elementary school teacher.

1. It was hot in the dentist's office, there was no air conditioning.
2. The desks in room 32 are in good shape, they aren't large enough for college students.
3. Dan went to church every Sunday when he was living at home in Bonberry, now that he is going to college and living away from home, he doesn't go to church as often.
4. Sal's sister's name is Marta, she is unmarried she is employed by Lockheed Aircraft.
5. I'm still full from all the chicken at the picnic, let's just have a salad tonight.
6. Alexandra is in better shape at thirty than she was at twenty, she's taking better care of herself.
7. Danielle began lifting weights just to firm up her muscles and tone her body now she is entering body-building tournaments and winning trophies.
8. All Soviet bloc nations boycotted the Olympic games many great athletes were unable to compete in Los Angeles.
9. You should vote against the tax relief bill, it is very poorly written.
10. The road was narrow it was curvy it was located east of Tulsa, it was dangerous.

Exercise 25 The following paragraph contains some run-on sentences that need correcting. Rewrite the paragraph and correct all run-ons using the methods suggested in this section. When you finish, compare your paragraph with the answer key.

Example The snow is falling harder and harder, it has covered the ground and the rooftops. If it continues this hard all night, we could be snowed in by morning, let's leave now and not take any chances.

Revised: The snow is falling harder and harder, and it has covered the ground and the rooftops. If it continues this hard all night, we could be snowed in by morning. Let's leave now and not take any chances.

Tad decided to start his own mail-order business, he had invented a disc that could be attached to the bottom of any hanging plant container to catch the water running out of the drainage holes. First, he found a company that could produce the plastic discs cheaply, then he looked around for magazines to advertise in. He finally decided on three gardening magazines, he took his money out of savings and bought three ads. Within a few days, the orders started coming in for his plant discs. He sold all the discs that had been made in two weeks, he had to increase production. At the end of a month, Tad had made enough money to buy three more ads for the following month. He hoped that sales would continue to increase, he knew he had to make a profit beyond advertising money to be successful.

Practice Quiz Take this picture quiz to prepare for the section quiz. Then compare your answers with the answer key. When you are ready for the section quiz, let your instructor know.

I. Circle the letter of the correctly punctuated sentence(s) in each group. Circle one letter in each group.

Example

a. I've always wanted to be a mechanic. Because all of my brothers are mechanics.

(b.) I've always wanted to be a mechanic because all of my brothers are mechanics.

1. a. The Halloween party at the cabin has been canceled. Because the cabin is snowed in.

   (b.) The Halloween party at the cabin has been canceled because the cabin is snowed in.

2. a. The Model T Club met in front of the church before the members left on their cross-country trip.

b. The Model T Club met in front of the church. Before the members left on their cross-country trip.

3. a. While I am mixing mortar for the bricks. You can be setting them out along the sidewalk.

   b. While I am mixing mortar for the bricks, you can be setting them out along the sidewalk.

4. a. The violent crime rate increased this year. While the "victimless" crime rate went down.

   b. The violent crime rate increased this year while the "victimless" crime rate went down.

5. a. Unless you want to catch a bad cold, don't go swimming in that freezing river.

   b. Unless you want to catch a bad cold. Don't go swimming in that freezing river.

6. a. It's hard feeding the chickens. Because the rain has made a quagmire of their pen.

   b. It's hard feeding the chickens because the rain has made a quagmire of their pen.

7. a. If the pollution gets any worse in the city, I'm going to move to the coast.

   b. If the pollution gets any worse in the city. I'm going to move to the coast.

8. a. Let's visit Aunt Minnie this weekend before she leaves for Mexico for a month.

   b. Let's visit Aunt Minnie this weekend. Before she leaves for Mexico for a month.

9. a. Melinda is feeling much better today. Although she still has a slight fever.

   b. Melinda is feeling much better today although she still has a slight fever.

10. a. Since the federal tax rate has been reduced, the federal deficit has increased.

    b. Since the federal tax rate has been reduced. The federal deficit has increased.

II. Circle the letter of the correctly punctuated sentence(s) in each group. Circle one letter per group.

Example

a. The footprints in the back alley were made by tennis shoes, they were at least size 13s.

b. The footprints in the back alley were made by tennis shoes they were at least size 13s.

(c.) The footprints in the back alley were made by tennis shoes. They were at least size 13s.

1. a. I'm having a hard time paying my rent this month, I had to pay $300 to get my car fixed.

   b. I'm having a hard time paying my rent this month, for I had to pay $300 to get my car fixed.

c. I'm having a hard time paying my rent this month I had to pay $300 to get my car fixed.

2. a. That Scotch tape that you wrapped around the water faucet has already come off. You need to take the faucet off and replace the washers if you want to stop the leak.

   b. That Scotch tape that you wrapped around the water faucet has already come off, you need to take the faucet off and replace the washers if you want to stop the leak.

   c. That Scotch tape that you wrapped around the water faucet has already come off you need to take the faucet off and replace the washers if you want to stop the leak.

3. a. Sally doesn't spend much time at home, she is either at school or at work most of the time.

   b. Sally doesn't spend much time at home she is either at school or at work most of the time.

   c. Sally doesn't spend much time at home because she is either at school or at work most of the time.

4. a. The dormitory rates haven't changed in two years, they are still very reasonable.

   b. The dormitory rates haven't changed in two years; they are still very reasonable.

   c. The dormitory rates haven't changed in two years they are still very reasonable.

5. a. Let's walk down to the pier this evening, we can watch the fishing boats come in.

   b. Let's walk down to the pier this evening we can watch the fishing boats come in.

   c. Let's walk down to the pier this evening; we can watch the fishing boats come in.

6. a. Diseases that have been wiped out in the United States are still a problem in other parts of the world. For example, cholera and malaria are still common illnesses in countries with poor sanitation conditions.

   b. Diseases that have been wiped out in the United States are still a problem in other parts of the world, for example, cholera and malaria are still common illnesses in countries with poor sanitation conditions.

   c. Diseases that have been wiped out in the United States are still a problem in other parts of the world for example, cholera and malaria are still common illnesses in countries with poor sanitation conditions.

The Word

The final section in each level deals with common wording errors that writers need to correct within their sentences before sharing their writing with readers. No matter how interesting and well-worded a paragraph may be, if it contains errors in areas such as spelling, subject-verb agreement, irregular verb usage, plural forms, or pronoun usage, much of the paragraph's effectiveness may be lost.

Verb Forms

Section Topics

Separated Subject and Verb
Irregular Verb List #2

Separated Subject and Verb

As you have learned in earlier levels, present tense verbs must agree with their singular or plural subjects. Problems arise for some writers when the subject and verb are separated by other words that may confuse the agreement issue. The most common group of words separating subjects and verbs is called a *prepositional phrase*.

Here is some information on prepositional phrases and a suggestion for handling subject-verb agreement when such phrases are involved:

1. A *prepositional phrase* is a group of words beginning with a preposition. Here is a list of the most common prepositions beginning phrases that separate subjects and verbs:

in	(*in* the room)	with	(*with* the white headband)
on	(*on* my right)	from	(*from* Dallas, Texas)
to	(*to* the north)	across	(*across* the table)
for	(*for* all seasons)	beside	(*beside* the small creek)
by	(*by* the drinking fountain)	behind	(*behind* the refrigerator)
of	(*of* all the boxers)	through	(*through* the west window)

2. The final word in a prepositional phrase (the *object* of the preposition) should *never be mistaken for the subject*. When dealing with subject-verb agreement, *ignore* the prepositional phrase between the subject and verb.

Here is a group of sentences with their prepositional phrases *underlined*. The subject comes before the phrase and the verb comes immediately after. All of the present tense verbs *agree* with their subjects.

One <u>of the dogs</u> eats potato salad. (Verb *eats* agrees with singular subject *one*.)

The view <u>of the mountains</u> is lovely. (Verb *is* agrees with singular subject *view*.)

Your nieces <u>from Brooklyn</u> speak with an accent. (Verb *speak* agrees with plural subject *nieces*.)

The dogs <u>in my yard</u> bark most of the time. (Verb *bark* agrees with plural subject *dogs*.)

A ladder <u>in the garage</u> is broken. (Verb *is* agrees with singular subject *ladder*.)

The camera <u>with the wide-angle lens</u> captures the action well. (Verb *captures* agrees with singular subject *camera*.)

Exercise 26 Each of the following sentences contains a prepositional phrase separating the subject and verb. First, draw a line through the prepositional phrase separating the subject and verb. Then, underline the subject. Finally, circle the present tense verb in parentheses ( ) that *agrees* with the subject. Remember, as a *general rule*, if the subject is *singular*, the verb ends in *s*, and if the subject is *plural*, the verb does *not* end in *s*. Compare your answers with the answer key.

Example The <u>mouse</u> ~~behind my cupboards~~ ((is), are) very crafty.

1. Your <u>sister</u> ~~from Glenview Heights~~ (wear, (wears)) strong perfume.

2. The books on the table in the hall (are, is) not for sale.
3. Your attitude about snakes and spiders (is, are) similar to mine.
4. The trees on the north and east sides of campus (is, are) in bloom.
5. That tractor in the back of the pasture (look, looks) like an antique.
6. Your old family album with many of your ancestors' pictures (fascinate, fascinates) me.
7. A crew of sixteen high school students (operate, operates) a weekend car wash.
8. One of those old clothes hampers (need, needs) to be thrown out.
9. The spirit of the two opposing soccer teams (is, are) very high.
10. The light from the new mercury lamps (brighten, brightens) the neighborhood.
11. Your brown shoes with the thick soles (need, needs) polishing.
12. A government of the people, by the people, and for the people (sound, sounds) perfect.

Exercise 27 Fill in an appropriate *present tense* verb in each of the following sentences. Cross out any *prepositional phrase* that separates the subject from the verb. Then show your sentences to your instructor.

Example The odors from the back of the kitchen *puzzle* the diners.

1. A friend in need *is* a friend indeed, but two friends in need *are* a problem.
2. Your trip to the Leeward Islands *sounds* exciting.
3. One of my projects this summer *is* to paint the fence.
4. A group of dogs *run* in front of my house daily, and one of them *eats* ~~*rolls*~~ my lawn.
5. While the cat in the bushes *hates* people, the cats on the sidewalk *need* them.
6. No one in any of the seven lines in front of the theaters *likes* standing in line.
7. A trip to the bank in the morning *is* very important for Carl.
8. Several of the painters from the new college *show* their artwork in the park.

9. When the man ~~from the cleaners~~ runs, the man ~~from the plumbing store~~ sweats
10. Two of the geese need medical attention, and one ~~of them~~ needs hospitalization.

Irregular Verb List #3

This is the third set of irregular verbs for you to learn. These words are grouped together because their past tense and past participle forms are similar.

Simple Form	*Past Tense*	*Past Participle*
break	broke	broken
choose	chose	chosen
drive	drove	driven
eat	ate	eaten
fall	fell	fallen
freeze	froze	frozen
get	got	gotten
give	gave	given
ride	rode	ridden
rise	rose	risen
shake	shook	shaken
speak	spoke	spoken
steal	stole	stolen
take	took	taken
write	wrote	written

Here are some tips on learning the past tense and past participle forms of these verbs:

1. *All past participle forms* end in *-en*. These are the most difficult forms to remember for many writers.
2. Many past tense forms have a long *o* and a silent ending *e*. (*broke, chose, drove, froze, rode, rose, spoke, stole, wrote*)
3. These are the most commonly used verbs on the list that give writers problems: *write/wrote/written, give/gave/given, eat/ate/eaten, drive/drove/driven,* and *choose/chose/chosen*. Give these verbs some special attention, *particularly* in the past participle form.

Exercise 28 Fill in the correct past tense or past participle form of each verb in parentheses. Remember, the past tense does *not* take a helping verb, and the past participle is used with *has, have,* and *had*. Compare your answers with the answer key.

Examples (take) I have ___taken___ the keys for the apartment to school.

(drive) I ___drove___ a tractor for ten hours yesterday.

1. (write) Have you ___wrote___ your grandmother lately?
2. (steal) Jack ___stole___ away quietly in the night.
3. (speak) Have you ___spoke___ to your boss about a Christmas bonus?
4. (shake) Mildred ___shoke___ with fear when her brakes gave way while she was driving downhill.
5. (rise) Your reputation with your classmates has ___rose___ steadily.
6. (ride) Jake ___rode___ his moped to school in a rainstorm.
7. (give) Have you ___given___ your writing assignment any thought?
8. (get) Sarah ___got___ a letter in the mail from the admissions office at Kent State.
9. (freeze) I nearly ___froze___ at the ice hockey rink last night.
10. (fall) The temperature ___fell___ 20 degrees from midday until dark.
11. (eat) I had ___eaten___ all of the french fries before Susie sat down.
12. (drive) William has ___driven___ everyone crazy with his moose impersonations.
13. (choose) Miriam ___chose___ to announce her candidacy for the city council on June 1.
14. (break) Sam's new car had ___broke___ down one week after the warranty had expired.
15. (take) Matty ___toke___ her time on every section of the calculus final.

Exercise 29 Fill in the appropriate tense—past, present perfect, or past perfect—of each verb in parentheses. Remember, the past tense is used when an action is *completed*, the present perfect when an action *continues* into the present, and the past perfect when one action is completed before another action occurs. Use no helping verbs with the past tense, use *has* or *have* with the present perfect, and use *had* with the past perfect. When you finish, compare your answers with the answer key.

Examples

(write) I have written my mother every Monday for three months.

(write) I wrote my mother a long letter last night.

(write) I had written my mother every Monday until I forgot last week.

1. (take) Last night I had taken a carload of boy scouts to Lookout Point.
2. (take) I take a carload of Boy Scouts to Lookout Point every summer.
3. (speak) John spoke to Pedro in the cafeteria just a minute ago.
4. (speak) John had spoken to Pedro before I walked into the cafeteria.
5. (rise) The river rose three inches last night.
6. (rise) The river already has risen six inches this month, and there are still ten days left.
7. (eat) Amelia has eaten at the same table in the cafeteria every morning this semester.
8. (eat) Amelia eate at the same table every morning until she quit eating breakfast.
9. (choose) Sarah chose to stay out of school for one semester.
10. (choose) Sarah has chosen to stay out of school until Harvey talked her into attending.
11. (drive) Last week Ike drove his Volkswagen cross-country from Washington to Florida.
12. (drive) Ike has driven cross-country from Washington to Florida every summer for the last four years.
13. (give) Mildred gave $100 to the Cancer Research Foundation.
14. (give) Mildred has given $100 to the Cancer Research Foundation before she was asked to contribute.
15. (break) Francine broke off her engagement to Max last Tuesday.
16. (break) Francine has broken off her engagement to Max twelve times already.

Exercise 30 Fill in an appropriate irregular verb from List #3 in each blank in the following paragraph. Use the correct past tense or past participle form. When you finish, compare your answers with the answer key.

Examples When Clyde __fell__ into the freezing water, his whole body __shook.__

He would have __frozen__ if Sally hadn't built a fire for him to thaw out.

Despite last night's snowstorm, Phyllis still __rode__ to school on her new motorcycle. Halfway to school, the motorcycle __broke__ down, and Phyllis sat on the icy sidewalk and __froze__. If Cliff hadn't __drove__ by, Phyllis wouldn't have made it to school. He __took__ her to campus, and she had her motorcycle __driven__ to the Honda service garage. Phyllis had __taken__ a chance driving her motorcycle under bad conditions, and she had __got__ a lesson she needed. At school, she was so hungry that she __ate__ three hamburgers, and then sat down and __wrote__ her boyfriend a letter asking him if he wanted to buy a motorcycle.

Practice Quiz Here is a practice quiz to help prepare you for the section quiz. Take the quiz, and compare your answers with the answer key. Then when you are ready for the section quiz, let your instructor know.

I. Circle the letter of the sentence that has correct subject-verb agreement.

Example

(a.) One of the doctors performs ten surgeries a day.

b. One of the doctors perform ten surgeries a day.

1. a. A letter from the Garcias arrive at our house every morning.
   (b.) A letter from the Garcias arrives at our house every morning.
2. (a.) Six boxes of grapes from Peru sit on your front porch.
   b. Six boxes of grapes from Peru sits on your front porch.
3. (a.) A group of housewives from the mountains drive into town every day to shop.
   b. A group of housewives from the mountains drives into town every day to shop.

4. a. Not one of the ivy shoots I planted look like it's going to live.
   b. Not one of the ivy shoots I planted looks like it's going to live.
5. a. The traffic on the two main freeways are backed up for miles.
   b. The traffic on the two main freeways is backed up for miles.
6. a. The nervousness of the zoo animals indicates a change of weather soon.
   b. The nervousness of the zoo animals indicate a change of weather soon.
7. a. A table at the new restaurant between the bank buildings are difficult to get.
   b. A table at the new restaurant between the bank buildings is difficult to get.
8. a. Those nails in the bottom drawer needs straightening.
   b. Those nails in the bottom drawer need straightening.
9. a. I don't know many people here, but the men in the greenhouse is my uncles from Texas.
   b. I don't know many people here, but the men in the greenhouse are my uncles from Texas.
10. a. One of the latest releases issued by the city councilmembers support the new tax laws.
    b. One of the latest releases issued by the city councilmembers supports the new tax laws.

II. Circle the letter of the correct irregular verb form for each sentence.

Example You have __________ none of your promises to me.

a. broken b. broke c. breaked

1. Have you __________ a college to attend for next semester?
   a. chose b. chosen c. choosed
2. You have __________ your mother crazy with your late-night escapades.
   a. drove b. drived c. driven
3. That rat __________ right through the bedroom wall last night.
   a. ate b. eated c. eaten
4. The temperature in Atherton __________ one degree in twenty-four hours.
   a. falled b. fallen c. fell
5. Our radiator water has __________ every night we have left the car out.
   a. frozen b. froze c. freezed
6. Have you __________ all of the classes you needed for the fall semester?
   a. got b. getted c. gotten

7. I ________________ you very specific instructions for locating the hidden treasure.

   a. gived b. gave c. given

8. Have you ________________ to anyone about working for the highway patrol after you graduate?

   a. speaked b. spoke c. spoken

9. Sam has ________________ his horse in every May Day parade since he was ten.

   a. rode b. ridden c. rided

10. The audience ________________ and greeted the president enthusiastically.

    a. rised b. raised c. rose

11. Have you ________________ all of the snow off your parka?

    a. shaken b. shook c. shaked

12. Mickey ________________ my Lifesavers when I went to the pencil sharpener.

    a. stolen b. stealed c. stole

13. Minnie has ________________ great precautions to avoid sunburn this summer.

    a. took b. taken c. taken

14. Have you ________________ your life story for your fans yet?

    a. written b. wrote c. writed

15. When Sal entered the courtroom, he ________________ to no one.

    a. speaked b. spoke c. spoken

Pronouns, Adjectives, and Adverbs

Section Topic

Comparative and Superlative Adjectives

Adjectives are often used by writers to compare things: people, cars, colleges, movies, jobs, cities, or religions. They may use adjectives to compare the size of four brothers, the speed of two sports cars, the cost of tuition at a number of colleges, the endings of Alfred Hitchcock movies, the difficulty of different jobs, the crime rate in different cities, or the creation myths in different religions. Adjectives that are used in comparisons take special forms, which are covered in this section on "Pronouns, Adjectives, and Adverbs."

Comparative and Superlative Adjectives

An adjective may be used to describe a single thing, to compare two things, or to compare one thing to many others. Here are examples of these three uses for adjectives and the three forms the adjectives take:

Sally is short. (*Short* describes Sally.)

Sally is shorter than Sue. (*Shorter* compares the size of Sally to Sue.)

Sally is the shortest person in her family. (*Shortest* compares the size of Sally to the rest of her family.)

Notice that with the one-syllable adjective *short*, the *-er* ending is added for comparing two things, and the *-est* ending is added for comparing *more than two things*. Here are three more examples of the uses for adjectives with a *longer* descriptive word:

Sally is considerate. (*Considerate* describes Sally.)

Sally is more considerate than Sue. (*More considerate* compares Sally to Sue.)

Sally is the most considerate person in the class. (*Most considerate* compares Sally to all of her classmates.)

Notice that with longer adjectives (two syllables or more), a *more* is added before the adjective for comparing two things, and a *most* is added before the adjective for comparing *more than two things*.

Now that you have a general idea of the forms that adjectives take, here are some basic rules for making comparisons with adjectives:

COMPARATIVE FORM (WHEN COMPARING *TWO THINGS*)

1. Add *-er* to *one-syllable adjectives*:

   I am shorter than you are.
   Sam is smarter than Phil.
   Mercury lights are brighter than fluorescent lights.

2. Add *more* in front of adjectives with *two or more syllables*:

   I am more depressed than you are.
   Sam is more graceful than Phil.
   Mercury lights are more effective than fluorescent lights.

3. Add *-er* to two-syllable words ending in *-y* or *-ow*. (drop the *y* and add *-ier*):

   I am lonelier than you are.
   Sam is sillier than Phil.
   Mercury lights are prettier than fluorescent lights.
   The river is shallower today than last week.

4. The word *than* often comes after the adjective in sentences comparing *two things*. (See all of the examples from 1, 2, and 3.)

5. *Never* use both *more* and an *-er* ending with an adjective:

   Wrong: You are more smarter than I am.
   Right: You are smarter than I am.

   Wrong: You are more beautifuler than ever.
   Right: You are more beautiful than ever.

SUPERLATIVE FORM (WHEN COMPARING *THREE OR MORE THINGS*)

1. Add *-est* to *one-syllable adjectives*:

   I am the shortest person in my family.
   Sam is the smartest elephant in the zoo.
   Mercury lights are the brightest lights for tennis courts.

2. Add *most* in front of adjectives with *two or more syllables*.

   I am the most dependable person in the family.
   Sam is the most curious elephant in the zoo.
   Mercury lights are the most expensive lights on the market.

3. Add *-est* to two-syllable words ending in *-y* or *-ow* (drop the *y* and add *-iest*).

   I am the rowdiest person in my family.
   Sam is the heaviest elephant in the zoo.
   Mercury lights give off the loveliest glow of any outdoor lights.
   That is the shallowest that I've ever seen Lake Placid.

4. The word *the* often comes before the adjective in sentences comparing three or more things. (See all of the examples in 1, 2, and 3.)

5. *Never* use both *most* and an *-est* ending with an adjective:

   Wrong: You are the most smartest person I know.
   Right: You are the smartest person I know.

   Wrong: Francine is the most remarkablest artist in the school.
   Right: Francine is the most remarkable artist in the school.

Exercise 31 Each of the following sentences compares *two things*. Fill in the correct *comparative* form of each adjective in parentheses depending on the number of syllables the adjective has. Add *-er* to one-syllable adjectives and two-syllable adjectives ending in *-y* or *-ow* and add *more* in front of adjectives of two syllables or more. When you finish, compare your answers with the answer key.

Examples (fast) You are a *faster* runner this year than last.

(beautiful) The petunias are *more beautiful* in the spring than in the summer.

1. (interesting) The first day of school was ______________ than I thought it would be.
2. (friendly) The students were ______________ than I imagined.
3. (fascinating) The classes were ______________ than my high school classes.
4. (short) The classes were also ______________ than usual since it was the first day.
5. (fast) The whole day went by ______________ than I expected.
6. (boring) I thought that college would be ______________ than it was.
7. (excited) Now I am ______________ than ever about coming back tomorrow.
8. (long) However, tomorrow's classes will be much ______________ than today's.
9. (hard) The homework will definitely be ______________ than today's.
10. (typical) Tomorrow will be ______________ of a regular college day than today was.

Exercise 32 Each of the following sentences compares *three or more things*. Fill in the correct *superlative* form of each adjective in parentheses, depending on the number of syllables the adjective has. Add *-est* to one-syllable adjectives and two-syllable adjectives ending in *-y* or *-ow* and add *most* in front of adjectives with two syllables or more. When you finish, compare your answers with the answer key.

Examples (fast) I felt the *fastest* today in track practice that I've ever felt.

(unusual) The antique knife display in the library is the *most unusual* display of the year.

1. (interesting) The first day of school was the ______________ of the week.
2. (friendly) I met some of the ______________ people I'd ever met.
3. (fascinating) The classes were the ______________ I'd ever taken.
4. (short) The classes were also the ______________ I'd ever attended.
5. (fast) It was the ______________ day of school I'd been through.

6. (boring) I thought college would be the ______________ part of my education.

7. (excited) Now I am the ______________ I've ever been about going to school.

8. (long) Although the classes tomorrow will be the ______________ I've had, I should still enjoy them.

9. (hard) Although the homework will be the ______________ I've done, I don't think I'll mind it.

10. (typical) Teachers say that the second week of college is the ______________ week to judge school by, so I hope it goes as well as the first.

Exercise 33 Fill in the correct comparative and superlative form of each adjective in parentheses in the following sentences. Use *-er* and *more* with adjectives comparing *two things*, and use *-est* and *most* with adjectives comparing three or more things. Remember, the word *than* follows the adjective in sentences comparing two things, and the word *the* comes before the adjective in sentences comparing three or more things. When you finish, compare your answers with the answer key.

Examples (quick) The *quickest* way to get to the library is across the weedy lot.

(quick) It is *quicker* to go through the lot than to stay on the sidewalk.

(sincere) Sarah seems *more sincere* in her compliments than her brother Tad.

(sincere) Sarah is the *most sincere* person I've met this semester.

1. (tall) The new men's dorm will be the ______________ building on campus.

2. (tall) It will be even ______________ than the eight-story women's dorm.

3. (beautiful) The dorm will be the ______________ building on the west side of campus.

4. (beautiful) It will not be ______________, however, than the fine art's building on the east side.

5. (large) The rooms inside the dorm will be ______________ than in the other dorms.

6. (large) The rooms will be the ______________ dorm rooms in the state.

7. (pretty) Built atop a large hill, the dorm will have the ______________ setting of any building on campus.

8. (pretty) The setting is even _______________ than the student union setting by the lagoon.

9. (expensive) The new dorm is the _______________ place to live on campus.

10. (expensive) It is even _______________ than the married students' quarters behind the lagoon.

Exercise 34 Fill in your own comparative and superlative adjectives in the following sentences. Use the correct form for the number of things compared in a sentence and for the number of syllables each adjective has. When you finish, show your fill-ins to your instructor.

Example That old car is the ugliest vehicle in the neighborhood.

The lake is more crowded than it was last year.

1. As the winter months approach, the days grow _______________ than at any other time of the year.
2. Samuel is _______________ as an adult than he was as a teenager.
3. That magnolia tree is the _______________ tree in the yard.
4. The movie *Blood Island* was the _______________ movie of the summer.
5. You seem to be _______________ in your schoolwork than last semester.
6. An alligator is _______________ than a crocodile.
7. The real estate seminar on limited partnerships was _______________ than the one on no-money-down investments.
8. Kay has behaved the _______________ of any of the preschool children in the child development lab.
9. The stretch of road between Crescent City and Vermiel is the _______________ section of Avenue 392.
10. Your younger sister is _______________ than your older sister.
11. That is the _______________-looking hat you've ever worn.
12. In the mileage test, Toyota performed _______________ than Datsun or Volkswagen.
13. Your new air conditioner is _______________ than your old one.
14. Those seedless grapes are the _______________ I've ever eaten.
15. The house on the corner is the _______________ house on the block.

Exercise 35 Write a paragraph or short essay about something that you regretted doing: quitting a job, ending a relationship, dropping a class, joining the service, getting married, taking a particular job, getting an apartment, breaking the law, and so on.

Write your paragraph for anyone who may be tempted to make the same mistake. (You may want to do some "free writing" on your topic before writing your first draft.

Sample Draft I made a mistake losing my temper at the league swim meet, our freestyle relay team had just won the league championship. When the last person on our relay finished the race we all jumped into the pool to celebrate. However, three of the other teams were still finishing when we jumped in so the starter disqualified our team for interference. We had to forfeit the league championship and the gold medal.

When we were disqualified, I totally lost control and cussed out the starter. Later, he reported the incident to my coach who reported it to the athletic director. Because of that incident, I lost an awful lot.

I regretted that incident for a long time but I did learn a lesson. From then on when I really got mad about something, I'd keep my mouth shut until I got control of myself. That has kept me out of a lot of trouble but I still blow up sometimes.

When you finish your draft, go over the sample draft with a classmate, analyzing the paragraphing, sentence wording and structure, and punctuation. What revisions would you suggest? Then analyze your own draft and make note of any revisions or corrections you want to make. Then write your final draft and share it with a classmate.

Practice Quiz Take this practice quiz to prepare for the section quiz. Then compare your answers with the answer key. When you are ready for the section quiz, let your instructor know.

Circle the letter of the correct adjective form that completes each of the following sentences.

Example Sam Snead has the ______________ golf swing of any professional golfer.

a. smoother　　b. most smooth　　(c.) smoothest

1. The first weeks away from home for a foreign exchange student are the ______________.

   a. most lonely　　b. lonelier　　c. loneliest

2. Montgomery Ward is having its ______________ clear-out sale of the year.

   a. most large　　b. largest　　c. larger

3. Your new lawn furniture is ______________ than the old wicker chairs.

   a. comfortabler　　b. more comfortable　　c. most comfortable

4. That sand trap shot was the ______________ of the golf tournament.

   a. most incredible b. more incredible c. incrediblest

5. I seem to get ______________ as the week progresses.

   a. sleepier b. more sleepy c. most sleepy

6. For most children, two is a ______________ age than three.

   a. most awkward b. awkwarder c. more awkward

7. I've never met a ______________-looking couple than Jan and Marcus.

   a. nicer b. more nice c. nicest

8. My new twelve-volt car battery is ______________ than my old ten-volt.

   a. more dependable b. most dependable c. dependabler

9. A burglary is ______________ to occur at 3:00 a.m. than at 1:00 a.m.

   a. more likely b. likelier c. more likelier

10. Thelma is ______________ of her posture than she used to be.

    a. more consciouser b. consciouser c. more conscious

Spelling

Section Topic

Problems with a Single Letter

This section on "Spelling" introduces a list of words that are commonly used and frequently misspelled by many writers. Learning to spell these words correctly will help you to eliminate a number of potential spelling problems in your writing.

Problems with a Single Letter

These words are grouped together because a single letter in each word is often involved in the most common misspellings.

beautiful	government	pleasant	separate
clothes	guess	pretty	similar
college	interesting	radio	sophomore
describe	mountain	remember	stereo
first	picture	schedule	temperature

Although there are no common spelling rules to learn these words by, here are some suggestions that may help:

1. If you spell the *endings* of the following words correctly, you will probably spell the word correctly: *clothes,* not *cloths; mountain,* not *mountin; radio,* not *radeo; stereo,* not *sterio;* and *college,* not *collage.*
2. If you *sound out* these words correctly and spell them as they sound, you will probably spell them correctly: *gov·ern·ment,* not *gov·er·ment; in·ter·est·ing,* not *in·trest·ing; pic·ture,* not *pi·ture; pret·ty,* not *per·ty; re·mem·ber,* not *re·me·ber; soph·o·more,* not *soph·more;* and *tem·per·a·ture,* not *tem·per·ture.*
3. Some words have one key letter that is often missed: *describe,* not *discribe; separate,* not *seperate;* and *similar,* not *simular.*
4. Some words have two key letters side by side: *beautiful,* not *butiful; first,* not *frist; guess,* not *geuss; pleasant,* not *plesant;* and *schedule,* not *shedule.*

Exercise 36 Underline the correctly spelled word from each group.

Example	hairy	harry	hiary
1.	temperature	temperture	temprature
2.	sterio	stereo	stero
3.	sophmore	sophemore	sophomore
4.	schedule	shedule	schedgule
5.	similar	simular	simaler
6.	seprate	seperate	separate
7.	remember	rember	remeber
8.	radeo	radio	radiio
9.	pertty	pretty	prety
10.	pleasant	plaesant	plesant
11.	piture	pikture	picture
12.	mountain	mountaine	mountin

13. intresting	interesting	intersting
14. guess	geuss	gess
15. goverment	govermnent	government
16. frist	first	ferst
17. describe	discribe	decribe
18. collage	colege	college
19. clothse	clothes	cloths
20. beautiful	butiful	beatiful

Exercise 37 Rewrite any of the following words that are misspelled. Then compare your spellings with the list words on pages 271–272.

Example ecsample example

1. discribe describe
2. similar ______
3. sophomore ______
4. mountain ______
5. intresting interesting
6. temperture temperature
7. separate ______
8. college ______
9. beatiful beautiful
10. clothse clothes
11. government ______
12. frist first
13. shedule schedule
14. picture ______
15. sterio stereo

Exercise 38

Write ten sentences using two different words in each sentence from the list on pages 271–272. Underline the list words, and use them in any order you wish. Then share your sentences with a classmate who is finished. Spell the list words correctly.

Examples The picture playing at the student union wasn't very interesting. I'd like to describe a mountain range that I traveled through this summer.

1.
2.
3.
4.
5.
6.
7.
8.
9.
10.

Practice Quiz

Take this practice quiz to prepare for the section quiz. Then compare your answers with the answer key. When you are ready for the section quiz, let your instructor know.

Circle the letter of the correctly spelled word in each group.

Example	a. chicken	b. chiken	c. chickin
1.	a. beatiful	b. beautiful	c. butiful
2.	a. clothes	b. cloths	c. clothse
3.	a. college	b. collage	c. colege
4.	a. describe	b. discribe	c. decribe
5.	a. frist	b. ferst	c. first
6.	a. goverment	b. government	c. govermnent
7.	a. geuss	b. guess	c. gess
8.	a. interesting	b. intresting	c. interresting

9. a. mountain	b. mountian	c. mountin
10. a. picture	b. piture	c. pikture
11. a. pleasant	b. plesant	c. pleasent
12. a. pertty	b. perty	c. pretty
13. a. radeo	b. raido	c. radio
14. a. remember	b. remeber	c. rememmber
15. a. schdule	b. schedule	c. shedule
16. a. simular	b. similur	c. similar
17. a. separate	b. seperate	c. seperete
18. a. sophmore	b. sophomore	c. sophemore
19. a. stero	b. sterio	c. stereo
20. a. temperture	b. temperature	c. temprature

Writing Review

In this "Writing Review" section, you have the opportunity to apply what you have learned in the first four levels to a composition assignment. Much of what you have learned about paragraphing, sentence development, and correct usage will be useful as you move step by step through the process of writing a composition.

Level 4 Composition Assignment

Select one of the following topics for writing a composition:

General Topic Areas:

1. a law that needs changing
2. spanking children
3. being a "housewife"
4. improving our school system
5. couples living together without marriage
6. body building for women
7. single parenting
8. cable television

Step One

1. Select a topic that you have an opinion on and would like to write about.
2. Consider a tentative *controlling idea*—a main idea you want to develop about your topic—to give your composition direction.
3. Do some form of prewriting (listing ideas, brainstorming, free writing) to prepare for your first draft.
4. Write the first draft of your composition beginning with an opening that includes your *controlling idea* and developing supporting points in separate paragraphs. *Your audience for this composition is your classmates.*

Step Two When you finish your first draft, read it over and apply these questions:

1. What is accomplished in the opening? Is it interesting? Is the controlling idea clearly stated?
2. Do you develop a different supporting point in each paragraph? Do you have a topic sentence for each paragraph? Do your paragraphs relate well to your controlling idea?
3. Is each paragraph developed, unified, and organized effectively? What can you add to make your draft clearer or more interesting?
4. Will your audience get anything out of the composition? Have you kept them in mind as you wrote?
5. Make a note of any changes in the content or organization you want to make for the next draft.

Step Three Now go over the individual sentences within each paragraph and follow these suggestions:

1. Make sure that your sentence structure is *varied*. Are you using compound and complex sentences? Do you have any pairs or groups of *short sentences* that need combining? Underline sentences for combining and insert joining words to form compound and complex sentences if necessary.
2. Are your sentences clearly, smoothly worded? Underline any sentence that appears awkward, wordy, or vague to revise in your next draft. Make sure you are using *concrete language* wherever appropriate.
3. Check paragraphs for run-on sentences and fragments. Also, make sure that you are using *commas* correctly in compound and complex sentences.

Step Four Now give your composition a final check for wording errors. Follow these suggestions:

1. Check each sentence for correct subject-verb agreement. Also, check past tense verbs for the *-ed* ending, and make sure all *irregular verbs* are spelled correctly.
2. Check your use of pronouns, including correct subject pronoun forms and pronoun-antecedent agreement. Also, make sure you are using correct comparative and superlative adjective forms.
3. Check your spelling. Are you adding the *-s* or *-es* ending to plural words? Are you spelling your *-ing*-ending words correctly? Are you using *there, their,* and *they're* correctly? Also, check your apostrophes on *possessive words* and *contractions*. Look up in the dictionary any words you are uncertain of.

Step Five Write the final draft of your composition, including all improvements and error corrections. Then share your final draft with a number of classmates.

LEVEL 5

In this final level, you cover some interesting and challenging aspects of writing. You learn to write an effective ending for a composition, you work with more sophisticated sentence structures, you cover a variety of punctuation situations, you learn some of the finer points of grammar usage, and you are introduced to some challenging spelling words. Then you write a final composition applying everything you have learned about writing compositions, paragraphs, and sentences. By the time you finish this level, you should have enough basic writing knowledge and experience to communicate effectively in any writing situation.

The Composition

Section Topic

Ending Paragraph

Most effective compositions have three definite parts—a beginning, a middle, and an end. The beginning is your opening paragraph, which was covered in Level 5. The middle is the heart of the composition—all of the information and ideas that develop and support the controlling idea for the composition. The ending paragraph provides a strong conclusion to your composition, leaving readers with something to think about.

Ending Paragraph

Most compositions conclude with an *ending paragraph* that leaves readers with some final thoughts on the topic of the composition. Although ending paragraphs vary in content, effective endings all follow logically from the previous paragraphs in the composition, support the controlling idea for the composition, and leave the reader with a sense that the topic has been thoughtfully concluded. A strong ending paragraph leaves a positive impression with the reader while a weak ending can hurt an otherwise effective composition.

Here are some different ways that compositions are frequently ended:

1. With compositions involving personal experiences, the ending paragraph often includes the *effects* or *results* of the experience and what, if anything, the writer may have *learned*.

Sample Composition

Too Many Moves

My first semester of college was the worst I've been through. Everything started out smoothly enough. I had made plans during the summer to share an apartment with two of my close friends from high school. We had found a nice enough apartment about two miles from campus, but before we even moved in, problems started developing that ended up keeping me on the move the entire semester.

One of the two girls I was to share an apartment with was going to work instead of going to college. However, a week before we were to move in, she found out that she didn't get the job she had been counting on. She was forced to live at home and look for work, and two of us were stuck with higher monthly rent payments. We lasted for a month and then agreed that we couldn't make it by ourselves. Joan moved in with her aunt and uncle who lived across town from college, and I started looking around.

I ended up finding lodging in a sorority house that took in boarders. Actually I lived in an old wooden cottage behind the main house with three other girls, so the rent wasn't bad. The room was small, there was one tiny bathroom for four people, and the place was noisy, but it was the best I could afford for the time. However, one day I returned from school and saw smoke coming from the back of the house. The cottage had caught fire, and the fire department was putting out the last flames. My room was a charred mess, and there was no way that anyone could live there for a long time. I was once more out of a place to stay, and there was still over a month of school left.

After looking around all weekend for lodging, I finally gave up and moved home. I ended up driving forty miles to school every day, so I almost spent as much on gas as I would have on lodging. I'd drive to school, go to classes, and come home and sit in an empty house for a few hours. I was very bored, and I'd also lost the will to study. It had been such a bad semester moving all over the place that my heart wasn't in school anymore. So the semester just played itself out.

Ending Paragraph:

I finished the semester with 2 C's and 2 D's, I'd lost ten pounds, and I'd had a lousy time. It was a wasted semester of college. I did learn a few things, though. First, when you plan on rooming with a noncollege person, you are taking the risk that she will not be around for an entire semester. Next, if you want to live with some peace and quiet, don't ever board in a sorority house. And if you want to be bored to death, live at home. I've now decided that the best place for me is the dormitories, and that's where I'm living next semester. That way I'll know exactly what I have to pay, I won't have to depend on getting roommates, and I'll have the cafeteria to eat in, the library to study in, and plenty of people around for social life. Besides, nothing could be worse than living in three different places in one semester.

2. With compositions involving a problem or problems the writer is analyzing, the ending paragraph often presents a possible solution(s) to the problem.

Sample Composition

A Dull Duty

I never did much cooking until I got married. I never liked working in the kitchen with my mom when I was growing up. I remember burning a couple of batches of cookies one summer, but that was about the extent of my cooking. Then in my sophomore year of college, I got married and started cooking regularly. My husband knew nothing about cooking, so being the wife, I figured it was my responsibility. Now I've been cooking for over a year, and it's the dullest duty I've ever had.

First, cooking takes up too much of my time. Making an evening meal, even for two people, usually takes me at least an hour. Then when my parents or his parents come over for dinner, or when we have friends over, I end up spending two or three hours in the kitchen. Even putting together sandwiches for lunch takes fifteen minutes by the time I get everything out and put it together. I never realized how much time mom spent in the kitchen, and now I'm stuck doing the same thing.

Second, cooking is hot work. We live in a small apartment with a water cooler, and from late spring through early fall, it is warm in the kitchen. Whenever I use the oven, the kitchen feels like a sauna. Even cooking over the gas range heats the kitchen up to over 100 degrees. I get dizzy standing over the stove with the heat and steam coming off the boiling vegetables or pasta. Sometimes I have to get out of the kitchen while I'm cooking and just cool off. As long as I'm in there, there's no escaping the heat.

Finally, cooking is boring. My husband is a meat and potatoes man. He doesn't like anything fancy or unusual. So I just cook him the basics: hamburgers, roasts, fried chicken, potatoes, green beans, salad, and so forth. It doesn't take much skill or imagination to boil potatoes or fry a hamburger. It might be more fun fixing a fancy casserole or some exotic foreign dish, but as long as I'm cooking for Matt, it's going to be boring.

Ending Paragraph:

Since cooking isn't going to be a favorite task and since I'm stuck with it, I've decided to make the job easier. First, I don't make Matt lunches anymore. He can make his own sandwiches or heat some soup, for I'm just as busy at school as he is. Second, we're going to eat TV dinners at least once a week. You can get pretty good meals, and they're not that expensive. Third, my husband has agreed to learn to fix at least two dishes so that he can cook dinner once a week. Fourth, I'm learning to cook two meals at a time so that we can eat leftovers the second night. Finally, Matt's agreed to let me experiment with casseroles once or twice a month to get out of the meat and potatoes rut. These changes should make my cooking situation more tolerable, and if they don't, I'll try something else.

3. With any composition involving a controlling idea and supporting points, the ending paragraph may *summarize the key points and reinforce and extend the controlling idea.*

Sample Composition

A Nice Place to Live

Some people think that the central Albion Valley is the worst place in the state to live. They say that it's hot, that it's ugly, and that there is nothing to do. However, most of the people who say those things don't live here. I've lived in the Albion Valley all of my life, and I happen to like it here. In fact, in some ways, it's a great place to live.

First, the Albion Valley is ideally located. We are only forty-five minutes from the mountains, an hour and a half from the ocean, and three hours from the large northern and southern metropolitan areas. We are in the best location for enjoying everything the state has to offer. There's snow skiing an hour away at Crescent Summit, surf fishing two hours away at Morley Beach, or sight-seeing at the state capital only two and a half hours away. The central Albion Valley is the best place to live for getting to anywhere in the state within a few hours.

Second, the weather is not as bad as outsiders say. All you hear about is how hot it gets here, but that's only three months in the summer. There are also the beautiful fall and spring seasons and the mild winters. And if you live in the valley long enough, you learn how to deal with the summer heat. There are swimming pools, water slides, lakes, and rivers for cooling off, and there is usually a nice breeze in the late afternoon and evening, even on the hottest days. You also learn to stay inside air-conditioned homes or apartments during the heat of the day. Once summer is over, you have about nine months of pleasant weather, so the valley doesn't deserve its bad reputation.

Third, there are lots of things to do in Albion, the largest city in the valley. Albion has a population of over 100,000, and it has plenty of movie theaters, good restaurants, nightclubs, and shopping malls. It also has a convention center, a philharmonic orchestra, a number of art galleries and museums, and several playhouses. For sports fans, the local state college has excellent football, basketball, and baseball teams. People who move to Albion from the larger metropolitan areas are pleasantly surprised at the number of things that the city has to offer. There's a lot more to do in Albion that most outsiders realize.

Ending Paragraph:

As you can see, the central Albion Valley certainly isn't as bad as some people would have you believe. In fact, most of the people who live here rate the area highly. They like the location, the mild weather, and activities available. They also like the idea of living in an area that is less crowded, less polluted, and less expensive than other parts of the state. I've lived in the Albion Valley for twenty-two years, and I'm not planning on moving. I figure I could do a lot worse.

4. With compositions that contain *comparisons* of different items, situations, or ideas, the ending paragraph may *draw a conclusion* based on the comparisons made within the composition.

Sample Composition

Looking for the Perfect Cookie

I love cookies. I grew up eating chocolate chip cookies and milk. I learned to bake them myself when I was about ten, and I could devour a whole panful in one sitting. I thought that nothing could be better than homemade chocolate chip cookies until I started trying the new cookie shops that are going up in most cities. Being a chocolate chip cookie expert for many years, I decided to sample the cookies at the three newest cookie shops in town in search of the best chocolate chip cookie in Akron.

First, I ate at Grandma's Pantry in the Farmer's Market Mall. Grandma's chocolate chip cookies are large, about five inches in diameter, but thin. They have an average amount of chips in them and finely chopped pieces of nuts. The cookies are chewy and fairly sweet. They cost forty cents apiece, and it took four of them to fill me up.

The next day I went downtown and ate at Harry's Snack Shop at the corner of E and Main. Harry's chocolate chip cookies are smaller than Grandma's but much thicker. They are loaded with chips, and the nuts are in large chunks. The cookies are crunchy instead of chewy, and they are sweeter than Grandma's. They cost forty-five cents apiece, and three of them filled me up.

The last place I tried was the Cookie Shoppe in the Westside Mall. The cookies are about the same size as Harry's, and they're also loaded with chips. The nuts are in large chunks, and you can choose among walnuts, almonds, peanuts, and macadamia nuts. The cookies are soft and chewy, and they are very sweet. The Cookie Shoppe serves only warm cookies, so the chocolate chips are nice and gooey. They cost forty-five cents apiece, and three of them were all I could eat.

Ending Paragraph:

For my taste, chocolate chip cookies at the Cookie Shoppe are the best in town. I like soft, thick, warm, chewy cookies with lots of chips, and that's the way the Cookie Shoppe makes them. However, if you don't like your cookies that sweet, I'd suggest Grandma's Pantry. And if you like crunchy cookies instead of chewy ones, then Harry's is the place to go. All three places serve freshly baked cookies seven days a week, so where you go depends on your cookie preference.

5. With any type of composition, the ending paragraph may project what the *future may hold* for the subject of the composition.

Sample Composition

The Changing Workweek

In the early 1900s in the United States, workers in large industries worked long days and long weeks. It was not uncommon for workers in the meat packing companies of Chicago, for example, to work from dawn to dark, twelve to fourteen hours, for six or seven days a week. Similar workweeks were common among miners in West Virginia and millinery workers in New York. As unions started exerting their influence, however, the working conditions of

American workers began improving, and the workweek was gradually shortened. Today, workers have workweek options that were unheard of earlier in the century.

The five-day workweek has become commonplace in American industry. However, the four-day workweek is becoming even more popular. Instead of spreading their forty hours a week over five eight-hour days, many workers are opting for four ten-hour days. This gives the workers longer working days, but it also gives them three-day weekends, an unheard-of luxury even twenty years ago. Management isn't complaining since the same amount of work gets accomplished, and in some cases a plant can be totally shut down on the fifth day, saving the company thousands of dollars in utilities.

Another change in the workweek is the variable hours option. While American workers have traditionally worked either day, swing, or night shifts, some companies are allowing workers to set their own hours within the workweek. A worker, for example, could work from 7:00 a.m. to noon, take the afternoon off, and then continue from 5:00 p.m. to 8:00 p.m. Another worker might work straight through from 6:00 a.m. to 2:00 p.m. and be off the rest of the day. Such flexible schedules are becoming more common in metropolitan areas with commuter-time traffic problems and in industries that are open around the clock. The advantage to the workers is that they can plan their hours around the days of their families. For example, a husband who takes each afternoon off could babysit the children while his wife works. The variable hours schedule also motivates workers because the company is letting them control their own time.

A third change in the workweek over the past twenty years is the use of overtime. While most workers do not have to work beyond a forty-hour week, many companies will pay them time and a half to do so. Although this is more expensive for the company, it is still cheaper than having to hire additional workers and providing benefits. On traditional nonworking days such as holidays, workers are often paid double-time or more to work. Overtime pay is a seasonal option in some industries, such as the U.S. mail service, but in others, workers may average fifteen to twenty hours of overtime a month per year. Overtime pay allows companies to meet their production needs at a given time without exploiting the workers. It allows workers to make extra money at a higher rate than they normally work for. Although overtime work often represents a return to longer working days and weeks, it is done on a voluntary basis and is usually negotiated willingly by the workers.

Ending Paragraph:

What does the future hold for American workers? As modern technology turns more and more work over to machines, the typical workweek may continue to shrink. Some companies have already gone to thirty-five-hour weeks, and before the turn of the century, the thirty-five-hour week may be standard. As the need to conserve resources increases, the incentive for companies to go to four-day weeks will be greater. Within twenty years, the most common workweek may be a four-day, thirty-two-hour workweek. The great advantage to shorter workweeks is that workers have more time off to themselves and with their families. However, given the financial demands upon American families in the future, it may also become common for workers to hold down two full-time jobs at one time. Given the American work ethic, most workers will probably fill their free time with more work instead of more leisure.

Exercise 1 Write your own ending paragraph for each of the following compositions. Create an ending that makes sense for the composition, that relates to the controlling idea, and that leaves the reader with something to think about. You may use any of the ending suggestions or combination found in this section. When you finish, share your ending paragraphs with your instructor.

Example

A Bad Accident

When I was in the first grade, I was playing on a piece of playground equipment called the ocean wave. It was a circular bench attached to a tall middle pole, and the bench swung back and forth as we rocked it. One day I made the mistake of putting my hand in the wrong place, and I ended up in the doctor's office. It was the worst day of my young life, and it also turned out badly for my mom.

As we rocked the bench back and forth, it clanged against the metal pole in the middle. Without thinking, I put my hand on the inside of the bench, and the next time the bench swung inward, the top of my index finger was smashed against the pole.

I let out a scream and fell off the bench. I looked at my finger and started sobbing. The fingernail was halfway torn off, and my hand was covered with blood. My finger was throbbing with pain, and I nearly vomited. The yard-duty teacher came over and helped me to the nurse's office, and the nurse covered my finger with gauze. Then the principal came and drove me to the nearest doctor's office.

My mother met me at the doctor's office, and we went into one of the little rooms with the padded table and the horrible instruments lined up neatly on trays. I lay on the table and sobbed as my mother tried to soothe me. The doctor came in, unwrapped the gauze, and said, "Boy, you did a bang-up job on that nail." I half laughed through my sobs and braced myself for what was to come. I closed my eyes and felt a sharp pain in my finger. I screamed, and my mother fainted, crumbling to the floor beside the table. The doctor had given me a shot of pain killer right into the red meat underneath the torn nail. Soon the flesh was deadened, and he pulled off the nail. Then he bandaged the finger and put a splint on it. In the meantime, a nurse was helping my mother.

Ending Paragraph: (effects of the accident)

We finally left the office with my finger feeling better and my mother carrying five stitches in her forehead where she had hit the floor. Once the numbness started wearing off, the tip of my finger began throbbing again, so I took pain pills every two hours until I went to sleep. It took over a year for my fingernail to grow back, and to this day the nail is still ridged and ugly. My mother carries a scar on her forehead where she cut herself. The ocean wave no longer sits on the playground. It was removed the year of my accident because it was too dangerous. If anything good came from my smashed finger, it was that no one else would ever get hurt on the ocean wave. But mother and I still carry reminders of that accident with her scarred forehead and my funny-looking finger.

1. Downward Slide

My first semester of college, I wanted to do well. I wanted to prove to myself that I could handle college classes, and I was determined to study hard to succeed. At least that's how I felt when the semester began. By the end of the semester my expectations had changed a lot, but I had learned a lesson.

My most challenging class of the semester was going to be Physical Science I. The class met daily at 8:00 a.m. and had a Wednesday evening lab. When the semester started, I went to class every morning, took notes on the lectures, and read my assignments. I studied hard for my first test and got a B on it. I was off to a great start.

Then I took a couple of mornings off from class to reward myself. When I returned, I realized the instructor hadn't noticed I'd been gone. There were about one hundred students in the class, and he never took roll. I figured I could sleep in once in a while, borrow someone's notes, and still do well.

I went from sleeping in once a week to two or three times. On the next test I got a low C, but it didn't bother me that much. After having gone to high school and almost never missing a class, the freedom to be able to sleep in and not get in trouble was too much for me. I continued my poor attendance, and then I went off the deep end and missed three weeks in a row. I vowed that I'd borrow all of the lectures notes I'd missed and that I'd catch up on the reading assignments. But deep down inside, I knew I was in trouble.

When the final exam finally came, I was a month behind in my note taking and three chapters behind in the book. The night before the final, I borrowed a friend's notes, took my book and headed to a vacant dorm room at the end of the building. I was determined to stay up all night copying notes and reading 120 pages in the text. I took a handful of No-Doze tablets with me to keep awake. However, after about an hour's studying, I realized that I had more work than I could do in a week, let alone a night. I gave up at about 2:00 a.m. and went to sleep. The next morning I took the final and was finished in twenty minutes. I had guessed on every answer.

Ending Paragraph:

2. One Vote for Cafeteria Lunches

At the beginning of the year, I'd go off campus with my friends to eat lunch. We'd rush downtown, grab a hamburger and Coke, and rush back to campus for our one o'clock class. Then one day I decided to stay on campus and eat because I had to study for a test. To my surprise, I enjoyed my lunch in the cafeteria. Now my friends still go off campus to eat most of the time, but I stay and eat in the cafeteria. I actually prefer eating lunch in the cafeteria to going off campus.

First, I can get a good meal in the cafeteria. When I ate downtown at a sandwich shop, I'd always get greasy hamburgers and french fries. At the cafeteria, I get better balanced lunches: salad, vegetables, chicken or fish, milk and occasionally yogurt. I'm not eating as much junk food or consuming as many calories, and that's good for me. I can get a more nutritious meal in the cafeteria.

Second, I save a lot of time eating on campus. Instead of wasting twenty minutes going downtown and returning, I have twenty more minutes to study or relax before class. I even save more time because in the cafeteria, there's no waiting for the food. So I take my time, eat slowly, and still have twenty to thirty minutes before class. I don't ever feel rushed anymore.

Third, I have met new friends eating in the cafeteria. Since my old high school friends eat downtown, I started eating with different people I'd met in class. Many of the people who eat in the cafeteria didn't graduate from the local high schools, so I've gotten to know people from all over the state. Now I can go into the cafeteria at lunchtime and sit down with two or three different groups of students and feel comfortable. I've gotten to know some really nice people that I wouldn't have known otherwise.

Ending Paragraph:

3. Racquetball or Tennis?

Tarpey College requires at least two semesters of PE classes for all graduates. Since I had to take PE, I decided to take classes I thought I'd enjoy. I also wanted to take classes where I'd get some exercise. So I took one semester of racquetball and one semester of tennis, and I found out that they are very different sports.

Racquetball is a fast-paced sport that keeps you moving. However, you don't move too far at once because of the size of the court. Racquetball requires a lot of short, quick bursts in one direction and then another. For me, that caused problems. First, I'm not very quick, so I had trouble getting to a well-placed ball. Second, I'm tall, and I had a hard time bending down to return the low, hard hits off the front wall. I also got dizzy trying to follow the ball bouncing off the walls like a pinball. Racquetball did give me a good workout, but I seldom won a game, and I didn't really enjoy it.

Tennis is a much different game. It's slower paced than racquetball, so it was easier for me to play. I takes much longer for a tennis ball to be returned over a net than for a racquetball to careen off a wall, and I was able to move into position to hit the ball most of the time. My height was also an advantage when I was at the net or when I was serving. I still got in a lot of running, but it wasn't the short, abrupt moves I made in racquetball, so my lack of quickness didn't hurt me as much. I was much better at tennis, I got good exercise, and it wasn't so hard on my body.

Ending Paragraph:

Exercise 2 Write a composition on one of the following topics. Include an opening paragraph with a controlling idea, three or four middle paragraphs for developing your topic, and an *ending paragraph* that follows logically from the other paragraphs and provides a definite conclusion to the composition. Remember, *the middle paragraphs are the heart of your composition*, but an effective opening and closing are also important. Your audience for this composition is your classmates. Write the composition with them in mind.

Select one of the following topics:

1. a satisfying experience
2. comparing three of something: three similar cars, three rock groups or singers, three classes, three living situations, three colleges, three friends, three forms of contraception, three similar restaurants, or three similar jobs
3. one school-related issue (campus police carrying guns, serving beer on campus, charging tuition, dropping the school paper, bookstore prices, apathy in school government, unfair requirements, paying parking fees, or another issue that concerns you)
4. a person you respect (or envy)
5. a particular store you can't resist

Before you begin, you may want to use some prewriting technique—listing supporting points, making a formal outline, brainstorming, or writing freely on the topic—to generate ideas. Use the technique that would be most useful for your topic.

When you finish your first draft, read it carefully and consider any revisions to strengthen your opening or closing paragraphs, to improve the unity, development, or organization of your middle paragraphs, or to make the composition in general clearer, more interesting, and more informative. Also, revise individual sentences for clarity, and correct any grammatical, structural, or spelling errors. Then if you'd like a second opinion, exchange drafts with a classmate or two. Mark all revisions on your draft and write the final draft to share with your instructor.

Sample Composition

Topic: a person I envied
Specific Subject: Bud Pinter
Controlling Idea: Bud Pinter was my idol in college.
Prewriting Work: (two examples)

Brainstorming:

great looks
very masculine
good body
intelligent
kind
mechanically inclined
great with the ladies
perfect skin
envied him
building homecoming float
playing poker
his kindness to me
set me up on dates
never met anyone like him
a man's man
don't know where he is
building the racing cart

Formal Outline: (from brainstorming)

I. Great-looking guy
  A. Tall and muscular
  B. Perfect skin
  C. Great eyes
  D. Perfect teeth and square jaw
  E. Hairy chest
II. Bud and the ladies
  A. Gone with lots of girls
  B. Fast starter at college
    1. Sophomore girlfriend
    2. Twenty-three-year-old waitress
    3. Visits from hometown girls
    4. The "Fonzie" of the dorms
III. Very intelligent
  A. College easy for him
  B. Mechanical whiz
    1. Fixed my bike and car
    2. Built a soap box racer
    3. Horse for homecoming float
IV. A nice guy
  A. Always good to me
    1. Helped me with the bike and car
    2. Got me dates
    3. Included me in poker games
  B. Nice to the girls
    1. Never led anyone on
    2. Happy to share him

Final Draft

My College Idol

I came from a small high school where I was one of the big shots. I thought I was a decent-looking guy and pretty cool until I went off to college. Then I met a guy from Florida who lived in my dormitory. The better I got to know him, the worse I felt about myself. He turned out to be everything I *thought* I was, and I turned out to be just another guy. Bud Pinter was my college idol.

First, there were his looks. Bud was six feet tall and muscular. He had deep blue eyes, perfect teeth, and a strong square jaw. A pimple had never touched his perfect complexion. To top it off, he had a hairy chest that I envied, being a hairless wonder myself. When I was around Bud, I felt like a skinny, buck-toothed case of walking acne.

Then there was Bud and the women. He had gone with more girls in high school than I had even known. And after two weeks of college, he already had a sophomore girl coming to his dorm room regularly. Then there was the girl from back home who visited during Thanksgiving and the twenty-three-year-old waitress he saw on weekends. Basically, Bud could have about any girl he was interested in. He was the stud of the dorms.

Bud was also bright. He breezed through his classes without working very hard. He was a mechanical and electrical whiz. He fixed my bicycle chain for me one week and adjusted my car carburetor the next. When our dorms entered the soap box derby, Bud built the racing car, and when we made a float for homecoming, Bud built a mechanical horse for it that raised up on its hind legs. While Bud built the horse, I stuffed the toilet paper in the chicken wire.

Finally, Bud was a nice guy. I had secretly hoped that he'd turn out to be mean or conceited, but he wasn't. Like I said, he helped me with bicycle and car problems. He always included me when some of the guys played poker in his room. He even set me up on a couple of dates with his girlfriends' roommates. And although he sure wasn't true to one girl, he was nice to all of them, and he didn't lead them on. They seemed glad to share him.

I transferred from Fayettville after my freshman year and went home to school. I never saw Bud after that or heard from him. I did go back to Fayettville after two years and checked up on some of my old friends, but Bud had apparently gone back to Florida by then. I've known a lot of sharp guys since then, but Bud still stands out as being really special. I've tried to imitate the way he was sometimes, but I'm just not a Bud. He seemed to have it all. At least that's the way I'll always remember him.

Practice Quiz

Take this practice quiz to prepare for the section quiz. Then compare your answers with the answer key. When you are ready for the section quiz, let your instructor know.

Circle the letter of the best *ending paragraph* for each composition.

Example

My junior year of high school I was on the varsity football team. I was tall, thin, and awkward, so I spent most of the season on the bench. We had a good team and I was glad to be on it, but like everyone else, I wanted to get out on the field and show the coach what I could do. I got my chance one game in the middle of the season when I was sent in on the punting team. I'm still trying to live down that one play.

When Coach Clawson yelled, "Johnson, get in for Jewell on the punting team," I jumped off the bench and raced onto the field to join the huddle. As an end, I had an important job. While the other players blocked for the punter, the other end and I were to run down field and cover the punt, hopefully tackling the runner for no gain. As I lined up and waited for the signals to be called, I was determined to make the tackle.

When the punter yelled "hike," I sprinted down the field, my eyes fixed on the punt returner. I heard the thud of the ball making contact with the kicker's foot and then saw it soaring high in the air toward the punt returner. I tried to keep my eye on the ball, on the returner, and on my course of direction. Finally, I just focused on the punt returner and raced straight at him. The ball reached him just before I did, and as soon as he caught it, I knocked him down with a flying tackle. The ball spurted out of his hands and I scrambled after it. As I fell on the ball, I realized I had not only made a great open-field tackle, I had also recovered the ball deep in the other team's territory. I leaped to my feet and ran triumphantly off the field.

As I neared the sidelines, I didn't near any cheers or see any players waiting to mob me. I saw the coach throw down his headphones angrily, and I knew something was wrong. As it turned out, I had paid too much attention to the ball and not enough to the punt returner, for he had signaled for a fair catch moments before I had crashed into him. Instead of making a great tackle and recovering a fumble, I had committed a fifteen-yard penalty and given the other team an automatic first down. The coach pulled me over and said a few choice words, but I was too humiliated to even care. I had made a fool out of myself.

(a.) Needless to say, I didn't play anymore that night, but fortunately we won the game despite my goof. The coach even came over after the game and said, "At least you were pursuing well." I got teased by some of the players, and I got more teasing at school the next day, but it was all good-natured. I began to feel a lot better. The next game I got into, I broke my hand trying to arm-tackle a 210-pound fullback, and that was the end of my football career. I didn't go out my senior year, and the coach never seemed too upset about it. Football just wasn't my game, but for about five seconds after that one punt coverage, I felt the thrill of making a great play.

b. Needless to say, I didn't play anymore that night. But the next game I got in, I played defensive end for about five plays. On the fifth play, the other team's fullback ran a dive off tackle, and I stupidly stuck out my arm instead of throwing my body toward him. He practically knocked my hand off, and I ran off the field in pain. Within fifteen minutes the back of my hand was badly swollen, and I kept an ice pack on it the rest of the game. The next day I went to the doctor's for X-rays, and he found two cracked bones in the top of my right hand. He put the hand in a cast, and I didn't play anymore football that year. In fact, I never played again. But I'll never forget covering that one punt return.

c. Needless to say, I didn't play anymore that night. However, the game turned out all right, so things weren't so bad for me. The coach even came over after the game and said something to me. Some of the guys talked to me in the locker room, and some kids talked to me at school the next day. Things were getting better for me. The next game I got to play in, I hurt myself, and that ended the season. I didn't go out my senior year, and the coach didn't say much about that.

1. Family Fishing

When I was a child, my family used to visit my aunt and uncle in Tarpey. We had to travel over a mountain ridge to get there, and there was a trout farm near the top of the ridge. My younger brother and I always begged my dad to let us stop there and fish on the way home, and sometimes he'd give in. It was a big thrill for us because it was the only fishing we ever did. However, there was one stop at the trout farm that I regretted.

The farm had four small ponds filled with hundreds of rainbow trout. We'd take these long bamboo poles with lines and hooks and put some gummy orange stuff on the hooks. Then we'd drop our hooks into the water, and instantly a whole school of trout would dart toward the bait. I'd feel a tug on my pole and in one big jerk, I'd pull the fish from the water and onto the concrete beach. My brother would pull one out at about the same time, and Dad would have a couple of nine- or ten-inch trout to pay for.

On that particular day, I threw my line into the water first and immediately pulled out an eight-incher. I stood proudly by my flopping fish and watched my brother put in his line about two feet from the shore. The big schools of fish in the middle of the pond didn't notice the bait, so it just sank in the water. Then my brother let out a whoop as his pole bent in two. A big trout had come up off the bottom and taken the hook. There was no way my brother could jerk the fish out of the water, so he walked backwards with his pole and dragged the biggest fish I'd ever seen onto the beach. Jeremy was yelling with joy, and I was standing by my eight-inch trout feeling miserable.

a. Dad ended up paying for Jeremy's six-pound, twenty-four-inch trout and my quarter-pound eight-incher. Jeremy was a celebrity at the trout farm. Everyone wanted to take pictures of the little boy with the huge fish. No one noticed his sister pouting in the shadows with tears in her eyes. I was being a brat and I knew it, but I couldn't stand my little brother catching that big fish and me catching a minnow. To my surprise, Jeremy called me over to hold the fish with him for some pictures. He even let me hold it by myself for a while, and I started thinking maybe it was *our* fish instead of Jeremy's. I started feeling better, thanks to my little brother's kindness. He was willing to share his glory with me, and I often wonder if I would have been as generous.

b. Dad ended up paying for a six-pound, twenty-four-inch trout and my quarter-pound eight-incher. Jeremy's fish was the biggest one ever caught at the farm, so everyone treated him specially. Jeremy was feeling one way and I was feeling another. But when Jeremy saw how I was feeling, he let me share his glory. Then I felt bad about the way I had acted. I'll never forget that day.

c. Dad ended up paying for a six-pound, twenty-four-inch trout and my quarter-pound eight-incher. Jeremy's fish was the biggest ever caught at the farm. The biggest fish before that was a four-pound, eighteen-inch brown trout. The interesting thing about the brown trout was that it wasn't a stocked fish. It had snuck in from an adjoining creek and joined the rainbows. The last time I drove over the ridge, the trout farm wasn't there anymore. It had been leveled, and a housing development was going up. A lot of new homes are being built on the ridge since they opened up the reservoir for fishing and skiing.

2. Cruising Money

At least once very couple of weeks, my friends and I pile into a car and cruise Mooney Boulevard in Vicksburg. Mooney is a wide four-lane street with malls, restaurants, and parking lots on each side along the three-mile cruising strip. When I tell my mom I'm going cruising, she always looks at me like I'm crazy. She'll say, "How can you spend the night driving up and down a road? Why don't you go to a movie or something?" Well, we do go to movies some weekends, and we also go to Zak's, a teenage nightclub. But on a lot of Friday nights, cruising is my favorite activity.

The biggest kick in cruising is checking out all the new guys. At school you're stuck with the same faces every day, but when you're cruising, you never know who's going to drive up next to you. Guys from all over the area come to cruise Mooney. It's fun to see a load of good-looking guys heading the other direction and try to figure out a way to catch them. We'll flip a U-turn just about anyplace to go after a car of "hunks." Most of the time we just check the guys out, but sometimes we'll pull over and talk to them or split up and ride in each other's cars. Nothing much ever happens, but it's fun riding around and talking with guys I've never met. And you never know. Maybe the next car that pulls up beside me will have Mr. Right in it. Anything's possible when you're cruising.

Another fun part of cruising is being with the gang. Patti, Marty, Charlotte, Vicki, and I have been pals since our freshman year in high school. We call ourselves the "Stubbs," and when we go cruising, we are very crazy. We turn the radio up full blast and sing our hearts out. We puff on cigarettes like real degenerates. We'll hang halfway out of the car to talk to guys, and we'll race them off the line when the light changes. And we laugh at anything and everything. Cruising brings out the craziness in us, and we have a blast together.

Then there's the practical side of cruising. It's pretty cheap entertainment. We split the gas five ways each time we go, and that's about a dollar apiece. Then we stop at Mearle's Drive-in on the way home and buy milk shakes and fries, which is another dollar or two. That's a pretty cheap night compared to going to the movies or a concert. Even when we're short on money, we can always pool enough cash to head for Mooney's.

a. Tomorrow night the Stubbs are heading to Mooney's Boulevard in Marty's 1978 Monte Carlo. We'll cruise for three or four hours, and we'll have a great time. Then we'll come home and sleep in on Saturday until about 10:00. Then we'll go to Patti's after lunch and plan what we want to do the rest of the weekend. The Stubbs spend a lot of time together, as you can tell.

b. Tomorrow night the Stubbs will head for Mooney's Boulevard in Marty's 1978 Monte Carlo. We may find some guys, and we may not. But we don't care either way. We'll have fun no matter what. We just like being together.

c. Tomorrow night the Stubbs will head for Mooney's Boulevard in Marty's 1978 Monte Carlo. We may find some great-looking guys, or we may strike out. But either way we'll have a lot of fun because we enjoy cruising and being together. And we'll still have plenty of money left for next weekend. So even though we're in college now, we're not too old to enjoy cruising. Luckily, a lot of college guys like it too.

3. The Right Shift

Since working for the Boren Chemical Company, I've been on three different shifts: the day shift, the swing shift, and the night shift. I started on the night shift in 1979, moved to the swing shift in 1982, and have been on the day shift since then. If you are considering taking a job that has different shifts available, I can give you some advice from my experience.

The night shift isn't the greatest, but at least you have your evenings at home, which is important if you are married and have kids like I do. I used to get off work at 5:00 a.m., come hope and sleep until about 1:00 p.m. Then I had the afternoon to relax and the evening to be with my family. By the time I left for work at 8:00 p.m., the boys were almost asleep and my wife wasn't long out of bed because she works during the day. So we had quite a bit of time together.

The swing shift was the worst for me. When I'd come home from work at 12:30 a.m., everyone was asleep. When I'd wake up at 9:00 a.m., my wife would be at work and the boys at the babysitter's. When I'd go back to work at 3:30 p.m., my wife wouldn't be home yet and neither would the boys. During the week, I was a stranger to my family. And I hated going to work in the afternoon and working through the evening, the time I enjoy being home. So the swing shift had nothing good about it.

The day shift that I'm on now is the best of all. I'm gone when my wife and sons are gone, and I'm home when they're home. I sleep at night like a normal person and work in the day. I never did get used to sleeping during the day when I worked the night shift. I feel better physically now that I'm on the day shift, and I'm in a better mood at work and at home. I'll stay on the day shift as long as I can.

a. If you're a family man like myself, I'd suggest trying for the day shift if possible and then volunteering for the night shift as a second choice. One time when I was on the night shift, I fell asleep on the job. I was supposed to add a certain tint to vats of dye when they rolled by me, and while I slept, at least ten vats moved on down the line. When they reached the end of the conveyor belt, the dye was a bright red color instead of the pastel pink it was supposed to be. Fortunately, that was my last night on the night shift, and I had a different foreman on the swing shift. I wouldn't recommend the swing shift for anyone.

b. If you're a family man like myself, I'd suggest trying for the day shift if possible and then volunteering for the night shift as a second choice. Stay away from the swing shift, or you'll seldom see your family. However, if you are single and like to save money, the swing shift might not be bad because you'll be working when you might otherwise be out partying. The night shift is the second-best choice for a family man because you have the evenings with your family, but if you are single and like to socialize, the night shift might kill you off. It really depends on the kind of person you are and whether you are single or married, but I don't think anyone can go wrong with the day shift. It's got all of the advantages.

c. Which shift you choose really depends on you. If you are married, like me, you might prefer one shift, but if you are single, you might prefer another. Also, you might prefer one shift in the summer and a totally different shift in the winter. Are you a night person or a day person? That might make a difference as to what shift you prefer. My suggestion is to take the shift you want.

4. Apartment Hunting

Two weeks before school started, I started hunting for an apartment along with my future roommate. Actually, I ended up doing most of the looking because she was still working at an ice house. I went into Monroe at least five times looking for a two-bedroom apartment to rent, and I usually came home discouraged. Luckily, I found a pretty nice place to rent three days before school began. But shopping for an apartment with a limited budget is hard work.

There are a lot of great apartments in Monroe, but they are all too expensive. I found a number of newer two-bedroom, two-bathroom apartments near the college with good-sized living rooms and kitchens, plenty of cupboard and closet space, and a swimming pool or jacuzzi on the grounds. I'd ask the landlord the rental price, and it would always be somewhere from $375 to $450 a month. Since the maximum we could pay was $325 a month, the apartments were out of our range. It was depressing going through these nice apartments we couldn't afford.

Then there's the problem of finding a good location. Obviously, the apartments nearer the college are the best located, but they are also the most expensive. Often when I'd find a decent-sounding apartment in the paper for $300, it would end up being halfway across town from the college or in some run-down neighborhood. The farther an apartment complex is away from the college, the less chance there is that it will have college students in it. We didn't want to end up in a complex with a bunch of older people or young married couples. I drove all over Monroe more than once tracking down a good-sounding deal, and usually the apartment ended up being beside a railroad track or a good twenty minutes from the campus.

Then there's the problem of size. The larger apartments are naturally the more expensive ones. Many of the nicer apartments in our price range felt like doll houses: tiny rooms and low ceilings. We had quite a bit of old furniture to move into an apartment, and we both slept on queen-sized beds. We needed adequate closet space for a semester's worth of clothes. We also planned on doing all of our own cooking, so we wanted a good-sized kitchen. Many of the apartments that sounded really nice turned out to be too small to consider. But as time began running out, I figured we'd probably end up taking a small apartment and stuffing everything into it that we could.

a. Luckily, all of the effort finally paid off. After looking at at least twenty-five different apartments and rejecting all of them, I found an apartment complex that was being remodeled. There were twelve apartments in two one-story buildings, and they had knocked out the ceilings in all the rooms and raised them a foot and a half. They had taken out the wall between each living room and small dining area so that it was all one larger area. They had paneled the walls in the living room with artificial oak paneling, and they had painted the walls and the new ceilings an off-white. The kitchen cupboards had been sanded and stained, and there were new curtains in all of the rooms. There was also a new light-green shag carpet in all the rooms but the kitchen, and the kitchen had new linoleum. I liked the looks of the apartments, the price was right, and they were close to the college. So I immediately put down a deposit on one.

b. Luckily, all of the effort finally paid off. After looking at a lot of apartments, I found an apartment complex that was being remodeled. It was an old complex that didn't look too hot from the outside, but inside it looked better. The apartments weren't small, and the rent wasn't bad. Besides, they weren't that far from the college. I put down a deposit immediately, and my search was over. What I thought would be an easy task turned out differently. I ended up spending two weeks doing a lot of things to find an apartment. Finding an apartment is different from what I imagined, and it may be different from what you imagine.

c. Luckily, all of the effort finally paid off. After looking at at least twenty-five different apartments and rejecting all of them, I found an apartment complex that was being remodeled. It was an old complex that didn't look too hot from the outside, but inside, the remodeled apartments were like new. The apartments were good-sized and rented for $310 a month, and they were only ten minutes from the college. I put down a deposit immediately, and my search was over. What I thought would be an easy task had turned into two weeks of driving around, making phone calls, scanning newspapers, and finding a lot of places I didn't like or couldn't afford. Finding an apartment is hard work when you can't spend much money, and you need to plan on spending a lot of time looking.

5. American Dream

When my aunt and uncle bought their house in 1973, it cost them $19,500. Today, the same house is worth $60,000. In a little more than ten years, the value of the house has increased 200 percent, or 20 percent a year. And that is a typical example of what has happened to house prices in the United States. Houses that were affordable for many people in 1970 are not affordable for many people today. The American dream of owning your own home is fading fast for many families.

In the early 1970s, a family could earn $20,000 a year and make a $250-a-month house payment on a nice three-bedroom house with a $5,000 down payment. The family spent about 20 percent of its earnings on house payments. Today, a family could earn $40,000, but house payments on the same-sized house would be $800 a month with a $15,000 down payment. That family would spend close to 50 percent of its earnings each month on house payments, a 30-percent increase over the 1970s couple. Today's family would have a very rough time making ends meet. And for families making much less than $40,000 a year, most of today's house payments are impossible.

People buying homes today are often walking into nightmares. They end up with such big house payments that they become strapped to their homes. After making house and property tax payments, they have little money left to live on, let alone enjoy life. In many cases, both the husband and wife are working to afford the house, and if one gets laid off, the payments can't be made. It is not surprising that there are more foreclosures on homes today than ever before. People still want a part of the American dream, but houses just aren't affordable for many couples who buy them and hope for the best.

a. The days of buying homes cheaply may be gone forever. People are just going to have to work harder to buy their homes. The husband and wife will both have to work, and they might have to take part-time jobs along with their main jobs. When the children get old enough, they can work too to help make the house payments. No family sacrifice is too great to own one's own home, and families should be willing to do anything possible to buy a home and make those payments. It's the American way.

b. The days of buying homes cheaply may be gone forever. People are going to have to look for different ways to buy homes in the future. Things will never be great, but that doesn't mean they have to be bad. In the 1970s, people bought homes cheaply, but that doesn't mean they were any happier than today's home buyers. In fact, studies show that people who live in their own homes aren't any happier than people who live in condominiums. Condominiums are actually apartment-sized homes, and they are bought and sold just like houses. I've never been in a condominium, but one of my friend's parents own one.

c. The days of buying homes cheaply may be gone forever. People looking for homes today much change their thinking. First of all, the dream house is going to have to be scaled-down in size. Since the 1950s, houses have kept getting larger and larger while families have gotten smaller and smaller. Americans think they need so much more room than they actually do. Many companies are now coming out with small, compact, space-efficient houses that are both affordable and adequate for most families. Second, more creative financing must be devised to help people make house payments without being strapped. The government should give homeowner's loans at low interest rates to young couples who qualify. There should also be variable payment plans where couples can make larger payments as they can afford them. And there should be strict regulations against speculators who buy and sell houses for profits and keep pushing the price of housing higher. Finally, couples may have to wait and save a few years before buying a house. In the 1940s and '50s, families might work for ten to fifteen years to buy a house. Families may have to be more patient and wait longer to buy their homes, like earlier generations did.

The Sentence

In this final section on "The Sentence," you are introduced to the most complex sentence patterns and structural problems found in the text. Then as a punctuation summary, you cover the most common uses for commas, semicolons, colons, and quotation marks. By the time you finish this section, you should be able to express yourself using a variety of clearly worded, correctly punctuated sentence forms.

Sentence Variety

Section Topic

Compound and Complex Combinations

Compound and Complex Combinations

Throughout the book you have been working with compound and complex sentences. It is also possible to create new sentence forms by using a combination of compound and complex structures within a sentence. In these sentences, you might use two subordinating conjunctions, two coordinating conjunctions, or a combination of subordinating and coordinating conjunctions.

Here are the basic compound and complex sentence variations that writers find useful:

1. *Complex-complex sentence:* a sentence containing two clauses beginning with subordinating conjunctions (or relative pronouns) and one independent clause that can stand alone

   Examples: (subordinating conjunctions and relative pronouns underlined)

   While we are investigating the effects that a swap meet would have on college parking, let's go ahead and take out an application with the school before we miss the deadline.

   Because the summer was so hot in June and July, the grapes ripened in early August whereas they usually ripen in early September.

   The men who planned the crosstown freeway didn't put in off-ramps where they were the most needed.

   We moved to the country because Dad bought a small farm that came with twenty head of cattle.

2. *Compound-compound sentence:* a sentence containing two clauses beginning with coordinating conjunctions and one independent clause that can stand alone

   Examples: (coordinating conjunctions underlined)

   Arnie was having trouble with his breathing, so he moved to Phoenix because of its dry air, but his breathing problem persisted.

   The new art show opening at Peach Plaza is startling, for all of the paintings are of nudes, and most of the drawings are quite explicit.

   Led Zeppelin, a heavy metal rock group, played some of their old standards, and then they played some new songs by lead singer Robert Plant, but the audience loved the oldies best.

   We could begin work at Wendy's this week or we could take a week off first, but I'd suggest we get started as soon as possible.

3. *Compound-complex sentence:* a compound sentence containing a subordinate clause in one or both of its halves

   Examples: (subordinating and coordinating conjunctions underlined)

   Before the year ends, let's take out an IRA, for we can reduce our taxable income for the year.

   Although Marie's old Ford looked terrible, it still ran well, so when she decided to sell it, she got a good price.

   The supervisor who hired Jan as a teller is a tough boss, for he never lets his tellers sit down.

   If you really want me to help you wash your windows, please give me a week's notice, for I'm very busy this month.

Exercise 3 Fill in subordinating conjunctions (*when, before, if, as, while, because, since, although, until, unless, where, wherever, whereas*) and relative pronouns (*who, which, that*) to complete the following complex-complex sentences. When you finish, compare your answers with the answer key.

Example *When* Matt and Celia got married, they honeymooned in Miami *until* their money ran out.

1. ________ there aren't many trees in the lower mountain area, ________ we climb another thousand feet, we'll be in a dense pine forest.
2. ________ you were taking aspirin for your headache, I was taking Tylenol for mine ________ I'm allergic to aspirin.
3. ________ Joanna spent two weeks in New York City, she was ready to return to Iowa ________ she missed her boyfriend Harley.
4. The apartment ________ I lived in last semester was noisy ________ it was located next to a train track.
5. The plumber ________ fixed our kitchen sink did a good job ________ he was very expensive.
6. ________ we get our bonus checks this month, we won't be able to make our car payments ________ we spent so much on Christmas presents.
7. ________ Joan is recovering well from her accident, she still needs to stay in bed ________ she can walk by herself.
8. ________ your aunt wants to live with us this summer, she'll have to sleep on the couch ________ all the beds are taken.

Exercise 4 Fill in coordinating conjunctions (*and, so, but, yet, for, or*) to complete the following compound-compound sentences. Then compare your answers with the answer key.

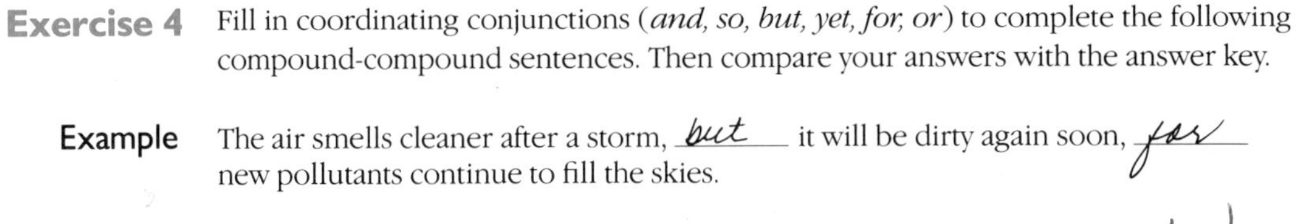

Example The air smells cleaner after a storm, *but* it will be dirty again soon, *for* new pollutants continue to fill the skies.

1. The cats can sleep in the garage, ________ they can sleep on the porch, ________ they can't sleep in the house.

2. The housing project on I Street is moving fast, ______ the prices for two-bedroom houses look reasonable, ______ let's take a look at their model home.
3. The water in the Tulle River is rising, ______ it is still lower than usual, ______ the farmers have been using a lot of water for irrigation.
4. Crimes of violence are decreasing in the United States, ______ the personal theft rate is increasing, ______ home burglaries are seldom solved by the police.
5. Thousands of refugees enter the United States every year, ______ we have a lenient emigration system, ______ America is seen by many as the promised land.
6. Samantha enjoys making dry flower arrangements, ______ she prefers sewing quilts, ______ she has more use for them.
7. The feminist group protested outside the beauty pageant arena, ______ they resented women being viewed as objects, ______ another group of pro-pageant women protested the protesters.
8. Meg and Stan's dinner party was quite small, ______ many of their old classmates they invited were out of town, ______ there was more than enough to eat for the rest of us.

Exercise 5 Fill in subordinating conjunctions, relative pronouns, and coordinating conjunctions to complete the following compound-complex sentences. Use coordinating conjunctions (*and, but, so, for, yet, but*) in the blanks *preceded by commas*. Then compare your answers with the answer key.

Example *If* Clyde wants his parents to trust him, he will have to be more honest, *but* it will take some time to rebuild the trust.

1. The land in the foothills was selling cheaply, ______ it had little grass on it ______ was fit for grazing.
2. Those new shoes ______ you wore to school looked comfortable, ______ please tell me ______ you bought them.
3. Mr. Herboldt, ______ teaches Comparative Religion I, is well educated,

_______ most students _______ take the class learn a great deal.

4. _______ Judd's family were very close, they were all independent, _______ they enjoyed doing things on their own.
5. _______ you make your car payments, don't take money from your new savings account, _______ your money is drawing 13 percent interest this month.
6. The new students _______ live in the area often find the local college boring, _______ students from out of the area seem to like it.
7. _______ you were cranking the homemade ice cream, I was cutting the pie, _______ the pie won't be ready to serve _______ it cools.
8. _______ you get more exercise, Harv, you are going to get heavy, _______ start jogging with me in the mornings _______ you aren't too busy.

Exercise 6 Complete the following complex-complex, compound-compound, and compound-complex sentences in your own words. Then share your sentences with a classmate who has finished and with your instructor.

Example When *you come to take the math test*, please bring plenty of paper and pencils, for *the test is twelve pages long*.

1. If you want to go to the football game tonight, we'd better leave early, for _______________.
2. The candidates for the legislature got nervous as _______________, but no one would know who won the election until early Sunday morning.
3. The girl in the old Levi's is the daughter of my history professor, and she came to school with him because _______________.
4. If _______________, you should only take nine to twelve units a semester because _______________.
5. Although _______________, the farmers still made very little money since _______________.
6. The meteorologists who _______________ were very accurate, for _______________.

7. If you want to walk to the wharf today, you'd better get started before

_______________________________.

8. I'll be in the barn feeding the cows unless _______________________________,

so come out and visit me before _______________________________.

9. Until the weather gets a lot warmer, _______________________________,

for _______________________________.

10. That woman who _______________________________ almost never smiles, but

yesterday I saw her laughing when _______________________________.

Exercise 7 Write your own sentences following the patterns provided. Put commas before coordinating conjunctions that join clauses and after clauses *beginning* with subordinating conjunctions. Then share your sentences with a classmate who is finished and with your instructor.

Example compound-compound using *and* and *but*

you're looking very nice this year, and you're also looking very healthy, but I heard you were in bed with pneumonia most of the summer.

1. complex-complex with *although* and *because*
2. compound-compound with *and* and *so*
3. compound-complex with *and* and *because*
4. complex-complex with *if* and *who*
5. compound-complex with *when* and *but*
6. compound-compound with *or* and *for*
7. complex-complex with *although* and *unless*
8. compound-complex with *if* and *for*
9. compound-compound with *and* and *yet*
10. complex-complex with *since* and *who*

Practice Quiz

Take this practice quiz to prepare for the section quiz. Then compare your answers with the answer key. When you are ready for the section quiz, let your instructor know.

Circle the letter of the sentence from each group with the most appropriate subordinating and coordinating conjunctions and relative pronouns.

Example

(a.) If you want to use my kiln to fire your pottery, you certainly may, but please turn it off when you are finished.

b. While you want to use my kiln to fire your pottery, you certainly may, or please turn it off when you are finished.

c. Because you want to use my kiln to fire your pottery, you certainly may, so please turn it off when you are finished.

1. a. Although Simon and Garfunkel were a popular singing team in the 1960s, Simon was the more talented, for he wrote the music and lyrics to their songs and played the guitar.

   b. Since Simon and Garfunkel were a popular singing team in the 1960s, Simon was the more talented, yet he wrote the music and lyrics to their songs and played the guitar.

   c. As Simon and Garfunkel were a popular singing team in the 1960s, Simon was the more talented, or he wrote the music and lyrics to their songs and played the guitar.

2. a. Although Charles lived in Sanger, he worked in a mortuary, so he didn't work there long as he hated being around dead bodies.

   b. While Charles lived in Sanger, he worked in a mortuary, but he didn't work there long because he hated being around dead bodies.

   c. As Charles lived in Sanger, he worked in a mortuary, so he didn't work there long since he hated being around dead bodies.

3. a. If you want to invest your money safely, put it into some kind of account who is government secured.

   b. Before you want to invest your money safely, put it into some kind of account who is government secured.

   c. If you want to invest your money safely, put it into some kind of account that is government secured.

4. a. Jim put his car in the shop because it was running roughly, but when he got it back, it still wasn't running well.

   b. Jim put his car in the shop while it was running roughly, for when he got it back, it still wasn't running well.

   c. Jim put his car into the shop before it was running roughly, so when he got it back, it still wasn't running well.

5. a. One job that Matilda was qualified for was lifeguarding, so she turned down the job with the city pool until it didn't pay very well.

b. One job that Matilda was qualified for was lifeguarding, but she turned down the job with the city pool because it didn't pay very well.

c. One job who Matilda was qualified for was lifeguarding, so she turned down the job with the city pool because it didn't pay very well.

6. a. After you invite anyone to the apartment, let's clean it up, yet let's also buy a kitchen table.

   b. While you invite anyone to the apartment, let's clean it up, for let's also buy a kitchen table.

   c. Before you invite anyone to the apartment, let's clean it up, and let's also buy a kitchen table.

7. a. Angie and Joe are thinking about splitting up, but I think they will stay together until the school year ends.

   b. Angie and Joe are thinking about splitting up, so I think they will stay together before the school year ends.

   c. Angie and Joe are thinking about splitting up, and I think they will stay together after the school year ends.

8. a. It's 90 degrees in the inland city of Tustin, so ten miles from here on the beach, it's 72 degrees until the sea breeze cools the air.

   b. It's 90 degrees in the inland city of Tustin, for ten miles from here on the beach, it's 72 degrees before the sea breeze cools the air.

   c. It's 90 degrees in the inland city of Tustin, but ten miles from here on the beach, it's 72 degrees because the sea breeze cools the air.

9. a. I hate putting disinfectant on cuts because it stings so badly, but I do it anyway to prevent infection.

   b. I hate putting disinfectant on cuts before it stings so badly, so I do it anyway to prevent infection.

   c. I hate putting disinfectant on cuts while it stings so badly, for I do it anyway to prevent infection.

10. a. Sam is planning a weekend trip to Buffalo when he moves to California while it will be the last time he will see his parents for a year.

    b. Sam is planning a weekend trip to Buffalo before he moves to California, for it will be the last time he will see his parents for a year.

    c. Sam is planning a weekend trip to Buffalo before he moves to California, or it will be the last time he will see his parents for a year.

Clear Sentences

Section Topic

Parallel Construction

To communicate with your readers most effectively, you need to write clear, smooth, direct sentences. In this section on "Clear Sentences," you learn an important feature of smoothly structured sentences: *parallel construction*.

Parallel Construction

When two or more words or groups of words are joined in a sentence, they should be *parallel* in construction: Each part should have the same *grammatical structure* and *word order*. Here are examples of sentences with their *parallel parts underlined*.

Minnie bought a ticket to the play, went out for dinner, and arrived at the theater by 7:00.
(Each parallel part begins with a *past tense verb* followed by a *prepositional phrase*.)

Sam enjoys sleeping, eating, watching television, and cruising Main Street.
(Each parallel part begins with an *-ing*-ending word.)

Thelma is friendly, cooperative, outgoing, and interesting.
(Each parallel part is an *adjective* describing Thelma.)

The English literature course requires that you read six novels, write book reports on four of them, write a critique on one, and write a thematic analysis on another.
(Each parallel part begins with a present tense verb followed by a *direct object*.)

When an item within a series is *not* parallel, the sentence sounds awkward and the reader has problems. Here are examples of sentences with parallel construction problems followed by their revised, parallel forms. The problem areas are underlined.

Horace is wise, patient, kind, and good manners. (*Good manners* is not parallel with *wise, patient,* and *kind*.)
Revised: Horace is wise, patient, kind, and well-mannered.

Mickey drove across town, picked up Mabel, and returns to his house. (*Returns* is not parallel with the *past tense* verbs *drove* and *picked*.)
Revised: Mickey drove across town, picked up Mabel, and returned to his house.

I'd like to travel across the country, stay at different campgrounds, and living as cheaply as possible. (*Living* is not parallel with *travel* and *stay*.)
Revised: I'd like to travel across the country, stay at different campgrounds, and live as cheaply as possible.

It is cold, windy, dark, and with gloom outside. (*With gloom* is not parallel with *cold, dark,* and *windy.*)
Revised: It is cold, windy, dark, and gloomy outside.

Sally walks out the door, calls a cab, in the backseat climbs, and heads for the opera. (*In the backseat climbs* does not have *parallel word order* with the other parts; the verb should come *first.*)
Revised: Sally walks out the door, calls a cab, climbs in the backseat, and heads for the opera.

Here are the main things to remember about parallel construction in your sentences:

1. When two or more groups of words are joined in a sentence, their structures should be *parallel*: the same grammatical constructions and the same word order.
2. To correct a parallel construction problem in a sentence, change the nonparallel part so that it is structurally the same as the other parts it is joined with.
3. Parallel construction is important because it makes your sentences smoother, clearer, and easier for readers to understand.

Exercise 8 Each of the following sentences has a parallel construction problem. Rewrite each sentence and correct the problem so that all parts of a series are parallel. Then compare your answers with the answer key.

Examples Thelma loves eating lasagna, spaghetti, ravioli, and loves eating fettuccini.
Revised: Thelma loves eating lasagna, spaghetti, ravioli, and fettuccini.

Swimming, ice skating, to play golf, and to throw knives are Harriet's hobbies.
Revised: Swimming, ice skating, playing golf, and throwing knives are Harriet's hobbies.

1. The snow fell slowly, lightly, and in a gentle way on the school grounds.
2. I never saw so many cheerful, courteous students and helpful.
3. Marvin is kind, gentle, responsible, and consideration.
4. After work I ate dinner, go to a show, came home, and to bed.
5. The jewel thief saw the diamonds on display and for the next morning planning the robbery.
6. I would like to become a nurse, raise a family, and to be financially comfortable.

7. At this stage, the pudding batter should be slightly runny, smoothly textured, and have hotness.
8. This cleansing cream will keep your skin healthy, glowing, and with softness.
9. She often wondered how she will pay the second semester's tuition.
10. Jonathan has green eyes, black hair, long sideburns, and tall.

Exercise 9 Complete the following sentences so that they are parallel in construction. When you finish, show your sentences to a classmate who is finished and to your instructor.

Examples I am tired of the noise, the filth, and *the heat* in the dorms.

Gertrude put on her tights, did her stretching exercises, and *left for her aerobic dancing class*.

1. Matthew walked into the house, turned on the television, and ________.
2. I enjoy bowling, skating, swimming, ________, and ________.
3. Minerva has brown hair, green eyes, ________, and ________.
4. Those swans are large, graceful, and ________.
5. Helen walked into the classroom and ________.
6. Sarah believes in democracy, capitalism, the draft, ________, and ________.
7. Clyde ran down the sidewalk, ducked into an alley, ________, and ________.
8. I'd like to know where you want to go, why you want to go, and ________.
9. Hanson knocked the wasp nest from the bush and ________.
10. The bus that you rode on is the bus ________.
11. Terence is not only cheap but ________.
12. You can put a TV dinner in the oven tonight or ________.

Exercise 10 The following paragraph contains some sentences with *parallel construction problems*. Rewrite the paragraph and correct any nonparallel sentence parts. When you finish, compare your paragraph with the answer key.

Example Mollie rode her bike to school and parks it in the front lot bike rack. Then she went to her classes, eats lunch, and rode back home on her bike.

Revised: Mollie rode her bike to school and parked it in the front lot bike rack. Then she went to her classes, ate lunch, and rode back home on her bike.

The three cats in the garage were being sneaky. Gerald wanted them out of the garage for the night and they not wanting to go. He called them and banged on their food dish, but they will not come. They'd hide under the parked cars in the garage, dart from one car to the other, and stayed a step ahead of Gerald. Finally, he was able to herd them out the side garage door, shut the door and lock it. The cats went out to the back porch for the night and slept on the redwood table or on the throw rug slept. They don't like the porch as well as the garage but getting used to it.

Practice Quiz

Take this practice quiz to prepare for the section quiz. Then compare your answers with the answer key. When you are ready for the section quiz, let your instructor know.

Circle the letter of the sentence in each group that has *parallel construction*.

Example

a. The kite lifted into the air, glided toward a power pole, and is caught on the line.

b. The kite lifted into the air, glided toward a power pole, and was caught on the line.

(c.) The kite lifted into the air, glided toward a power pole, and caught on the line.

1. a. Bothered by bad weather, bad scheduling, and a record that wasn't good, the football franchise in Milwaukee folded.

   b. Bothered by bad weather, bad scheduling, and a not good record, the football franchise in Milwaukee folded.

   c. Bothered by bad weather, bad scheduling, and a bad record, the football franchise in Milwaukee folded.

2. a. I ran in the Surburban Teachers' Marathon last Saturday and did have a good time.

   b. I ran in the Surburban Teachers' Marathon last Saturday and having a good time.

   c. I ran in the Surburban Teacher's Marathon last Saturday and had a good time.

3. a. Malaga is a small, poor, town of rural location.

   b. Malaga is a small, poor, rural town.

   c. Malaga is a small, poor town that is rural.

4. a. Your aunt has nice flowers, well-trimmed bushes, and a clean swimming pool.
   b. Your aunt has nice flowers, well-trimmed bushes, and a swimming pool that is clean.
   c. Your aunt has nice flowers, well-trimmed bushes, and a not dirty swimming pool.
5. a. It's important to know your strengths, to know your weaknesses, and what you want from life.
   b. It's important to know your strengths, to know your weaknesses, and to know what you want from life.
   c. It's important to know your strengths, your weaknesses, and to know what you want from life.
6. a. We could go to the movies, go miniature golfing, or will stay home and read.
   b. We could go to the movies go miniature golfing, or at home stay and read.
   c. We could go to the movies, go miniature golfing, or stay home and read.
7. a. Your car is sleek, fast, sporty, and carries a big price tag.
   b. Your car is sleek, fast, sporty, and costs a lot.
   c. Your car is sleek, fast, sporty, and expensive.
8. a. I'd like a lot of ketchup on my hamburger but no mustard.
   b. I'd like a lot of ketchup on my hamburger but mustard, no thank you.
   c. I'd like a lot of ketchup on my hamburger but a lot of mustard I don't want.
9. a. Millicent reached for the pickle jar on the top shelf, sprained her back, lay in bed for a week, going back to work, and feeling terrible.
   b. Millicent reached for the pickle jar on the top shelf, sprained her back, lay in bed for a week, went back to work, and felt terrible.
   c. Millicent reached for the pickle jar on the top shelf, sprained her back, in bed for a week lay, to work went, and terrible felt.

Correct Sentences

Section Topics

Commas

Colons and Semicolons

Quotation Marks

This final "Correct Sentences" section covers different uses for the comma, semicolon, and colon, and it also introduces the use of *quotation marks* for punctuating conversation in your writing.

Commas

Throughout the text, you have learned to use commas in a number of situations. First, this section will review what you have already learned. Then you will learn two new uses for commas.

Here is a review of comma usage from the previous levels:

1. Put a comma before the coordinating conjunction (*and, or, but, so, for, yet*) in a *compound sentence*.

   I'd like to get a job this semester, but I'm too busy with my science labs.
   The cost of living has increased 5 percent this year, and it is expected to go higher next year.

2. Put a comma after an *introductory phrase* or *subordinate clause*.

   Since I've owned this 1972 Malibu, I haven't had to change the oil once.
   Because you have had so many jobs, you've gained a lot of different skills.
   Although Barry enjoys socializing, he is basically a loner.
   Shopping for a wedding gown at Macy's, Marie found nothing to her liking.
   Troubled by the steep climb up the mountain, Harry decided not to go all the way to the top.
   Behind the truck seat on the driver's side, Marian stashes her collection of tobacco pouches.

3. Put commas around a *relative clause* beginning with *who* or *which* if the modified word is *clearly named or identified*.

   Jason Broemmel, who takes medicine for his allergies, lives next to a large meadow.
   The new Coke, which replaced the old Coke, doesn's taste any different to me.

4. Put commas after items in a series.

   This summer we'll take a trip to the coast, the mountains, the city, or the desert.
   You can find vacant apartments on N Street, on Avenue 392, and on Campus Drive.
   Ironing, washing dishes, vacuuming the carpet, and taking out the garbage were Ned's chores.

Exercise 11 Put commas in the following sentences, following the five comma usage rules just presented. Then check your answers with the answer key.

Example When you finish doing the dishes, meet me on the patio for dessert.

1. If you want to save money paint the apartment yourself instead of hiring someone.
2. Lionel made $2,000 working in the cannery but he blew it all on one trip to Atlantic City.
3. Sally Enright who got chicken pox from her brother was out of school for ten days.
4. Uncle Clyde has given up smoking drinking chewing tobacco and eating fried foods.
5. Driving along Highway 52 in Oregon you can go for miles without seeing any litter.
6. The Vancouver Zoo the only zoo in Canada with albino whales is popular with tourists.
7. Digging in the soft mud in the shallow water Phillis found four large clams.
8. While you were sleeping in the bedroom a thief came into the house and stole your pants.
9. Stamp collecting which requires great patience is as popular among girls as boys.
10. Walking to school cramming for tests eating in the cafeteria and baby-sitting her cousins are things that Matilda hates to do.
11. I didn't get home from the slumber party until 7:00 a.m. so I slept until noon that day.
12. The minister's J Street parsonage which was built in 1902 has been restored many times.

Here are two more uses for commas that you will find useful in your writing:

MORE USES FOR COMMAS

1. Place commas around an "interrupter" in a sentence: a word or group of words that adds information to the sentence but isn't absolutely necessary. The "interrupter" may come in the beginning of a sentence or within it. Here are some of the more common interrupting expressions: *as a matter of fact, as you know, by the way, for example, incidentally, in fact, naturally, needless to say, of course,* and *on the other hand.*

Examples:

By the way, are you going to the real estate seminar tomorrow?
That new dress, as a matter of fact, cost me two weeks' allowance.
The Barnum and Bailey circus is, of course, known throughout the world.
Needless to say, carrying twenty units in one semester was difficult.
That fern, for example, can live either indoors or on a shaded patio.

2. If a person is spoken to directly in a sentence, set that person's name off with commas:

James, do you want to move out of the dorms and room with me in an apartment?
I'd like another piece of your apple pie, Sarah.
Do you think, Mr. Parsons, that we could take the test next week?

Exercise 12 Put commas in the following sentences to set off "interrupters" or the name of a person directly spoken to.

Examples Clyde, why do you always order the same thing on the menu?

The students in the corner, by the way, are all from the same town.

1. Mariam the coffee is too strong to drink unless you add cream.
2. Incidentally have you heard that Professor Branscom is marrying one of his students?
3. I believe Melissa that you enjoy playing football more than I do.
4. President Reagan of course had little trouble defeating Walter Mondale.
5. I'll be glad to baby-sit your daughter tonight Suzanne.
6. Last summer in the foothills for example there were sixteen separate fires reported.
7. The wheat crop as you probably know has been badly stunted by lack of moisture.
8. Would you mind Jackie if I rested here while you went on to the camp?
9. A trip to Chicago I imagine would cost us more than we can afford.

Exercise 13 Each of the following sentences contains at least two different comma usage situations. Put in commas where they are needed, and then compare your punctuation to the answer key.

Example If you want to visit the county fair, I'd go on Tuesday afternoon, Michael. (Introductory subordinate clause and name of person spoken to set off.)

1. Jack's sunburn is making him miserable so he is staying indoors resting keeping cool and using sunburn ointment.
2. While the museum was closed for repairs we started visiting the aquarium a large building containing a 100,000-gallon tank.
3. Mr. Jackson who plays saxophone in the city band has a full-time job of course.
4. Sally's mail-order business which she began in early July is doing very well and she is considering doubling her advertising budget.
5. Responding to the President's operation the stock market dropped three points Tuesday but it rebounded five points by the weekend.
6. Harriet I'd like you to ride in this new Mazda a smooth-handling little car.
7. Incidentally that part-time college custodial job which is a good job for a student is still open.
8. Mildred I'd like you to meet my best friend Hal Gipson.
9. When the Joneses got married last spring I was really surprised Mary.
10. Looking at the foothills now you'd never guess they will be green in a month but the spring rains revive the grass quickly.

Colons and Semicolons

Colons and semicolons are not used nearly as often as commas, but they do come in handy in certain situations. Here are the most common uses for colons and semicolons:

1. A *colon* indicates that an example or examples are going to follow in support of the statement made. A colon always comes after a *complete statement*:

   A lot of things need repairing in the cabin: the kitchen window, the bathroom floor, and the hallway walls.
   There is one thing that I could use: more money.
   Everything in the hospital smelled funny: the rooms, the medicine, the nurses, and the food.
   I have one relative that I've never met: Aunt Minnie.
   All of the apartments around here are similar: one-bedroom, small, furnished, and expensive.

2. A semicolon is used to join *two closely related sentences*. A semicolon takes the place of a joining word or of a period and capital letter. *Don't capitalize* the word following the semicolon.

   We're going shopping in Tucson this morning; then we're having lunch at Alfredo's Pizzeria.
   The Plaza Apartments is a pretty ritzy place to live; it has a swimming pool, a jacuzzi, and a sauna.
   I don't mind getting tuberculosis shots; however, I hate polio shots.
   Gretchen is a great student; she is intelligent, hardworking, and well organized.

Exercise 14 Put in semicolons (;) and colons (:) in the following sentences where they are needed. When you finish, compare your punctuation with the answer key.

Examples Carl is really loaded with the one quality: charm.

We left for school at 7:30; we were still late because we got a flat tire.

1. Someone has been scribbling graffiti on the walls in the theater bathroom they need washing off badly.
2. You actually have too many interests you never have enough time to complete any one project.
3. Extreme right-wing politicians believe that one thing hurts their cause negative press.
4. Invite all of these people to the party Ted, Clara, Homer, Cleo, and Penelope.
5. Sam's parents are great people warm, generous, kind, and forgiving.
6. The lots by the river are selling fast they were reduced in price after last year's flood.
7. You can wear your new cords to the play tonight they will look fine with your blue blazer.
8. There are three things I hate about the ferris wheel going up over the top, getting stuck at the top, and rocking back and forth.
9. There is one class at this college I can't seem to pass zoology.
10. Maria was having trouble getting her parents to accept her new boyfriend then one day they started treating him decently.

Quotation Marks

When writers share personal experiences with a reader, they often use segments of conversations from an experience to make it more lifelike and interesting. Any time you have someone speaking in your writing, you need to use *quotation marks*.

Here are some basic rules for using quotation marks that will help you punctuate *direct quotations* correctly:

1. A direct quotation is the actual words of the speaker. An indirect quotation, which does not require quotation marks, does *not* include the actual words of the speaker; it relates what the speaker said in the *writer's* words.

   Direct Quotation: "I'm going to the dog races this evening," said Willie.
   Indirect Quotation: Willie said that he was going to the dog races this evening.

   Direct Quotation: Freda asked, "Where's the beef in this hamburger?"
   Indirect Quotation: Freda wanted to know where the beef was in the hamburger.

2. Place quotation marks (" ") around the actual spoken words, and capitalize the first word of the quotation.

   Thelma explained, "The test will take two hours, one for the essay and one for the matching section."
   "I've never eaten at a luau," said Tony.
   Millie said, "The last time I enrolled in Tucker's class, the class was canceled."
   "When will we get to the top of this hill?" asked Millicent.

3. Always identify the speaker by putting his or her name in front, in the middle, or after the quote. Put a *comma* after the speaker introduction in the beginning of the sentence. When the speaker is identified in the middle, use quotation marks to begin the quote again.

   Minnie replied, "We'll put them in the back shed for the time being."
   "They'll get mighty hot in the back shed," said Malcolm.
   "That's all right," said Minnie. "We'll eat all of them before they spoil."

4. Put a comma after the quoted words if the sentence continues and a period if the quote ends the sentence. If the quote asks a question, always put a question mark after it. Always put the quotation marks *outside* of the ending punctuation mark.

   "We'll be late for class if we stay behind this slow traffic," said Felix.
   Mary said, "I'd rather be late for class than get a speeding ticket."
   "Why don't we take a side road and beat the traffic?" asked Felix.

Exercise 15 Put quotation marks around the speaker's words in each of the following sentences. Then compare your punctuation with the answer key.

Example Harold said, "When will we start picking peaches this summer?"

1. Jethro said, I'm tired of smoking these straws all the time, Ned.
2. Ned replied, They're okay if you don't inhale the flames with the smoke.
3. Yeah, but it's not like smoking the real thing, said Jethro.
4. Well, I guess you're right, said Ned. Let's get some real cigars.
5. Jethro said, I'll swipe some from my father's cigar box.
6. Okay, said Ned. But don't let him catch you.
7. We can smoke them behind the barn tonight, said Jethro.
8. I'll meet you there at 9:00, said Ned. I'll bring the matches.

Exercise 16 Put in all necessary punctuation and capital letters to punctuate the following quotations correctly. Then compare your answers with the answer key.

Example We won't be coming for dinner Thursday said Monica.

I'm sorry you can't make it said Gertrude we were looking forward to having you over.

1. Maggie said when are we going to see a movie, Fred
2. Fred answered I'm willing to go any time you are
3. Why don't we go this Saturday asked Maggie I don't have any plans
4. Fred said I'm free on Saturday too. What do you want to see
5. There's a double horror feature playing at the Midway Drive-in said Maggie
6. Fred said I thought you hated horror movies
7. I used to replied Maggie now I kind of enjoy them
8. Then we'll go to the drive-in on Saturday said Fred I'll pick you up at 8:30.

Exercise 17 Write your own conversation between any two people: two friends, a husband and wife, a boyfriend and girlfriend, a teacher and student, a boss and employee, a brother and sister, or two strangers. Punctuate your conversation correctly. Then share your writing with a classmate who is finished and with your instructor.

Example Gloria said, "Freddie, I want to take the car tonight. I'm going to a show."

Freddie replied, "I need the car because I'm taking Rosalie roller skating in New Trier."

"Rosalie has her own car," said Gloria. "Let her drive for once."

"Her car isn't running well, and she hasn't been taking it to school," said Freddie.

"Well, just this once I get the car," said Gloria. "You take it every weekend."

"I'll flip you for it," said Freddie. "Heads, I get the car and tails, you get it."

"No way," said Gloria. "You're not going to use that two-headed coin on me."

Exercise 18 Write a composition about a personal experience where you had a conflict with another person(s): a teacher, friend, boss, parents, husband or wife, brother or sister. Include an opening paragraph that *sets up* the experience (time, place, situation) and an ending paragraph that *reflects* on the experience in some way. As you write your draft, change paragraphs as you move from one time, place, or incident to another.

To practice punctuating dialogue, include some *conversation* between yourself and the other person(s) to dramatize the situation for the reader, and punctuate the conversation with quotation marks. Write the composition for a classmate whom you have shared work with throughout the semester.

Before you begin, you may want to write freely on your topic for fifteen minutes to discover what things are most memorable about the experience.

When you finish your first draft, apply everything you have learned about revising and correcting a composition, and when you are ready, write a final draft that includes all of your improvements and corrections.

Sample Composition (Final Draft)

The Secret Smoker

When I was in junior high school, I had a real fascination with smoking. Some of the more "sophisticated" girls would smoke in the bathrooms at lunch or recess, and I secretly envied them. I wanted to be in there puffing away too, but I was too good a girl for that sort of thing. Neither of my parents smoked, and if I was ever caught smoking, I knew they would be shocked. Yet, I was determined to have a cigarette sooner or later.

On Saturday afternoons I'd often go to the bowling alley with friends and stay there until 7:00 or 8:00 p.m. We'd bowl, play the pinball machines, and talk to the guys from school. One afternoon, I noticed some cigarette butts in these tall metal ashtrays filled with sand. The cigarettes were stuck in the sand, and some of them looked pretty long, like someone had just taken a puff or two and tossed them away. When no one was looking, I put a few of the longer ones in my pocket and waited until dark. Then I snuck out behind the bowling alley, lit a cigarette, and puffed away. It was a filthy habit, smoking cigarettes that had been in other people's mouths, but I got a thrill from it. I started sneaking smokes every time we went to the bowling alley.

After a few weeks of smoking at the bowling alley, one day I noticed a small sample pack of cigarettes in my dad's work car, probably left there by a business client. I swiped the pack and headed for the school grounds across from our house. I hid behind a baseball backstop and proceeded to smoke all five cigarettes in the pack, the first clean cigarettes I'd ever had. Then I went back to the house and started watching TV.

Later that day, dad apparently noticed that the cigarette pack wasn't in his car. He came in and sat down beside me. I must have smelled like stale tobacco because he immediately asked me, "Cellie, do you have anything you want to tell me?" I felt a tightening in my chest, and I managed to whisper, "Nope." Then Dad said, "Cellie, I know you took the cigarettes from the car and smoked them because you smell like tobacco. There's no use denying it." Well, I knew I was caught, but I just couldn't admit it to him. Trying to keep from crying, I blurted out, "I didn't take any cigarettes from anywhere and I don't know what you're talking about. I don't smoke!" Dad looked at me for a long time with this disappointed look, and then he finally said, "Well, when you're ready to tell the truth, I'm ready to listen." I walked out the front door and stayed away for a couple of hours.

I never did admit to my parents that I'd smoked those cigarettes, and they never asked me about them again. I went back to smoking cigarette butts at the bowling alley, and it took me over a year to lose my interest. But to this day I still feel bad about telling dad such an obvious lie. I should have told him the truth and taken the consequences, but I didn't want him to think that his "angel" had stooped to stealing cigarettes and smoking. The trouble is, he knew anyway, and I came out even worse by lying. I never was the perfect girl that my dad made me out to be.

Practice Quiz

Take this practice quiz to prepare for the section quiz. Then compare your answers with the answer key. When you are ready for the section quiz, let your instructor know.

Circle the letter of the correctly punctuated sentence in each group.

Example

(a.) Mandy Brady, who used to live behind me, got married and moved to Tuskegee.

b. Mandy Brady, who used to live behind me got married and moved to Tuskegee.

c. Mandy Brady who used to live behind me, got married and moved to Tuskegee.

1. (a.) While I was trying to register for the spring semester, six classes closed in fifteen minutes.

   b. While, I was trying to register for the spring semester six classes closed in fifteen minutes.

   c. While I was trying to register for the spring semester six classes closed in fifteen minutes.

2. a. I paid for all of my fees out of my own money but my grant will cover tuition.

   b. I paid for all of my fees out of my own money but, my grant will cover tuition.

   (c.) I paid for all of my fees out of my own money, but my grant will cover tuition.

3. a. Students who drop after the first two weeks, I believe must pay a twenty-dollar drop fee.

   (b.) Students who drop after the first two weeks, I believe, must pay a twenty-dollar drop fee.

   c. Students who drop after the first two weeks I believe, must pay a twenty-dollar drop fee.

4. a. I'd like pork chops a baked potato green beans garlic bread and tea for dinner.

   b. I'd like pork chops, a baked, potato, green, beans, garlic bread and tea, for dinner.

   (c.) I'd like pork chops, a baked potato, green beans, garlic bread, and tea for dinner.

5. (a.) Mounting the exercise beam in the gymnasium, Phyllis slipped and fell to the mat.

   b. Mounting the exercise beam in the gymnasium Phyllis slipped and fell to the mat.

   c. Mounting the exercise beam in the gymnasium Phyllis, slipped and fell to the mat.

6. (a.) You only need to bring one thing to the football game, a thermos of coffee.

   b. You only need to bring one thing to the football game; a thermos of coffee.

   c. You only need to bring one thing to the football game: a thermos of coffee.

7. a. The children played four-square the first half of recess then they played dodge ball until the bell rang.

   b. The children played four-square the first half of recess, then they played dodge ball until the bell rang.

c. The children played four-square the first half of recess; then they played dodge ball until the bell rang.

8. a. "The birds have ruined most of the cherries on our backyard trees, said Mavis.

   b. The birds have ruined most of the cherries on our backyard trees, "said Mavis."

   c. "The birds have ruined most of the cherries on our backyard trees," said Mavis.

9. a. If you want to keep from getting sunstroke today, drink a lot of liquids and wear a hat.

   b. If you want to keep from getting sunstroke today drink a lot of liquids and wear a hat.

   c. If, you want to keep from getting sunstroke today, drink a lot of liquids and wear a hat.

10. a. The line at the concert arena is two blocks long and, it is getting longer by the minute.

    b. The line at the concert arena is two blocks long, and it is getting longer by the minute.

    c. The line at the concert arena is two blocks long and it is getting longer by the minute.

11. a. There's lots to do in the country; swim, hunt, ride three-wheelers, or float the river.

    b. There's lots to do in the country, swim, hunt, ride three-wheelers, or float the river.

    c. There's lots to do in the country: swim, hunt, ride three-wheelers, or float the river.

12. a. Maria has been feeling great lately; she's been getting plenty of exercise.

    b. Maria has been feeling great lately, she's been getting plenty of exercise.

    c. Maria has been feeling great lately she's been getting plenty of exercise.

13. a. "That's an unusual painting," said Mel. "I've never seen a dog with three heads."

    b. "That's an unusual painting, said Mel. I've never seen a dog with three heads."

    c. That's an unusual painting, "said Mel." I've never seen a dog with three heads.

14. a. The Colter Tower, which is the largest building in Cheyenne was built by two hundred workers.

    b. The Colter Tower which is the largest building in Cheyenne was built by two hundred workers.

    c. The Colter Tower, which is the largest building in Cheyenne, was built by two hundred workers.

15. a. Uncle Fabian, who used to race go-carts in Florida, retired on his army pension.

b. Uncle Fabian, who used to race go-carts in Florida retired on his army pension.

c. Uncle Fabian who used to race go-carts in Florida, retired on his army pension.

The Word

The final step in the writing process is proofreading your composition and editing out any errors that you haven't caught in earlier steps. This final section on "The Word" covers four problem areas that could be handled in the editing phase: shifts in verb tense, irregular verbs, comparative and superlative adjectives, and spelling words involving double letters.

Verb Forms

Section Topics

Shifting Verb Tenses

Irregular Verb List #4

A common problem for many writers is beginning a paragraph using one verb tense and then shifting to a different tense within the paragraph. The problem of shifting tenses is most common in personal experience writing where a writer tries to relate something that happened in the past and dramatize it as if it was happening in the present. What results is a paragraph or composition that shifts back and forth between past and present tenses, a confusing situation for readers. This section shows you how to avoid shifting verb tenses and also introduces a final list of irregular verbs.

Shifting Verb Tenses

When you write a composition, you may write about something that has already happened, about something that is currently happening or existing, or about something that may happen or exist in the future. In each situation, you rely mainly on one particular verb tense: the past, the present, or the future. Writers have problems when they needlessly shift verb tenses within a paragraph or a composition. Such tense shifts can create awkward paragraphs and confuse readers.

Here are some suggestions for keeping tense shifts to a minimum in your writing:

1. When you are writing about something that has already happened or that existed in the past, stick mainly to the *past tense*.

   Sample Topics for Past Tense: yesterday's history final
   the Battle of Bunker Hill
   dinosaurs of the Northern Hemisphere

2. When you are writing about something that is currently happening or existing, stick mainly to the *present tense*.

   Sample Topics for Present Tense: my life in the dormitories
   the trouble with night classes
   Mayville's downtown parking problem
   the new Mayfair Mall in Toledo

3. When you are writing about something that may happen or exist in the future, stick mainly to the *future tense*.

   Sample Topics for Future Tense: my life ten years from now
   the future of nuclear weapons
   marriage and divorce in the 1990s

4. Most tense-shifting problems occur between the past and present tenses. Don't begin a paragraph writing *about something that has happened* in the past tense and then shift to the present tense to continue relating the same incident.

   Example of Past-Present Shift: (shifts to present tense underlined)

   Last summer I worked at the city pool in Shreveport. In the mornings I taught swim lessons and then in the afternoon I lifeguarded during free-swim hours. I have the deep-end station from the diving boards to the buoy line. Mainly, I have to watch for wall crawlers who venture into the deep end but can't swim. I saved three youngsters last summer, but none of the rescues was difficult.

5. To correct tense-shifting problems in a paragraph, change the tense of verbs that have shifted tenses so that they are consistent with the rest of the verbs in the paragraph.

   Example of Tense-Shifting Corrections: (revising paragraph in 4)

Last summer I worked at the city pool in Shreveport. In the mornings I taught swim lessons and then in the afternoon I lifeguarded during free-swim hours. I had the deep-end station from the diving boards to the buoy line. Mainly, I had to watch for wall crawlers who ventured into the deep end but couldn't swim. I saved three youngsters last summer, but none of the rescues was difficult.

6. Some tense shifting within a paragraph or composition is acceptable as you move from the past to the present or from the present to the future in your experience.

Example of Acceptable Tense Shifting in a Paragraph: (tense shifts underlined)

Last night, I had a bad headache and felt terrible. I went to bed early and slept for twelve hours. Today, I feel much better. My headache is gone, and I am well rested. If I continue feeling good, I will go to the library tonight, and tomorrow I will head for the mountains for some hiking.
(Tense shifts from *past* to present to future.)

Here are some examples of paragraphs with tense-shifting problems, followed by their correct versions.

Wrong: (tense shift: past to present to past)

I spent most of Saturday morning watching the U.S. Open Tennis Championships on television. Then I ate lunch and studied in my room for an hour and a half. At 3:00 I went shopping at Beno's. I buy some toothpaste, a magazine, and a six-pack of Pepsi. Then I return home and work in the kitchen until dinnertime. After dinner, I watched a movie on television until 8:00 and then went to my room to read. I fell asleep around 10:30.

Revised: (all verbs in past tense)

I spent most of Saturday morning watching the U.S. Open Tennis Championships on television. Then I ate lunch and studied in my room for an hour and a half. At 3:00 I went shopping at Beno's. I bought some toothpaste, a magazine, and a six-pack of Pepsi. Then I returned home and worked in the kitchen until dinnertime. After dinner, I watched a movie on television until 8:00 and then went to my room to read. I fell asleep around 10:30.

Wrong: (tense shift: present to past to present)

A good sledding area is near the Azalea Campground. You have to drive about five miles down a small winding road to reach the campground, so it is seldom crowded. Both behind and in front of the small campground are good sledding hills. The hills were covered with three or four feet of snow, and there were wide open areas between the pine trees. Some of the runs were long and steep, and others are short and gradually sloped, so there is a place for everyone to sled, from beginners to experts. When we finish sledding, we barbecue hot dogs at the campground and build a big fire to warm up.

Revised: (all verbs in present tense)

A good sledding area is near the Azalea Campground. You have to drive about five miles down a small winding road to reach the campground, so it is seldom crowded. Both behind and in front of the small campground are good sledding hills. The hills are covered with three or four feet of snow, and there are wide open areas between the pine trees. Some of the runs are long and steep, and others are short and gradually sloped, so there is a place for everyone to sled, from beginners to experts. When we finish sledding, we barbecue hot dogs at the campground and build a big fire to warm up.

Wrong: (tense shift: from present to future to present)

To get to the Manchester Mall in Riordan from the college, you head west on the narrow street beside the dorms until you reach Manning Avenue. Turn right on Manning, cross the bridge, and then drive about twelve miles until you reach Highway 99. Turn right on 99 heading north, and drive about ten miles to the city limits of Riordan. Then you will look for a Highway 41 turnoff sign. You will turn right on the Highway 41 exit and will drive about three miles across the city until you will reach the Shields Avenue turnoff. You will turn right off the freeway to Shields, and then you will make a left on Shields at the stop sign. Drive one long block down Shields, and the Manchester Mall is on your right. Turn right at the first stop sign by Macy's, and park wherever you want.

Revised: (all verbs in present tense)

To get to the Manchester Mall in Riordan from the college, you head west on the narrow street beside the dorms until you reach Manning Avenue. Turn right on Manning, cross the bridge, and then drive about twelve miles until you reach Highway 99. Turn right on 99 heading north, and drive about ten miles to the city limits of Riordan. Then you look for a Highway 41 turnoff sign. You turn right on the Highway 41 exit and drive about three miles across the city until you reach the Shields Avenue turnoff. You turn right off the freeway to Shields, and then you make a left on Shields at the stop sign. Drive one long block down Shields, and the Manchester Mall is on your right. Turn right at the first stop sign by Macy's, and park wherever you want.

Exercise 19 Each of the following sentences contains a shift in verb tenses. Revise each sentence and correct the shift by changing the second verb so that it is the same tense as the first. Then compare your answers to the answer key.

Example Sally walks down the sidewalk by the bookstore and stopped by a drinking fountain.

Revised: Sally walks down the sidewalk by the bookstore and stops by a drinking fountain.

1. Yesterday, Sammy went to his English class in the morning, and he goes to his science lab that evening.
2. Mildred had trouble starting her Mazda, so she calls her neighbor to get a ride to work.
3. I will buy your lunch today, and I also buy your dinner.
4. Meg worked out for a half hour in the weight room, and then she eats a banana split.
5. Football is a big sport at Colin College, and the team usually won most of its games.
6. Ralph Burns runs for the city council every year, and he always lost.
7. The children cleared the plot of weeds, and then they plant watermelon seeds.
8. Offshore oil drilling was the biggest issue before the legislature, and supporters argue strongly for government approval.
9. Harold's father bought a new harvesting machine for his wine grapes, and he borrows money from Guaranteed Savings to pay for it.
10. New York gets very hot in the late summer, but it didn't get as hot as Atlanta.

Exercise 20 Rewrite the following short paragraphs and correct any shifts in verb tenses so that all verbs in each paragraph are the same tense. Then compare your paragraphs to the answer key.

Example When I stayed with my cousin on his family's farm, I helped him with the chores. First, we fed the chickens, pigs, and turkeys in the pens behind the house. Then we move the cows to a different grazing field. Finally, we milk the two dairy cows and store the milk in the walk-in icebox in the barn.

Revised: When I stayed with my cousin on his family's farm, I helped him with the chores. First, we fed the chickens, pigs, and turkeys in the pens behind the house. Then we moved the cows to a different grazing field. Finally, we milked the two dairy cows and stored the milk in the walk-in icebox in the barn.

1. At sixty-eight, Sarah Garcia is in better shape than her twenty-five-year-old daughter. Every morning, Sarah gets up at 5:30 and walks for an hour. At 9:30, she turns on public television and does thirty minutes of aerobic exercises with the instructor. In the evening after dinner, she walked another hour, and then she did twenty sit-ups before going to bed. She follows this routine Monday through Friday.

2. There were some strange rock groups at the concert audition last night. One group of guys called Flake all had their hair dyed purple and wore pink ballet tutus. Another group from England called Pain had all kinds of safety pins stuck in their ears and noses. Three girls from Cheyenne called Arrested Development come out dressed in bibs and hot pink diapers. A solo performer named Body has nothing on but a loincloth and a quart of body oil. Most of the groups are more interesting to watch than to listen to.

3. Mel did everything possible to increase business at this car wash. He offers 50 percent off on small cars like Volkswagens and Honda Civics. He gives a free wash to every tenth car that comes through. He gave away a chamois cloth to every customer and had free helium balloons for the kids. He installed a pool table and a ping-pong table in the waiting room for customers. He even keeps the place open twenty-four hours a day on weekends. Mel tried everything to make the business go.

4. Mary Ann and Grace are having problems with their partnership. They own a gift shop together, and they have different opinions on what they need to stock. Mary Ann wants to invest a lot in collectible dolls and figurines, and Grace feels they should specialize more in silver and china. Mary Ann feels they should keep the same store hours as the other shops downtown, but Grace feels they should stay open during the evenings and on Sunday afternoons. Mary Ann wanted both of them to work the shop together, but Grace wanted them to trade off every other week and hire a girl to help out. Mary Ann felt they should reinvest most of their first-year profits in advertisements while Grace wanted to save the money for future shop expansion. They are realizing that partnerships aren't perfect.

5. Last week my friends and I floated down the Kings River. We started at the Goodfellow Bridge and floated for six hours until we reached Kelly's Beach. Along the way, we dodged a lot of motorboats hauling skiers behind them. When a boat whizzed by, it created waves that nearly capsized our inner tubes. At one point about halfway between Goodfellow and Kelly's, a boat heads straight for us. We yell and wave our hands, but it just keeps coming. We paddled furiously to get out of the way, and it swerves at the last second to avoid us. The driver of the boat was laughing, and everyone in the boat looked drunk. We climbed out of the water and ran to a nearby melon patch, and when the boat returns, we bomb it with cantaloupes.

Exercise 21

The following composition moves in time from the past (first paragraph) to the present (second paragraph) to the future (third paragraph). However, there are some unnecessary tense shifts within each paragraph that need correcting. Rewrite the composition and correct any tense shifts within each paragraph. Then show your corrections to your instructor.

When I was a young, I hated bedtime. I was afraid of the dark, and I had to sleep with a light on. Even then, I was afraid that monsters would come through my bedroom window and kill me. And every sound I heard in the house was someone sneaking back into my room to stab me through the heart. I hide under the bed, or more often I run from the room and end up sleeping at the foot of my parents' bed.

Now that I am almost twenty, I obviously do better than when I was a child. However, I am still a scaredy-cat. When my parents leave for a weekend, I hate staying at home alone, and I usually invite a friend over to stay with me. I still need a light on when I sleep although I settle for a tiny night-light in the hall. And before I go to bed, I double-check every door and window in the house to make sure they are locked. I knew no monsters were outside my bedroom window, but I still worried about guys with hatchets, guns, and chain saws just waiting to get at me. My imagination was as bad as ever.

Sometime in the future, I will solve my problem. I will marry a big, strong fellow who won't be a chicken like me. Then I'll never have to sleep alone again. I wouldn't need a night-light then, either. And I wouldn't have to dread going to sleep ever again.

Exercise 22 Write a paragraph about a fear or concern you had when you were young. When you finish, exchange paragraphs with a classmate and check each other's verb usage. Are there any *shifts in tense* that need changing? Correct any shifts in tense in your paragraph, and then share it with other classmates.

Sample Paragraph

When I was growing up, I was always afraid of getting into a fight. I was big for my age and a pretty good athlete, so I felt I could probably hold my own. However, there were some guys who seemed to get into fights all the time, and I figured they knew a lot more about fighting than I did. I was afraid that if one of them took me on, he'd probably beat me up. That would not do much for my reputation, which was what I was really worried about. As the years passed and I avoided fights, I grew more and more paranoid about the day that I would be challenged. Well, the day never came, or at least I was able to maneuver out of any possible conflicts. To this day, I've never been in a fight, and I still wonder if I have what it takes. I may never find out.

Irregular Verb List #4

Here is a fourth set of irregular verbs to work on. Each verb changes form from the past tense to the past participle. The verbs are grouped together because their forms change similarly.

Simple Form	*Past Tense*	*Past Participle*
blow	blew	blown
do	did	done
draw	drew	drawn
fly	flew	flown
go	went	gone
grow	grew	grown
know	knew	known
lie	lay	lain
see	saw	seen
tear	tore	torn
throw	threw	thrown
wear	wore	worn

Note the following features on this list of irregular verbs:

1. Most of the verbs end in *-ew* in the past tense and *-own* in the past participle: *blew/blown, flew/flown, grew/grown, knew/known, threw/thrown*.
2. Two of the most commonly used (and misused) verb forms are on this list: *go/went/gone* and *do/did/done*. The most common mistake is using the past tense form instead of the past participle form with a helping verb. (I have went shopping. You have did well.) These verbs should be given extra attention.
3. The most difficult verb forms on the list are *lie/lay/lain*, which are often confused with *lay/laid/laid*. Here are the differences between the two verbs:

   lie/lay/lain: in a reclining or resting position; no action shown

   Henry is lying on the sofa.
   Mollie lay down for a nap an hour ago.
   That old tree has lain on the ground for years.

   lay/laid/laid: place or set something down; show action

   Jonathan is laying place mats on the kitchen table.
   Felix laid his books on the table and sat down.
   Maria has laid down twelve yards of carpet in the living room.

Exercise 23 Fill in the correct past tense or past participle form of the verb in parentheses in each sentence. Remember, the past participle (third column) is used with the helping verbs *has, have,* and *had* to form the present perfect and past perfect tenses. The past tense (second column) does *not* take a helping verb. When you finish, compare your answers with the answer key.

Example (tear) The carpenters have *torn* the roof off of the cathedral.

1. (go) Have you ________ to the latest Eddie Murphy movie?
2. (fly) The TWA 747 ________ over aiport hotel.
3. (draw) We have ________ some strange-looking sketches of human bodies.
4. (do) Have you ________ everything possible to burglarproof your house?
5. (blow) The wind ________ in from center field of Ebbets Field.
6. (throw) Hortensia has ________ a fit every time her boyfriend hasn't called on time.
7. (see) Have you ________ the pictures of Clarence in the post office downtown?
8. (lie) Sarah ________ on the sofa and planned her future.
9. (know) Jack ________ that he would have a hard time learning Russian.
10. (grow) You have ________ older with grace and dignity.

Exercise 24 Fill in past tense and past participle verbs from List #4 in the following sentences. Select the verb that makes the most sense to complete each sentence. Remember, the past tense does *not* take a helping verb and the past participle form *does*. When you finish, compare your answers with the answer key.

Examples

Have you *flown* in a small plane before?

Bert's aunt *grew* tulips on both sides of her house.

1. Have you ________________ to the district fair yet this fall?
2. Clyde ________________ a large hole in the seat of his tuxedo pants.
3. Jim's campaign for homecoming queen has ________________ the attention of the city press.
4. The young pitcher ________________ the ball to first base and picked off the runner.
5. Amelia has ________________ in all kinds of planes and gliders.
6. Those plants have ________________ over every time the wind comes up at night.

7. You have ______________ exceptionally well on your landscaping projects this semester.
8. Have you ______________ the way that Stella twirls two batons at once?
9. That dog ______________ in the backseat of my car all night.
10. Freda ______________ that her job at the bank was in jeopardy.
11. Tammy has ______________ the same pants to school every day this week.
12. I have ______________ accustomed to your strange remarks.

Exercise 25 Write your own sentences using the list #4 irregular verbs in their past tense, present perfect, and past perfect tenses as directed. Remember, the past tense does not take a helping verb, the present perfect includes *has* or *have* + past participle, and the past perfect includes *had* + past participle. When you finish, show your sentences to your instructor.

Examples

past tense of *tear*

Sally tore her dress last night jumping the barbed wire fence.

past perfect of *grow*

Sam had grown six inches in the last six months.

past perfect of *fly*

Salley has flown all over the world in a hot air balloon.

1. past tense of *grow*
2. present perfect of *know*
3. past tense of *lie*
4. present perfect of *see*
5. past perfect of *do*
6. past tense of *throw*
7. past tense of *fly*
8. present perfect of *blow*
9. present perfect of *draw*
10. past perfect of *tear*

11. past perfect of *go*

12. past tense of *blow*

Practice Quiz

Take this practice quiz to prepare for the section quiz. Then compare your answers with the answer key. When you are ready for the section quiz, let your instructor know.

I. Circle the letter of the paragraph that does *not* contain a shift in verb tenses.

Example

(a.) During the Olympic summer, everything went smoothly in Los Angeles. Thanks to the cooperation of motorists and industry, air pollution was at a minimum, and it didn't affect the athletes' performances. A cool afternoon breeze kept the Coliseum and the USC campus in the 70s for the track-and-field and swimming competition. Merchants in the Coliseum area decked out their stores in Olympic colors and painted over any graffiti, and neighborhood gangs sold Olympic souvenirs instead of hassling spectators. Finally, regular commuter traffic was down about 30 percent, so there were no bad traffic snarls for the athletes or spectators. Residents began to wonder why every summer in Los Angeles couldn't be just as good.

b. During the Olympic summer, everything went smoothly in Los Angeles. Thanks to the cooperation of motorists and industry, air pollution was at a minimum, and it didn't affect the athletes' performances. A cool afternoon breeze kept the Coliseum and the USC campus in the 70s for the track-and-field and swimming competition. Merchants in the Coliseum area deck out their stores in Olympic colors and paint over any graffiti, and neighborhood gangs sell Olympic souvenirs instead of hassling spectators. Finally, regular commuter traffic is down about 30 percent, so there are no bad traffic snarls for the athletes or spectators. Residents begin to wonder why every summer in Los Angeles can't be just as good.

c. During the Olympic summer, everything goes smoothly in Los Angeles. Thanks to the cooperation of motorists and industry, air pollution is kept at a minimum, and it doesn't affect the athletes' performances. A cool afternoon breeze keeps the Coliseum and the USC campus in the 70s for the track-and-field and swimming competition. Merchants in the Coliseum area decked out their stores in Olympic colors and painted over any graffiti, and neighborhood gangs sold Olympic souvenirs instead of hassling spectators. Finally, regular commuter traffic was down about 30 percent, so there were no bad traffic snarls for the athletes or spectators. Residents began to wonder why every summer in Los Angeles couldn't be just as good.

1. a. The latest craze in the beauty business is the tanning salon. These salons are opening up across the country in big cities and small towns. They are for people who want to get that year-round tanned look. What's more, they claim to be safer for the skin than the sun's rays. In the tanning booth, the cancer-causing ultraviolet rays are supposedly filtered out so that the tanning lamps spread a harmless light over the body. There is no question that the tanning

booths work, for patrons who spend a week of twenty-minute sessions in a booth come out with great tans in December. However, most skin specialists believe that the tanning lamps are just as dangerous as sunlight because it is the ultraviolet light that causes the tanning. Tanning salon patrons apparently are taking the same chances with their skin as summer sunbathers.

b. The latest craze in the beauty business is the tanning salon. These salons are opening up across the country in big cities and small towns. They are for people who want to get that year-round tanned look. What's more, they claim to be safer for the skin than the sun's rays. In the tanning booth, the cancer-causing ultraviolet rays are supposedly filtered out so that the tanning lamps spread a harmless light over the body. There was no question that tanning booths worked, for patrons who spent a week of twenty-minute sessions in a booth came out with great tans in December. However, most skin specialists believed that the tanning lamps are just as dangerous as sunlight because it is the ultraviolet light that caused the tanning. Tanning salon patrons apparently were taking the same chances with their skin as summer sunbathers.

c. The latest craze in the beauty business is the tanning salon. These salons are opening up across the country in big cities and small towns. They will be for people who want to get that year-round tanned look. What's more, they claim to be safer for the skin than the sun's rays are. In the tanning booth, the cancer-causing ultraviolet rays will be supposedly filtered out so that the tanning lamps will spread a harmless light over the body. There is no question that the tanning booths work, for patrons who spend a week of twenty-minute sessions in a booth come out with great tans in December. However, most skin specialists believe that the tanning lamps are just as dangerous as sunlight because it is the ultraviolet light that causes the tanning. Tanning salon patrons apparently will be taking the same chances with their skin as summer sunbathers.

2. a. Hurricane Elena hit the coast of Mississippi around Biloxi last summer and caused great damage. The hurricane brought winds up to 120 miles an hour and six inches of rain. Ocean waves grow to twenty feet in height and crash over the seawall protecting residents along the Gulf. Homes are flooded, roofs cave in, and cars float down the streets. Thousands of families evacuate their homes and return days later to find them nearly destroyed by the wind and water. Elena was the worst hurricane to hit Mississippi in fifty years.

b. Hurricane Elena hit the coast of Mississippi around Biloxi last summer and caused great damage. The hurricane brought winds up to 120 miles an hour and six inches of rain. Ocean waves grew to twenty feet in height and crashed over the seawall protecting residents along the Gulf. Homes were flooded, roofs caved in, and cars floated down the streets. Thousands of families evacuated their homes and returned days later to find them nearly destroyed by the wind and water. Elena was the worst hurricane to hit Mississippi in fifty years.

c. Hurricane Elena hit the coast of Mississippi around Biloxi last summer and caused great damage. The hurricane will bring winds up to 120 miles an hour and six inches of rain. Ocean waves will grow to twenty feet in height and crash over the seawall protecting residents along the Gulf. Homes will be flooded, roofs will cave in, and cars will float down the streets. Thousands of families evacuated their homes and returned days later to find them nearly destroyed by the wind and water. Elena was the worst hurricane to hit Mississippi in fifty years.

3. a. We need to get a lot of things for the apartment before we settle in. In the kitchen, we need a table to eat on and some chairs. We also need a paper towel rack and an electric can opener. We could also use a toaster oven if we can find a used one. In the living room, we will need a table for our lamp and something to hang on the walls. We will also need some kind of rack to set the black-and-white TV on. You have your bedroom in good shape, but I will need a nightstand for my clock radio and a chest of drawers for my clothes. The bathroom is pretty well stocked, but we need to replace the towel rack and buy some washcloths.

   b. We needed a lot of things for the apartment before we settled in. In the kitchen, we needed a table to eat on and some chairs. We also needed a paper towel rack and an electric can opener. We could also use a toaster oven if we could find a used one. In the living room, we need a table for our lamp and something to hang on the walls. We will also need some kind of rack to set the black-and-white TV on. You have your bedroom in good shape, but I still need a nightstand for my clock radio and a chest of drawers for my clothes. The bathroom is pretty well stocked, but we need to replace the towel rack and buy some washcloths.

   c. We need to get a lot of things for the apartment before we settle in. In the kitchen, we need a table to eat on and some chairs. We also need a paper towel rack and an electric can opener. We could also use a toaster oven if we can find a used one. In the living room, we need a table for our lamp and something to hang on the walls. We also need some kind of rack to set the black-and-white TV on. You have your bedroom in good shape, but I still need a nightstand for my radio and a chest of drawers for my clothes. The bathroom is pretty well stocked, but we need to replace the towel rack and buy some washcloths.

4. a. Eating at the new restaurant called Spoons was quite an experience. First, they had a strange menu. They had twenty different kinds of hamburgers, three kinds of tacos, a Mexican pizza, and spareribs. That was all the food on the menu. I'd never tried a Mexican pizza before, so I ordered one with a mug of beer. After a twenty-minute wait, I got my Mexican pizza. It had cheese and hamburger meat on it covered with green onions, tomatoes, olives, and three kinds of green peppers. I took a big bite out of one slice, and my mouth was on fire. I had bitten into some of the peppers. I reach for my beer mug and can barely lift it it's so heavy. I gulp down the beer to put out the fire, but after three gulps, the beer is gone. The mug is so thick that there's only enough room for a few ounces of beer. I holler to the waitress for some water, and she says water is twenty-five cents extra. I yell for a dollar's worth and throw down four glasses of water in fifteen seconds. Finally the fire was put out in my mouth, but I wasn't about to take another bite of that pizza.

   b. Eating at the new restaurant called Spoons was quite an experience. First, they had a strange menu. They had about twenty different kinds of hamburgers, three kinds of tacos, a Mexican pizza, and spareribs. That was all the food on the menu. I'd never tried a Mexican pizza before, so I ordered one with a mug of beer. After a twenty-minute wait, I got my Mexican pizza. It had cheese and hamburger meat on it covered with green onions, tomatoes, olives, and three kinds of green peppers. I took a big bite out of one slice, and my mouth was on fire. I had bitten into some of the peppers. I reached for my beer mug and could barely lift it it was so heavy. I gulped down the beer to put out the fire, but after three gulps, the beer was gone. The mug was so thick that there was only enough room for a few ounces of beer. I hollered to the waitress for some water, and she said water was twenty-five cents extra. I yelled for a dollar's worth and threw down four glasses of water in fifteen seconds. Finally, the fire was put out in my mouth, but I wasn't about to take another bite of that pizza.

c. Eating at the new restaurant called Spoons is quite an experience. First, they have a strange menu. They have about twenty different kinds of hamburgers, three kinds of tacos, a Mexican pizza, and spareribs. That is all the food on the menu. I have never tried a Mexican pizza before, so I order one with a mug of beer. After a twenty-minute wait, I get my Mexican pizza. It has cheese and hamburger meat on it covered with green onions, tomatoes, olives, and three kinds of green peppers. I take a big bite out of one slice, and my mouth is on fire. I have bitten into some of the peppers. I reach for my beer mug and can barely lift it it is so heavy. I gulped down the beer to put out the fire, but after three gulps, the beer was gone. The mug was so thick that there was only enough room for a few ounces of beer. I holler to the waitress for some water, and she says water is twenty-five cents extra. I yell for a dollar's worth and throw down four glasses of water in fifteen seconds. Finally, the fire is put out in my mouth, but I am not about to take another bite of that pizza.

5. a. The area around our family's old place had really changed. The peach orchard that used to grow across the street had been pulled out and replaced by a housing tract. We had two acres of pasture land behind our house, but that land was bought by the school district, and a junior high school was built on it about five years ago. The narrow two-lane road at the end of the block that used to be Road 38 was rebuilt into a six-lane avenue and renamed Harper Boulevard. Every orchard, vineyard, or open pasture in the area was torn out long ago and replaced with apartment buildings, surburban houses, and small shopping centers.

b. The area around our family's old place has really changed. The peach orchard that used to grow across the street had been pulled out and is replaced by a housing tract. We had two acres of pasture land behind our house, but that land is bought by the school district, and a junior high school is built on it about five years ago. The narrow two-lane road at the end of the block that used to be Road 38 was rebuilt into a six-lane avenue and renamed Harper Boulevard. Every orchard, vineyard, or open pasture in the area is torn down long ago and is replaced with apartment buildings, surburban houses, and small shopping centers.

c. The area around our family's old place has really changed. The peach orchard that used to grow across the street is pulled out and replaced by a housing tract. We had two acres of pasture land behind our house, but that land was bought by the school district, and a junior high school was built on it about five years ago. The narrow two-lane road at the end of the block that used to be Road 38 was rebuilt into a six-lane avenue and renamed Harper Boulevard. Every orchard, vineyard, or open pasture in the area will be torn down long ago and will be replaced with apartment buildings, surburban houses, and small shopping centers.

II. Circle the letter of the sentence with the correct irregular verb form.

Example

a. Have you wore your new tennis shoes to practice yet?

(b.) Have you worn your new tennis shoes to practice yet?

1. a. The skin from Henry's knuckles torn when he scraped them against the wall.
   b. The skin from Henry's knuckles tore when he scraped them against the wall.
2. a. The wind has blown most of the smog away from the city.
   b. The wind has blew most of the smog away from the city.
3. a. The modern art museum in Gellespie has grown tremendously in the last year.
   b. The modern art museum in Gellespie has grew tremendously in the last year.
4. a. No one knowed exactly when Elton John would take the stage at Wembley Stadium.
   b. No one knew exactly when Elton John would take the stage at Wembley Stadium.
5. a. Matilda has lain around the house doing nothing for three days now.
   b. Matilda has lay around the house doing nothing for three days now.
6. a. Have you saw the work that the Joneses have done on the old house?
   b. Have you seen the work that the Joneses have done on the old house?
7. a. The governor of Rhode Island throwed out the first pitch of the World Series.
   b. The governor of Rhode Island threw out the first pitch of the World Series.
8. a. Sarah has did all of her reports on CIA activities in Central America.
   b. Sarah has done all of her reports on CIA activities in Central America.
9. a. Tad drew sketches of peacocks strutting around the Milpitas Zoo.
   b. Tad drawed sketches of peacocks strutting around the Milpitas Zoo.
10. a. We have went to every anthropology lecture that has been offered this semester.
    b. We have gone to every anthropology lecture that has been offered this semester.
11. a. Marty was tore between going out for the tennis team or playing in the band.
    b. Marty was torn between going out for the tennis team or playing in the band.
12. a. The model plane flied around in circles and then dived straight toward the ground.
    b. The model plane flew around in circles and then dived straight toward the ground.

Pronouns, Adjectives, and Adverbs

Section Topics

Switching Pronouns
-ly Adverbs

Switching Pronouns

A common problem writers have is switching to different pronouns within the same sentence or paragraph. Here is an example of a paragraph containing a number of *pronoun shifts*. The pronouns are underlined.

I always enjoy watching tag team wrestling on television. You can really get into the excitement when there are four wrestlers to watch, two on each team. When we watch wrestling, we root for one team against the other, and we hoot and holler like it's the Super Bowl. You can really see a lot of eye gouging, hair pulling, kicking, and kidney punching in a big match. I also like tag team because when one guy is getting killed, his teammate can come in and get revenge. We drink beer, yell at the referees, and grunt and groan with the wrestlers every Monday night that tag team wrestling is on.

As you can see, the writer begins with the personal pronoun *I*, switches to *you*, then to *we*, back to *you*, back to *I*, and back to *we* again. All of this pronoun shifting within a single paragraph can confuse readers.

Here is the same paragraph with the pronoun shifts eliminated.

I always enjoy watching tag team wrestling on television. I can really get into the excitement when there are four wrestlers to watch, two on each team. When I watch wrestling, I root for one team against the other, and I hoot and holler like it's the Super Bowl. I can really see a lot of eye gouging, hair pulling, kicking, and kidney punching in a big match. I also like tag team because when one guy is getting killed, his teammate can come in and get revenge. My friends and I drink beer, yell at the referees, and grunt and groan with the wrestlers every Monday night that tag team wrestling is on.

Now the pronoun shifting has been eliminated from the paragraph, and the writer has used the first person *I* form that is most appropriate for sharing his viewpoint.

Here are some points to remember concerning the problem of pronoun shifts:

1. Stay with the same basic pronoun form in a paragraph. (For example, if you begin with *I*, stay with *I* and other first person pronouns such as *me, my,* and *mine.*)

2. If you start with *I* and then introduce other people in the paragraph, you change pronouns as you refer to others than yourself. (For example, you would use *we* to refer to yourself and others as a group, *they* to refer to others beside yourself, and *he* or *she* to refer to an individual other than yourself.)

3. You can use the pronoun *you* to refer to *people in general* and then change to *I* to refer to yourself within the same paragraph. (Example: Getting to the Skills Center from here is easy. *You* can walk diagonally across the grass, or *you* can follow the north sidewalk that curves around the lawn. On nice days, *I* usually cut across the lawn because it's quicker, but when it's wet, *I* take the sidewalk.)

4. There are four ways to refer to *people in general: you, people, a person,* or *one*. Choose only one form for a paragraph rather than shifting from one to another. *One* is the *most formal* and *least used* of the four references.

   Example of *incorrect pronoun shifting:*

   You can make a lot of money selling door to door if you have the right personality. A person can't get easily discouraged or he or she will have little success. If one is determined and willing to be rejected, you can do quite well. People who make money selling door-to-door realize that rejection is a big part of one's life as a salesperson.

   To correct the pronoun-shifting problem in the sample paragraph, the pronoun *you* should be used throughout the paragraph in place of other options.

Exercise 26 Change any pronouns in the following sentences to avoid unnecessary pronoun shifts. Also, change any word such as *people* or *a person* if it represents a shift in the sentence. If the pronouns in a sentence are used correctly, mark *C* in front of the sentence. Then compare your answers to the answer key.

Example You should try to save a little money each month. One can stay out of debt that way.

Revised:

1. I am not going to use that mouthwash any more, for one could burn one's tongue with it.

2. They left for the movies about an hour ago, so he probably won't be home until after midnight.
3. I really enjoy going to the mall on Sundays. We just sit around and watch all the people.
4. You can get great bargains on canned goods at Rasco's, and a person can save some money.
5. I have always wanted to test my skills at quarterback, but no coach has let me.
6. If you really want to do well in life, one should set one's goals high.
7. People who attend Grateful Dead concerts are strange. They seem like they're from another planet.
8. I've always enjoyed the view of the city from my apartment. You can see the entire skyline of Minneapolis from the balcony.
9. I enjoyed visiting with the president of the college yesterday. We talked to him for a half hour about student involvement in hiring teachers.
10. You can really lose a lot of money gambling in Atlantic City if a person gets carried away.

Exercise 27 Rewrite the following paragraph and correct any inappropriate shifts in pronouns or in the use of *people* or *a person*. Then show your paragraph to your instructor.

Example I left for school at 7:30 and picked up John and Joe. We drove to school and parked in the west parking lot. You can always find a parking place in the west lot because it's a little farther from most classrooms than the other lots. However, one saves enough time by not having to search for a parking place that a person can get to one's classes on time easily.

Revised: I left for school at 7:30 and picked up John and Joe. We drove to school and parked in the west parking lot. We can always find a parking place in the west lot because its a little farther from most classrooms than the other lots. However, we save enough time by not having to search for a parking place that we can get to our classes on time easily.

I applied for a grant to Waco State College. We filled out a lot of grant forms and mailed them to Waco State. You can get anywhere from $100 to $1,000 in grant money, and one can renew a grant every year if a person remains scholastically eligible. I am hoping to get at least $500 a semester so we don't have to work every day after school. If I don't get the grant, we will go to Waco State anyway because one feels the college has an excellent aeronautics program. I plan on being a jet mechanic.

-ly Adverbs

An *adverb* is used to *modify a verb*. Adverbs often supply information crucial to a reader's understanding of the action occurring in a sentence. Here are some sentences that are identical except for the underlined adverbs. Notice how each adverb changes the meaning of the sentence.

John hit the ball powerfully into the outfield.

John barely hit the ball into the outfield.

John hit the ball gracefully into the outfield.

John hit the ball clumsily into the outfield.

John hit the ball weakly into the outfield.

John hit the ball intelligently into the outfield.

The verb in each of the sentences is *hit*. The adverbs modify *hit* in ways that drastically change the meaning of the sentence.

Here are some points to remember about adverbs:

1. Most adverbs modify verbs by telling how the action occurred. In the sample sentences above, each adverb tells how John hit the ball: powerfully, barely, gracefully, clumsily, weakly, and intelligently.
2. Some adverbs modify verbs by telling when or how often the action occurred. (Examples: Come to my house immediately. We frequently attended lectures at the college. Maria will arrive momentarily. Lately I've been getting headaches.)
3. Most adverbs end in *-ly*, including all of the adverbs in this section. A common error is to leave off the *-ly* ending on an adverb. (Examples: I played the piano bad last night. Then rain came down very rapid. Maria fixed her hair neat. He threw the football graceful.)
4. Adverbs can be located in different places within a sentence. Different adverb locations provide for *different emphases* within a sentence. (Example: Quietly I snuck downstairs to the refrigerator. I quietly snuck downstairs to the refrigerator. I snuck quietly downstairs to the refrigerator. I snuck downstairs to the refrigerator quietly.)
5. Adverbs are extremely useful for providing *exact information* about the action in a sentence. They are powerful enough to change the entire meaning of a sentence. (Examples: Janet sang the national anthem beautifully. Janet sang the national anthem terribly. Janet sang the national anthem hurriedly. Janet sang the national anthem slowly. Janet sang the national anthem mournfully. Janet sang the national anthem amateurishly. Janet sang the national anthem emotionally. Janet sang the national anthem humorously.

Exercise 28 Fill in the following sentences with *-ly*-ending adverbs that fit sensibly. Try to use as many different adverbs as you can. Show your answers to your instructor.

Examples I watched my first tennis match *ignorantly*.

Nero fiddled *crazily* while Rome burned.

Jan ran *rapidly* down the stairs.

1. You play the guitar ______________.
2. Janette ______________ stormed out of the house.
3. The cat played with the mouse ______________.
4. You have been looking very tired ______________.
5. Jack visits Almira's dormitory room ______________.
6. Manual ate the spinach on his plate ______________.
7. The thunder roared ______________ in the eastern sky.
8. Freddie behaved ______________ after returning from boot camp.
9. Marsha ______________ called her mother every Sunday night.
10. Gretchen ______________ struggled with her math homework.
11. ______________ your car has been looking very clean.
12. Please turn over the keys to the rest room ______________.

Exercise 29 The following paragraph contains some *adverb errors*. Rewrite the paragraph and add the *-ly* ending to any adverb that needs it. Compare your answers to the answer key.

Example Mack did very poor on his history final, so he lay on his bed disgusted.
Revised: Mack did very poorly on his history final, so he lay on his bed disguistedly.

The morning was going very bad for Allison. First, her alarm didn't go off, so she got up an hour late. She had to rush about frantic to get to work on time. When she arrived at work, her boss was waiting for her angry. She had forgotten to close the back door of the grocery store tight the night before, and someone had snuck in quiet and stolen four loaves of bread. Her boss told her that she would have to pay for the bread herself. He also told her that if she was late again, she would lose her job quick. Allison nodded her head rapid and went to work stocking the shelves. She worked quiet all morning without stopping for a break. When lunchtime came, she walked proud out the front door and never returned.

Practice Quiz

Take this practice quiz to help prepare for the section quiz. Then compare your answers with the answer key. When you are ready for the section quiz, let your instructor know.

I. Circle the letter of the best-worded sentence(s) from each group.

Example

a. I wanted to send you a Christmas card, but we forgot at the last moment.

b. I wanted to send you a Christmas card, but people forget at the last moment.

(c.) I wanted to send you a Christmas card, but I forgot at the last moment.

1. a. You can get rid of dandruff with the right shampoo, and a person should try his best.

   b. You can get rid of dandruff with the right shampoo, and one should try one's best.

   c. You can get rid of dandruff with the right shampoo, and you should try your best.

2. a. I wanted to take a trip across the channel, but we didn't have the time.

   b. I wanted to take a trip across the channel, but I didn't have the time.

   c. I wanted to take a trip across the channel, but you don't have enough time.

3. a. Sarah decided to return to college in the spring. You made a very smart decision.

   b. Sarah decided to return to college in the spring. She made a very smart decision.

   c. Sarah decided to return to college in the spring. One makes a very smart decision.

4. a. We haven't done anything for relaxation all week. You need to unwind and enjoy yourself.

   b. We haven't done anything for relaxation all week. I need to unwind and enjoy myself.

   c. We haven't done anything for relaxation all week. We need to unwind and enjoy ourselves.

5. a. You could take a taxi to the front of the hotel, or one could take the trolley instead.

   b. You could take a taxi to the front of the hotel, or a person could take the trolley instead.

c. You could take a taxi to the front of the hotel, or you could take the trolley instead.

6. a. I really miss sharing my lunch with Mack at work, for we really enjoyed eating together.

   b. I really miss sharing my lunch with Mack at work, for one really enjoys eating together.

   c. I really miss sharing my lunch with Mack at work, for I really enjoy eating together.

7. a. We gathered in the courtyard for a family picture because you get the best light there.

   b. We gathered in the courtyard for a family picture because we get the best light there.

   c. We gathered in the courtyard for a family picture because one gets the best light there.

8. a. I have never heard of a shampoo that gets rid of all dandruff. I don't think there is one.

   b. I have never heard of a shampoo that gets rid of all dandruff. You don't think there is one.

   c. I have never heard of a shampoo that gets rid of all dandruff. We don't think there is one.

9. a. I left for the coast on the 7:00 bus. We traveled for an hour and then stopped for lunch.

   b. I left for the coast on the 7:00 bus. You travel for an hour and then stop for lunch.

   c. I left for the coast on the 7:00 bus. I traveled for an hour and then stopped for lunch.

10. a. You should really watch out for falling rocks in the hills, for one could get badly injured.

    b. You should really watch out for falling rocks in the hills, for you could get badly injured.

    c. You should really watch out for falling rocks in the hills, for a person could get badly injured.

II. Circle the letter of the sentence with the correct adverb form.

Example

a. The baseball team played terrible last night.

(b.) The baseball team played terribly last night.

1. a. You have behaved strange since you came back from vacation.

   b. You have behaved strangely since you came back from vacation.

2. a. The irises are growing beautifully along the north fence.

   b. The irises are growing beautiful along the north fence.

3. a. Let's all study very diligent for the next six days.
   b. Let's all study very diligently for the next six days.
4. a. We left the dock as rapid as we could because of the storm.
   b. We left the dock as rapidly as we could because of the storm.
5. a. Judy combs her hair neat before going out on a date.
   b. Judy combs her hair neatly before going out on a date.
6. a. The choir wanted to perform perfect during the county festival.
   b. The choir wanted to perform perfectly during the county festival.
7. a. Your payment for your car insurance was unusually late this month.
   b. Your payment for your car insurance was unusual late this month.
8. a. John covered third base in the playoff game very smart.
   b. John covered third base in the playoff game very smartly.
9. a. Melinda tiptoed into the house very quietly so as not to awaken her parents.
   b. Melinda tiptoed into the house very quiet so as not to awaken her parents.
10. a. Hilda speaks four languages fluent.
    b. Hilda speaks four languages fluently.

Spelling

Section Topics

Double-Letter Words
Final Spelling List

This final spelling section introduces a list of the most challenging words in the text. The words all have one thing in common: double letters that give many writers problems.

Double-Letter Words

Here are the spelling words for this section:

across
appropriate
arrangement
business

different
difficult
disappoint
especially
embarrass
immediate
impossible
occasion
occurred
opposite
opponent
parallel
succeed
surround
terrible
tomorrow

Unfortunately, there are no spelling rules to cover the wide range of double-letter occurrences in this list. To learn to spell them correctly, you need to practice spelling them, to learn to visualize their correct spellings, and to come up with your own gimmicks for spelling certain words correctly. (For example, the word *parallel* has two parallel lines [double *l*] within it. You don't find the double letter in *across* until you get "across" the word. The double letter in *immediate* comes "immediately" in the word. You open your "business" with only one *s*, but you close your "business" with two *s*'s.)

Exercise 30 Underline the correctly spelled word in each group. Then compare your answers with the list for this section.

Example attitude atittude attittude

1. tommorow	tomorrow	tommorrow
2. teribble	terrible	terribble
3. surround	suround	surounnd
4. suceed	succed	succeed
5. parallel	parallell	paralell
6. oponnent	oponent	opponent
7. opposite	opossite	oppossite
8. ocurred	occured	occurred
9. occasion	ocassion	occassion
10. impposible	imposibble	impossible
11. immediate	imeddiate	immediatte
12. embarras	embarass	embarrass
13. especialy	esppecially	especially
14. disappoint	dissappoint	dissapoint

15. dificult	difficult	dificcult
16. diferent	differrent	different
17. business	bussiness	busness
18. arrangment	aranngement	arrangement
19. aproppriate	appropriate	approppriate
20. accros	across	accross

Exercise 31 Respell any word that is spelled incorrectly. Put *C* in the space if the word is spelled correctly. Then check your spellings with the list for the section.

Example dinner *c*

letucce *lettuce*

1. across
2. diferrent
3. dissapoint
4. embarass
5. occurred
6. paralell
7. tommorow
8. opponent
9. ocassion
10. imposible
11. especially
12. suceed
13. teribble
14. aproppriate
15. immediate

Practice Quiz

Take this practice quiz to prepare for the section quiz. Then compare your answers with the answer key. When you are ready for the section quiz, let your instructor know.

Circle the letter of the correctly spelled word in each group.

Example a. letter b. leter c. leterr

1. a. accros	b. accross	c. across
2. a. approppriate	b. appropriate	c. aproppriate
3. a. arrangment	b. aranngement	c. arrangement
4. a. business	b. bussiness	c. busness
5. a. different	b. diferrent	c. differrent
6. a. dificcult	b. dificult	c. difficult
7. a. dissapoint	b. disappoint	c. dissappoint
8. a. especially	b. esspecialy	c. especialy
9. a. embarass	b. embarrass	c. emmbarrass
10. a. immediate	b. imeddiate	c. immeddiate
11. a. impossible	b. immposible	c. imposible
12. a. occasion	b. occassion	c. ocassion
13. a. ocurred	b. occured	c. occurred
14. a. opossite	b. opposite	c. oppossite
15. a. opponent	b. oponnent	c. opponnent
16. a. parallel	b. parallell	c. paralell
17. a. suceed	b. succeed	c. succed
18. a. suround	b. surrounnd	c. surround
19. a. teribble	b. terrible	c. terribble
20. a. tomorrow	b. tommorrow	c. tommorow

Final Spelling List

This final list of words contains 120 of the most frequently misspelled words that writers tend to rely on. You may use it as a convenient spelling reference when proofreading your drafts for errors.

accommodate
achievement
acquaintance
acquire
actual
amateur
against
alleys
amount
apparent
appearance
approach
argument
attendance
beginner
believe
benefit
boundary
business
certain
chief
comparative
conscience
controversy
convenience
criticism
dealt
dependent
describe
despair
disappoint
disease
divine
efficient
embarrass
exaggerate
exercise
existence
expense
experience
explanation
extremely
fascinate
forty
friend
government
grammar
guarantee
height
heroes
huge
ignorant
imaginary
immediately
independent
intelligent
interest
interrupt
knowledge
laid
led
leisure
license
loneliness
loose
lose
luxury
maintenance
marriage
meant
mere
naturally
necessary
ninety
noticeable
obstacle
occasion
occurrence
operate
opinion
original
paid
parallel
particular
performance
personal
physical
piece
planned
possess
practical
preferred
prejudice
preparation
principal
principle
privilege
probably
procedure
prominent
promise
psychology
pursue
really
receive
recommend
repetition
sense
separate
shining
similar
studying
success
surprise
tries
truly
villain
weather
whether
writing

Writing Review

Here is a final composition assignment that allows you to apply everything you have learned about effective writing. The writing skills you have developed throughout this course should serve you well for most writing that you will do both in and out of school.

Level 5 Composition Assignment

Select one of the following general topics for writing a composition:

1. an issue you feel strongly about
2. a problem that needs solving
3. the causes of ________ (acid rain, ozone depletion, high teenage suicide rate, divorce, rising tuition costs)
4. the effects of ________ (child abuse, cocaine use, dropping out of school, the warming environment, divorce on children, getting a college education)
5. four or five kinds of ________ (teachers, drinkers, students, salespeople, comics, relationships, religious types, friends)
6. a philosophy to live by

Step One

1. Select a specific topic. Pick one that interests you, that you know something about, and that you can develop into a composition.
2. Decide on a tentative *controlling idea* for the composition.
3. Consider the supporting ideas, incidents, steps, or details you may want to include in your composition by doing some prewriting work: listing points, making a formal outline, brainstorming, or writing freely on your topic.
4. Decide on a tentative organization for your composition.

Prewriting Example: the problem of teenage pregnancy
Controlling Idea: The high rate of teenage pregnancy can be lowered.

Free Writing A lot of girls at my high school have gotten pregnant. Some have the babies and others get abortions. Either way, it is usually a bad situation and the girls regret getting pregnant. Boys and girls need more information on birth control. Most boys don't take any responsibility, and the girls usually count on the boys to know what they are doing. The results are obvious. Since boys and girls are having sex in high school, the schools should face up to it and educate them about birth control—the ones that work best. They should also let students know that there is a shared responsibility and that it's up to both the boy and girl to avoid a pregnancy. Girls should see the effects that pregnancy has on their lives: being an outcast, dropping out of school, having an abortion, or raising a kid when you're not ready. Girls don't think of all these consequences. Boys should learn that they can't just walk away from it all—that they shared in the making, so they share in the consequences. Birth control pills should be available at the school, and anyone should be able to get them without the parents' approval. Most girls who have sex never let their parents know. At a school that gave out birth control pills, the pregnancy rate went down. To cut down on all of the sex, schools should scare students about venereal disease just like they do about alcoholism, smoking, and driving accidents. Those horror movies they show about the insides of people's lungs and cut-off heads in accidents would work just as well for syphilis or herpes. Also, schools should educate students against early sex: that it isn't all that it's cracked up to be, that it can ruin relationships, that a lot of people feel forced into it, that being a virgin isn't something to be ashamed of. The schools have to do it because parents just don't.

5. Now write the first draft of your composition, beginning with an opening paragraph that includes your controlling idea. Develop your main ideas in separate paragraphs. Your *audience* for the composition is any group of people that *you* feel could profit from reading it. Name your reading audience here: ______________________________

Step Two Read over your draft, following these suggestions:

1. Is your opening paragraph effective? It should have a clear lead-in, introduce your topic, and contain your controlling idea for the composition. Make any changes in your opening to make it more interesting or clearer.

2. Check your paragraphing. Do you develop a separate point, step, or incident in each middle paragraph? Do most paragraphs have topic sentences? Is the main point of each paragraph well developed? Do you use enough details and examples to make your points?

3. Do you use *transitional wording* to tie your sentences and paragraphs together?

4. Do you have a strong ending paragraph? Does it relate to the controlling idea of your composition? Does it leave your readers something to think about? Does it make them aware of the importance of the composition's subject to you?

5. Will your readers find the draft interesting? Is it written so that they can clearly understand your ideas? What can you do to make your composition more interesting or informative and your ideas more easily understood?

Make note of all possible revisions you might include in your final draft.

Step Three Now go over your individual sentences within your composition and follow these suggestions:

1. Is your sentence structure varied? Are you using compound and complex sentences? Do you have any pairs or groups of short sentences that need combining? Underline any sentences that need restructuring or combining.
2. Are your sentences clearly, smoothly worded? Eliminate unnecessary words, smooth out awkward phrasing, and replace vague wording with *concrete language*. Also, correct any problems with misplaced modifiers, nonparallel construction, and dangling modifiers.
3. Check your punctuation. Eliminate any run-on sentence or fragment. Check your comma usage. Also, make sure you are using semicolons, colons, and quotation marks correctly. Make any punctuation changes necessary so that your final draft will contain complete, correctly punctuated sentences.

Step Four Now proofread your composition for errors. Follow these suggestions:

1. Check sentences for subject-verb agreement, for the *-ed* on regular past tense verbs, for the correct irregular verb forms, and for *unnecessary shifts in verb tenses within a paragraph*.
2. Check your use of pronouns, making sure you are using subject pronouns correctly and that all pronouns agree with their antecedents. Also, make sure that you have the *-ly* ending on adverbs, that you are using comparative and superlative adjectives correctly, and that you are using *good/well* and *bad/badly* correctly.
3. Check your spelling. Make sure you have the *-s* or *-es* ending on plural words and that your *-ing*-ending and *-ly*-ending words are spelled correctly. Are you using *there, their,* and *they're* correctly? Have you put apostrophes in contractions and possessive words? Look up any word you are uncertain of.

Step Five Write the final draft of your composition, including all improvements and error corrections noted in Steps Two, Three, and Four. Be prepared to share your composition with your classmates and with your instructor.

Sample Final Draft (from Prewriting Example)

Reducing Teen Pregnancies

This year alone, over twenty thousand teenage girls, from ages thirteen to seventeen, will become pregnant. The disastrous effects of these pregnancies will include abortions, unwanted babies, single, jobless mothers, high school drop-outs, and doomed marriages. Teenage pregnancy has reached epidemic proportions, and something must be done to reduce the numbers before thousands more lives are ruined.

Girls and boys are having more sex at earlier ages than ever before. However, their desire for sex isn't matched by their knowledge of birth control, their emotional maturity, or their sense of responsibility. Girls often foolishly believe that boys know what they're doing, and boys often aren't thinking about anything but sex, and seldom about the consequences. A couple has sex a few times without the girl getting pregnant, and they start thinking there's no problem. Then before they know it, bang! The girl misses a period and the nightmare begins.

Boys might take more responsibility if they felt the weight of the consequences, but unfortunately teenage pregnancy is primarily a female tragedy. It is the girl who has to get the abortion or take the pregnancy to term. It is the girl who has to drop out of school. It is the girl who faces the stigma of pregnancy and who often becomes a single, jobless, uneducated mother. Many girls who become pregnant already have two strikes against them: they are often poor and come from badly educated, and often split, families. The third strike—pregnancy—puts them out of the game, on welfare and in poverty, maybe for a lifetime.

What can be done to change this tragic pattern? First of all, families need to be strengthened. Mothers and fathers need to be taught how to parent. Perhaps the responsibility for teaching parents needs to lie in the community. Churches and school districts often provide parenting effectiveness courses for families. Public health clinics offer counselling. Support groups can provide a sense of kinship. Through these, parents can learn how to communicate with their children and to give them the love they are seeking, which will turn them from premature sexual involvement.

Children need affirmation of their identity and of their worth. When they have this, they can say "no" to sexual pressure, and they can respect the "no" of another. They have a reason: their bodies and emotions are valuable and are not to be exploited. In our society, we have linked the sale of products from cars to toothpaste with sex. We have made sexual activity a standard. Kids need to know there is love and life outside the bedroom.

Teens also need to be taught the physical consequences of early sexual involvement. Herpes and other sexually transmitted diseases which have no cure are on the rise. Is a night of passion worth a life with herpes? Is this encounter worth conceiving a child the teen is unprepared to care for? Abortion has been the standard answer to that question for years, but abortion has other tragic effects which include sterility, tubal pregnancies, and emotional problems.

Teens need to learn to take responsibility for their actions. It does not take intelligence, maturity, or worldliness to have intercourse—flies do it with amazing proficiency—but it does take intelligence and maturity to practice self control, whether that means saying "no" and respecting another's "no" or practicing contraception.

We do not have to assume that this problem will be with us forever; we can make a difference in our communities by providing parents with information and support as they raise their children, by affirming the worth of each member of the family, and by providing teenagers with practical and moral education.

Appendix

This section is especially useful for students who are learning English as a second language. It contains exercises dealing with the use of *articles* (*a, an, the*) and *prepositions* (*in, on, at, to, of*), and with two pronoun problems: left-out subject pronouns and unnecessary pronouns.

Small Words

The small words covered in this section are among the most commonly used words in writing. Seldom will you write a sentence without including one or more of these words. They are used primarily to identify or locate the main items within a sentence. Since they appear so frequently, it is important that you be able to use them correctly.

A, An, The Here are the most common uses for the *articles a, an,* and *the* and a fourth situation when *no article* is used.

A

used with *singular* words that begin with a *consonant* and refer to *no particular person or thing*
(singular: *one* of anything: a boy, a dog, a cat, a wallet, a scarf)
(consonant: any letter *other* than a, e, i, o, u.)

Sam would like a car for Christmas.
You played a good game of chess.
A boy in the library just checked out twenty books.
Do you think a tutor would help me?
Joanne has a bad toothache.

AN

used with *singular* words that begin with a *vowel* and refer to *no particular person or thing*
(vowel: the letters *a, e, i, o,* and *u*.)

An apple would sure taste good right now.
Maria would like an answer to her question.
There was an avalanche on the north side of the mountain.
Do you think an eggplant sandwich would taste good?
George has an appetite you wouldn't believe.

THE

used with *singular* and *plural* words that refer to *one particular person, group of people, thing, or group of things*
(plural: *more than one of anything:* cars, dogs, clouds, wallets, socks)

The boy standing behind me is very tall.
I'll take the meatball sandwich at the end of the counter.
The grapes you just picked are sweet and juicy.
Do you know the answers to yesterday's math assignment?
The news about John's scholarship pleased his parents.

NO ARTICLE USED

in front of *plural* words that refer to *no particular persons or things*

Girls tend to mature earlier than boys.
Ted thinks that turtles make great pets.
Football players have more injuries than swimmers.
Cows are not as smart as monkeys.

Exercise 1 Fill in the correct word—*a, an,* or *the*—in each space. *Leave the space blank if no word is needed.* Then check your answers with the key in the back of the book.

Examples

We have __a__ long way to go before we reach Milpitas.

Harry saw __an__ octopus at the aquarium.

1. I believe that ________ only train leaving for Chicago today will be late.
2. Do you know what time ________ basketball game at the Spectrum begins?
3. John would like to find ________ nice woman to settle down with.
4. Maria went to ________ small shop and bought ________ orchid.
5. ________ first six minutes of ________ relationship are very important.
6. ________ moon is just a sliver tonight, but ________ stars around it are bright.
7. Jeanne packed ________ apple, ________ sandwich, and ________ piece of pie for lunch.
8. Do you want ________ strawberries on your cornflakes this morning?

9. ________ funny thing happened to Mr. Gomez when he checked out ________ book.

10. ________ last bus to Chinatown leaves ________ station in ________ short time.

11. ________ tacos and ________ enchiladas are a good combination to eat.

12. ________ doctors have ________ highest rate of alcoholism among professional groups.

Exercise 2 A problem some writers have is leaving out an *a, an,* or *the* that is needed in a sentence. Rewrite the following paragraph and add any *a, an,* or *the* that is needed. Then compare your answers with the key in the back of the book.

Example I'll have hamburger and piece of pie for lunch.

Revised: I'll have a hamburger and a piece of pie for lunch.

Melissa enjoys working at only restaurant across from the campus. She is only waitress, but crowd is never too large. She takes the customers' orders, gives them to cook, and then takes food to the customers. Then she bills them, takes their money, and returns their change. Finally, she clears tables before next customers sit down. Between customers, she has time for short break. Since she is only waitress, she gets all the tips. On good day, she'll get over twenty dollars in tips. That is unusually high amount for waitress in small restaurant.

In, On, At, To, Of Five other commonly used small words are the prepositions *in, on, at, to,* and *of.* Some writers have trouble deciding which word to use in a particular situation. Here are the most common uses for these words.

IN:

inside of or *within*

We were sitting in the car.
The packages are in the closet.
Your big feet are in the doorway.
We have six dogs in the backyard.
We will need your help in ten minutes.

ON:

on top of or *upon*

There was a lizard sitting on the porch.
Put the poster on the bulletin board.
Set all of the dishes on the table.
You will find your keys on top of the icebox.

a member of

We are on the same team.
John took his seat on the jury.
You are on the list of students for graduation.

AT:

a specific location or *time*

I'll meet you at 7:00 p.m. at the high school.
Everyone will arrive at your house by dawn.
Lab class will begin on Thursday morning at 9:00.
Let's meet at the corner of 16th and R Street.

TO:

toward a specific place or *person*

We are going to the show this afternoon.
No one went to the library from our geology class.
My sister's baby goes to bed at 12:00 a.m.
Give this gift to Jill when you see her.
The letter was sent to Henry from his mother.

OF:

used to specify a particular person, group of people, thing, or things

Only one of the boys is missing his sweatshirt.
A box of matches was left on the fireplace.
A lot of your problems are caused by poor eyesight.
All of the cake was eaten before the party.

Exercise 3 Fill in the best word—*on, in, to, at, of*—to complete each of the following sentences. Then compare your answers with the key in the back of the book.

Example Six __of__ the starting players were home with the flu.

1. You have a lot ________ bugs ________ your windshield.
2. I will meet Freddie ________ the corner of 10th and L ________ 10:00.
3. We are going ________ the bakery after we drop off Sue ________ her aunt's.
4. We have been working ________ this science project for six hours ________ a row.
5. None ________ your friends were ________ the park when we got there.
6. We left ________ the car very early so we could get ________ class ________ time.
7. We were living ________ an island located ________ the Indian Ocean.
8. ________ six o'clock, all ________ the workers will leave ________ their cars.
9. ________ the last few hours, John has accomplished many ________ his goals.
10. Let's go ________ the store and park ________ the north lot.

Exercise 4 The following paragraph needs *revising* to correct errors in the use of *in, on, at, to,* and *of.* Rewrite the paragraph and make any necessary changes. Then check your revised paragraph with the key in the back of the book.

Example We went to the feedstore on our old truck.

Revised: We went to the feedstore in our old truck.

Our geology class took a field trip at the Mojave Desert. Some of us rode on a station wagon, and others rode on a van. It was warm at night, so we slept in top of our sleeping bags. The next morning we went hiking at the nearby foothills, and we camped on the hills overnight. It rained that night, so we all slept on the main tent. The next morning we returned at our main campsite and spent the morning drying out our food and clothing. We had to be in our way home by 2:00 p.m. to reach the college by midnight. The station wagon got a flat tire on the way, so we didn't get at the college until 2:00 a.m.

Practice Quiz

Here is a practice quiz on "small words." Take the quiz and compare your answers with the key in the back of the book.

Fill in the best word in the blank to complete each sentence.

Example One _of_ your friends went into the navy last month.

a. of b. at c. to d. on

1. I want _______ word with you, Clare, about your plans for the weekend.
   a. a b. an c. to d. on
2. No one wants to believe _______ truth about Harry's unusual past.
   a. a b. an c. the d. none needed
3. Do you want to eat _______ apple for breakfast this morning?
   a. a b. an c. the d. none needed
4. I don't really think that _______ anteaters make the best pets.
   a. a b. an c. the d. none needed
5. _______ elm trees in your front yard are beautiful.
   a. a b. an c. the d. none needed
6. We met _______ young man from Australia this morning at the airport.
   a. a b. an c. the d. none needed
7. Henrietta has just met _______ man of her dreams.
   a. a b. an c. the d. none needed
8. _______ cats are very independent animals.
   a. a b. an c. the d. none needed
9. I'll meet Thelma _______ her locker in ten minutes.
   a. in b. on c. at d. to
10. We are all going _______ the circus tonight with the Bronlee family.
    a. in b. on c. at d. to
11. The new tractor got stuck _______ the deep mud behind the barn.
    a. in b. on c. at d. of
12. All _______ the prizes for the contest were claimed in fifteen seconds.
    a. in b. on c. at d. of
13. Most students were really _______ a hurry to finish their algebra test Monday.
    a. in b. on c. at d. to

14. Please put all of the chips ________ top of the table.
    a. in b. on c. at d. to
15. I think I have given you all ________ the advice you'll ever need.
    a. in b. on c. at d. of
16. People don't always understand the value ________ an education.
    a. in b. on c. at d. of
17. Let's throw the saddles ________ the horses and head for the high country.
    a. in b. on c. at d. of
18. The dance will be held ________ the gymnasium immediately after the game.
    a. in b. on c. at d. to
19. Please drop me off ________ the bank on your way home tomorrow.
    a. in b. on c. at d. to
20. No one is going ________ the racetrack today without a lot of money.
    a. in b. on c. at d. to

Unnecessary Pronouns

In the first section of the text on *pronouns*, you learned that it is better to replace a word with a pronoun than to repeat the word needlessly in a sentence or paragraph. However, it is an error to add an *unnecessary* pronoun that *replaces nothing* in a sentence. Here are examples of four sentences with unnecessary pronouns underlined.

That plane <u>it</u> looks like it is going to crash.

The dog that you own <u>he</u> is very friendly to strangers.

Your daughter <u>she</u> is going to be a very good actress.

Those boys in the back room <u>they</u> are playing poker.

John and I <u>we</u> both enjoy fishing in the reservoir.

Here are two suggestions for eliminating unnecessary pronouns in a sentence.

1. If a pronoun can be dropped from a sentence and the sentence is still complete and makes sense, the pronoun isn't needed.
2. If the pronoun in a sentence isn't needed to replace another word, it should be deleted.

Here are four more sentences with unnecessary pronouns, followed by revised versions that eliminate the problem.

The woman who works at the laundromat she is my aunt.
Revised: The woman who works at the laundromat is my aunt.

The lobster you ate for dinner it came from the East Coast.
Revised: The lobster you ate for dinner came from the East Coast.

Some people they prefer getting lost to asking for directions.
Revised: Some people prefer getting lost to asking for directions.

Those doors in the back of the store they are falling apart.
Revised: Those doors in the back of the store are falling apart.

Exercise 5 Rewrite any of the following sentences that contain an unnecessary pronoun, and eliminate the pronoun. Mark *C* for correct sentences. Then check your answers with the answer key.

Example Lucinda she was working hard at the doctor's office all day.
Revised: Lucinda was working hard at the doctor's office all day.

1. Gary he got a six-month warranty on his new Volkswagen engine.
2. Fifty housewives they protested the closing of the day-care center at school.
3. The art collection in the cafeteria it was done by a graduate student.
4. Louie he will have to register for the draft next week.
5. My grandmother from Chicago she still drives a car at eighty-six years of age.
6. The women didn't get back into the same limousines that they arrived in.
7. Tim hates getting up early the next morning after he has been to night class.
8. The boxes in the alley they aren't of any use because they smell like sardines.
9. That flower that you have in a vase on your mantel it looks like a rare orchid.
10. The men who jammed into the boxing arena they rooted for the local favorite.

Exercise 6 Rewrite the following paragraph, and *eliminate* any *unnecessary pronouns* that you find. Then compare your paragraph with the answer key.

Example Homer and I we walk to school on sunny mornings. The walk to school it isn't too bad, and we enjoy getting some exercise before class.

Revised: Homer and I walk to school on sunny mornings. The walk to school isn't too bad, and we enjoy getting some exercise before class.

The students they arrive in front of the school at 8:00 a.m. The flatbed truck it rolls up at 8:05, and they climb aboard. The truck heads to the outskirts of town. Then it stops, and the students they unload with their gunnysacks. They divide into two groups, and each group of students it covers one side of the road. They walk down the sides of the road picking up bottles and cans. After they fill their gunnysacks, they return to the truck and unload them. After a half day of work, they climb aboard the truck with over a ton of cans and bottles. The rest of the afternoon it is spent separating cans from bottles so the students they can take them to different recycling plants.

Left-Out Pronouns

Another problem some writers have is *leaving out* a pronoun that is necessary to complete a sentence. In some languages, you may leave out a subject pronoun if it is clear what the subject is. In English, the subject pronoun can never be left out.

Here are examples of sentences with pronouns incorrectly left out.

Is important to find a regular place to study every night (Beginning *It* left out)

It is cold outside, and that is why is necessary to dress warmly. (*it* left out before third *is*)

Marian is very nice. Is kind, generous, and loving. (*She* left out in second sentence)

Check your brakes to make sure are good enough for the trip. (*they* left out after *sure*)

Here are three basic points to help you remember to include necessary pronouns.

NECESSARY PRONOUNS

1. Subject pronouns can never be left out: *I, he, she, it, we, they, you.*
   Wrong: Is very cold out today.
   Right: It is very cold out today.

2. Subject pronouns frequently are incorrectly left out before the verb forms *is* and *are*.
   Wrong: The test will be difficult, and are going to have to study.
   Right: The test will be difficult, and we are going to have to study.

3. Subject pronouns are incorrectly left out *most frequently* in the middle of sentences.
   Wrong: When you buy a car, make sure is checked by a mechanic.
   Right: When you buy a car, make sure it is checked by a mechanic.

Exercise 7 Rewrite the following sentences by *adding* the left-out pronoun in each sentence. Then compare your sentences with the answer key.

Example I think is very important to eat food with fiber in it.

Revised: I think it is very important to eat food with fiber in it.

1. I borrowed the family car for the weekend, so was very happy.
2. Denise has done poorly in algebra. That's why is thinking of dropping the class.
3. That's a beautiful statue in the park, and is over three hundred years old.
4. That girl is only sixteen years old, and bought 50 shares of computer stocks.
5. That cat belongs in the jungles of Africa, but share our house with it.
6. Is necessary for everyone to fill out a grant application before February 1.
7. When you go buy the tires, make sure are in stock at the store.
8. The Joneses won't be going to the game tonight because are in Las Vegas.
9. Because Marie had a very hard time at the dentist, is worried about her next visit.
10. Although the tax increase hurts everyone, hurts the lower-income people the most.

Exercise 8 The following paragraph has some pronoun problems. Some sentences contain *unnecessary* pronouns and others leave out *needed pronouns*. Rewrite the paragraph and correct the pronoun errors by eliminating unnecessary pronouns and adding needed subject pronouns. Then compare your sentences with the answer key.

Millie she has been enjoying school this semester. Although her classes are difficult, is doing well in them. Her geometry class in the morning it is her most difficult class, but is getting a B in it. She isn't getting worse than a C in any class. She is also making more friends. One boy in her English class he eats lunch with her on Mondays and Fridays. He has also introduced her to some of his friends, and are very nice people. Is a much better semester for Millie than in the fall. Next semester it could be even better, for some of her friends from high school they are enrolling.

Practice Quiz

Take this practice quiz, and check your answers with the answer key. Circle the letter of the best-worded sentence in each pair.

Example

a. Maria she is a drama student at Kellogg University.

(b.) Maria is a drama student at Kellogg University.

1. a. The girls who lives next door she works at Bank of America on C Street.

   b. The girls who lives next door works at Bank of America on C Street.

2. a. Some people enjoy working outdoors on weekends, and others they prefer staying inside.

   b. Some people enjoy working outdoors on weekends, and others prefer staying inside.

3. a. Physics is a tough subject, and that's why is important not to get behind.

   b. Physics is a tough subject, and that's why it is important not to get behind.

4. a. Although the library has good reference books, it doesn't have a good fiction section.

   b. Although the library has good reference books, doesn't have a good fiction section.

5. a. The spiders that I found in the bathtub they are called daddy longlegs.

   b. The spiders that I found in the bathtub are called daddy longlegs.

6. a. The first step in getting a loan is filling out an application, and the second step it is to go for an interview.

   b. The first step in getting a loan is filling out an application, and the second step is to go for an interview.

7. a. Sam enjoys riding motorcycles in the desert because is so peaceful in the early mornings.

   b. Sam enjoys riding motorcycles in the desert because it is so peaceful in the early mornings.

8. a. Before changing your car's oil, first make sure is dirty enough to need changing.

   b. Before changing your car's oil, first make sure it is dirty enough to need changing.

9. a. You'll have to dig up the pipe to find out where is leaking.

   b. You'll have to dig up the pipe to find out where it is leaking.

10. a. Open the door to the attic to find out what it is making that noise.

    b. Open the door to the attic to find out what is making that noise.

11. a. The girl from the Virgin Islands she is living in the dorms this semester.

    b. The girl from the Virgin Islands is living in the dorms this semester.

12. a. Henry couldn't find time to do all of his homework, so was very frustrated.

    b. Henry couldn't find time to do all of his homework, so he was very frustrated.

13. a. My Oldsmobile runs on regular gas. That's why is not too expensive to own.

    b. My Oldsmobile runs on regular gas. That's why it is not too expensive to own.

14. a. When you want to take a shower, is important to let the water run a while to get hot.

    b. When you want to take a shower, it is important to let the water run a while to get hot.

15. a. The sweater you wore to school on Friday it is an alpaca, isn't it?

    b. The sweater you wore to school on Friday is an alpaca, isn't it?

Answer Key

Level One

Exercise 1

1. e	3. c	5. c	7. e
2. d	4. b	6. a	8. e

Exercise 2

1. The view from the windows was great. The cupboard space was adequate.
2. He disliked running in the Troborg Invitational Marathon last summer.
3. She also expects us to know a lot from our high school math classes.
4. He helps me with my homework.
5. She is a gray, long-haired cat with normal eating habits.
6. Then we'll move on to the shower and caulk the cracks between the tiles.

Practice Quiz The Paragraph

1. c	3. a	5. c	7. c
2. d	4. e	6. c	8. e

Practice Quiz Sentence Variety

1. b	3. c	5. a	7. b
2. a	4. a	6. d	8. d

Practice Quiz Clear Sentences

1. a	3. a	5. c	7. b	9. c
2. c	4. b	6. b	8. b	10. b

Exercise 10

1. night. They	5. Oscar. They	9. mall. It
2. warm. It	6. bright. It	10. conditions. They
3. duplex. They	7. tomorrow. We	
4. diet. She	8. Scott. I	

Exercise 11

Alicia worked as a secretary for an accounting firm. She started as a typist but later helped with the bookkeeping.

She decided to enroll at San Joaquin Night School in their accounting program. The classes met four evenings a week for two sixteen-week semesters.

Today, Alicia is a certified public accountant. She is working for the same firm that hired her as a secretary ten years ago.

Practice Quiz Correct Sentences

1. b
2. a
3. b
4. b
5. a
6. b
7. c
8. b

Exercise 12

1. Aunt Clarice makes
2. door needs
3. trees fell
4. Marvin accepted
5. hurricane tore
6. hamster bit
7. building collapsed
8. ideas startle
9. sign shakes
10. news bothered
11. shoes make
12. actions speak
13. Terry behaved
14. looks attract
15. One fell
16. man reads
17. call prevented
18. nose dripped
19. opener works
20. head flew

Exercise 14

1. belongs
2. break
3. needs
4. sneak
5. goes
6. has
7. need
8. slips
9. carry
10. hosts
11. plans
12. enjoy
13. belong
14. answers
15. looks
16. sells
17. fit
18. complain
19. gives
20. eat

Exercise 16

1. sisters enjoy
2. ducks waddle
3. nail scratches
4. fence needs
5. dogs sleep
6. eyebrow arches
7. teachers bring
8. hamsters bite
9. storms blow
10. motorcycles lean
11. boxers want
12. labs last

Practice Quiz Verb Forms

I.

1. d
2. c
3. a
4. b
5. c
6. b
7. d
8. a
9. c
10. b

II.

1. a
2. b
3. b
4. a
5. b
6. b
7. b
8. a
9. b
10. b
11. b
12. b
13. b
14. a
15. a

Exercise 17

1. she
2. he himself
3. them
4. its it
5. his he himself
6. we
7. they them
8. their them
9. it
10. they their them
11. you your yourselves
12. we our them ourselves

Exercise 18

Rita enjoys living in her new apartment. She moved in two months ago with her friend Gwendolyn. They share the one-bedroom apartment, and they take turns cleaning it. All of the apartments in the complex have one bedroom, and all of them rent for $250 a month. Rita and Gwendolyn's apartment has a microwave oven, and they enjoy cooking in it. They do all of their own cooking because they enjoy cooking for themselves. Rita would like an apartment to herself some day, but until she can afford it, she is happy to share an apartment with Gwendolyn.

Practice Quiz Pronouns, Adjectives, and Adverbs

1. a
2. b
3. c
4. b
5. b
6. b
7. b
8. a
9. a
10. c

Exercise 20

1. donkeys
2. children
3. women
4. hutches
5. mice
6. foxes
7. bodies
8. men
9. monkeys
10. salaries
11. people
12. places
13. reasons
14. armies
15. alleys
16. classes
17. parties
18. grasses
19. duties
20. latches

Exercise 21

1. jerseys
2. batches
3. lobbies
4. glasses
5. faces
6. lawns
7. journeys
8. flies
9. couches
10. turkeys

Practice Quiz Spelling

1. b
2. c
3. b
4. a
5. d
6. a
7. c
8. d
9. c
10. b
11. c
12. b
13. d
14. d
15. a

Level Two

Exercise 1

1. Freddie is very shy.
2. I'll never work in a commercial laundry again.
3. It must finally be spring.
4. But I'm enjoying my raquetball class a lot.
5. Suzette's the only person I know who likes marmalade jelly on her eggs.
6. The sidewalks in the neighborhood are filthy.

Exercise 2

1. b
2. c
3. c
4. c
5. b
6. b
7. c
8. c
9. b
10. c

Exercise 7

1. A. She loves to play jokes on friends.
    1. She painted her roommate's feet green while her roommate was sleeping.
    2. She tied a cow to her brother's bed one night.

   B. She's good at imitating people.
    1. She does a great Fat Albert imitation.
    2. She can laugh just like Eddie Murphy.

2. A. Ocean tides and undertow can be very dangerous.
    1. Rip tides can take you miles down the coastline.
    2. An undertow can carry you far out into the ocean.

   B. The surf can be very powerful.
    1. The surf can hold you underwater for a long time.
    2. The surf can flip you around like a rag doll.

3. A. The restaurant does special things for children.
    1. Each child gets a special coloring book.
    2. Each child gets a free dessert with dinner.

B. Senior citizens get special treatment.
   1. Anyone over sixty gets a 50% discount.
   2. Anyone over sixty gets seated immediately on arrival.

4. A. The lingerie buys are excellent.
   1. You can buy slips at a thirty percent discount.
   2. There's a two-for-one sale on underwear.

   B. There's also a special sale in the sports department.
   1. Fishing poles are marked wáy down.
   2. A $100 weight set costs only $42.99.

5. A. Henry is in the best shape of his life.
   1. He can do fifty push-ups.
   2. He can run over three miles without getting exhausted.

   B. He likes the fellows in his platoon.
   1. He grew up with many of them.
   2. They all stick together and help each other.

6. A. The two main negotiators didn't get along.
   1. One was very emotional and the other was very calm.
   2. They never trusted each other.

   B. Neither side wanted to make the first move.
   1. The U.S. waited for Russia to make a land missile concession.
   2. Russia waited for the U.S. to make a nuclear submarine concession.

Practice Quiz The Paragraph

I.

1. c
2. a
3. c
4. c
5. c
6. a
7. c
8. b
9. a
10. c

II.

1. b
2. a
3. b
4. b
5. a

Exercise 10

1. and
2. so
3. and
4. but *or* yet
5. but *or* yet
6. for
7. but *or* yet
8. and
9. for
10. so
11. but *or* yet
12. so *or* and
13. or
14. so *or* and
15. for

Exercise 14

(sample revision)

Frank bought ten acres of wheat, and he paid $800 an acre.
Then there were two years of drought, so his crops were very small.
The next year was a little better, but it wasn't good enough for Frank to clear his debt.
He sold the farm the next month, and he moved to the city and bought a grocery store.
He is happy to be free of the farm, but he misses living in the country.

Practice Quiz Sentence Variety

I.

1. b
2. a
3. c
4. c
5. b
6. c
7. c
8. a
9. c
10. a

II.

1. c
2. a
3. b
4. b
5. a
6. b
7. b
8. b
9. b
10. c

Practice Quiz Clear Sentences

1. b
2. c
3. b
4. c
5. c
6. a
7. a
8. b
9. c
10. c

Exercise 17

1. test. The
2. freeway. The
3. meet. This
4. breeding. There
5. weekends. The
6. evening. There
7. spring. That
8. hours. Then

Exercise 18

1. Wednesday, but
2. loud music, and
3. evening, and *or* for
4. tonight, so
5. city, and
6. town, but
7. yesterday, so
8. hour, and

Practice Quiz Correct Sentences

1. c
2. a
3. a
4. b
5. b
6. a
7. c
8. c
9. b
10. b

Exercise 20

1. is
2. was
3. are
4. were
5. is
6. was
7. is
8. was
9. are
10. were
11. is
12. was
13. are
14. were
15. is
16. was
17. are
18. were
19. are
20. were

Exercise 22

1. talked
2. freed
3. denied
4. fried
5. hated
6. delayed
7. displayed
8. skated
9. prayed
10. loved
11. used
12. slipped
13. dried
14. angered
15. robbed
16. sobbed

Exercise 23

1. worked
2. looked
3. changed
4. destroyed
5. learned
6. disturbed
7. removed
8. planned
9. covered
10. rammed
11. baked
12. denied collected

Exercise 24

Mabel believed in the basic goodness of people. She accepted them with their faults, and she never tried to change anyone. She enjoyed talking to people, and she never tired of listening to their problems. Because of her kindness, people loved Mabel. They showed her only their best side. They acted kinder and behaved more gently around her than normally. Men purchased gifts for her, and women sewed her clothing. She lived in Plaines, Illinois, and everyone who visited her there remembered her well. Mabel offered everyone her best, and she received the same in return.

Practice Quiz Verb Forms

I.

1. b
2. a
3. b
4. b
5. a
6. a
7. b
8. b

II.

1. b
2. b
3. a
4. a
5. c
6. a
7. c
8. b
9. a
10. a

Exercise 26

1. we
2. I
3. she
4. we
5. he
6. she
7. I
8. he
9. they
10. we
11. he we
12. I

Exercise 28

1. Phyllis and he
2. Gertie and I
3. Sarah, Henry, and I
4. Mr. Sanchez and he
5. correct (c)
6. correct (c)
7. Clyde and I
8. Henry and she
9. Mick and I
10. Melissa and she

Practice Quiz Pronouns, Adjectives, Adverbs

1. b
2. b
3. b
4. a
5. b
6. b
7. b
8. b

Exercise 29

1. caring
2. jumping
3. planning
4. beginning
5. dating
6. delaying
7. studying
8. cutting
9. coming
10. running
11. waiting
12. enjoying
13. carrying
14. hitting
15. having
16. flying
17. wearing
18. driving
19. writing
20. putting

Exercise 31

1. There
2. Their
3. They're
4. Their
5. There
6. they're
7. There their
8. They're their
9. there there there
10. their there

Practice Quiz Spelling

I.

1. b
2. a
3. a
4. b
5. c
6. c
7. a
8. b
9. b
10. a
11. a
12. a
13. b
14. b
15. a
16. a
17. c
18. a
19. c
20. b

II.

1. a
2. a
3. a
4. a
5. a
6. a
7. b
8. a

Level Three

Exercise 1

1. deer in herds
   an occasional fox
   rabbits and squirrels
   bluejays everywhere
   lizards darting around
   crickets chirping
2. monthly income way down
   special sales aren't working
   good help hard to find
   store needs some fixing up
   electric bill going up slightly
3. good for the heart
   good for the lungs
   builds endurance
   good for the muscles
   loosens tendons
   doesn't hurt body joints
   lose weight
   shrinks waistline
4. sun peeking through clouds
   white, puffy clouds
   birds flying above the trees
   tall elm trees everywhere
   lush green grass
   ducks on the lake
   large, sunken lake in middle
5. buy a dress
   buy wedding gift
   shower
   wash her hair
   get dressed
   put on makeup
   pick up her sister
   drive an hour to the party

Exercise 4

(sample responses)

First	One	next	Then	Despite
Next	First	First	always	However
However	After	Then	Finally	

Exercise 5

(sample responses)

however	in fact	In addition	therefore
First	For example	As you can see	

Practice Quiz The Paragraph

I.

1. a	3. a	5. b	7. a
2. b	4. a	6. a	8. b

II.

1. a	3. a	5. a	7. c	9. a
2. a	4. a	6. a	8. a	10. a

Exercise 8

1. As	4. until	7. while	10. before
2. When	5. As	8. When	11. whenever
3. After	6. While	9. After	12. where

Exercise 9

1. If is,	5. Since mountains,	9. unless
2. because	6. because	10. If higher,
3. Unless Street,	7. If beard,	11. Since Samantha,
4. although	8. since	12. although

Practice Quiz Sentence Variety

1. c
2. a
3. c
4. b
5. a
6. b
7. a
8. a
9. a
10. b
11. c
12. a
13. a
14. b

Practice Quiz Clear Sentences

1. a
2. b
3. a
4. b
5. c
6. c
7. c
8. c
9. b
10. b

Exercise 16

1. F
2. F
3. S
4. F
5. S
6. F
7. S
8. F
9. F
10. F
11. F
12. S
13. S
14. F
15. S

Practice Quiz Correct Sentences

1. c
2. b
3. b
4. b
5. c
6. c
7. a
8. b
9. b
10. b

Exercise 19

1. boarder — comes goes
2. car — spins crashes
3. mother — wants needs
4. Ivan — believes preaches
5. rocket — lifts veers crashes
6. We — are want
7. No one — knows cares
8. sun — drops turns
9. I — observe record
10. Teachers — expect encourage are disappointed

Exercise 22

1. found
2. have found
3. had found
4. has heard
5. heard
6. had heard
7. had laid
8. has laid
9. laid
10. have stood
11. stood
12. had stood
13. won
14. has won
15. had won

Exercise 23

1. have bought
2. bought
3. had bought
4. caught
5. has caught
6. had caught
7. had kept
8. kept
9. has kept
10. taught
11. has taught
12. had taught

Exercise 24

1. thought
2. taught
3. spent
4. slept
5. sat
6. sent
7. met
8. lost
9. left
10. kept
11. fought
12. won
13. told
14. stood
15. sold
16. said
17. read
18. paid
19. made
20. led
21. laid
22. held
23. heard
24. had
25. found

Practice Quiz Verb Forms

I.

1. a
2. b
3. b
4. b
5. a
6. b
7. b
8. a
9. b
10. a

II.

1. b
2. a
3. b
4. b
5. b
6. b
7. b
8. b
9. a
10. b
11. b
12. b
13. b
14. b
15. b
16. a
17. b
18. b
19. b
20. b
21. a
22. b
23. b
24. a

Exercise 25

1. his he
2. it
3. their them
4. it
5. his or her
6. her
7. our we
8. his or her his or her
9. their they
10. its it
11. they their
12. its

Exercise 26

1. their
2. his
3. their
4. his
5. his or her
6. their
7. his or her
8. it
9. his him
10. their

Exercise 28

1. good
2. well
3. good
4. well
5. well
6. good
7. well
8. good
9. well
10. good

Practice Quiz Pronouns, Adjectives, Adverbs

I.

1. b
2. a
3. c
4. b
5. b
6. b
7. b
8. a
9. b
10. a

II.

1. b
2. b
3. a
4. b
5. b
6. b
7. b
8. a
9. b
10. a

Exercise 34

1. sister's
2. trout's
3. pastor's
4. pigeons'
5. soldiers'
6. correct
7. correct
8. street's
9. newspaper's
10. parents'
11. men's
12. Maria's
13. Clyde's
14. students'
15. boxes'
16. correct
17. correct
18. wind's
19. school's
20. grandparents'

Exercise 35

1. month's
2. custodian's
3. girl's
4. squirrels' Mitchell's
5. Uncle's doctor's
6. children's women's
7. year's
8. hamster's brother's
9. nation's civilians'
10. Sally's

Practice Quiz Spelling

I.

1. c
2. b
3. c
4. a
5. b
6. c
7. c
8. c
9. c
10. c
11. a
12. c
13. c
14. b
15. c

II.

1. c	3. b	5. a	7. c	9. a
2. c	4. b	6. b	8. b	

Level Four

Exercise 1

1. *Paragraph 2:* Begin with "Italian food is one of my favorites."
   Paragraph 3: Begin with, "Japanese food is my second favorite."
   Paragraph 4: Begin with, "Probably my favorite ethnic food is Mexican."
   Topic Sentences: Italian food is one of my favorites.
   Japanese food is my second favorite.
   Probably my favorite ethnic food is Mexican.
2. *Paragraph 2:* Begin with, "When I went to school, the students looked like the cast from the movie 'Grease.'"
   Paragraph 3: Begin with, "The cars parked in the school lot were vintage 1950s."
   Paragraph 4: Begin with, "When I went to a department store downtown, I got my biggest shock."
   Topic Sentences: When I went to school, the students looked like the cast from the movie "Grease."
   The cars parked in the school lot were vintage 1950s.
   When I went to a department store downtown, I got my biggest shock.
3. *Paragraph 2:* Begin with, "First, find out about the pay and benefits for the job."
   Paragraph 3: Begin with, "Second, it's important to find out about the hours."
   Paragraph 4: Begin with, "Finally, it is important to look into the working conditions."
   Topic Sentences: First, find out about the pay and benefits for a job.
   Second, it's important to find out about the hours.
   Finally, it is important to look into the working conditions.
4. *Paragraph 2:* Begin with, "In P.E. class the first semester, he was doing the rope climb in the gym when the rope came off the ceiling hook."
   Paragraph 3: Begin with, "Then during Christmas vacation, Monte went ice skating at Mill Pond."
   Paragraph 4: Begin with, "Monte's worst mishap came in the spring."
   Topic Sentences: In P’.. class the first semester, he was doing the rope climb in the gym when the rope came off the ceiling hook.
   Then during Christmas vacation, Monte went ice skating at Mill Pond.
   Monte's worst mishap came in the spring.

Exercise 4

1. b	3. c	5. b	7. c	9. c
2. c	4. a	6. b	8. b	10. b

Practice Quiz
The Composition

I.

1. b
2. b

II.

1. b
2. b
3. c
4. c
5. a
6. c
7. c
8. a
9. b
10. a

III.

1. a
2. b
3. c
4. c
5. a
6. c

Exercise 9

1. that
2. who
3. who
4. which
5. which
6. that
7. that or who
8. who
9. that
10. which
11. who
12. which

Exercise 11

1. c
2. c
3. Park, Wyoming,
4. Walker,
5. c
6. Lewis, store,
7. Ford, owned,
8. c
9. Collins,
10. c

Practice Quiz Sentence Variety

I.

1. a
2. b
3. b
4. b
5. a
6. b
7. a
8. b
9. b
10. b

II.

1. b
2. b
3. b
4. a
5. a
6. a
7. b
8. c
9. a
10. b

Exercise 14

1. treatment for implanting hair
2. firewood that is on the back porch
3. Nervous and excited, John
4. John took twenty letters of recommendation
5. president of the Ajax Employment Agency
6. breeze from the ocean
7. wash all of their clothes on the rocks
8. rug in the den
9. meadow just beyond that hill
10. results of the election
11. shirt that you gave me
12. talking to on the patio
13. woman who invited you to her party
14. cat sleeping in her basket
15. clouds blowing in from the north

Exercise 15

1. students that you introduced me to
2. plants in the back of the classroom
3. chair that we just bought

4. guy who stole my French notes.
5. water running in the garden.
6. manager that moved to Naples.
7. players from the opposing team
8. Relaxed and confident, Marta
9. man who introduced us
10. Everyone in pink pajamas

Exercise 16

1. While the children were playing on the monkey bars on the playground, it got very hot.
2. While Milton was trying to pass a bill on child abuse through Congress, his wife became his secretary.
3. Since Simon was delighted by his new tractor rig, a second one was purchased.
4. As Mary was planning for the hot weather ahead, the weather suddenly cooled.
5. While Ted and Celia were traveling through six cities in one week, their luggage was lost twice.
6. As Grace was inspired by the countryside, her sketches were better than ever.
7. Since Alice was worried about her failing health, her doctor's glowing report was welcome.
8. As Harvey was finding a place to display his statues on the courthouse lawn, tourists followed him around.

Practice Quiz Clear Sentences

I.

1. b
2. a
3. c
4. a
5. c
6. a
7. c
8. a
9. a
10. c
11. a
12. c

II.

1. b
2. b
3. c
4. a
5. a
6. b
7. a
8. c
9. b
10. a

Exercise 20

1. Aunt Hilda worries about her roses when the neighbor boys are playing outside.
2. When the Olympic Games were in Los Angeles, air pollution was minimal.
3. Then it surfaced twenty yards downstream where the river splits in half.
4. When she was asleep last night, her dog broke a sprinkler line, and water gushed out all night long.
5. The thief broke into the house through the back door while the family was sleeping inside.
6. While drought and starvation continued in Ethiopia, American and British rock groups raised millions of dollars through concerts televised worldwide.
7. He has accumulated over two hundred bottles from all over the world since he began collecting three years ago.
8. When the election results were in, Sarah had run a close second to the incumbent.
9. If you want to go to Harvey's barn party tonight, I'll be glad to pick you up.
10. Mark's health science lab was canceled yesterday because the instructor was ill.

Exercise 23

A. 1. year. They
2. Oregon. The
3. week. Now

B. 1. outside, for
2. Since I'm
3. 9:00 p.m., or

C. 1. park; it
2. today; television
3. stocks; they

D. 1. Ted is short, handsome, and lonely.
2. Mary is a 15-year-old blonde from Missouri.
3. The tide came in and went out with the moon.

Exercise 24 (suggested corrections)

1. office, for
2. shape, but
3. Bonberry. Now
4. Sal's sister Marta is unmarried and employed by Lockheed Aircraft.
5. picnic, so
6. twenty; she's
7. body. Now
8. Olympic Games; many
9. bill; it
10. The narrow, curvy, dangerous road was located east of Tulsa.

Exercise 25 (suggested run-on corrections)

business. He
cheaply; then
magazines, so he
in two weeks, so he
increase, for he

Practice Quiz Correct Sentences

I.

1. b
2. a
3. b
4. b
5. a
6. b
7. a
8. a
9. b
10. a

II.

1. b
2. a
3. c
4. b
5. c
6. a

Exercise 26

1. wears
2. are
3. is
4. are
5. looks
6. fascinates
7. operates
8. needs
9. is
10. brightens
11. need
12. sounds

Exercise 28

1. written
2. stole
3. spoken
4. shook
5. risen
6. rode
7. given
8. got
9. froze
10. fell
11. eaten
12. driven
13. chose
14. broken
15. took

Exercise 29

1. took
2. have taken
3. spoke
4. had spoken
5. rose
6. has risen
7. has eaten
8. had eaten
9. chose
10. had chosen
11. drove
12. has driven
13. gave
14. had given
15. broke
16. has broken

Practice Quiz Verb Forms

I.

1. b	3. b	5. b	7. b	9. b
2. a	4. b	6. a	8. b	10. b

II.

1. b	4. c	7. b	10. c	13. c
2. c	5. a	8. c	11. a	14. a
3. a	6. c	9. b	12. c	15. b

Exercise 31

1. more interesting
2. friendlier
3. more fascinating
4. shorter
5. faster
6. more boring
7. more excited
8. longer
9. harder
10. more typical

Exercise 32

1. most interesting
2. friendliest
3. most fascinating
4. shortest
5. fastest
6. most boring
7. most excited
8. longest
9. hardest
10. most typical

Exercise 33

1. tallest
2. taller
3. most beautiful
4. more beautiful
5. larger
6. largest
7. prettiest
8. prettier
9. most expensive
10. more expensive

Practice Quiz Pronouns, Adjectives, Adverbs

1. c
2. b
3. b
4. a
5. a
6. c
7. a
8. a
9. a
10. c

Practice Quiz Spelling

1. b	5. c	9. a	13. c	17. a
2. a	6. b	10. a	14. a	18. b
3. a	7. b	11. a	15. b	19. c
4. a	8. a	12. c	16. c	20. b

Level Five

Practice Quiz The Composition

1. a
2. c
3. b
4. c
5. c

Exercise 3 (suggested responses)

1. Although	when or if	5. who	although
2. While	because	6. Unless	because
3. After	because	7. Although	until
4. that	since or because	8. If	because

Exercise 4 (suggested responses)

1. or	but	5. for	and
2. and	so	6. but	for
3. yet	for	7. for	but
4. but	and	8. for	so

Exercise 5 (suggested responses)

1. for	that	5. When	for
2. that so	where	6. who	yet
3. who and	who	7. While but	until
4. Although	and	8. Unless so	when

Practice Quiz Sentence Variety

1. a	3. c	5. b	7. a	9. a
2. b	4. a	6. c	8. c	10. b

Exercise 8

1. The snow fell slowly, lightly, and gently on the school grounds.
2. I never saw so many cheerful, courteous, helpful students.
3. Marvin is kind, gentle, responsible, and considerate.
4. After work I ate dinner, went to a show, came home, and went to bed.
5. The jewel thief saw the diamonds on display and planned the robbery for the next morning.
6. I would like to become a nurse, raise a family, and be financially comfortable.
7. At this stage, the pudding batter should be slightly runny, smoothly textured, and hot.
8. This cleansing cream will keep your skin healthy, glowing, and soft.
9. She often wondered how she would pay the second semester's tuition.
10. Jonathan has green eyes, black hair, and long sideburns, and he is tall.

Exercise 10 (nonparallel sentences revised)

1. Gerald wanted them out of the garage for the night, and they didn't want to go.
2. He called them and banged on their food dish, but they would not come.
3. They'd hide under the parked cars in the garage, dart from one car to the other, and stay a step ahead of Gerald.
4. The cats went out on the back porch for the night and slept on the redwood table or on the throw rug.
5. They don't like the porch as well as the garage but are getting used to it.

Practice Quiz Clear Sentences

1. c	4. a	7. c
2. c	5. b	8. a
3. b	6. c	9. b

Exercise 11

1. money, paint
2. cannery, but
3. Sally Enright, brother,
4. smoking, drinking, chewing tobacco, and
5. Oregon, you
6. Vancouver Zoo, whales,
7. water, Phillis
8. bedroom, a thief
9. collecting, patience,
10. Walking to school, cramming for tests, eating in the cafeteria, and
11. 7:00 a.m., so
12. parsonage, 1902,

Exercise 12

1. Mariam,
2. Incidentally,
3. believe, Melissa,
4. , of course,
5. tonight, Suzanne
6. foothills, for example,
7. crop, as you probably know,
8. mind, Jackie,
9. Chicago, I imagine,

Exercise 13

1. miserable, so staying indoors, resting, keeping cool, and
2. repairs, aquarium,
3. Mr. Jackson, band, job,
4. business, July, well, and
5. operation, Tuesday, but
6. Harriet, Mazda,
7. Incidentally, job, student,
8. Mildred, friend,
9. spring, surprised,
10. now, month, but

Exercise 14

1. bathroom; they
2. interests; you
3. cause:
4. party:
5. people:
6. fast; they
7. tonight; they
8. wheel:
9. pass:
10. boyfriend; then

Exercise 15

1. "I'm . . . Ned."
2. "They're . . . smoke."
3. "Yeah . . . thing,"
4. "Well . . . right," "Let's . . . cigars."
5. "I'll . . . box."
6. "Okay," "But . . . you."
7. "We . . . tonight,"
8. "I'll . . . 9:00," "I'll . . . matches."

Exercise 16

1. Maggie said, "When . . . Fred?"
2. Fred answered, "I'm willing . . . are."
3. "Why don't . . . Saturday?" asked Maggie. "I . . . plans."
4. Fred said, "I'm free . . . too. What do . . . see?"
5. "There's a . . . Drive-in," said Maggie.
6. Fred said, "I thought . . . movies."
7. "I used to," replied Maggie. "Now I . . . them."
8. "Then we'll . . . Saturday," said Fred. "I'll . . . 8:30."

Practice Quiz Correct Sentences

1. a
2. c
3. b
4. c
5. a
6. c
7. c
8. c
9. a
10. b
11. c
12. a
13. a
14. c
15. a

Exercise 19

1. he went
2. she called
3. I also will buy
4. she ate
5. team usually wins
6. he always loses
7. they planted
8. supporters argued
9. he borrowed
10. it doesn't

Exercise 20

(shifts corrected)

1. she walks another hour
   then she does twenty sit-ups
2. Arrested Development came out
   Body had nothing on
   groups were more interesting
3. He offered 50% off
   He gave a free wash
   He even kept the place
4. Mary Ann wants both of them
   Grace wants them to trade
   Mary Ann feels they
   Grace wants to save
5. a boat headed straight for us
   We yelled and waved our hands
   it just kept coming
   it swerved at the last second
   when the boat returned
   we bombed it

Exercise 23

1. gone
2. flew
3. drawn
4. done
5. blew
6. thrown
7. seen
8. lay
9. knew
10. grown

Exercise 24

(suggested responses)

1. gone
2. tore
3. drawn
4. threw
5. flown
6. blown
7. done
8. seen
9. lay
10. knew
11. worn
12. grown

Practice Quiz Verb Forms

I.

1. a
2. b
3. c
4. b
5. a

II.

1. b
2. a
3. a
4. b
5. a
6. b
7. b
8. b
9. a
10. b
11. b
12. b

Exercise 26

1. my tongue
2. so they
3. Sundays. I
4. and you
5. Correct
6. life, you
7. Correct
8. apartment. I
9. yesterday. I
10. if you

Exercise 29

going very badly
rush about frantically
waiting for her angrily
of the grocery store tightly
snuck in quietly
lose her job quickly
nodded her head rapidly
worked quietly
walked proudly

Practice Quiz Pronouns, Adjectives, Adverbs

I.

1. c	3. b	5. c	7. b	9. c
2. b	4. c	6. c	8. a	10. b

II.

1. b	3. b	5. b	7. a	9. a
2. a	4. b	6. b	8. b	10. b

Practice Quiz Spelling

1. c	5. a	9. b	13. c	17. b
2. b	6. c	10. a	14. b	18. c
3. c	7. b	11. a	15. a	19. b
4. a	8. a	12. a	16. a	20. a

Appendix

Exercise 1

1. the	5. The a	9. A a
2. the	6. The the	10. The the a
3. a	7. an a a	11. (no articles)
4. a an	8. (no article)	12. (no article) the

Exercise 2

Melissa enjoys working at the only restaurant across from the campus. She is the only waitress, but the crowd is never too large. She takes the customers' orders, gives them to the cook, and then takes the food to the customers. Then she bills them, takes their money, and returns their change. Finally, she clears the tables before the next customers sit down. Between customers, she has time to eat a snack and take a rest. Since she is the only waitress, she gets all the tips. On a good day, she'll get over twenty dollars in tips. That is an unusually high amount for a waitress in a small restaurant.

Exercise 3

1. of on	5. of (in, at)	9. In of
2. (on, at) at	6. in to on	10. to in
3. to at	7. on in	
4. on in	8. at of in	

Exercise 4

Our geology class took a field trip to the Mojave Desert. Some of us rode in a station wagon, and others rode in a van. It was warm at night, so we slept on top of our sleeping bags. The next morning we went hiking in the nearby foothills, and we camped in the hills overnight. It rained that night, so we all slept in the main tent. The next morning we returned to our main campsite and spent the morning drying out our food and clothing. We had to be on our way home by 2:00 p.m. to reach the college by midnight. The station wagon got a flat tire on the way, so we didn't get to the college until 2:00 a.m.

Practice Quiz

1. a	5. c	9. c	13. a	17. b
2. c	6. a	10. d	14. b	18. a
3. b	7. c	11. a	15. d	19. c
4. d	8. d	12. d	16. d	20. d

Exercise 5 (eliminate)

1. he	3. it	5. she	7. c	9. it
2. they	4. he	6. c	8. they	10. they

Exercise 6 The students arrive in front of the school at 8:00 a.m. The flatbed truck rolls up at 8:05, and they climb aboard. The truck heads to the outskirts of town. Then it stops, and the students unload with their gunnysacks. They divide into two groups, and each group of students covers one side of the road. They walk down the sides of the road picking up bottles and cans. After they fill their gunnysacks, they return to the truck and unload them. After a half day of work, they climb aboard the truck with over a ton of cans and bottles. The rest of the afternoon is spent separating cans from bottles so the students can take them to different recycling plants.

Exercise 7

1. I was
2. she is
3. it is
4. she bought
5. we share
6. It is
7. they are
8. they are
9. she is
10. it hurts

Exercise 8 Millie has been enjoying school this semester. Although her classes are difficult, she is doing well in them. Her geometry class in the morning is her most difficult class, but she is getting a B in it. She isn't getting worse than a C in any class. She is also making more friends. One boy in her English class eats lunch with her on Mondays and Fridays. He has also introduced her to some of his friends, and they are very nice people. It is a much better semester for Millie than in the fall. Next semester could be even better, for some of her friends from high school are enrolling.

Practice Quiz

1. b	4. a	7. b	10. b	13. b
2. b	5. b	8. b	11. b	14. b
3. b	6. b	9. b	12. b	15. b

Index